PATERNOSTER THEOLOGICAL

Kenosis and Priesthood

Towards a Protestant Re-Evaluation of the Ordained Ministry

PATERNOSTER THEOLOGICAL MONOGRAPHS

A full listing of titles in this series and Paternoster
Biblical Monographs
appears at the end of this book

PATERNOSTER THEOLOGICAL MONAGRAPHS

Kenosis and Priesthood

Towards a Protestant Re-Evaluation of the Ordained Ministry

T. D. Herbert

Foreword by Graham Ward

MILTON KEYNES · COLORADO SPRINGS · HYDERABAD

Copyright © T. D. Herbert 2008

First published 2008 by Paternoster

Paternoster is an imprint of Authentic Media
9 Haldom Avenue, Bletchley, Milton Keynes, MK1 1QR, UK
1820 Jetstream Drive, Colorado Springs, CO 80921, USA
and
OM Authentic Media, Medchal Road, Jeedimetha Village,
Secunderabad 500 055, A.P., India
Authentic Media is a division of IBS-STL UK, a compamy limited by guarantee
(registered charity no. 270162)

14 13 12 11 10 09 08   7 6 5 4 3 2 1

The right of T. D. Herbert to be identified as the Author of this Work
has been asserted by him in accordance with the Copyright, Designs
and Patents Act 1988.

All rights reserved. No part of this publication may be reproduced, stored in a retrieval system, or transmitted, in any form or by any means, electronic, mechanical, photocopying, recording or otherwise, without the prior permission of the publisher or a license permitting restricted copying. In the UK such licenses are issued by the Copyright Licensing Agency, 90 Tottenham Court Road, London W1P 9HE.

British Library Cataloguing in Publication Data
A catalogue record for this book is available from the British Library

ISBN 978-1-84227-565-8

Typeset by T. D. Herbert
Printed and bound in Great Britain
by AlphaGraphics Nottingham

PATERNOSTER THEOLOGICAL MONOGRAPHS

Series Preface

In the West the churches may be declining, but theology—serious, academic (mostly doctoral level) and mainstream orthodox in evaluative commitment—shows no sign of withering on the vine. This series of *Paternoster Theological Monographs* extends the expertise of the Press especially to first-time authors whose work stands broadly within the parameters created by fidelity to Scripture and has satisfied the critical scrutiny of respected assessors in the academy. Such theology may come in several distinct intellectual disciplines—historical, dogmatic, pastoral, apologetic, missional, aesthetic and no doubt others also. The series will be particularly hospitable to promising constructive theology within an evangelical frame, for it is of this that the church's need seems to be greatest. Quality writing will be published across the confessions—Anabaptist, Episcopalian, Reformed, Arminian and Orthodox—across the ages—patristic, medieval, reformation, modern and counter-modern—and across the continents. The aim of the series is theology written in the twofold conviction that the church needs theology and theology needs the church—which in reality means theology done for the glory of God.

Series Editors

† David F. Wright, Emeritus Professor of Patristic and Reformed Christianity, University of Edinburgh, Scotland, UK

Trevor A. Hart, Head of School and Principal of St Mary's College School of Divinity, University of St Andrews, Scotland, UK

Anthony N.S. Lane, Professor of Historical Theology and Director of Research, London School of Theology, UK

Anthony C. Thiselton, Emeritus Professor of Christian Theology, University of Nottingham, Research Professor in Christian Theology, University College Chester, and Canon Theologian of Leicester Cathedral and Southwell Minster, UK

Kevin J. Vanhoozer, Research Professor of Systematic Theology, Trinity Evangelical Divinity School, Deerfield, Illinois, USA

*To Pam, James and Tom
with loving gratitude*

Contents

Foreword by Graham Ward	xiii
Preface	xvii
Acknowledgements	xix
Abbreviations	xxi

Chapter 1: Introduction : The Reality of Priesthood	1
Representation and Realism	3
Realistic Representation: Kenosis and Priesthood	4
Anti-Realistic Representation: Kenosis and Priesthood	7
Critically Realistic Representation: Kenosis and Priesthood	8
Narrative and Critical Realism	11
Narrative and Identity	14
Summary of the Argument	16

Part I: Kenosis and God's Graceful Self-revelation to Humanity	19

Chapter 2: The Story of the Doctrine of Kenosis	21
Classic Kenotic Theory and Human Identity in Christology	22
Kenosis as the Death of God	27
'Truly God and truly man'?	31
Luther and Divine Identity in Christology	42
Conclusion	46

Chapter 3: Kenosis and the Theology of Barth, Balthasar and Moltmann	47
Kenosis in the Theology of Karl Barth	48
Kenosis in the Theology of Hans Urs von Balthasar	55
Kenosis in the Theology of Jürgen Moltmann	62

Conclusion	71

Chapter 4: Philippians as a Narrative Account of Identity in Kenosis — 75

Some Introductory Remarks	76
Assumptions about the Epistle to the Philippians	76
Narrative and the Text of Philippians	77
Narrative and the Structure of Philippians	79
Identity in the Epistle to the Philippians: Setting the Theme (1.1-2)	81
Paul's Identification with the Philippians (1.3-11)	82
Paul's Identification with Christ (1.12-26)	83
Christian Living as Self-identification with Christ (1.27-2.18)	84
True and False Identity (3.1-4.9)	86
True Identification involves Participation in the Other (4.10-20)	90
The *Carmen Christi*	92
Adamic Christology and the Divine Identity	92
Philippians 2.6-11	96
Philippians as a Mimetic Narrative of Priestly Identity	101
Conclusion	103

Part II: Priesthood and the Grateful Human Response to the Divine Self-revelation — 105

Chapter 5: Vocation and Priesthood — 107

Vocation in the Theology of Hans Urs von Balthasar	108
Vocation in the Theology of Jürgen Moltmann	120
Vocation in the Theology of Karl Barth	129
Election, Priesthood and Covenant in 1 Peter 2.4-10	138
Conclusion	145

Chapter 6: Covenant, Sacrifice and Priesthood — 147

The Priestly Testimony and Counter-testimony of the First Testament	148
The Priestly Testimony	148
Priesthood and Covenant	151
Counter-testimony in the First Testament against the Priests	154

Contents   xi

The Testimony and Counter-testimony of the Priesthood of Jesus in the Letter to the Hebrews	158
Priestly Testimony in Hebrews	160
Counter-testimony against the Priestly in Hebrews	162
The Testimony and Counter-testimony of Sacrifice	166
The Testimony and Counter-testimony of the Divine *pro nobis* in Jesus Christ	173
Conclusion	185

Part III: Priesthood: The Imaginative and Human Retelling of God's Story — 189

Chapter 7: Narrative and Imagination	**191**
Different Conceptions of Priesthood and Sacrifice	191
The Dialectical Imagination	197
Chapter 8: Priesthood and the Ordained	**207**
Priesthood and Analogy	208
Analogy and the Dialectical	208
The Particularism of Priesthood in the Bible	211
Exemplarism and Interchange	215
A Representative Priesthood	219
The Particular and the General	219
Bishops and Deacons at Philippi	222
The Eucharist and Priesthood	225
The Asymmetrical Representation of the Priesthood	231
Representation and Participation	237
Tracing the Priestly Representation	238
Κοινωνία as Participation	243
Participation, Κοινωνία and the Eucharist as a Theologia Crucis	248
Conclusion	250

Part IV: Conclusion — 257

Chapter 9 Priesthood: Tracing the Promise of God's Saving Act	**259**
Identity and Recognition	260

Character and Diversity 263
The Eucharist, Sacrifice and Externalisation 267

Bibliography **271**

Index **287**

Foreword

New moves are occurring with the theological imagination, both Roman Catholic and Protestant. With the decline of liberal Christianity (entrenched in the legacies of modernity) there has been a return to tradition, no where more so than in Protestant and particularly Anglican circles. In the wake of this new ecumenical notes are being sounded. This trend is not without forerunners: Karl Barth, who has an important role to play in this book, was of considerable interest to Roman Catholic theologians of *nouvelle théologie* sympathies and found himself in conversations with major theological voices such as Erich Przywara and Hans Urs von Balthasar. But today we find a new weaving of the Protestant tradition, with its inheritance from Luther and Calvin, back into the Early Greek and Latin Fathers. New readings of Luther and Calvin have facilitated these theological moves, particularly the Finnish school's work on Luther's metaphysics and new emphases on Calvin's more Roman Catholic leanings. What was best about liberal theologies – their concern with the cultural (in the widest sense of that term) – is retained. But rather than theology apologising for itself in the triumphant stare of these other sciences, theology is addressing the economic, gender, political and ecological sensibilities of the times from its own distinct perspective. As a result Protestant theology is richer and more diverse. It has, to my mind, stopped being defensive – either about its own reformed rather than Roman Catholic agenda or the threatened incursions of the secular. Protestant theology has rather become more confident – able to explore the questions it repressed (such as sacramentality and doctrines of creation), engage and learn from theologies from other Christian traditions and able to experiment with new methodologies arising from philosophy, both analytic and Continental (such as deconstruction, phenomenologies of desire and Wittgensteinian accounts of language).

The book we have before us is a further expression of this new imaginative turn in Protestant theology. It takes up a repressed question – the question of priesthood; it explores what, since Hegel, has been an influential doctrine for Protestantism – kenosis – but returns us to Patristic Trinitarian reflections upon *perichoresis, processio* and *missio* that characterise the intra-Trinitarian *dunamis*; it engages and learns from the

Roman Catholic theology of Hans Urs von Balthasar and the Lutheran liberal theology of Jürgen Moltmann; and it undertakes these three explorations with the assistance of narrative theories of identity. But what are also important, and constitutes an important background in this study, are material questions related to ordained ministry in the Reformation tradition. This book, then, is not a piece of systematic theology that nestles towards the top of some mountain of abstraction. It is an engaged systematics that issues from long practical engagement with liturgical life. It is from reflection upon being a priest that the theology of priesthood emerges. And it returns to priestly activity in a way that gives new meaning (and new coherence) to priesthood for Protestantism. This is to my mind how theology should proceed, even (perhaps particularly) in a culture of professional theologians stationed in universities across the world. In the same way, in the past, the Cappodocian reflection upon the ascetic life arose from critical reflections upon the eremitic withdrawal from the world and Augustine's theology of friendship from the several communities which he both lived in and created. Even the high-flown speculations on intra-Trinitarian life that commenced in Alexandria and flourished in both pre- and post- Nicaea theologies were rooted not only in contemporary battles with docetism and Gnosticism, but also (and primarily) in concerns to value the created order and the material practices of human existence. In was in those speculations that mediations upon the *carmen Christi* of Philippians 2 gave rise to a doctrine of kenosis – a doctrine that, closely related to creation and incarnation, explored the relationship between the immanent life of God and God's operations in the world created by Him. It is a doctrine of utmost importance for this book.

Priesthood has been given a number of theological evaluations in the Christian church. As understood by the Roman Catholics it refers to a mediating role in the church's sacramental ministry of Christ to the secular world, the world of the laity. In particular, the priest mediates the grace of God in the sacraments, with the mass, in which the atoning sacrifice of Christ is enacted, operating as the daily heart around which the six other sacraments (that order the course of human life) are situated. As understood by the Orthodox church the liturgical role of the priest is extended sacramentally. The priest has a role in a cosmic liturgy; for the priest vocalizes the hymn of thanksgiving and praise that all creation sings. This role too is mediatory for the song sung participates in the unfolding salvation of humankind. It articulates the promise of salvation that human beings are elevated into a condition of *theosis* – conformity to Christ the divine Logos. In contrast, in the Protestant tradition, in which the mediating role of the priesthood is played down in a quite legitimate desire to emphasize the sovereignty of God and the profound *diastasis* that separates the divine from the human, priests have no mediatory function. The cultic role they fulfil in the economy of salvation is indirect – they are called in

Foreword xv

their profession of Christ to preach the Word of God. It is that Word, in its sheer graciousness, that saves. Priest, then, cannot be the title for a distinct ecclesial office for, on Scriptural witness, it refers to the "priesthood of all believers". The ordained minister in the Protestant tradition is not separated out from the community of such believers, but one among them called to serve in the ecclesial institution that builds up the common faith. And yet ecclesiology cannot be disassociated from a doctrine of the triune God and Christ is frequently described in priestly and cultic language (as this volume makes clear). He is specifically referred to the Psalmist's account of the "priest after the order of Melchizidek" in Hebrews. Since believers are then disciples and imitators of Christ how then does priesthood function for Protestants? How does it relate to atonement and vocation? If, in the past, Protestantism has shied away from such questions and not clearly viewed vocation as related to Trinitarian *missio*, it is one of the important contributions of this volume that those questions are answered in terms of the effective work of testimony and counter-testimony that takes place in the dialectic between the divine and the human. So at a time when the Protestant ordained ministry (like ordained ministries in the Roman Catholic and Orthodox traditions) is experiencing difficulty in terms of declining vocations and at least two generations of people unschooled in theological teaching it is extremely valuable to show how the language of priesthood assists in the development of a Christian sacerdotal identity. It enriches Protestant ecclesiology and Protestant theology more generally. Furthermore, in rooting this ecclesiology within a doctrine of the Trinity there is a move towards a greater catholicity that I hope also enriches ecumenical debate.

That Christian identity, as again this volume shows, is intimately associated with a kenotic Christology – that is, an account of the Christ who is sent into the world by the Father to be obedient even on to death that all things may be made subject to Him. The narrative of kenosis is nothing less than the narrative of divine identity – this is the revelation of what is God to and for us. It is another contribution of this book to expound this association and its implications for the doctrine of atonement. Most particularly because at this time a number of contemporary theologians (like Thomas T. Altizer and John D. Caputo) and philosophers (like Gianni Vattimo), following a certain secularised understanding of Hegel, are employing the figure of kenosis to describe a purely immanent and negative process that erases the transcendence of God, and baptises the secular. Several theologians examining these discourses have warned that ultimately such gestures, bound to conceptions of endless sacrifice towards the other, lead to a destructive nihilism. Ironically, it was Hegel who called this a bad infinite and it was a characteristic of an Unhappy Consciousness. To recover then the doctrine of kenosis for Christianity in a way that emphasises the operations of a triune God who, as creator and sustainer of the world, is never conflated with that world, is very important. To develop an understanding of that kenosis, which we each enter into as Christian believers following Christ, as an affirmative rather than negative process within an economy of God's giving to us and our response is also important. The act of producing such a theology is itself nothing less than a counter-testimony – an act of priesthood. This book then performs what its argument sets out demonstrate. Tim Herbert, in and through this theological investigation, is serving the tradition in which he stands *in a priestly manner*, and his sacrifice of time and intellectual energy is returned to him transfigured. One can only hope that such service for the church is accepted with gratitude.

Graham Ward
Professor of Contextual Theology and Ethics at The University of Manchester, September 2008

Preface

This study was submitted to the University of Manchester in 2004 as a PhD thesis. I am very grateful to Paternoster that it is now published in book form.

This work is partly the result of being a Protestant with over twenty years experience as an ordained Anglican priest. This reflection has been focused latterly first as a result of involvement in the selection of men and women for ordination and secondly, as Principal of a regional training course responsible for preparing men and women for ordination. In this work I wish to try and break out of the sterile ontological/functional or biblical/tradition focused debates that have almost universally dominated this issue. As a Protestant I have sought to take seriously the biblical basis for theology but to suggest that as with hermeneutics, the key issue is located in the nature of the divine-human encounter and the representational nature of the language employed to articulate these key relationships.

As is evident I have a long standing interest in the nature of ministry and in particular the nature of the ordained ministry. In particular I have come to recognize that one of the problems with much of the debate as it is engaged with by evangelical or Protestant writers is the lack of theology. By which I mean that because the focus is often upon issues like leadership or functionalism theology gets left to one side or adduced merely to support the desired outcome. However, as students on the *Lancashire and Cumbria Theological Partnership* are no doubt tired of hearing ministry is above all a theological activity. It is the theological nature of ministry which identifies it as distinctively Christian activity. In this context I understand theology very simply as being concerned with how the community of faith speaks logically and therefore coherently about God. In this context ministry, and therefore the priesthood of the ordained can be understood as enacted speech about God. Such enacted speech takes place in a double context. First, it takes place in the context of the communities of those people who desire to be the faithful people of God and secondly in the face of the wider world which is God's beloved creation.

The problem, however, is the lack of theological imagination which is often consequential upon the fact that much speech about ministry is driven by either pragmatism or perceived notions of orthodoxy. In this context this work is intended to give the debate a bit of a jolt in the hope that we, that is those of us who are privileged to be called to the ordained ministry – in whatever church – may continue to wrestle with our calling in all its apostolicity and catholicity in order to fulfil it all the better.

Tim Herbert
Cotehill
Petertide, 2007.

Acknowledgements

I am very grateful that I have had the opportunity to engage with what for me has been a fascinating area of study. That this has been possible has been due to many people. In particular I must acknowledge my gratitude to my colleagues on the staff of the *Lancashire and Cumbria Theological Partnership* (formerly the *Carlisle and Blackburn Diocesan Training Institute* and students who have helped me to think through some of the issues and bearing with my theological obsessions over a number of years. I would also like to thank the Ecclesiastical Insurance Group for a very generous grant towards the cost of the studies, as well as to Rt. Revd. Ian Harland and the Rt. Revd. Graham Dow for invaluable support. I would also wish to record an immense debt of gratitude to the Revd. Dr. Jim Garrard, Dr. John Todd, Dr. Margaret Ives for their valiant proof reading of the text and Dr Karl Möller for helping me to correct the pagination while retaining blame for any remaining errors. Above all, however, it remains for me to thank Professor Graham Ward who has provided unstinting and stimulating supervision throughout this research from its inception to completion. Finally, to record my thanks to Tom whose endless questioning has encouraged my own questioning, to James for the recognition of the complexity and importance of language and its usage, which is so often taken for granted and not least to Pam for her love and support over many years.

Abbreviations

AR	*God's Reign and Our Unity*, The Report of the Anglican-Reformed International Commission 1981-1984,
ARCIC	The Anglican-Roman Catholic Commission
BEM	*Baptism, Eucharist and Ministry*, WCC, Faith and Order Paper 111,
CD	Barth, Karl, *Church Dogmatics* (ET), 1936-1969
FOAG	Faith And Order Group
HTR	*Harvard Theological Review*
Laws	Richard Hooker, *The Laws of Ecclesiastical Polity*
LXX	The Septuaguint
JSNT	*Journal for the Study of the New Testament*
JTS	*Journal of Theological Studies*
NTS	*New Testament Studies*
PI	Wittgenstein, Ludwig, *Philosophical Investigations* (ET, G E M Anscombe)
RSV	Revised Standard Version
SJT	*Scottish Journal of Theology*
Syst	Pannenberg, Wolfhart, *Systematic Theology* (ET), 1988-1998
TD	Balthasar, Hans Urs von, *Theo-Drama,* (ET,), 1988-1998
TDNT	*Theological Dictionary of the New Testament* (ET)
WCC	World Council of Churches

CD ROM
CCEL   *Christian Classics Ethereal Library*, 2000

Bible Usage
Unless otherwise stated biblical quotations are from the *Revised Standard Version* of the Bible, copyright 1946, 1952, © 1957, 1971, 1973 by the Division of Christian Education of the National Council of the Churches of Christ in the USA.

Chapter 1

Introduction: The Reality of Priesthood

Ministerial priesthood remains a sharply divisive concept for the Christian Churches. Whereas Protestantism is hermeneutically suspicious of priesthood for historical,[1] biblical[2] and theological[3] reasons Roman Catholicism, in its official accounts,[4] maintains a doctrine of ministerial priesthood which appears not to address these concerns. One significant consequence has been the inability of those arguing from either Reformed Protestant or Catholic backgrounds to reach a consensus.[5] This has in turn,

---

[1] Historical objections normally focus upon the lateness of the emergence of the application of the title 'priest' to the ordained ministry and the history of the Reformation.

[2] Biblically grounded objections to the priesthood of the ordained usually focus upon the apparent absence of references to a ministerial priesthood in the New Testament account of the emerging Church.

[3] Theological objections focus upon the understanding that priesthood undermines divine sovereignty and the primacy of grace by interposing a 'sacrificial tribe or class between God and man, by whose intervention alone God is reconciled and man forgiven.' (J. B. Lightfoot. 'The Christian Ministry', in *St Paul's Epistle to the Philippians* (Revd. Edn.), London, Macmillan and Co, 1879, 181.)

[4] According to the Second Vatican Council the ordained ministry is a divinely instituted and historically traceable hierarchical succession through Peter and his successors the papacy which is shared with the episcopate with whom priests, 'as helpers took on the ministry'. (*Lumen Gentium*, 20. Austin Flannery OP (ed.), *The Basic Sixteen Documents Vatican Council II: Constitutions Decrees Declarations* (Revised Translation), Dublin, Dominican Publications, 1996, 27.) For a recent accounts of the Roman Catholic understanding of ordination and priesthood see: Aidan Nichols, *Holy Order*, Dublin, Veritas Publications, 1990, 137, Benedict M. Ashley OP, 'The Priesthood of Christ, the Baptised and the Ordained', Donald J. Goergen, Ann Garrido (ed), *The Theology Of Priesthood*, The Liturgical Press, Collegeville (Minnesota), 2000, 164. Dissenting voices are most notably: Hans Küng, *Why Priests?* (ET), London, Fontana, 1972; Edward Schillebeeckx, *The Church With A Human Face* (ET), London, SCM, 1985.

[5] Notable ecumenical statements are provided by: The Anglo-Roman Catholic International Commission (ARCIC), *The Final Report*, London, CTS/SPCK, 1982; *Baptism, Eucharist and Ministry*, Faith and Order Paper 111, Geneva, WCC, 1982; *Anglican-Lutheran Dialogue*, London, SPCK, 1983; *God's Reign Our Unity*,

been a powerful negative force in ecumenism.[6] Nevertheless the debate concerning the ordination of women has shown the significance attached to the doctrine of the priesthood in the Church.[7] In this thesis I shall question the linguistic and representational understanding of kenosis in order to re-examine the biblical and theological parameters of priesthood.

The contention of this thesis is that by rejecting both the naively realistic account and resisting the alternative of an anti-realistic account of kenosis it is possible to construct a critically realistic dialectical account of kenosis[8] and priesthood.[9] In the critically realistic account I propose that priesthood and kenosis are linked through a common narrative of the divine/human encounter.[10] However, this approach resists any claims that either priesthood or kenosis can be stated in a series of logical propositions. Furthermore narrative[11] provides a framework in which objective facts are structured and therefore interpreted by inclusion within a discernible and coherent plot, and bounded by the limitations of characterisation. It is therefore possible to assess the validity of kenosis and the priesthood of the ordained within the broader worldview or metanarrative of the Christian story.

I shall further argue that the traditional Protestant account is limited by an adherence to a naively realistic epistemology of biblical language which distorted its account of priesthood.[12] As James Dunn notes, Paul's use of priestly language in the service of the gospel[13] has intriguing possibilities for the concept of ministry.[14] While Dunn's primary concern is not ministerial priesthood but the hermeneutics of good exposition, his wish is that the text should speak and be heard. Thus the expositor "functions as a priest precisely by functioning at the point"[15] on the edge of the divine human encounter. However, he concludes that neither of these can be

---

London/Edinburgh, SPCK/The Saint Andrew Press, 1984; *The Nature and Purpose of the Church*, Faith and Order Paper 181, Geneva, WCC, 1998. *The Meissen Common Statement* (1988) and *The Porvoo Common Statement* (1993).

[6] In England both the Anglican-Methodist Re-Union Scheme (1968) and the Ten Propositions (1982) failed over the recognition of orders.

[7] Negatively see: Nichols, 1990, 152. Positively see: Robin Greenwood, *Transforming Priesthood*, London, SPCK, 1994, 43.

[8] See: Chapters 2 and 3 below.

[9] See: Chapters 4 and 5 below.

[10] See: Chapters 4 and 5 below.

[11] Aristotle, *Poetics*, London, Penguin, 1996. See: Chapter 4 below on narrative and Philippians.

[12] Karl Barth, *The Knowledge of God and the Service of God According to the Teaching of the Reformation* (ET), London, Hodder and Stoughton, 1949, 213.

[13] James D. G. Dunn, 'What Makes a Good Exposition', *The Expository Times* (114), 2003, 155.

[14] See: Chapters 4 and 8 below.

[15] Dunn, 2003, 156.

achieved independently of the community within which exposition and hearing take place.

I shall argue therefore that the divine-human encounter is primarily an event of the Word and can be articulated with priestly language.[16] Priesthood is a sign of the mutual participation of the divine and human. It is in human words that the divine Word is represented but without any confusion of form. The human word may speak the Word of God but it does not become the Word. The human proclamation of the Word of God is therefore kenotic. Not because the word is negated by the Word, nor is the Word surrendered to the human word, but rather filled by the Word, while retaining their own words and provenance.[17] Each participates in the other; boundaries are crossed in the communicative act and salvation announced. Kenosis, as a critically realistic account of the divine-human, represents the participation of the divine in the human sphere within a trinitarian account of God's saving grace. The priesthood of the ordained is a public testimony to God's prior sovereign grace. The priestly sacrifice is one of grateful response, recognisable in relation to Christ, Christ like, but remaining a distinctly human activity.[18] Priesthood therefore embraces the ordering of the community by modelling the Christian identity of the whole people of God. It is not a status but a way of life transformed by the presence of God.

In order to proceed it is important to clarify a number of methodological issues that have emerged. First, there is the question of the representation of the mutual participation of the divine and the human. Secondly, there are the implications of different models of representation for accounts of kenosis and priesthood. Thirdly, it is important to examine the nature and role of narrative as a vehicle for meaning. Fourthly, to explore the nature of the divine-human encounter as the basis of both kenosis and the priesthood. Finally I shall summarise my argument.

Representation and Realism

Baldly stated representation is concerned with the depiction of reality. On the one hand realists believe the language of representation corresponds to an external objective reality. Thus according to Wittgenstein's early theories of language it is the "simplest kind of proposition... [which] asserts the existence of a state of affairs."[19] Consequently, if "an elementary

---

[16] See: Chapters 6 and 7 below.
[17] See: Chapter 8 below.
[18] See: Chapter 6 and 8 below.
[19] Ludwig Wittgenstein, *Tractatus Logic-Philosophicus* (ET), London, Routledge & Kegan Paul Ltd, 1988, 4.21. Wittgenstein designates such a proposition an 'elementary proposition'.

proposition is true, the state of affairs exists".[20] Wittgenstein wishes to establish that for language to be meaningful it requires logical and structural connection between objects and the name which denotes them.[21] The realist claims that propositions correspond[22] to reality. Facts, states of affairs, and propositions are usually introduced "by means of a clause beginning with 'that'".[23] On the other hand anti-realists believe that language can never correspond to any external and objective truth or fact. God is not "a metaphysical entity 'out there'. Such a God is too small" rather God is "and always was a metaphor for the values generated by human culture".[24]

Between these two extremes it is possible to suggest a middle way which is neither the naïve realism of Wittgenstein's elementary propositionalism nor the expressivist relativism of the Sea of Faith community. This alternative is found in the *Philosophical Investigations* which Wittgenstein begins with a long quote from Augustine[25] in order to recapitulate the linguistic theory he himself had espoused in *Tractatus*. In this later work Wittgenstein rejects his earlier theory according to which words name and therefore describe objective realities replacing it with the notion of what he calls 'language games' emphasising "that the speaking of a language is part of an activity, or a form of life."[26] Language as an activity is not dependent upon some perceived common essence but "similarities, relationships and a whole series of them at that." Wittgenstein asked his readers not to think but to "*look and see*"[27] 'similarities and relationships' which he called "family resemblances".[28] This third understanding of representation denies an overly simplistic realism of sameness replacing it with an analogical realism of likeness or similarity.[29]

Realistic Representation: Priesthood and Kenosis

So how is priesthood represented? It might be represented negatively:

---

[20] Wittgenstein, 1988, 4.25.

[21] In the *Tractatus* Wittgenstein developed a picture theory of representation. (See: 2.12; 2.131; 2.14; 2.15, 2.161, 2.17.)

[22] Roger Scruton, *Modern Philosophy*, London, Pimlico, 1994, 99.

[23] Scruton, 1994, 100.

[24] Andrew Moore, *Realism and Christian Faith*, Cambridge, CUP, 2003, 3, quoting David Boulton, *A Reasonable Faith: Introducing the Sea of Faith Network*, Loughborough, Sea of Faith, 1997, 9.

[25] *PI*. 1. Quoting: Augustine, Confessions, I. 8.

[26] *PI*. 23.

[27] *PI*. 66 – his italics.

[28] *PI*. 67.

[29] See: Chapters 7 and 8 below.

The Reality of Priesthood 5

[A] survey of the relevant NT material has shown *that* a priesthood of church leaders separate or different from that of the Christian community is absent from the earliest church's writings... [indeed] *that* ideas are present in the NT which tell against the presence of a priestly group within the church.[30]

Or it might be represented positively: Jesus Christ not only founded the Church but endowed it with a form of Christian ministry in which

the fullness of the Spirit's presence and operation once for all granted to the Church, in the visible society once for all instituted; and is at least therefore a 'tenable proposition' *that* it should have been expressed in a once for all empowered and commissioned ministry.

That it is more than a 'tenable proposition' – it is a proposition which states a fact of history.[31]

Clearly, these two representations are irreconcilable. Nonetheless both authors believe they are making statements that correspond to an objective truth.[32] In the first statement Colin Bulley makes a claim that appeals to the *objective* Bible reader, whereas Charles Gore makes a claim that appeals to the *objective* theological historian. It is no coincidence the authors quoted

---

[30] Colin Bulley, *The Priesthood of Some Believers*, Carlisle, Paternoster, 2000, 48 – my italics.

[31] Charles Gore, *The Church and the Ministry* (4th Edn.), London, Longmans, Green and Co., 1900, 58-9. - my italics.

[32] Charles Gore and Colin Bulley are not alone in adopting a naively realistic approach. Thus according to R. C. Moberly his argument stands or falls 'according to its own attempt to give an intelligent, rational, and judicial marshalling and interpretation of the evidence of actual historical facts.' (R. C. Moberly, *Ministerial Priesthood* (2nd Edn.), London, John Murray, 1919, vi.) Edwin Hatch argued that his account of the ministry was based upon 'historical science' and 'the testing of the documents which contain the evidence.' (E. Hatch, *The Organization Of The Early Christian Churches* (2nd Edn.), London, Rivingtons, 1882, 3.) C. H. Turner spoke of the attempt to conduct a 'strictly scientific and historical' examination of the emergence of the ordained ministry. (H. B. Swete (ed.), *Essays On The Early History Of The Church And The Ministry* (2nd Edn.), London, Macmillan and Co., 1921, xxi.) Another example is the argument that the ordained might enable 'the proper fulfillment [sic.] of the apostolic mission that had been entrusted to it by Christ.' *Presbyterorum Ordinis*, 2, Flannery, 1996, 318.) Ecumenically the Lima Statement also addresses the question of the ordained ministry, by means, though not exclusively, of a historical approach. However, it acknowledges that the ordination of women (*Baptism, Eucharist and Ministry* (*BEM*), Faith and Order Paper 111, Geneva, WCC, 1982, para. 18.) requires it to question the significance of the traditional historical account for validating different ministerial patterns.

above preface the claims they make with *that*. According to Gore historians simply re-present the past - events but also intellectual, social and cultural ideas, norms and movements - as it was. According to Bulley the omission by the Bible writers of an account of a designated ministerial priesthood is a fact which describes the reality of the Church in the apostolic era.

The same realism, evident in articulations of priesthood, is evident in accounts of kenosis – both in its German[33] and then later its British form[34] - that attempt to depict the nature of the divine-human encounter in Incarnation of Jesus Christ. The kenoticists believed they were offering a realistic depiction of the Incarnation. The reality of the divine-human encounter in the person of Jesus Christ logically required there was some necessary emptying or renunciation of the divine nature if the human nature was not to be a mirage.[35]

This position I shall call naïve realism. The naïve realist, for example Gore, assumes that it is possible to represent reality *as it is*. The theologian who is able to apply a scientific historical method is able to demonstrate "'what is essential'... from 'what can be called truly accidental'"[36] for the Christian religion. For Gore (and others) historical "research demonstrated that there had always been a distinct ministerial office" substantiating "the primitive 'institutions of bishops [and] presbyters'".[37]

Likewise Bulley, assumes that the Bible represents reality, as it is, because it is the Word of God and immune from human bias. Such foundationalism[38] understands "the meaning of the Bible... as a set of propositional statements, each expressing a divine affirmation, valid always and everywhere."[39] This "biblical theology" is "a kind of biblical positivism".[40] Applied to Scripture's apparent absence of interest in the doctrine of ministerial priesthood this is damning.[41] For the realist

---

[33] Gottfried Thomasius.
[34] Notably: Charles Gore, Frank Weston (both Anglican), and P. T. Forsyth (Congregationalist).
[35] See: Chapter 2 below.
[36] Jaroslav Pelikan, *Christian Doctrine and Modern Culture (since 1700)*, Chicago, Chicago University Press, 1989, 102.
[37] Pelikan, 1989, 87. See: Chapter 7 below.
[38] Foundationalism is the belief that knowledge must be grounded upon certain and therefore objective foundations. Classically Protestants foundationalism presumes a notion of biblical inerrancy.
[39] Avery Dulles, *Models of Revelation*, Dublin, Gill and Macmillan, 1983, 39. See also: Colin J. D. Greene, '"In the Arms of the Angels": Biblical Interpretation, Christology and the Philosophy of History', Craig Bartholomew, Colin Greene, Karl Möller (ed), *Renewing Biblical Interpretation*, Carlisle, Paternoster, 2000, 202.
[40] David H. Kelsey, *The Uses of Scripture In Recent Theology*, London, SCM, 1975, 23, quoting B. B. Warfield's preferred epithet.
[41] Kelsey, 1975, 21.

epistemologically "church doctrines function as informative propositions or truth claims about objective realities."[42]

Anti-Realistic Representation: Kenosis and Priesthood

In the Preface to *Radical Theology and the Death of God* Thomas J. J. Altizer and William Hamilton asked whether it was "possible to conceive of a form of Christianity coming to expression without belief in God."[43] According to Altizer the "disappearance of the historical Jesus is but a particular expression of a far deeper reality, the death of God."[44] Kenosis is the emptying of and therefore the absence of the divine. Existence "is not an appropriate word to ascribe to God, [so] therefore he cannot be said to exist".[45] Altizer and Hamilton denied that theological language which speaks of God can in any realistic sense be said to describe the divine. For Altizer realism, and in particular the claim to have access to the historical Jesus, is bogus. The time has past and is irrevocable so that "the Christian faith" must "transcend the language of images".[46] Similarly Don Cupitt argues the depiction offered is of the observer's perceptions of reality, as they understand it.

> Religion is not metaphysics but salvation, and salvation is the state of the self. It has to be appropriated subjectively or existentially. There is no such thing as religious truth and there cannot be. The view that religious truth consists in ideological correctness or in the objective correspondence of doctrinal statements with historical and metaphysical facts is a modern aberration, and a product of the decline of religious seriousness.[47]

In an article published to accompany the television series *The Sea of Faith*, Cupitt suggests that anti-realism is a consequence of the emergence of scepticism which is the child of modern science. Therefore instead "of being able to recognise eternal reality beyond the world, it was now

---

[42] George Lindbeck, *The Nature of Doctrine*, Philadelphia, The Westminster Press, 1984, 16.
[43] Thomas J. J. Altizer and William Hamilton, *Radical Theology and the Death of God*, London, Pelican, 1968, 9. See: Chapter 2 below.
[44] Thomas J. J. Altizer, 'Word and History', in Altizer and Hamilton, 1968, 128.
[45] William Hamilton, 'The Death of God Theologies Today', in Altizer and Hamilton, 1968, 39.
[46] Thomas J. J. Altizer, in Altizer and Hamilton, 1968, 131.
[47] Don Cupitt, *Taking Leave of God*, London, SCM, 43, (Quoted: Moore, 2003, 4).

restricted to recognising mathematical patterns in experience."[48] The Death of God theologians' and Cupitt's anti-realism suggests that truth - far from being given, objective, and external - is to be discovered and named. This reflects Lindbeck's second theory of religion and doctrine, the "experiential-expressivist", which "interprets doctrines as noninformative and nondiscursive symbols of inner feelings, attitudes, or existential orientations."[49] The result is an understanding of doctrine and religion, which potentially can be expressivist and relativist, in which meaning is an individual construct.[50]

Both the realist and anti-realist positions are flawed when discussing both the priesthood and kenosis.[51] On the one hand naïve realism demands a greater degree of correspondence between the external and objective original and its representation. So for example for Protestant theology no account of priesthood can go, beyond the New Testament evidence. Equally, according to Protestant theology, priesthood cannot be justified by the appeal that it is the way things are. On the other hand, an anti-realistic account of kenosis presumes there can be no objective reality which is God, and therefore only the divine absence can be pointed to. Therefore what is the alternative?

Critically Realistic Representation: Kenosis and Priesthood

'Critically realistic dialectic' is the epithet Bruce McCormack applies to the theological methodology of Karl Barth. According to McCormack Barth regarded God as

> a Reality which is complete and whole in itself apart from and prior to the knowing activity of human individuals. He conceived of the relation to God to the world in terms of a fundamental *diastasis*.[52]

In representations of God and the world Barth's realism, McCormack argues, is *critical*: it is beyond the empirically observable. The "truly 'real' is the wholly otherness of the *Self*-revealing God in comparison with whom

---

[48] Don Cupitt, 'Religion without superstition', *The Listener*, 13.9.84. The *Sea of Faith* was broadcast by the BBC, September 1984.
[49] Lindbeck, 1984, 16.
[50] Mooe, 2003, 3-7.
[51] See: Chapters 2 and 7 below.
[52] McCormack defines *diastasis* as 'a relation in which the two members stand over and against each other with no possibility of a final synthesis into a higher form of being.' (Bruce McCormack, *Karl Barth's Critically Realistic Dialectical Theology*, Oxford, OUP, 1997, 129.)

the empirical world is a mere shadow and appearance."[53] Concluding his study, McCormack draws attention to three aspects of Barth's methodology. First, it is "a strictly theological epistemology" which like "the Chalcedon formula ... points out errors" but without claiming to give "positive expression to the truth in the middle."[54] Secondly, McCormack argues that "to the extent that Barth concerned himself with philosophical epistemology at all he was an idealist."[55] Thirdly, that "dialectical theology in the form in which it was taught by Barth was a thoroughly modern option."[56] Barth's dialectical theology is to be understood in the light of his rejection of natural theology and apologetics, historicism the fundamentals of nineteenth-century liberal theology as embodied by Wilhelm Herrmann.

Critical realism frees kenosis from a trinitarianly naïve Christology according to which either Jesus Christ is either truly God or truly man but to be both is ultimately self-cancelling. It acknowledges the limitation of human language to depict accurately divine reality. Kenosis proposes a different language game governed by the otherness of God, while articulating the "mystery" which "must be spoken."[57] Kenosis seeks to hold together the *a priori* otherness of God and humanity in the divine-human encounter in the Father's self-revelation by sending the Son.[58] Likewise, it requires that priesthood, understood within a trinitarian and not simply christological context, articulates the human-divine encounter.[59] A critically realistic account of priesthood frees it from the naively realistic assumption that it can effect salvation so blurring the otherness of God from humanity. Rather priesthood can only ever signify salvation.

Critical realism permits a more complex understanding of representation while denying the extreme relativism of anti-realism. Barth, for example, understands representation in three distinct ways. According to Graham Ward there is first, "the knowledge of God presented in [*eintreten*] any creaturely encounter by the particularity of the revelatory event."[60]

---

[53] McCormack, 1997, 130 – his italics.
[54] McCormack, 1997, 464.
[55] McCormack, 1997, 465. Indeed McCormack suggests that Barth's philosophical foundations are essentially Kantian and of the nineteenth century. (McCormack, 1997, 130, 465.)
[56] McCormack, 1997, 466.
[57] Eberhard Jüngel, *Theological Essays I* (ET), Edinburgh, T & T Clark, 1989, 67.
[58] See: Chapter 3 below.
[59] See: Chapters 5 and 8 below.
[60] Graham, Ward, *Barth, Derrida and the Language of Theology*, Cambridge, CUP, 1998, 237. A variant form associated with the verb '*vertreten*' relates specifically to the work of Jesus Christ and carries significant overtones of substitution. So Barth speaks of Jesus' salvific action wherein he 'represents [*vertritt*] us at the right hand of the Father in our flesh' (*CD* II.1, 156; quoted by Ward, 1998, 237). Interestingly, the same passage Barth draws attention both to Jesus' high-priestly office within his representative role

Secondly, there is '*darstellen*' which is used "'to give an account', a narrated description"[61] concerned with the possibility of human representation. Therefore priesthood could represent humanity before God leading a sacrifice of praise and thanksgiving for his saving grace in Jesus Christ. Thirdly this would accord with '*repraesentieren*' a "much more general word" which includes both the first and second types[62] and which "is linked to a discourse's ability to repeat and present the eschatological promise of full and immediate self-presence, 'I am with you always.'"[63] Thus for Barth, God's Yes to humanity "is a representation [*Repraesentation*] of God's Word"[64] which culminates in "the sacrificial part of our public worship".[65] Barth regards preaching[66] and sacrament as proclamation[67] and therefore signs, "of the promise of the Gospel."[68] Proclamation is the "representation of God's Word"[69] in human words which points to the "very Word of God" which is always a "divine event"[70] transforming the human word by its participation in the divine Word. The priestly task, like kenosis, is the representation of the signs of the divine presence. However, the transformation effected is neither such that the Word of God is absorbed into the human nor yet a human word divinized. Both retain their particular identity within this incarnational moment so that the critically realistic dialectic is maintained.[71]

Representation, which is critically realistic, can also be articulated in terms of both 'fitting' and 'tracking' theories. The former suggests "signs... in virtue of resembling other things and they point to what they resemble", [72] while the latter because they track other objects or ideas "point to what they track."[73] Applying this to Barth's understanding; *eintreten* and

---

and his priestly representation of humanity before God (*CD* II.1, 156.) See: Chapter 8 below and the particularity of the accounts of priesthood in Paul.

[61] Ward, 1998, 239. In contradistinction to the first group which are primarily concerned with the divine 'modes of representation and knowing' (Ward, 1998, 240). See: Chapters 5 and 6 below.

[62] Ward, 1998, 242.

[63] Ward, 1998, 243. See: Chapter 8 below.

[64] *CD* I.1, 59 [1975]; quoted, Ward, 1998, 242-3.

[65] *CD* I.1, 58.

[66] *CD* I.1, 61.

[67] *CD* I.1, 61,

[68] *CD* I.1, 62.

[69] *CD* I.1, 64 – my italics.

[70] *CD* I.1, 65.

[71] See: Chapter 8 below.

[72] Donna M. Summerfield, 'Fitting versus tracking: Wittgenstein on representation', in Hans Sluga, David G. Stern (ed), *The Cambridge Companion to Wittgenstein*, Cambridge, CUP, 1999, 102.

[73] Summerfield, 1999, 103.

vertreten presume a fitting understanding whereas *darstellen* presumes tracking while *repraesentieren* appears to combine both in a dialectic ambiguity. Donna Summerfield suggests that there are three important contrasts between these two theories. First, tracking theories are dependent upon the occurrence of what is represented. Secondly, therefore, whereas fitting theories are dependent upon internal likeness, tracking theory is externally determined.[74] Thirdly,

> not surprisingly, fitting theories also tend to suppose that the properties that confer semantic value on signs are epistemically accessible in some privileged or special way to the 'meaner' (i.e., the person doing the meaning), whereas tracking theorists tend to suppose that the properties that confer semantic value on signs need not be epistemically accessible in any special way."[75]

In this thesis therefore I shall argue that a critically realistic dialectic permits speech which is meaningful in the context of Protestant theology concerning kenosis and priesthood.

Narrative and Critical Realism

Explicitly kenotic accounts of the Incarnation first appeared in the mid-nineteenth century[76] as a reaction to the anti-realist Zeitgeist of the age encapsulated in the work of Feuerbach[77] and Marx.[78] The Incarnation was no longer a mystery but the encounter of "the 'natural' and the 'supernatural'". The traditional case "for the divinity of Christ" no longer appeared credible so that theologians felt "driven to make it by emphasizing his humanity."[79] In countering anti-realism some theologians responded by emphasizing the realism of theological language.

In Britain there emerged a debate about the priesthood in the latter part of the nineteenth century.[80] Among the disputants were Charles Gore and P. T. Forsyth who, it so happened, were also leading British proponents of

---

[74] Summerfield, 1999, 103-4.
[75] Summerfield, 1999, 105.
[76] Gottfried Thomasius, *Christi Person und Werk*, 1853-57. See: Chapter 2 below.
[77] L. A. Feuerbach, *The Essence of Christianity*, (1841) argued that religious belief was the false projection of the individual psychology.
[78] Karl Marx, (*Critique of Hegel's Philosophy of Right*, 1844, and *Theses on Feuerbach* 1845), argued that religion was a social construct.
[79] John Kent, 'Christian Theology in the Eighteenth to the Twentieth Century', Hubert Cunliffe-Jones with Benjamin Drewery (ed.), *A History of Christian Doctrine*, Edinburgh, T & T Clark, 1978, 508.
[80] See: Chapter 7 below.

kenotic Christology.[81] However, while Gore and Forsyth both advocated kenosis they held very different understandings of priesthood. What they shared was a desire for realism, according to which kenosis was an account which asserted that this is the way the incarnation is. Whereas Gore's historically grounded realism led him to claim this is the way priesthood is, Forsyth and other Protestants reading of the Bible claimed that this is not the way priesthood is.[82] However, both were guilty of "a premature fusion of horizons... before readers have listened in openness with respect for the tension between the horizons of the text and the horizon of the reader." Consequently, the "textual horizon has collapsed into that of the reader's narrative biography and is unable to do more than to speak back his or her own values and desires."[83]

The collapse of the textual horizon resulted in the 'thin description' which underlies the accounts of both kenosis and priesthood.[84] Thin description restricts itself to the objective account, that this is the way it is as the locus for the meaning of an event whereas thick description[85] recognises that events and ideas are given their meaning by a whole range of cultural and interpretative understandings.[86]

Fergus Kerr suggests, Barth, who was "the original practitioner of 'narrative theology'" denounced "the rationalist epistemological bias"[87] which has permeated biblical reading and theology. According to Barth,

> the human possibility of knowing is not exhausted by the ability to perceive and comprehend. Imagination, too, belongs no less legitimately in its way to the human possibility of knowing. A man without

---

[81] See: Chapter 2 below.
[82] See: Chapter 7 below.
[83] Thiselton, 1992, 531 – his italics.
[84] Both of which were established in the period which extended from roughly the middle of the nineteenth century until approximately the end of the First World War. See: Chapters 2, 7 below.
[85] See: Chapters 7 and 8 below.
[86] Clifford Geertz, 'Thick Description: Toward an Interpretive Theory of Culture', in *The Interpretation of Cultures*, New York, Basic Books Inc., 1973, 3-30. Geertz begins by rehearsing Gilbert Ryle's analysis of the 'two boys rapidly contracting the eyelids of their right eye' (Geertz, 1973, 6) and the ability differentiate between a wink and an involuntary twitch or with the introduction of third boy who parodies the act. The point being that 'thin description' of the empirical sees all three acts as essentially the same, whereas a 'thick description' is able to acknowledge the significantly different meanings in each case. According to Karl Möller 'the "unbiased view" of the historical-critical approach has turned out to be a chimaera'. (Karl Möller, 'Renewing Historical Criticism', Craig Bartholomew, Colin Greene, Karl Möller (ed), *Renewing Biblical Interpretation*, Carlisle, Paternoster, 2000, 166.)
[87] Fergus Kerr, *Theology after Wittgenstein* (2nd Edn), London, SPCK, 1997, 9.

The Reality of Priesthood

imagination is more of an invalid than one who lacks a leg... there are more things... in the human capacity and of perception and presentation – than are dreamed of in their philosophy.[88]

A critically realistic dialectical theology, denies a positivist epistemology in which "what is of permanent value... must be reducible in the final analysis either to fact (history) or eternal truths that can be shown to be rationally and morally satisfying."[89] It neither seeks to cut itself loose from its moorings to realism. Nor does it believe "that only one historical or doctrinal expression of the faith expresses it definitively",[90] rather it recognizes like an analogy of an incomplete jigsaw, narrative can only represent 'possible actions.'[91]

Gerard Loughlin summarizes Ricoeur's theory of narrative as providing a framework "by which human life [and therefore events, intellectual, social and cultural ideas, norms and movements] is rendered significant." Narrative provides the possibility for presenting "a possible world for our dwelling,"[92] a worldview[93] which enables the imaginative completion of an otherwise incomplete jigsaw.[94] A Christian worldview is grounded in the objective reality of God represented by the understanding that this is God's world and human beings are his creatures. However, while human beings have turned their back upon God, this failure is resolved by His gracious gift of salvation.[95] Accordingly this narrative believes itself to be realistic,

---

[88] *CD* III.1, 91.
[89] Trevor Hart, 'Imagining Evangelical Theology', in John G. Stackhouse (ed), *Evangelical Futures*, Leicester, Apollos, 2000, 193.
[90] Moore, 2003, 5.
[91] Richard Evans writing about naïve realism, anti-realism and critical realism offers the analogy of completing a jigsaw where different pieces are scattered and first have to be brought together and even then when assembled the picture is incomplete. His point is that we may imagine what the picture ought to look like, but our imagining is not boundless but limited by the picture as we have it. Therefore 'if they only fit together to produce a picture of a steam-engine, for instance, it is no good trying to put them together to make a suburban garden: it simply will not work.' (Richard J. Evans, *In Defense Of History*, London, Granta Books, 2000, 89.)
[92] Gerard Loughlin, *Telling God's Story*, London, SPCK, 1999, 147.
[93] See: Chapters 4, 5 and 6 below.
[94] Butterfield using a different analogy but for similar ends describes the work of the historian as like that of the detective who creates a story in which facts are brought together and emplotted through the telling of stories whose plausibility can then be judged and accepted or rejected. (Herbert Butterfield, *Christianity And History*, London, G. Bell and Sons Ltd., 1949, 12, 14.)
[95] J. Richard Middleton and Brian J. Walsh, *Truth is stranger than it used to be*, London, SPCK, 1995, 11. According to Middleton and Walsh a worldview must answer four

but critically so, wishing to resist the relativism of the anti-realist. Consequently, "if the triune God reveals his independent reality to humans, it is likely that this will be detected by attending to the practices" and therefore beliefs "which together make up the Christian faith."[96]

Narrative and Identity

It is necessary, at this point, to make some very brief observations concerning the nature of identity. Identity is an important concept in this thesis[97] which serves to bring together kenosis and priesthood. First kenosis is concerned with the divine identity, and therefore the knowability of God. The danger inherent in kenosis is the implicit emptying, and consequent loss or surrender of identity.[98] Secondly, I shall argue that in the Letter to the Philippians a series of questions are posed concerning not only the identity of Jesus Christ, in relation to God, but also of Paul and the Philippians in relation both to one another but, above all, in relation to Jesus Christ. However, a third strand in the epistle is Paul's notion of the priestly identity of both Timothy and Epaphroditus but also the Philippians.[99] Thirdly, that the vocation of the church is to be a priestly people which is identifiable in relation God's covenant people, Israel.[100] Fourthly, that in the Scriptures priestly identity is not naively realistic but critically and dialectically realistic.[101] Finally, that the identity of priesthood if it is to be described thickly must look not simply to the meaning of the language of priesthood, important though that is, but to its essential roles and practices.[102]

It is ironic that 'identity' has a number of non-identical meanings. First, 'identity' can be understood in terms of objective 'sameness' in which one thing corresponds directly to another, in which case naïve realism is appropriate.[103] Secondly, identity can also be corporate, a shared resemblance. Thirdly, to 'identify' can mean to regard different objects as having an essential sameness. Finally, to 'identify' is also to determine 'the identity of an object or person'. Identity and therefore recognition needs to

---

fundamental questions: Where are we? Who are we? What's wrong? What's the remedy?

[96] Moore, 2003, 8-9. See: Chapter 6 below.
[97] See: Chapter 4 below.
[98] See: Chapters 2 and 3 below.
[99] See: Chapter 4 below.
[100] See: Chapter 5 below.
[101] See: Chapter 6 below.
[102] See: Chapters 7 and 8 below.
[103] For example, all first class stamps are identical, each one exactly the same and interchangeable.

The Reality of Priesthood 15

be elastic and able to encompass the variety of appearances that may be found within any family likeness.[104]

Paul Ricoeur suggests that identity, which is grounded in narrative through the establishment of character and by the keeping of the subject's word, offers the possibility of thick description so that both similarity and dissimilarity can be held together across the passage of time.[105] 'Identity' is not about one thing being 'the same as' an other thing (*idem*), but rather of repeatability and oneness (*ipse*). Identity is depends upon recognition and the correct naming the subject and its assignment to its proper genus.[106] Narrative, in recounting the experiences of the person, "constructs the identity of the character"[107] within the framework of the individual's participation within the story. According to Ricoeur identity consists of "the permanence in time of character and that of self-constancy."[108] By allusion to Paul, he suggests that between

> the imagination that says 'I can try anything' and the voice that says, 'Everything is possible but not everything is beneficial…' a muted discord is sounded. It is this discord that the act of promising transforms into a fragile concordance: 'I can try anything' to be sure, but 'Here is where I stand!'[109]

---

[104] So for example the *Dactylorhiza fuchsii* (common spotted orchid) whose flowers can be anything from 'white to reddish-purple' (Marjorie Blamey, Christopher Grey-Wilson, *The Illustrated Flora of Britain and Northern Europe*, London, Hodder and Stoughton, 1989, 480).

[105] Ricoeur proposes there are two possible expressions of identity 'that are both descriptive and emblematic: character and keeping one's word' (Paul Ricoeur, *Oneself As Another* (ET), Chicago, Chicago University Press, 1994, 118.) where idem and ipse meet one another. Character he defines as 'the set of distinctive marks which permit the re-identification of a human individual as being the same' (Ricoeur, 1994, 119.) through time and the 'set of lasting dispositions by which a person is recognized.' (Ricoeur, 1994, 121.) The second model of permanence other than character proposed by Ricoeur is that of 'keeping one's word' as an expression of 'self-constancy'. (Ricoeur, 1994, 123.)

[106] Paul Ricoeur, 1994, 149.

[107] Ricoeur, 1994, 147. See: Chapters 2 and 3 below.

[108] Ricoeur, 1994, 166. According to Barth, the disciples 'saw and heard Jesus again after His death, and that as they saw and heard Him they recognized Him, and they recognized Him on the basis of His identity with the One they had known before.' (*CD* .IV.2, 145.)

[109] Ricoeur, 1994, 167. (See: 1 Cor 10.23.) Charles Taylor suggests that to 'know who I am is a species of knowing where I stand. My identity is defined by the commitments and identifications which provide… the horizon within which I am capable of taking a stand.' So as we shall see in Chapter 4 below Paul speaks of being 'in Christ' which serves 'to determine where they stand on questions of what is good or worthwhile, or admirable or of value.' (Charles Taylor, *Sources of the Self*, Cambridge, CUP, 2000,

Identity, like the incomplete jigsaw, is shaped by the worldview (metanarrative) of the one to be identified and by the particular narrative in which it is located. So in this thesis I shall argue that the identity of the priesthood is primarily defined by reference, on the one hand, to the priority of God's sovereign grace[110] and, on the other hand, by human being's dependent and therefore responsive relationship as God's covenant partner.[111]

There remain two further aspects of identity which it is necessary to clarify briefly. First, narrative identity, as defined by Paul Ricoeur in terms of character, permits a degree of fluidity[112] or elasticity of identity, by denying absolute fixity.[113] But like the analogy of an incomplete jigsaw there is sufficient of the picture for recognition to remain a possibility[114] not least because the extant pieces do not permit rearrangement into an alternative image. Elasticity – and therefore fluidity – is suggestive of a critical realism, of likeness, similarity or family resemblance in which the notion of objective fact is maintained. Secondly, participation speaks of taking, the form of or part in or engaging with another.[115] So, for example, the intra-trinitarian relations are participatory, grounded in the movement between the divine persons. Similarly in Christian prayer one prays to the Father through the Son in the power of the Spirit. So kenosis speaks of the divine-human encounter and priesthood of the participation of God's people in the divine mission. Participation therefore permits interchange[116] but without any consequent loss of identity and is itself grounded in the Trinity.

Summary of the Argument

The contention of this thesis is that it is possible to construct a critically realistic dialectical account of kenosis and priesthood, within the context of the narrative of the divine-human encounter. I shall draw attention to the critically realistic and dialectical nature of the biblical language concerning priesthood. Furthermore I will demonstrate that priesthood and kenosis are signs of the mutual participation of the divine and human. It is in the

---

27.) Furthermore Taylor asserts that the 'full definition of someone's identity...involves...some reference to a defining community.' (Taylor, 2000, 36.)

[110] See: Chapters 2 and 3 below.

[111] See: Chapter 5 below.

[112] Herbert Butterfield suggested that its 'appearance of definiteness and finality is an optical illusion' and that the interpretation of historical material required both 'imagination and elasticity of mind'. (Butterfield, 1949, 15. See also: 127, 140.)

[113] See: Chapters 4 and 8 below.

[114] See: Chapter 5 below.

[115] Mirosalv Volf, *After Our Likeness*, Grand Rapids, Eerdmans, 1998, 195.

[116] See: Chapter 8 below.

kenosis of human words that the divine Word is represented but without any confusion of form.

In Part I I shall establish a narrative account of the doctrine of kenosis that is critically realistic. Therefore in Chapter 2 I shall briefly examine the failure of the naively realistic accounts of kenosis by both Thomasius and later by the English kenoticists. I shall also explore the failure of the Death of God theologians to articulate an anti-realist account of kenosis. Finally by reference to the Arian controversy and the Luther's theology of the cross I shall suggest that it is possible to construct a rather different, fundamentally trinitarian account of kenosis. In Chapter 3 therefore I shall explore the trinitarian and critically realistic accounts of the kenotic nature of God's self-revelation in Jesus Christ within the theologies of Karl Barth, Hans Urs von Balthasar and Jürgen Moltmann. Whereas in Chapter 1 kenosis provides a flawed analogy for the divine-human encounter, which proceeds from the human to the divine, Chapter 3 provides an analogy in which kenosis as event of divinely sovereign grace points to an altogether different understanding of priesthood. Finally in Chapter 4 I shall offer a study of Paul's letter to the Philippians in which kenosis is set in the context of an account of Christian identity and the priestly identity of public ministry.

Whereas Part I explores God's kenotic and sovereign self revelation, Part II concentrates upon the priestly human response. In Chapter 5 I shall seek to explore the accounts of the Church, vocation and anthropology understood kenotically in the theologies of Barth, Balthasar and Moltmann and the implications of these for the understanding of the priest as a human being in relation both to God but also the Church. This I shall do by reading 1 Peter 2.4-10 particularly in the light of Barth's critically realistic dialectical theology. In Chapter 6 I shall first examine the critically realistic dialectical account of priesthood in the Bible. Secondly, I shall propose that the relationship between kenosis, sacrifice and priesthood and finally the Christ's priestly role in the atonement as an analogy for ministerial priesthood.

Finally in Part III I shall seek to draw together Parts I and II in order to offer an account of ministerial priesthood that is acceptable to Protestant theology. In Chapter 7 I shall explore in greater depth the failure of the naively realistic account of ministerial priesthood. This I shall challenge by drawing attention to the possibilities offered by analogical and metaphorical language for the re-creation of imaginative and critically realistic dialectical accounts of the Christian story of the divine-human encounter, not least through the account of kenosis and priesthood. Finally in Chapter 8 I shall offer a critically realistic account of the ministerial priesthood based upon its roles and practices, most notably in terms of the eucharist as itself kenotic leading an expression of praise to the prior event of God's saving grace.

PART I

Kenosis and God's Graceful Self-revelation to Humanity

Chapter 2

The Story of the Doctrine of Kenosis

The fundamental concern of theology is the question of salvation. At its heart is the knowability of God and the divine-human relationship. Priesthood is an attempt to articulate the divine-human relationship and therefore salvation.[1] However, to what extent can God and humanity participate with one another while maintaining their distinct identities and integrities? In this chapter I offer a critical account of the emergence of the doctrine of kenosis as an attempt to provide an account of salvation through the participation of the divine in the human in Jesus Christ. According to the Chalcedonian Definition of the Faith[2] in Christ the two natures ensure that:

> one and the same Son, the same perfect in Godhead, and the same perfect in manhood, truly God and truly man, the same consisting of a reasonable soul and body, of one substance with the Father as touching the Godhead, the same of one substance with us as touching the manhood[.][3]

The Definition upholds the completeness of Christ's humanity and his full divinity. Grammatically God is the subject in the account of salvation, which takes its form in the incarnation of Jesus Christ, the divine self-revelation of which humanity is the object. It is only Jesus Christ who reveals the divine, being both truly God and truly man. Only Jesus Christ can effect salvation. For this reason Protestants have questioned the validity of priestly language when applied to the ordained ministry as implying needful human cooperation in the divine plan of salvation. In this Chapter I shall examine the christological account of kenosis as the crossing of the boundaries that distinguish the divine and the human. From this three questions will emerge. First, whether in crossing the boundaries and effecting salvation God and humanity co-exist unconfused, or whether the divine-human dialectic is dissolved in a final synthesis? Secondly, is kenosis a fundamentally christological event or an event of God as Trinity?

---

[1] Eberhard Jüngel, *Justification* (ET), Edinburgh, T & T Clark, 2001, 251.
[2] 451 CE.
[3] J. Stevenson (ed), *Creeds, Councils and Controversies*, London, SPCK, 1973, 337.

Thirdly, does kenosis, understood christologically, under-emphasize the vocational nature of the Incarnation? First, it is necessary for the subsequent discussion of priesthood, to establish that it can not involve any divine-human synthesis in the ordained. Secondly that priesthood, while christological, is not exclusively so, and thirdly its vocational nature.

In order to achieve these aims I shall first explore the classic form of the doctrine as developed in the work of Gottfried Thomasius and subsequently in the work of the British kenoticists. Secondly, I examine the development of radical kenosis in Death of God theology as the consequence of a propositional account of kenosis taken to its logical conclusion. These will illustrate how attention has been diverted from what I suggest is the real concern of kenosis, which is the divine identity. As a result I shall take a step back in order to outline an alternative history. Therefore, thirdly I shall examine the antecedents of kenosis - initially the Arian controversy and the emergence of classical Christology in the early Greek and Latin Fathers and its dependence upon and its implications for the understanding of God as Trinity. Finally I shall examine Luther's theology of the cross for the understanding of God.

Classic Kenotic Theory and Human Identity in Christology

The Lutheran Gottfried Thomasius was the most significant exponent of a kenotic Christology. In engagement with the contemporary debates he sought to recast classical Christian debates in within modern thought. Thomasius rightly identified the key problem as being the nature of the incarnation and what it meant to speak of Jesus Christ as 'truly God and truly man'. In order to uphold this declaration he suggested that the answer lay in the doctrine of kenosis. Thomasius understood that kenosis was evidence of the divine transcendence and "the divinely self-actualized nature of this union."[4] Accordingly he believed that Jesus Christ being 'truly man'

> can only have originated through God's determining of himself to actual participation in the human mode of being, i.e. in the human form of life and consciousness... And thus we shall have to posit the incarnation itself precisely in the fact that he, the eternal Son of God, the second person of the deity gave himself over into the form of human limitation and thereby the limits of spatio-temporal existence, under the conditions of a human development, in the bounds of an historical concrete being... is manifestly a self-limitation for the eternal Son of God. It is certainly not a divesting.[5]

---

[4] Jon K. Cooley, 'Gottfried Thomasius', Trevor A. Hart (ed), *The Dictionary of Historical Theology*, Carlisle, Paternoster, 2000, 543.

[5] Claude Welch (ed), *God and Incarnation in Mid-Nineteenth Century German*

However Thomasius account of kenosis appeared to propose a naively realistic account of the Lutheran doctrine of the communicatio idiomata. At the Reformation the discussion of the *communicatio idiomata* was primarily concerned with the consequences of the unity of Jesus Christ as God and man, and the implications for the relations between the two natures. Luther's account tended to a more propositional account than for example Zwingli for whom it is to be understood figuratively.[6] For Thomasius kenosis was essentially the process whereby the divine becomes human. To do this Thomasius distinguishes between the immanent and relative attributes of God. He argues that God's immanent attributes "are absolute power, truth, holiness and love." God's "relative attributes are omnipotence, omniscience and omnipresence, and arise in God's dealing with the world."[7]

Thomasius argued that the relative attributes can be divested without affecting the divinity of the incarnate Christ. God emptied himself of these in the Incarnation, exercising "no other lordship at all than the ethical one of truth and love... his whole exercise of power was absorbed in his world-redeeming activity."[8] Thomasius stressed this was an act of self-limitation and not the renunciation of being divine at the Incarnation.

Isaak Dorner was Thomasius' sharpest critic. Arguing from God's impassibility Dorner immediately recognized that "modern kenoticism... seeks to assert... the self-impartation or surrender of God to humanity."[9] In his rebuttal of Thomasius, Dorner referred to the Formula of Concord[10] and its explicit rejection of divine self-emptying as the "relinquishment of the eternal Logos himself of his divine glory."[11] He asserted that Thomasius and the kenoticists had fallen into the same trap as Arius, by reducing the person of Jesus Christ to a single nature. Furthermore, that kenoticism originated in an erroneous understanding of the necessary distinction between the being of God and of man, "such that God is the perfect man, and at least in Christ man is the God who becomes, the distinction being thus only a quantitative one".[12] The relinquishment "of the 'relative' divine attributes results in 'relative de-deification' of Christ."[13] However, the most acute criticism is that kenoticism has trinitarian consequences and not just

---

Theology, New York, OUP, 1965, 47-48.

[6] Wolfhart Pannenberg, *Jesus God and Man* (ET), London, SCM 1968, 299.

[7] J. Macquarrie, 'Kenoticism Reconsidered', *Theology*, LXXVII, (1974), 120.

[8] Welch, 1965, 70.

[9] Welch, 1965, 191.

[10] 1577.

[11] Pannenberg, 1968, 311.

[12] Welch, 1965, 192.

[13] Pannenberg, 1968, 311.

christological.[14]

The emergence of Kenotic Christology in the nineteenth century, and especially in the British kenoticists, coincided with a renewed interest in the doctrine of the priesthood of the ordained.[15] Set in the broader context of nineteenth century intellectual life, kenosis attempts to answer a number of questions concerning the 'truly human' nature of Jesus Christ. First there is the dominance of the Enlightenment view of reason and the relationship between 'I think' and its consequence for "man's understanding of himself and the world but also man's understanding of God".[16] Secondly, the emergence of historico-critical study of the New Testament "pointed up the reality of Jesus' humanity, particularly as revealed in His limitation of knowledge."[17] Thirdly, Thomasius emerges in the immediate aftermath of both Hegel and Schleiermacher, for whom the divine is revealed in human experience.[18] It is these factors which provide the stimulus for Thomasius and the recognition of the need to address all these issues.[19]

Like Thomasius, the British kenoticists fell into the same trap of falsely imagining the identity of Jesus. Within the Zeitgeist of an age in which Freud was developing his theories of the self and self-consciousness Charles Gore, Frank Weston and P. T. Forsyth understood kenosis by analogy with human experience in order to explore the self-awareness of Jesus Christ as both divine and yet fully human.[20] So, for example, Gore speaks of "sympathy love"[21] which he illustrates with the image of the well-educated person who relates to the uneducated one by the ability "to leave behind"[22] his superiority. Similarly, Frank Weston[23] uses analogies of the

---

[14] Graham Ward, 'Kenosis: Death, Discourse and Resurrection', Lucy Gardiner, Ben Quash, Graham Ward, *Balthasar at the End of Modernity*, Edinburgh, T & T Clark, 1999, 29.

[15] See: Chapter 7 below

[16] Eberhard Jüngel, *God as the Mystery of the World* (ET), Grand Rapids, Eerdmans, 1983, 111.

[17] D. G. Dawes, 'A Fresh Look at the Kenotic Christologies', SJT, Vol XV, 1962, 342.

[18] Karl Barth, *Protestant Theology in the Nineteenth Century* (ET, New Edn), London, SCM, 2001, compare 371, 405, 412, 435.)

[19] Thomasius work is partly a response to the *Life of Jesus Critically Examined* by D. F. Strauss (1835).

[20] Sarah Coakley, 'Kenosis and Subversion: On the Repression of Vulnerability in Christian Feminist Writing', Daphne Hampson (ed), *Swallowing a Fishbone?* London, SPCK, 1996, 82-111. The influence of the work of Thomasius upon the British kenoticists is debatable. However, Gore draws attention to the work of Thomasius, though his knowledge may have been second-hand (A. B. Bruce, *The Humiliation of Christ*, 1876, see: C. Gore, *Dissertations on Subjects Connected with the Incarnation*, London, John Murray, 1895, 189, n. 2).

[21] Gore, 1895, 218.

[22] Gore, 1895, 219.

The Story of the Doctrine of Kenosis

African king reduced to slavery, the favourite son of a commanding officer placed under the command of his father and the implications of being both a son and a soldier under authority. The obvious weaknesses of the analogies used by both Gore and Weston are their Victorian understanding of superiority and inferiority. The image of God conveyed is essentially patronizing.[24]

P. T. Forsyth's analogies are somewhat more subtle.[25] He concedes that the "difficulty of conceiving psychologically the kenotic process in the divine consciousness is certainly an impediment, but it is not an obstacle".[26] However, "Forsyth's point, which is movingly and persuasively argued, is that a restriction on human freedom, consciously and resolutely accepted by an act of 'supernatural' will, can in due course be seen as a means of glory."[27] Kenosis "declares the profound truth that 'the form of a servant' is not a derogation from or even a modification of the glory of God, but precisely the fullest expression of that glory as love."[28]

Forsyth observes:

God is God not physically but morally, not by power but by love... The nature of the Godhead is love... To this end the Son of God sympathetically renounces the glory of his Heavenly state... for God's sake.[29]

Although Forsyth hints at a Trinitarian understanding, he does not develop it. His concept of kenosis remains essentially christological.

Gore, Weston and Forsyth are all orthodox since they all struggle to express kenosis within the Antiochene christological framework of the person of Christ. This emerges "from a desire to realign the orthodox conception of Christ as one person in two natures with the newly emerging conception of personality." The consequence of this was that "a person was not defined simply in terms of antecedent natures, either human or divine,

---

[23] Frank Weston, *The One Christ*, London, 1907, see: Brenda Cross, 'The Christology of Bishop Frank Weston', *Theology*, LXXIV, 387-391.
[24] Sarah Coakley, 'Kenosis: Theological Meanings and Gender Connotations', John Polkinghorne (ed), *The Work of Love*, London, SPCK, 2001, 207
[25] These include: the venerable vizier who takes poison in place of the foolish young Sultan; the Russian concert violinist in pre-Revolution Russia who undergoes exile and loss of career in commitment to the poor; and the philosophy student who sets aside his promising academic career to provide for his family. (P. T. Forsyth, *The Person and Place of Jesus Christ*, London, Independent Press, 1946, 296-298).
[26] Forsyth, 1946, 305.
[27] Coakley, 1996, 98.
[28] 'This was the great emphasis of Forsyth... which makes his book a lasting contribution.' (J. A. T. Robinson, *The Human Face of God*, London, SCM, 1994, 208.)
[29] Forsyth, 1946, 313.

of which the person is an individualization. Rather a person was defined in terms of various forms of consciousness of the self." This in turn posed the problem: "How could a limited human consciousness coexist in a single person with the full actuality of the divine consciousness?"[30]

What is apparent is the assumption that the doctrine of kenosis as outlined presumes a naively realistic account of the Incarnation. This reflects a major break in hermeneutic practice fundamentally altering the way the authoritative texts of the Christian traditions, and especially the Bible, were read. This break occurred in the nineteenth century. Garrett Green, discussing Paul Ricoeur's identification of Marx, Nietzsche and Freud as the three masters of suspicion, adds Feuerbach. Green suggests that the emerging hermeneutic of suspicion "can be summarised in Marx's term false consciousness."[31] The authoritative paradigms offered by the masters of suspicion and their successors, and by which reality is understood, were advanced as scientific and therefore factual, being based in reality.[32] As a result the imagination and reality are regarded as being mutually opposed. For Thomasius, the nature of the unity in Christ of the divine and human was a conundrum to be solved. Kenosis was essentially an attempt to make a propositional christological statement, which plausibly articulated the concept of the participation of the divine in the human that was Jesus Christ. According to the hermeneutics of suspicion, to be such a human-divine figure was unimaginable unless the divine imposed strict self-limitation. The attempt to hold together the two natures and the implicit assumptions about Christ as 'truly God and truly man' in the light of the emerging modern understanding of the person and personality led Gore, Weston and Forsyth to propose kenosis as a possible solution.

So far four weaknesses of kenoticism have emerged. First, the classic nineteenth and early twentieth century exponents of kenoticism understood Jesus Christ, the historic figure whose story is narrated by the gospels, as identified in his incarnation as 'truly man'. Such a designation, it was assumed, necessarily qualified what it means to be 'truly God' at the same time. Because the two states are distinct, the kenoticists undermined the possible co-existence of the two natures in the one person.

Secondly, as Dorner recognised, there can be no true participation of the human directly in the divine. The attempt to overcome this by focusing on the sacrifice of Christ as the loss of the divine attributes of omnipotence, omniscience and omnipresence in order to become 'truly man' is docetic in its failure to maintain the divine-human diastasis. The depotentiation of Jesus Christ is matched by the divinization of humanity. However, this fails

---

[30] Dawes, 1962, 342.
[31] Garrett Green, *Theology, Hermeneutics, and Imagination*, Cambridge, Cambridge University Press, 2000, 12 – his italics.
[32] Green, 2000, 14.

to take the effects of sin seriously and underestimates the necessity of grace. It falls into the same trap as Pelagianism, viewing Jesus Christ as a second Adam,[33] assuming that human beings can cooperate with God in effecting their own salvation. Such an account resonates with the fundamental Protestant objection to the priesthood of the ordained as commonly understood.

Thirdly, if vocation is understood in terms of character, the incarnation of the second person of the Trinity cannot be understood in terms of divine divestment or self-limitation because that would be self-contradictory. For Jesus to remain true to himself, then he is necessarily 'truly God and truly man'. To be other requires him to become an altogether different person. In seeking to build upon Luther's *theologia crucis* Thomasius failed to recognize its essential trinitarianism.

Finally, and most significantly, traditional Kenoticism understands doctrine as functioning as "informative propositions or truth claims about objective realities."[34] This naively realistic account of Kenosis was advocated as being a rational and modern account of how God could be in Christ without undermining the reality of his true humanity. Kenosis was therefore understood in terms of the process of Incarnation.[35] This in turn leads to a Christology of mediation. Christ is the one who stands between God and man, with all the attendant implications. So one objection to priesthood is that it establishes an intermediary class, which exists to mediate the divine-human encounter.

Kenosis as the Death of God

Wolfgang Friedrich Gess went further than Thomasius by arguing that to become truly human required the total emptying of the divine at the Incarnation. Anything less was prey to what Biedermann called Docetic Gnosticism. The doctrine of kenosis,

> must take the last step toward its completion and allow the Logos to divest himself not only of his divine mode of being but also his divine essence, in order to begin from the beginning wholly as a true human soul... It is Gess who has brought the kenosis to this final conclusion.[36]

Consequently Gess "extends the kenosis to immanent attributes also. The self-depotentiation of the logos is absolute: 'He reduces Himself to the

---

[33] See: the fuller discussion in Chapter 4, 92-96 below.
[34] George Lindbeck, *The Nature of Doctrine*, Philadelphia, Westminster Press, 1984, 16.
[35] The later British kenoticists appear to confuse the emerging concept of personality and the Chalcedonian use of the word.
[36] Welch, 1965, 304-05.

germ of a human soul.'" Indeed Gess believed that "the incarnation affected the internal relations of the Trinity".[37] However, he does not accept that kenosis simply reduces Jesus to "a merely human conscious life", rather that "on any terms the experience of Jesus transcends that of other men insofar as He is aware that once He was more than man and will return some day to His former high estate." The divine remains – if at all – as the remembrance of his attributes of "power and knowledge which for the time being he has laid aside."[38] What he proposes is a temporary renunciation of the divine prior to the resurrection, consequently it is the man Jesus of Nazareth who is crucified, not the divine. Thomas J. J. Altizer proposes an even more extreme version, with the emergence of the Death of God theology.

Altizer says that the twentieth century is marked by "a passage through the death of God, the collapse of any meaning or reality beyond the newly discovered radical immanence of modern man".[39] He understands the death of God to be necessary on two counts. First, it is the rejection of the theological dualism, implicit in traditional Christology. Altizer states that he wishes "to speak of God as a dialectical process rather than as an existent Being... of the God who has emptied himself of God in Christ."[40] Secondly, because, "God has fully and totally become incarnate in Christ"[41] so the cross is the death of God. This is salvific because it liberates man from "the most alien, the most distant, and the most oppressive deity".[42] This has two consequences. First, it acts as 'informative propositions or truth claims about objective realities'[43] for it offers a dialectic in which there is thesis and antithesis resulting in a final synthesis. Secondly, humanity therefore does not simply cooperate in its own salvation but is its own salvation. To support this claim Altizer looks to Dietrich Bonhoeffer's notion of "religionless Christianity"[44] believing that in the notion of man come of age "the world itself is the source of the solutions"[45] and its own salvation.

However, Bonhoeffer's notion of 'religionless Christianity' is not that of the Death of God theologians.[46] In a series of letters Bonhoeffer asks, "How

---

[37] H. R. Mackintosh, *The Person of Jesus Christ*, Edinburgh, T & T Clark, 1912, 267.
[38] Mackintosh, 1912, 268.
[39] Thomas J. J. Altizer, *The Gospel of Christian Atheism*, London, Collins, 1967, 22.
[40] Altizer, 1967, 90.
[41] Altizer, 1967, 103.
[42] Altizer, 1967, 110.
[43] Lindbeck, quoted 25, n 33.
[44] D Bonhoeffer, *Letters and Papers From Prison* (ET), London, SCM, 1971 280.
[45] Altizer, 1967, 121
[46] William Hamilton, 'The Death of God Theologies Today', Thomas J. J. Altizer and William Hamilton, *Radical Theology and the Death of God*, London, Pelican, 1966, 51

do we speak of God – without religion".[47] His concern is to extricate Christ from being the object of religion in order that "Christ [might be]... the Lord of the world."[48] For Bonhoeffer this is the radical alternative to the naiveté and the pomposity of Christians who believe they need "to reserve some space for God".[49] Returning to the idea, he suggests that religion looks to "the power of God... God is the deus ex machina." Whereas the "Bible directs man to God's powerlessness and suffering".[50] Humanity's coming of age is not the removal of God but the willingness to let go of false gods. Kenosis is God's willingness to give himself for and to the world.[51] In Jesus Christ upon the cross God is the subject who, in an act of sovereign grace gives himself to effect salvation. This is very different from the Death of God theologians, for whom kenosis *is* the emptying or removal of God and therefore the liberation of the world by his death. Altizer looks not so much to the Lutheran Bonhoeffer but rather repeats the claim of Nietzsche's madman that God is dead.

Altizer also built his thesis on the work of the Lutheran Hegel.[52] At the start of the nineteenth century Hegel famously declared that "God is dead"[53] in a statement which has been variously construed by a number of theologians.[54] For Hegel "the incarnation is then immediately related to the death of Jesus Christ." Thus it "is not this man who dies, but the divine; that is how it becomes man."[55] As Jüngel has argued it would seem that Hegel's notion of the death of God is not essentially atheistic, as Altizer believes.[56] The problem is the complex nature of Hegel's understanding of the Trinity. He considers the idea of the Trinity to be a numerical problem, that "the Idea-three equals one" but that "only the absolute autonomy on the numerical one hovers before understanding, [signifying] absolute separation and splintering." Logical "reflection shows the numerical one rather to be

---

who admits, 'we don't really know what Bonhoeffer meant by religion' but two paragraphs later states '[a]t no point is the later Bonhoeffer of greater importance than in helping us work out a truly theological understanding of the problem of religionlessness.'

[47] Bonhoeffer, 1971, 280.
[48] Bonhoeffer, 1971, 281.
[49] Bonhoeffer, 1971, 282.
[50] Bonhoeffer, 1971, 361.
[51] Bonhoeffer, 1971, 360.
[52] Altizer, 1967, 62-69.
[53] G. W. F. Hegel, *The Phenomenology of the Mind* (ET 2nd Edn), London, Allen and Unwin, 1971, 753.
[54] Barth, 2001, 385; John Macquarrie, *Jesus Christ in Modern Thought*, London, SCM, 1997, 212.
[55] Jüngel, 1983, 77 quoting Hegel, *Jenaer Realphilosophie*.
[56] See: John Macquarrie, 1997, 219; Jürgen Moltmann, *The Crucified God* (ET), London, SCM, 1974, 234.

dialectical in itself and not something autonomous".[57] God "differentiates himself within himself, but in the process remains identical with himself."[58] Thus the death of Christ is not the death of God. It is what Moltmann speaks of as "death in God".[59] Therefore:

> God has died: this is the negation, and this is a moment of the divine nature, of God himself. In this death, accordingly, God is satisfied. God cannot be satisfied by something else, only by himself... God is the true God, Spirit, because he is not merely Father, enclosed within himself, but rather because he is Son, because he becomes the other and sublates this other. The negation is perceived as a moment of divine nature; therein all are reconciled.[60]

Hegel articulates divine kenpsis as an intra-trinitarian event, and therefore different from that proposed by the Death of God theologians. God is not dead; instead God has included death within the totality of the divine persona. However, in the process Hegel turns "the mystery of the cross into a piece of philosophy" wherein "the God-man (the primordial Man), by his self-revelation coincides in the last analysis with the self-understanding of man himself."[61] But for Altizer the death of God is the absence of God which he claims is the radical theological atheism announced by both Nietzsche and Hegel.[62] However, Altizer is mistaken on two counts, since Nietzsche is neither Christian nor is Hegel an atheist.

Altizer and his fellow Death of God theologians reject the traditional christological and trinitarian doctrine in their atheistic reading. Both Hegel and Bonhoeffer recognize the rise of atheistic thought and its strengths but neither is seduced by its claims. According to Hegel, "everything depends on grasping and expressing the ultimate truth not as Substance but as Subject as well."[63] Indeed the use of the language of subject and substance provides an echo of the terminology within which the "formulation of the Christian doctrine of Trinity took place" as Jüngel suggests.[64] This is very different from Altizer's reading.

---

[57] G. W. F. Hegel, *The Christian Religion, Lectures on the Philosophy of Religion* (Part III, ET Peter C. Hodgson), Missoula [Montana], Scholars Press, 1979, 71.
[58] Hegel, 1979, 78.
[59] Moltmann, 1974, 207.
[60] Hegel, 1979, 210.
[61] Hans Urs von Balthasar, *Mysterium Paschale* (ET), Edinburgh, T & T Clark, 1990b, 62. See also: Macquarrie, 1997, 212.
[62] Altizer, 1967, 137.
[63] Hegel, 1971, 80 (in the preface).
[64] Jüngel, 1983, 82; see: also Hans Küng, *The Incarnation of God* (ET), Edinburgh, T & T Clark, 1987, 209.

For Altizer God is unidentifiable because he has died and is absent, whereas for Bonhoeffer God is identified in the theology of the cross. For Altizer God is a question of abstract speculation. For Bonhoeffer God is not to be found in an "an abstract belief in God, in his omnipotence etc. That is not a genuine experience of God". Instead God is found in the "[e]ncounter with Jesus Christ."[65] The experience of God is possible only in the event of the Trinity; God who goes out of himself and who becomes the man for others, "the Crucified, the man who lives out of the transcendent."[66] However, if God is dead there can be no participation between God and humanity, for there is nothing to be participated in. God is a past event, and not a story to be engaged with.[67] For Bonhoeffer the story remains and participation in it is invited, "to live in Christ, to exist for others."[68]

In summary, in exploring nineteenth century kenotic theology I concluded that, first, the concern was the assumption that if Jesus Christ is truly God this must necessarily negate his being truly man. Secondly, the elevation of Christ's humanity at the expense of his divine nature rather than resolving the problem suggests that humanity is a partner in its own salvation. Thirdly, both objections erode the vocation of both Jesus Christ as saviour and a human being by undermining his essential character. Finally, kenosis as a propositional account of Jesus Christ's saving work results in the establishment of an intermediary figure or figures, who stand between God and humanity. These four objections are replicated in the traditional Protestant objections to the validity of the concept of a Christian ministerial priesthood.

In the second section, Altizer and the Death of God theologians push kenosis to its logical conclusion. This, it was argued, is the result of misunderstanding both Hegel's philosophical account of the death of God and Bonhoeffer's account of religionless Christianity. The result is an anti-realistic account in which humanity is understood as being the author of its salvation.

'Truly God and truly man'?

However, it is possible to trace an alternative, rather more tangential account of kenosis. To this end I shall first explore the identification of Jesus Christ as both God and man and the emergence of the doctrine of the Trinity during the first five centuries of Christian theology. As a result the doctrine of the Trinity provides an alternative framework in which it is

---

[65] Bonhoeffer, 1971, 381.
[66] Bonhoeffer, 1971, 382.
[67] Altizer falls into the trap Barth identifies with Hegel of a 'philosophy of *self-confidence*' (Barth, 2001, 377).
[68] Bonhoeffer, 1971, 383.

possible to articulate the divine-human relationship in Jesus Christ, as the God-man. Secondly, I shall explore Luther's emphasis upon the *theologia crucis* as rendering God knowable. Both of these in turn raise questions about both the possibility and the limitations of the intermediary role of Jesus Christ, which, as has already been suggested is a significant problem for Protestants in the articulation of priesthood.[69]

Arius was the dominant theological writer about Jesus Christ as both God and man in the Patristic period.[70] Arius brought to a head the consequences of the developing relationship between existing Greek philosophical thought and theology. The development of a Logos Christology served to enable the differentiation of the Father and the Son[71] but the weakness of the doctrine of the Logos as "Platonically conceived"[72] meant it was always prey to subordinationist tendencies. From Origen, Arius inherited an exegetical method, which he then developed.[73] What Origen proposed was a "theory of the intermediary, and mediating, status of the Logos".[74] According to Origen, the incarnate Christ is "intermediate between all created things and God".[75] Secondly, he sought to explore, how

> that mighty power of divine majesty, that very Word of the Father, and that very wisdom of God, in which were created all things, visible and invisible, can be believed to have existed within the limits of that man who appeared in Judea.[76]

For Origen the key is found in the concept of the pre-existent soul which in the case of Christ

> elected to love righteousness, so that in proportion to the immensity of its love it clung to it unchangeably and inseparably... that there existed in Christ a human and rational soul, without supposing that it had any feeling or possibility of sin.[77]

Origen recognizes the importance of questions of identity and participation for soteriology in any coherent understanding of God. He attempts to weave

---

[69] See: 27 above.
[70] Rowan Williams, *Arius* (2nd Edn), London, SCM, 2001, 82. According to Williams Arianism cannot be understood as a single coherent system dependent upon one leader.
[71] Pannenberg, 1968, 160.
[72] Pannenberg, 1968, 164.
[73] Williams, 1987, 148.
[74] G. W. H. Lampe, 'Christian Theology in the Patristic Period', H Cunliffe-Jones with Benjamin Drewery (ed), *A History of Christian Doctrine*, Edinburgh, T & T Clark, 1980, 76.
[75] CCEL CD Rom (2000), Origen, *de Principiis*, 2.6. 1.
[76] CCEL CD Rom (2000), Origen, *de Principiis*, 2.6. 2.
[77] CCEL CD Rom (2000), Origen, *de Principiis*, 2.6. 5.

together John 17.5 and Philippians 2 assuming the pre-existent glory of the Son as a prior necessity to the act of emptying which is the Incarnation. The divine Logos is the connecting "link between uncreated deity and created nature... that he contains in himself the logoi, that is the rational principles or (Platonic) ideas, of all creatures. Whereas the Father is absolute unity the Son contains in himself the many."[78] According to Origen the earthly Christ came

> taking the form of a servant, was made obedient unto death, that He might teach obedience to those who could not otherwise than by obedience obtain salvation. ...He became obedient to the Father, not only to the death of the cross, but also, in the end of the world, embracing in Himself all whom He subjects to the Father, and who by Him come to salvation, He Himself, along with them, and in them, is said also to be subject to the Father; all things subsisting in Him, and He Himself being the Head of all things, and in Him being the salvation and the fullness of those who obtain salvation.[79]

In this passage Origen appears to suggest that Christ is the incarnate Word, the one identified by God who participates in the Godhead but who is himself identified with humanity and participated in by those who are being saved. Platonism and Gnosticism both influenced Origen's theology and therefore like his contemporaries he "faced the problem of linking God with the world, the absolute with the contingent."[80] Consequently Origen appears to flirt with subordinationism whereby in the divine hierarchy Christ stands between God and man in every sense.

> The Son is both subordinate and equal to the Father, a double affirmation... subordination arises in the first place from the fact that the Father is Father, origin of the two other Persons and initiator of the Trinity. The latter role concerns the 'economy'... The Father gives the orders, the Son and the Spirit receive them... Thus the subordination of the Son and the Spirit is closely linked to their 'divine missions'.[81]

Kenosis makes possible the conjunction of the human soul and the divine Logos within Jesus Christ. Grillmeier suggests that for Origen, in the humanity of Christ "the fullness of the Godhead is present, even if hidden

---

[78] Lampe, 1980, 76-77.
[79] CCEL CD Rom (2000), Origen, *de Principiis*, 3. 5. 6.
[80] J. A. Lyons, *The Cosmic Christ in Origen and Teilhard de Chardin*, Oxford, OUP, 1982, 89.
[81] Henri Crouzel, *Origen* (ET), Edinburgh, T & T Clark, 1989, 188.

in the kenosis."[82] Origen believed that in this he was being faithful to the New Testament.[83] However, Origin does "seem to make the incarnation (and the corporeality) of Christ relative"[84] so that despite his effort to hold together the two natures he seems "to preserve a complete balance because of his Platonism."[85]

Origen wrestled with the same problem that was later to concern Arius and which was rooted in his indebtedness to Platonic conceptualization. What is evident in both the Arian controversy, and in the prior work of Origen, is the struggle to articulate the event of God in Jesus Christ within the confines of a pre-existing philosophical school of thought. Philosophically Origen can say "that the Saviour and the Spirit transcend all creatures, not in degree only but in kind, but that they are in their turn transcended by the Father".[86] Despite their similarity,

> the crucial difference remains that Arius' God requires a created individual for his self-revelation, while Origen's God is eternally and almost 'necessarily' one who manifests himself in his Word simply to respond to and glorify and rejoice in his own being, before and beyond creation.[87]

One influence of Greek philosophical thought was to lead to an understanding of the nature of God as being essentially apophatic. However, it must be remembered that Origen is not so much a systematic theologian as an explorer, whose writings can be used equally by either side of a controversy.[88] While the "thoughtful Christian might find himself in substantial agreement with the cultured pagan in his definition of God's changeless nature and eternal being", at "the heart of his faith [was] the meaning of Christ and of his work."[89]

The heart of the Arian controversy concerned the identity of the divine, and his participation in the human sphere. Consequently for Arius "the notion of sovereign divine will resolves the problem of the monad's relation to all else... The natural gulf between God and the world remains unqualified, and God is indeed beyond all natural relation".[90] It is this

---

[82] A. Grillmeier, *Christ in Christian Tradition* (Vol 1, ET), Oxford, Mowbrays, 1975, 145f.
[83] Phil 2.5-8; Col 2.9.
[84] Grillmeier, 1975, 145.
[85] Grillmeier, 1975, 146.
[86] Lampe, 1980, 77.
[87] Williams, 2001, 146.
[88] Lyons, 1982, 116.
[89] Maurice Wiles, *The Christian Fathers*, London, SCM, 1977, 24.
[90] Williams, 2001, 197-98.

understanding of God which, according to Williams, lies at the root of the three basic theological points that Arius broaches:

(i)   The Son is a creature, that is, a product of God's will;
(ii) 'Son' is therefore a *metaphor* for the second hypostasis, and must be understood in the light of comparable metaphorical usage in scripture;
(iii) The Son's status, like his very existence, depends upon God's will.[91]

In a complex argument Williams explores ideas of analogy, identity and participation through the Platonic concept of form. In particular he seeks to trace the influence of the thinking of the Middle Platonic writers Philo, Plotinus and Porphyry upon Arius' understanding of God and its repercussions for the doctrine of the Logos, the divine Son.[92]

Williams illustrates Arius' understanding of form, identity and representation by drawing upon the work of R. E. Allen, whom he suggests

> illuminatingly discusses this issue with reference to reflections in a mirror: the scarf is red, and its mirror image is red, but in the latter case, 'you cannot mean the *same* thing you mean when you call its original red'. The image does not stand alongside the original exemplifying the same characteristics: what it is is entirely defined by its being a reproduction of the original.[93]

The form and the image are similar, but not the same. They are essentially different. So that

> form goes out from its own reality not to produce imitations of itself but to cause certain related and purposive activities in a lower reality. There is not and cannot be any question of participation between form and particular in the sense of their simply exhibiting a common structure in different degrees.[94]

The upshot of all this, however precisely it is expressed, is that the substance of God cannot be participated, cannot enter into any definition of any other substance or admit any qualification by any other substance... Arius... condemns the fusion of substances into a 'consubstantial'

---

[91] Williams, 2001, 109.
[92] Williams, 2001, 216-22.
[93] Williams, 2001, 216.
[94] Williams, 2001, 220.

compound: the Son is not a *homoousios* 'portion' of the Father.[95]

> In the last analysis, the God of Arius, beyond all analogy and participation, can only be an empty abstraction... The problems set up by the extreme apophatic consequences of the third-century shift in philosophical thinking cannot be sidestepped by the appeal to will without a fundamental irrationality being introduced into the Godhead itself.[96]

Williams does not consider the Arian controversy simply a struggle to deal with either a heresy or a heretic. It is essentially a debate about language and how God is spoken of, and therefore identified and represented in the past and present, and whether God can be spoken of in new ways that are congruent with tradition. Furthermore it is important that the language employed maintains the primacy of the divine in the account of salvation. Thus, according to Pannenberg, patristic theology was most concerned to articulate the true divinity of Christ (contra Arius) in terms of God's saving act. "Athanasius especially expressed this concern: if the Most High God himself is not present in Jesus, then we do not gain a share in the divine life through Jesus nor are we reconciled with God himself through Jesus."[97]

The Arian controversy sharply focuses the issues raised by kenosis and what it means to speak of God becoming incarnate in the historical person Jesus Christ. First, Arianism undermines kenosis as vocation because the Son's status is reduced to that of a semi-divine intermediary. The Son is sent but no corresponding obedience is required on his part. Secondly, there is a linguistic problem. The language of kenosis, as the articulation of the divine-human encounter in the incarnation of Jesus Christ, is unable to encompass the necessary dialectic of the two natures. However, the Nicene settlement failed to resolve once and for all the problems of Trinitarian language and the relationship of the infinite with the finite through the Incarnation.

The period between Nicaea and Chalcedon saw the continuing development of the debate about the Incarnation and the relationship of Jesus Christ to the second person of the Trinity. In the West Hilary of Poitiers sought to incorporate the doctrine of the incarnation into the "framework of his trinitarian doctrine. For him, the incarnation is a revelation of the threefold God, especially of the Sonship in God."[98] Hilary seeks to maintain the traditional Christology of the Church. However, the Trinitarian emphasis and the dimension "of the Persons and their

---

[95] Williams, 2001, 222.
[96] Williams, 2001, 229.
[97] Pannenberg, 1968, 164.
[98] Grillmeier, 1975, 395.

The Story of the Doctrine of Kenosis 37

processions, relations and missions" is still not sufficiently recognised.[99] For Hilary, the Nicene settlement and the notion of *homoousios* "was not that the Father and Son are numerically one in substance, but that they share the same divine nature."[100] Hilary understands identity not in terms of sameness but of self-constancy. This is reminiscent of Athanasius' insistence upon 'identity' as a "more appropriate term than 'likeness' and that the Father and Son must be 'one (en) in substance'".[101] But does Hilary engage in conflict with the Arians at the cost of the real humanity of Jesus as the second person of the Trinity?

The problem with the doctrine of the two natures is its presumption that they "stand ontologically on the same level and have nothing to do with one another apart from their union in the person of the God-man."[102] Hilary seeks to circumvent this, but instead falls into an historical or sequential approach. Hilary "distinguishes three times: pre-existence, kenosis, and exhalation" preferring a historical approach "which is of course closely bound up with the ontic one, to a static view of the two natures in Christ."[103] It is important for Hilary that these states are clearly distinguished.[104]

Hilary's concern is to demonstrate that "the divine 'power' is so ordered that it can make room for a possible self-exteriorisation, as can be found in the Incarnation and the Cross."[105] In the Incarnation, the *Logos* accepts the limitation of being human. His true divinity remains but is concealed. What Hilary appears to be suggesting is not so much *kenosis*, as emptying, but *krypsis*, or concealment. The result of this is a changed emphasis in his understanding of the Incarnation, not as a necessary divesting of the divine

---

[99] Balthasar, 1990b, 27.

[100] J. N. D. Kelly, *Early Christian Doctrines* (5th Edn), London, A & C Black, 1977, 254.

[101] Kelly, 1977, 245.

[102] *Syst.* II, 385. See also: *CD* IV.2, 61.

[103] Grillmeier, 1975, 396.

[104] It 'is one thing, that he was God before he was man, another that he was man and God, and another that after being man and God, he was perfect man and perfect God. Do not then confuse the times and natures in the mystery of the dispensation' (Hilary, On the Trinity, 9.6, quoted by Jaroslav Pelikan, *The Emergence of the Catholic Tradition (100-600)*, Chicago, Chicago University Press, 1971, 257).

[105] Balthasar, 1990b, 29. According to Grillmeier, Hilary articulates a concept 'which consists in the renunciation of the *forma Dei* and the acceptance of the *forma servi*,' but which presupposes that, 'the subject remains in his divine nature. For by this "*in forma Dei esse*" he expresses what the Antiochenes, especially Nestorius and Theodoret, and even Alexandrians like Didymus understand by "*prosopon*" in its relationship to "*physis*": an emanation, a manner of appearance, a visible representation of a nature of being. In the kenosis, then, Christ abstained from 'showing' himself completely in his identity of substance with the Father, in the "*splendor gloriae*", although the fact he was God shone through the servant's form in the miracles.' (Grillmeier, 1975, 396.)

but rather the elevation of the human. Hilary's significance is his recognition of the dependence of Christology upon the Trinity.

It was the Cappadocian Fathers, notably Gregory of Nyssa, who further sought to articulate the doctrine of God through the development of the notion of Trinity. For Gregory "the word 'Godhead' is not significant of nature but of operation".[106] That "God who is over all, is the Saviour of all, while the Son works salvation by means of the grace of the Spirit, and yet they are not on this account called in Scripture three Saviours".[107] For Gregory differentiation and cause within the Godhead can only indicate "the fact that the Son does not exist without generation, nor the Father by generation".[108] But to speak of divine generation is in no way intended to imply this results from any suggestion of divine passibility.[109] Gregory, who is also influenced by Origen, is concerned to establish the nature of Spirit within the Godhead and the "'oneness of nature' shared by the three Persons".[110] He needed to avoid the accusations of the Arians that "the *homoousion* of the Spirit seemed to involve the Father having two Sons," and "to differentiate between the mode of origin of the Son and that of the Spirit."[111] Gregory of Nyssa provided what was to prove the definitive statement of the divine *processio*: namely the "Spirit, he teaches [*C Maced.* 2; 10; 12; 24], is out of God and is of Christ; He proceeds out of the Father and receives from the Son; He cannot be separated from the Word."[112]

But it is here that Origen's thought and the philosophical tradition that Gregory inherited appear to loom largest. According to Gregory "the Son acts as an agent, no doubt in subordination to the Father, Who is the fountainhead of the Trinity, in the production of the Spirit."[113] The divine nature remains "unlimited and incomprehensible, conceive no comprehension of it (sic), but declare that the nature is to be conceived in all respects as infinite... not limited even by name."[114] The co-existence of the divine and the human is acknowledged but not easily articulated. "He has the form of God and the form of a servant, being something according to His supreme nature, becoming other things in His dispensation of love to

---

[106] *Quod non sint tres dii*, P. Schaff and H. Wace (ed), *The Nicene and Post-Nicene Fathers of the Christian Church*, (Second Series, Vol V), Grand Rapids, Eerdmans, 1994, 333.
[107] *Quod non sint tres dii*, Schaff and Wace, 1994, 335.
[108] *Quod non sint tres dii*, Schaff and Wace, 1994, 336.
[109] *Contra Eunomius*, 4. 4, Schaff and Wace, 1994, 159-161.
[110] Kelly, 1978, 261.
[111] Kelly, 1978, 262.
[112] Kelly, 1978, 262.
[113] Kelly, 1978, 263.
[114] *Quod non sint tres dii*, Schaff and Wace, 1994, 335.

man".[115]

If Gregory of Nyssa seemingly speaks of the Son as the agent of the Father, Augustine asks, in what way does the Father send the Son and indeed what does such language mean? He finds the answer in the notion of missio, arguing that the Son is sent but that,

> whatever way it was done, it was certainly done by word. But God's Word is his Son. So when the Father sent him by word, what happened was that he was sent by the Father and his Word. Hence it is by the Father and the Son that the Son was sent, because the Son is sent, because the Son is the Father's Word.[116]

Augustine emphasized vocation, which the Arian account of Jesus Christ as a semi-divine mediatory figure had previously undermined. The Son accepts he is sent by the Father. The Arian controversy focused upon the nature of identity with, and participation of the divine in the human sphere. But Augustine is clear that the divine Logos 'taking the form of a servant' suggests that "He did not so take the form of a servant that he lost the form of God".[117] Therefore

> the Son is equal to the Father and that the Father is greater than the Son. The one is to be understood in virtue of the form of God, the other in virtue of the form of the servant, without any confusion.[118]

The emptying[119] is simply the necessary consequence of the incarnation. He "did this by being born of the virgin."[120] Kenosis means that "he could be a model for those who can see him as God above, a model for those who can admire him as man below".[121]

This is important especially in terms of the work of Christ in the atonement. The Son is not sacrificed in order to propitiate an angry god but atonement is the Son's vocation together with the Father who offers his only Son. Hence "we should understand that is was not just the man who the Word became that was sent, but that the Word was sent to become man."[122] Augustine is equally clear that "there is no modification in God

---

[115] *Contra Eunomius* 4. 3, Schaff and Wace, 1994, 158.

[116] Augustine, *de Trinitate*, II.9, (tr) Edmund Hill, *The Trinity*, New York, New City Press, 1991, 103.

[117] *de Trinitate*, I.14, 74.

[118] *de Trinitate,* I.14, 74.

[119] Here Augustine is discussing Phil 2.6.

[120] *de Trinitate* II.20, 111.

[121] *de Trinitate* VII. 5, 223.

[122] *de Trinitate* IV.27, 172.

because there is nothing in him that can be changed or lost."[123] Therefore he refutes the Arian understanding that the Father and Son are different in substance as unbegotten and begotten:

> let us believe that Father, Son and Holy Spirit are one God, maker and ruler of all creation: and that the Father is not the Son, and the Holy Spirit is neither the Father nor the Son, but that they are a trinity of persons related to each other, and a unity of equal being.[124]

In approaching the Trinity through "the economy or plan of creation and salvation, Augustine took seriously and spoke primarily of the distinctiveness of Persons in the Trinity".[125] Augustine makes a clear distinction between the immanent Trinity, as whatever could be learned of the inner relationships of the three, and the economic Trinity, as the divine presence in salvation history. What we appear to see in Augustine is someone who is struggling for a social image of the Trinity. This he describes in terms of the grammar of love which "means someone loving and something loved with love. There you are with three, the lover, what is being loved, and love."[126]

The discussion of the doctrine of God is necessarily undertaken within the parameters of Greek philosophical thinking. It was not until Luther that alternative concepts began to emerge. For Augustine, God is defined negatively - impassible and immutable. Like Gregory of Nyssa, he avoids the trap of subordinationism within the Godhead. However, the danger is that the Son remains essentially participant within the divine while failing to engage quite so fully with the human side of his nature. It is possible therefore to detect the emergence of one significant concern central to Protestant theology, the nature and importance of the sovereignty of God.

Although the Cappodocian Fathers and Augustine set the pattern for the doctrine of the Trinity, the preceding conflicts were by no means resolved. On the one hand, Nestorianism upheld the notion that there were two separate persons in the Incarnate Christ, human and divine. On the other, the Monophysites, held that in the person of the Incarnate Christ there was but a single, divine nature. The struggle of the Fathers was the result of the recognition that in the person of Jesus Christ "they had to do immediately with God, who unreservedly communicated *himself* to them... face to face in Christ who is the face of the Father turned toward them."

---

[123] *de Trinitate* V.5, 191.
[124] *de Trinitate* IX.1, 271.
[125] Mary T. Clark, *Augustine*, London, Geoffrey Chapman, 1996, 67.
[126] *de Trinitate* VIII.14, 255.

The Story of the Doctrine of Kenosis 41

Thus there is established "a profound reciprocity between God and man"[127] which is not mediated by a third party. It is the result of God's knowing self-revelation in the hypostatic union of God and man in the one person of Christ.

> Jesus Christ is thus not a mere symbol, some representation of God detached from God, but God in his own Being and Act come among us, expressing in our human form the Word which he is eternally in himself, so that in our relations with Jesus Christ we have to do directly with the ultimate Reality of God.[128]

Jesus Christ is the priest who crosses the diastasis separating God and humanity in his own person. But in order to do so God can only make himself known "within the modes of our creaturely"[129] reality.

The Chalcedonian Definition sought "to discover the solution of just *one* disputed question: *how* the confessions of the '*one Christ*' may be reconciled with belief in the '*true God and true man*', 'perfect in Godhead, perfect in manhood'."[130] Though the Chalcedonian Definition of Faith did not refer explicitly to either Arius or Arianism they are present by implication nonetheless. First this is shown by the reiteration of the creeds of Nicea and Constantinople. Secondly they are contained in its rejection of "those who attempt to pervert the mystery of the Incarnation"[131] by stating that because Christ was born a man a double Sonship co-exists in the Incarnate Christ, the human and the divine. By stating the incarnate Son is passable those who either mix or confuse the two natures of Christ are in error. The definition is not an original statement but rather a mosaic assembled from existing statements of the faith.[132] Furthermore it was "an agreement to disagree…" in order to produce a statement of the theology of pre-existence, kenosis, and exaltation, formulated in such a way as "to transcend speculative alternatives" so that consequently there emerged a dialectic wherein the "various contending doctrines of Christ vied with one another".[133]

---

[127] Thomas F. Torrance, *The Ground and Grammar of Theology*, Belfast, Christian Journals Limited, 1980, 159.
[128] Torrance, 1980, 160.
[129] Torrance, 1980, 163.
[130] Grillmeier, 1975, 545 – his italics.
[131] Stevenson, 1973, 366.
[132] Pelikan, 1971, 264.
[133] Pelikan, 1971, 266.

Luther and Divine Identity in Christology

It is no coincidence that Gottfried Thomasius was a Lutheran. It is possible to discern in him elements of Luther's christological thinking which, though not overtly kenotic, nonetheless incline towards an exploration of the cross in terms of the identity of God and his self-revelation through his saving activity in Jesus Christ. However, Luther's *theologia crucis* only makes sense in the light of the doctrine of the Trinity. Luther understands the theology of the cross as the antithesis of a 'theology of glory' by which he means the vain endeavour which assumes it is possible to penetrate the mystery of God either by means of reason or through mystic experience. Luther is clear that God can be known only by his self-revelation. It

> is not sufficient for anyone, and it does him no good to recognize God in his glory and majesty, unless he recognizes him in the humility and shame of the cross... So, also, in *John* XIV [.8], where Philip spoke according to the theology of glory: 'Show us the Father.' Christ forthwith set aside his flighty thought about seeing God elsewhere and led him to himself, saying, 'Philip, he who has seen me has seen the Father' [John XIV.9]. For this reason true theology and recognition of God are in the crucified Christ.[134]

At "the basis of the theology of the cross was the proposition that 'God can be found only in suffering and the cross,' so that 'he who does not know Christ does not know God hidden in suffering.'"[135] What Luther presents is krypsis not kenosis. In the humiliation of the cross God is both revealed yet remains hidden. In the exegesis of Galatians 3.13, Luther says Christ's saving action is that he "took all our sins upon him, and for them died upon the cross".[136] This is undertaken "of his [Christ's] own accord and by the will of his Father".[137] Atonement is as an act of the economic Trinity.[138].

For Luther, Christ is the "companion of sinners, taking upon himself the flesh and blood of those which were sinners and transgressors.[139] Christ's vocation "to overcome the sin of the world, death, the curse, and the wrath of God in himself [Christ], is not the work of any creature, but" is the work

---

[134] The Heidelberg Disputation, Theses and their Proofs, proof 20. (E. G. Rupp and Benjamin Drewery (ed), *Martin Luther*, London, Edward Arnold, 1971, 28 – their italics).

[135] Jaroslav Pelikan, *The Reformation of the Church and Dogma (1300-1700)*, Chicago, University of Chicago Press, London, 1985, 155-56 - my italics.

[136] M. Luther, *A Commentary on St Paul's Epistle to the Galatians*, (Middleton Edition, 1575), London, James Clarke & Co Ltd, 1953, 269.

[137] Luther, 1953, 269.

[138] Pelikan, 1984, 157.

[139] Luther, 1953, 269-70.

The Story of the Doctrine of Kenosis 43

"of the divine power alone."[140] Here Luther has two targets in mind for his polemic. First, "popish sophisters",[141] and secondly Arius' denial of the true divinity of Christ.[142] In describing this Luther paraphrases Christ's self-understanding,

> touching mine own person [Jesus Christ], both as human and divine, I am blessed and need nothing; but I will empty myself and will put upon me your person, that is to say, your human nature, and will walk in the same among you, and will suffer death to deliver you from death.[143]

According to Luther, God's action, and therefore God's being, is seen only in Christ upon the cross.

> Christ is apprehended, ... not in the foolish imagination of the sophisters and monks... but it is a spiritual faithful and divine beholding... of Christ hanging on the cross for my sins, thy sins, and the sins of the whole world.[144]

The issue concerning the self-revelation of and therefore the possibility of God's participation in creation is the same one found at the heart of the Arian controversy.[145]

> True it is indeed that Christ is a person most pure and unspotted: but thou must not stay there; for thou hast not yet Christ, although thou knowest him to be God and man: but then thou hast him indeed, when thou believest that this most pure and innocent person is freely given unto thee of the Father to be thy High Priest and Saviour, yea rather thy servant, that he putting off his innocency and holiness, and taking thy sinful person upon him, might bear thy sin, thy death, thy curse, and might be made a sacrifice and curse for thee, that by this means he might deliver thee from the curse of the law.[146]

However, the reference to Christ as 'High Priest' does not imply a mediatory role. Similarly that Christ 'puts off' his divine attributes in order to achieve a fuller humanity is not intended to suggest any notion of

---

[140] Luther, 1953, 274.
[141] Luther, 1953, 270.
[142] Luther, 1953, 274.
[143] Luther, 1953, 276.
[144] Luther, 1953, 278.
[145] Williams, 2001, 106.
[146] Luther, 1953, 278

divestment by the divine in the Incarnation.[147] Luther's concern is to speak of the incarnation of Christ in terms of the two natures conjoined in the one person. On the one hand, for the Antiochene theologians and Reformed theology, the *communicatio idiomata* occurred at the level of the person and not between the natures and was thus understood to be *in concreto*. On the other hand, the notion of the *communicatio idiomata abstracta*, refers to the abstract consideration of the relationship of the two natures, but distinct from their union in the person and in particular the communication of the divine properties to the human nature. This was of particular importance in the Alexandrian and Cappodocian christological understandings. Whereas the former taken to its extreme raises the spectre of Nestorianism and questions the very unity of Christ's person, conversely the latter position as developed by the Monophysites threatens the integrity of the two natures themselves. Both are logical but neither is an adequate proposition. Luther recognizes that it is necessary to move beyond this dialectic; recognizing the unity of the two natures in Christ's person demands a real communication or sharing of attributes. The problem is how precisely such a doctrine might be formulated. Luther criticizes Nestorius' failure to identify fully Jesus Christ and God as being one. He is clear that whatever is predicated of God must also be predicated of humanity in the specific case of Christ.[148]

According to Luther the answer is the *communicatio idiomata*, without which Christ would be merely a ghost either seemingly human or only divine in appearance.[149] Consequently the doctrine of the person of Christ stands "in apposition to the subject but the doctrine of the work of Christ formed the predicate: Christ was what he was in order to do what he did."[150] The *communicatio idiomata* enables Luther to articulate the completeness of Jesus Christ as being both 'truly man' while yet 'truly God'. The difficulty lies in its belief that it is possible to offer an unmediated and realistic account of the two natures in Christ. What seems to emerge is an implicit questioning of the use of language as determined by Greek philosophical thinking, according to which God can only be understood in any meaningful sense as apophatic. Luther's vision of God, is of one who is deeply concerned for the world and therefore "the subject of theology is guilty and lost man and the justifying and redeeming God."[151]

In conclusion, it is Luther's theology of the cross and its emphasis upon

---

[147] Bernard Lohse, *Martin Luther's Theology* (ET), Edinburgh, T & T Clark, 1999, 229.

[148] 'Martin Luther's Critique of Nestorianism', Alister McGrath, *The Christian Theology Reader*, Oxford, Blackwells, 1995, 152.

[149] Martin Luther, 'The Short Catechism' [1529], Henry Bettenson (ed), *Documents of the Christian Church* (2nd Edn), Oxford, OUP, 1975, 205.

[150] Pelikan, 1985, 161.

[151] Lohse, 1999, 40.

The Story of the Doctrine of Kenosis 45

the true humanity of Jesus which Thomasius and the kenoticists misappropriated. For Luther the *communicatio idiomata* provides for the articulation of the co-existence of the divine and human within Jesus Christ. This enabled him to state explicitly that it is in Jesus Christ on the cross that God is encountered. Nowhere in his writings is there any suggestion that Jesus Christ, as the Son of God, divests or empties himself of the divine attributes as a necessary condition of the incarnation. Furthermore Luther was able to make this step because he understood Jesus Christ as the incarnate Son of God who is the second person of the Trinity. Consequently he locates the saving event of the cross within the Trinity. Luther thereby escaped the constraints of a purely christological understanding which so hampered some of his later followers. The result of Luther's trinitarian understanding is that Jesus' "identity with the eternal Son, and therefore participation in deity and its attributes, is mediated by the self distinction of Jesus from the Father".[152] Consequently Luther is able to draw upon the language of priesthood, as signifying how in his saving action, Christ is able to cross the divine-human boundaries. This is the opposite of Thomasius and the kenoticists who, in elevating the role of the human Jesus, undermined the role of divine sovereignty within salvation.

Like Augustine, Luther's *theologia crucis* is also vocational. Commenting upon the phrase that the 'Son of God, loved me and gave himself for me' Luther can only emphasize, it was the lot of "the Son of God delivered... even to the death of the cross"[153] for the salvation of mankind. For this reason the Son is sent out from the Father. Luther can only return again and again to the word 'love' to describe what has been effected for mankind. Christ is found on earth "of his own accord and by the will of the Father".[154] The priesthood of Christ is "to make intercession for sinners, to offer himself a sacrifice for their sins".[155] For Luther the sacrifice is real and is once for all upon the cross. But God in Jesus Christ makes the sacrifice for mankind in an act of divine sovereignty and therefore an act of prevenient grace. Though he rejects the notion that humanity cooperates in its salvation nonetheless in the divine-human reciprocity Christ is *sacramentum* and *exemplum*, "his death is to be realized in me and I am to die with him before I can imitate him."[156]

---

[152] *Syst.* II, 387.
[153] Luther, 1953, 176.
[154] Luther, 1953, 269.
[155] Luther, 1953, 178.
[156] Marc Lienhard, *Luther, Witness to Jesus Christ*, Minneapolis, quoted, Lohse, 1999, 222.

Conclusion

In this thesis I shall argue that kenosis provides the primary analogy for the development of an understanding of priesthood, acceptable within a Protestant theological framework. Kenosis has the potential to provide such an analogy because its fundamental concern is the possibility and therefore the nature of the divine-human relationship. The first two sections demonstrated, by reference to traditional kenotic and Death of God theologies, that a neither a naively realistic nor anti-realistic understandings of kenosis provide a way ahead because they seek to resolve the divine-human dialectic of Jesus Christ as truly God and truly man. The effect of this in terms of priesthood is to either suggest humanity is responsible for its own salvation (Death of God theology) or to require some form of intermediary figure who mediates the divine-human relationship. Furthermore, both undermine the vocational nature of Jesus'
ministry by denying his essential character, as both truly divine and truly human.

However, the alternative, and rather more tangential account, provides the possibility of a more fruitful way forward. First, by setting the christological firmly within the trinitarian framework. Secondly, by setting the divine-human encounter within the context of the accounts of the immanent and economic Trinity. Thirdly, these firmly ground the saving act of Jesus Christ as vocational and an essential aspect of his character. Fourthly, together these expressly deny the possibility that Jesus Christ can be understood as being in any sense a semi-divine or intermediary figure. Instead kenosis is to be understood in terms of the identity of Jesus Christ.

I shall argue that it is this notion of the identity of God in relation to humanity, which is fundamental to any notion of priesthood. Priesthood does not occupy an intermediary role between humanity and God. Priesthood is human and this forms a parameter which defines its character. However, this is itself defined by the divine-human relationship within which it exists.

In order to explore more fully the trinitarian account of kenosis to develop further the analogy between kenosis and priesthood I shall now turn to the theology of Karl Barth, Hans Urs von Balthasar and Jürgen Moltmann.

Chapter 3

Kenosis and the Theology of Barth, Balthasar and Moltmann

Karl Barth, Hans Urs von Balthasar and Jürgen Moltmann have all developed kenotic theologies in the context of explicitly trinitarian accounts of the cross in the divine-human encounter. Furthermore they have approached the issue in ways which are both complementary and yet distinctive. Barth wrote from a Reformed perspective but within an explicitly Chalcedonian framework, Balthasar as a Roman Catholic but indebted to Patristic theology, and though Moltmann describes himself as a Reformed theologian I shall demonstrate that much of his thinking is influenced by Luther's *theologia crucis*. Thus they continue the debate that began in Chapter 1. Secondly, all three are committed to the exploration of the nature of the divine-human relationship in the context of a trinitarian soteriology. Thirdly, I shall explore their work in chronological order, as to some extent each is responding to their predecessors.[1]

What will emerge is the establishment of a number of simple boundary markers that will shape the subsequent discussion of the priesthood of the ordained. These are first, the primacy of the divine sovereignty. Secondly, the Chalcedonian Definition of Faith in relation to Jesus Christ as 'truly God and truly man', rooting Christology firmly within the doctrine of the Trinity. Thirdly, the dialectical nature of the divine-human encounter that understands kenosis as neither naively realistic nor an anti-realist account of Christ's saving act. In terms of priesthood therefore it requires the recognition that salvation is an act of sovereign grace which proceeds from God to humanity, and in which humanity's cooperation is not required. It repeats the Chalcedonian pattern ensuring that both God and man retain

---

[1] This is perhaps most evident in relation to Balthasar and Barth and Moltmann and Barth. However, Moltmann acknowledges the importance of Balthasar's contribution in the rehabilitation of kenosis not 'in the framework of the two natures, but in the context of the doctrine of the Trinity.' (Jürgen Moltmann, 'God's Kenosis in the Creation and Consummation of the World', John Polkinghorne (ed), *The Work of Love*, London, SPCK, 2001, 140-41.)

their essential characters and therefore maintains the essential *diastasis*. Finally, priesthood exists within the unresolved dialectic of the divine-human encounter.

Kenosis in the Theology of Karl Barth

It seems paradoxical that Barth who explicitly rejects the "modern kenotics"[2] should employ kenotic language and imagery to represent God's saving activity in Jesus Christ.[3] Central to Barth's theological narrative is the importance he attaches to the consistency of God's character. Barth draws on Aristotle's analysis of the four key attributes of characterisation required for satisfactory emplotment. First, there is goodness. A good character is one who fulfils their purpose. Secondly, it is important that a character is appropriate; that they are what they ought to be. Thirdly, Aristotle says a character should be 'like'. While his exact meaning is not clear, the implication is that the character must be one to whom one can relate. Finally, a character must be consistent.[4] Indeed Barth's distinctive hermeneutic "has much in common with literary criticism of the genre of realistic narrative."[5] So responding to critics of the first edition of *The Epistle to the Romans*, he suggests his system is:

> limited to a recognition of what Kierkegaard called 'the infinite qualitative distinction' between time and eternity... 'God is in heaven, and thou art on earth.' The relation between such a God and such a man, and the relation between such a man and such a God, is for me the theme of the Bible and the essence of philosophy.[6]

Barth believed that historical criticism alone is insufficient in interpreting the text.[7] Rather what is required, is "a creative straining of the sinews" through the application of a dialectical reading,

---

[2] According to Barth nineteenth century kenoticism was a theological absurdity. See: *CD* IV.1, 183.
[3] Wolfhart Pannenberg, *Jesus, God and Man* (ET), London, SCM, 1968, 313. See also: the prominence of references to Philippians 2.5-11 in the Scriptural Index, *CD* Index Volume, 160.
[4] Aristotle, *Poetics*, 8.1. This may seem curious given Barth's somewhat ambivalent attitude to Aristotle. (See: *CD* III.3 107, 334, IV.2, 758.) For the purposes of the argument I shall pay particular attention to *C D*. IV.1, sections 57-59.
[5] David Ford, 'Barth's interpretation of the Bible', S. W. Sykes (ed), *Karl Barth, Studies in his Theological Method*, Oxford, Clarendon Press, 1979, 57.
[6] Karl Barth, *The Epistle to the Romans* (6th Edn, ET), Oxford, Oxford University Press, 1957, 10.
[7] Barth, 1957, 6.

till the document seems hardly to exist as a document; till I have almost forgotten that I am not its author; till I know the author so well that I allow it to speak in my name and am even able to speak in his name myself. [8]

For Barth the Biblical narrative is a story into which the interpreter is drawn. The interpreter is not simply an external observer of the story but a participant. In Garrett Green's words, to "read the Bible as scripture is to interpret it – and to interpret the world and oneself at the same time" and therefore an act of exteriorisation. Further, the "literal sense of the biblical text tells us (if we are reading scripturally) what God *says*; but it requires an active interpretation to discern what God *means*."[9] This stands in direct opposition to the hermeneutics of suspicion which Green identifies as understanding religious belief to be "a form of false consciousness – not a deliberate falsehood but rather a systematic misunderstanding of one's own experience of the world." This is an understanding, which he believes "might be summarised in the claim that religion is 'bad imagination.'" [10]

So for Barth reading the Bible is not the "mere deciphering of words"[11] but the imaginative engagement with the text by the reader. The interpretative process includes the living of the text in response to God's self-revelation. The "helplessness of the theologian, unable to secure the truth of his or her teaching by means of apologetic argument, mirrors the helplessness of the crucified Christ" whereby God "has revealed Himself to our *imagination*".[12]

Imagination is not understood in its modern fictive sense. Imagination describes the tracing or plotting necessary either for the completion of an incomplete text or for forming images in the mind, which are coherent with the narrative as it is known but which is not otherwise specified.[13] Narrative emplotment by recourse to the imagination provides a way to reconfigure otherwise independent events and experiences into a coherent whole. Barth's hermeneutic is, using Lindbeck's expression, intratextual; it "is the text, so to speak, which absorbs the world, rather than the world the text." It

---

[8] Barth, 1957, 8.
[9] Garrett Green, *Theology, Hermeneutics and Imagination*, Cambridge, CUP, 2000, 176.
[10] Green, 2000, 171. Green's identified Feuerbach Marx, Nietzsche and Freud as exponents of a hermeneutic of suspicion for whom imagination and reality 'compromise a problematic duality...[being] opposed and mutually exclusive terms.' (92)
[11] Barth, 1957, 7.
[12] Green, 2000, 204 – his italics.
[13] N. T. Wright, *The New Testament and the People of God*, London, SPCK, 1996, 140-143 or a literary example is William Horwood, *The Willows in Winter*, London, HarperCollins, 1995.

"redescribes reality within the scriptural framework"[14] witnessing to the fact that God is and reveals himself in his Word.

Barth's imaginative narrative is rooted in a trinitarian understanding of God, revealed in Scripture. This is evident in the particularity of his account of how God is identified and therefore represented. The doctrine of reconciliation does not talk in abstract terms of the second 'person' of the Trinity or the Son of God but of Jesus Christ.[15] Hermeneutically this will form a key aspect for developing a Protestant understanding of priesthood. I shall argue that priesthood cannot– any more than the doctrine of reconciliation – be understood either speculatively or idealistically but only in relation to God as Father, Son and Holy Spirit. So, according to Barth, the "whole being and life of God is an activity both in eternity and in worldly time, both in Himself as Father, Son and Holy Spirit, and in His relation to man and all creation."[16] This is how "'God with us' speaks."[17] The agenda set for the discussion of salvation takes form in God's address to humanity, Jesus Christ.[18] Here God and humanity meet, such that boundaries are crossed and humans can participate in the "being of God" which can only be effected as a sovereign act of his grace.[19] Barth faces the apparent inherent contradictions of the God-man. On the one hand "that in Jesus Christ we have to do with very God. The reconciliation of man with God takes place as God Himself actively intervenes... God became man."[20] On the other, "that in Jesus Christ we have to do with a true man".[21] Although there is resolution there is no final synthesis because "the third Christological aspect" is

> the source of the two first, and it comprehends them both... as the one who is very God and very man in this concrete sense, Jesus Christ Himself is one. He is the 'God-man,' that is, the Son of God who as such is this man, this man who as such is the Son of God.[22]

Barth therefore delineates the parameters for his narrative by explicit reference to the Chalcedonian Definition of faith.

Barth's method is overtly dialectical, constantly proposing and opposing

---

[14] George Lindbeck, *The Nature of Doctrine*, London, SPCK, 1984, 118.
[15] *CD* IV.1, 52.
[16] *CD* IV.1, 7.
[17] *CD* IV.1, 8.
[18] *CD* IV.1, 122.
[19] 'Since salvation ... consists in participation in the being of God it can only come from God.' (*CD* IV.1, 8.)
[20] *CD* IV.1, 128.
[21] *CD* IV.1, 130.
[22] *CD* IV.1, 135

statements which he sets in tension, in which truth is to be sought between both while including the opposites themselves. We must therefore ask: "How can the humanity of Jesus Christ be different from and yet identify with our humanity in order to effect redemption and our adoption by the Godhead?"[23] Barth's answer is that when

> we say God we say the Creator and Lord of all things. And we can say all that without reservation or diminution of Jesus Christ... [which – his divinity] corresponds to the Godhead of God active and revealed in Him. No general idea of 'Godhead' developed abstractly from such concepts... we must learn from Jesus Christ...
>
> ...He is God as He takes part in the event...
>
> ... in the light of the fact it pleased God - and this is what corresponds outwardly to and reveals the inward divine being and event - Himself to become man. In this way, *in this condescension*, He is the eternal Son of the eternal Father. This is the will of this Father, of this Son and of the Holy Spirit who is the Spirit of the Father and the Son. This is how God is, this is His freedom, this is His distinctiveness from and superiority to all other reality.[24]

Seven things are apparent in this quote. First, there is particularism. Second, the revelation of God in Jesus Christ does not entail (*pace* Thomasius *et al.*) the renunciation of any divine attributes. Third, the use of the language of kenosis represents the Incarnation as an act of divine *condescension*. Fourth, this is an act of divine sovereignty from God to humanity. Fifth, it is essentially a Trinitarian event. Sixth, this can only be told as a narrative account.[25] Finally, it is dialectic. Jesus Christ is recognizable as a human being while remaining unchanged and therefore distinct in his divinity.

Barth represents the movement of the narrative as "the way of God into a far country" in which God goes out of himself in order to reveal himself in an act of divinely sovereign grace. He reinterprets the parable of the prodigal son as God's journey into an alien place, by becoming man, announcing God's love in which the Son goes out from the Father to humanity. In the story the Father is the subject who sends out the Son who

---

[23] Graham Ward, *Barth, Derrida and the Language of Theology*, Cambridge, CUP, 1998, 162.

[24] *CD* IV.1, 129 – my italics.

[25] 'The point is surely this: we cannot say what God is in himself; all we have is the narrative of God with us. And that is the narrative of a journey into a far country... the story of God's Son as a creatur' (Rowan Williams, *On Christian Theology*, Oxford, Blackwell, 2000, 159.)

is the object of the Father's love and is willingly received back.[26] It encapsulates Barth's characterization of Jesus Christ and the crossing of the divine-human boundaries. First, the journey of God into a far country in Jesus Christ is a matter of goodness, through the fulfilment of his vocation, which is the divine plan, framed in God's eternal covenant and election of his people. Jesus therefore fulfils the divine intention.[27] Secondly, in Jesus, God does not cease to be what he ought.[28] Thirdly, in the incarnation, God in Jesus Christ represents and participates in being human to the extent that to "be flesh is to be in a state of perishing before this God."[29] Finally, God is above all consistent "He does not cease to be God."[30] The journey of the Son of God into a far country "is in continuity with His grace as already demonstrated and revealed."[31] As Aristotle says, this does not preclude reversals but nonetheless the characters must still conform to their essential attributes if they are not to become incredible.

Barth returns[32] to a discussion of Philippians 2 as an account of Jesus as the Son of God who takes on being in the flesh, in real time while remaining obedient to God. In the humiliation "He emptied Himself... and became obedient unto death, even the death of the cross... [wherein] is found the deity of Jesus Christ".[33] As Barth stresses, the narrative "prevents the rounding off of the picture of Jesus into a kind of ideal-picture of human existence"[34] that is ultimately ahistorical. It is in the particular man Jesus Christ "and in Him alone that the Father is revealed."[35]

Barth's trinitarian framework therefore establishes the parameters within which he employs kenosis. This also provides the narrative structure within which he explores God's atonement in Jesus Christ. This structure is determined by the need to retain effective characterisation, within the structure of the plot[36] as delineated by the Chalcedonian Definition, which outlines the story of God's atoning and reconciling activity. 'The way of God into a far country' represents the encounter of the divine and the human, only possible in Jesus Christ. Furthermore he says that in Jesus

---

[26] *CD* IV.1, 183.

[27] 'What takes place is the divine fulfillment of a divine decree. It takes place in the freedom of God'. (*CD* IV.1, 195.)

[28] *CD* IV.1, 186.

[29] *CD* IV.1, 175.

[30] *CD* IV.1, 158.

[31] *CD* IV.1, 172, *CD* II.1, 397. See also: *CD* II.1, 490-608. The constancy of God in the Incarnation is explicitly an expression of God's being in Trinity (*CD* II.1, 515).

[32] Barth has already discussed Phil 2 see: *CD* II.1, 515-518.

[33] *CD* IV.1, 165f.

[34] *CD* IV.1, 167.

[35] *CD* IV.1, 166-167 (see: *CD* I.2, 872).

[36] Aristotle suggests that characterisation is only secondary to plot. (See: Aristotle, *Poetics*, 1996, 12 [4.3].)

Christ both God and humanity participate so that neither is diminished, and because they meet and are identified in mutual participation, so atonement and reconciliation become possible.[37] However, while both participate, the initiative remains firmly with God, humanity's role remains essentially consequential. In this Barth provides for the possibility of the divine-human encounter. Furthermore an aspect of Barth's theology of history is located in the entry of the eternal God into the temporal, created world through the incarnation. In this the "work of the Holy Spirit is to bring and hold together that which is different".[38] God's revelatory self-identity in the man Jesus makes possible for his entry into history through his participation in the created world:

> God gives Himself, but He does not give Himself away. He does not give up being God in becoming a creature, in becoming a man... when He dies in His unity with this man, death does not gain any power over Him. He exists as God in the righteousness and the life, the obedience and resurrection of this man. He makes His own the being of man in contradiction against Him, but He does not make common cause with it... He overcomes the flesh in becoming flesh. He reconciles the world with Himself as He is in Christ. He is not untrue to Himself but true to Himself in this condescension, in this way into a far country. If it were otherwise, if in it He set Himself in contradiction with Himself, how could He reconcile the world with Himself?[39]

The kenotic action of God is not the relinquishment of the divine attributes (*pace* Thomasius *et al.*) but the giving of himself in the economy of the Trinity. The sovereignty of God is absolute. God cannot be against or in disunity with Himself. His self-revelation must be true to his divine nature. Therefore, "God does not have to dishonour Himself when He goes into the far country, and conceals His glory... His condescension as such, is the image and reflection in which we see Him as He is."[40] It is an act of grace. Atonement is a Christological doctrine but trinitarian in operation. It is "a matter of the mystery of the inner being of God as the being of the Son in relation to the Father... an obedience of suffering, of the self-humiliation of Jesus Christ, of the way of the Son into a far country".[41] So God the Father gives himself to the Son through the Spirit. Kenosis is a statement of the divine identity.

---

[37] *CD* IV.1, 184.
[38] *CD* IV.3, 761.
[39] *CD* IV.1, 185.
[40] *CD* IV.1, 188.
[41] *CD* IV.1, 177.

> If then, God is in Christ, if what the man Jesus does is God's own work, this aspect of *the self-emptying and self-humbling of Jesus Christ as an act of obedience cannot be alien to God*. But in this case we have to see here the other and inner side of the mystery of the divine nature of Christ and therefore of the nature of the one true God - that He himself is also able and free to render obedience.[42]

The 'self-emptying and self-humbling of Jesus Christ', the kenosis spoken of in Philippians 2 is an intra-trinitarian event and therefore 'as an act of obedience cannot be alien to God'. It is an event that takes place within the Godhead, externalized in and through the person of Jesus Christ. Likewise it is an act of obedience which presupposes an above and a below, one who wills and one who obeys. But does this therefore necessarily compromise trinitarian equality within the Godhead? Here Barth's dialectic, the "is" and "is not", between which no permanent meanings (only impermanent moments of meaning) are possible comes into play directly. Kenotic language becomes the means by which it is possible to represent that which cannot be said. It becomes the imaginative key by which it is possible to identify the divine and thereby narrate the story of God in Jesus Christ, which ultimately can only be recounted and believed.[43]

As Barth acknowledges, there is an apparent offensiveness in such thinking, which touches the very heart of kenotic thought. As Pannenberg observes, any "derivation of the plurality of trinitarian persons from the essence of one God... leads to problems of either modalism on the one hand or subordinationism on the other."[44] If Origen's philosophical need to preserve the essential attributes of God as immutable and impassible resulted in suggestions of subordinationism, Barth appears to incline towards modalism. This is a consequence of his concept of revelation as essentially self-revelation by the divine.

Within his trinitarian understanding Barth appears to understand kenosis as offering a critically realistic narrative of Jesus Christ who is truly God and truly man, so remaining faithful to Chalcedon, and not as divine absence or surrender. Kenosis articulates the act of love revealed in the Word made flesh. But this is not simply enfleshment as the physical clothing of the divine. Instead it expresses the dialectic of the God-man, which is beyond any final synthesis into a higher truth. So if "we are to speak of God in terms of Jesus, we must say that in God there is that which makes possible the identity-in-difference - indeed, identity in distance or absence".[45]

---

[42] *CD* IV.1, 193 - my italics.
[43] *CD* IV.1, 200f.
[44] *Syst.* I, 298.
[45] Williams, 2000, 158.

Kenosis in the Theology of Hans Urs von Balthasar

I have postulated that Barth as an inheritor of the Reformed tradition advances kenosis as a trinitarian narrative of God's saving action in Christ to humanity, shaped by the biblical account. It is in the particular person of Jesus Christ, as 'truly God and truly man' that God reveals himself. Balthasar, a Roman Catholic, proposes a model, which is both dramatic and reliant upon the tradition of the Church, notably the Fathers. Balthasar's remains a literary and a narrative account but his emphasis upon the dramatic underlines its mimetic economy. Balthasar therefore adds further facets in the understanding of kenosis, which will further enrich the analogical possibilities with regards to the understanding of priesthood. However, it would be simplistic to suggest that the understanding of priesthood divides along Roman Catholic-Protestant lines, nonetheless this does at least suggest a major fault line in understanding.

According to Balthasar, theo-dramatic theory is the attempt "to create a network of related concepts and images" which in some sense express "the singular divine action."[46] This is necessary as that which stands between on the one hand aesthetics and on the other (theo)logic.[47] That all the world is a stage is both a powerful and enduring metaphor "attracting to itself all the ultimate imitations concerning the meaning and structure of existence."[48] However, if "the boundaries between" life and the stage "are blurred, so it is in God's dealings with mankind." Despite the blurring of the boundaries what God does for man "is simply good."[49] This goodness is God's act towards humanity in his saving act, which takes place upon "the world stage".[50] Drama provides a means of representing reality and presenting the drama of existence by acting as a mirror "in which existence can directly behold itself."[51] In the light of this he proposes four dramatic themes which frame the mimetic process. First, in the dialectic between the finitude in the play, which is performed, and its nonfinite meaning "the play harmonizes the various accents from determinism to freedom... that corresponds to the ambiguity between time and eternity".[52] Secondly, there is the distinction between the 'I' and the actor's allotted role. Crucial to this is that "the central task is to maintain identity while preserving distinction and distance."[53] Thirdly, in emphasizing the actor's responsibility for his own

---

[46] *TD* I, 17.
[47] *TD* I, 15.
[48] *TD* I, 135.
[49] *TD* I, 18.
[50] *TD* I, 19.
[51] *TD* I, 249.
[52] *TD* I, 251-52.
[53] *TD* I, 252. As we shall see this is important in the theologies of vocation and kenosis (see: Chapter 5 below).

performance and yet his responsibility to a director the "stage metaphor preserves the relationship between God's transcendence and immanence vis-à-vis the play... which Christian theology will express in the concept of the economic Trinity."[54] The content of the drama is not randomly constructed, but emerges from the first three points. Fourthly, therefore, the result is the creation of dramatic tension. But according to Balthasar, first and foremost "the content can only be man himself, caught between his 'I' and his role, between what he is and what he represents". However, he acknowledges that "what he is cannot be totally separated from what he represents; indeed his 'I' must responsibly realize itself in this representational role."[55] For Balthasar God's revelation is not an object to be viewed but "his action upon the world, and the world can only respond."[56]

What is apparent is that Balthasar has a greater sense of the creature's relative autonomy under God than did Barth. Whereas according to Barth the guiding movement in the narrative is always from God to humanity, for Balthasar, humanity is a more active participant. While this is important for his understanding of vocation it also has implications for his understanding of humanity in relation to God.[57] In a fictional drama an actor can represent anything, the 'I' and the representational role can be separated. But is this also true of man theologically? Nonetheless according to Balthasar "man is always an 'I'... action on the world stage will always be determined in part by how the man in the lowly role is viewed".[58] However, this is important for his account of the kenotic drama as it unfolds in the passion narrative.

> In the first place, if God is to 'play' through human beings and, ultimately, at the plot's turning-point (the incarnation), *as* a human being, then he must, to a greater or lesser extent, go incognito[59]

Kenosis provides a 'model' for representing the divine drama, in which Jesus Christ, the second person of the Trinity, is the self-representation of God's revelation to the world culminating in the event of his death and resurrection. Following Aquinas, Balthasar argues that "in Christ the *processio* within the Godhead, which constitutes the Son as the Father's dialogue partner, is identical in God's going-out-from-himself toward the

---

[54] *TD* I, 255.
[55] *TD* I, 256.
[56] Angelo Scola, *Hans Urs von Balthasar* (ET), Edinburgh, T & T Clark, 1995, 41.
[57] See: Chapter 5 below.
[58] *TD* I, 257.
[59] Aidan Nichols, *No Bloodless Myth*, Edinburgh, T & T Clark, 2000, 12.

word, with the *missio*, the sending of the Son to mankind."[60] Kenosis provides a means in the context of a trinitarian understanding of the Godhead whereby this can be told and represented in the relation to the world. But what

> is decisive at this point is the revelation of the Trinity which takes place in that it is precisely the *person* of the Son who manifests the person of the Father, the latter appearing in him. If it belongs to the supreme obedience of the Son that he lets himself be raised by the Father, it belongs no less to the completion of his obedience that he lets it be 'granted' him by the Father to 'have life in himself' (John 5.26) - and even, indeed, to *become* clothed in all the apparel of his own divine sovereignty, despite the fact that the apparel in question was already his own 'before the world was made' (Philippians 2.6; John 17.5). That Jesus thus *became* what he already was, both before the world's foundation and during his earthly ministry: this must be taken with absolute seriousness by every Christology.[61]

Balthasar, like Barth, rejects nineteenth century liberal Protestant kenotic theory seeking instead to "link their views rather with Patristic theology which sees the whole divine drama of our salvation as kenosis."[62] Kenosis is the revelation of Christ as human through the act of dying but also the confirmation of his divinity so that "it is precisely and supremely that he is known as God always in the light of the resurrection."[63] In this way Balthasar locates the kenotic event in the economy of the divine Trinity as the moment in which God offers himself to become recognisable within creation.

Although profoundly influenced by Karl Barth, Balthasar's theology is not simply derivative. He is perhaps more explicit in his Trinitarian formulation of the action of Christ. This enables him to be much more overtly kenotic. Secondly, he recognizes the necessary dialectic in any christological theory in order to balance the claims of Christ as truly divine while yet remaining truly human as the Jesus of history. Hence one of his stated aims is to avoid the extremes of Nestorianism on the one hand and Monophysitism on the other, believing:

---

[60] *TD* I, 646 - his italics. Balthasar completes his statement by drawing upon Aquinas and adding '(This *missio* is completed by the sending of the Spirit into the world, proceeding from both the Father and the Son).' – author's brackets.
[61] Hans von Balthasar, *Mysterium Paschale* (ET), Edinburgh, T & T Clark, 1990b, 207.
[62] John Thompson, 'Barth and Balthasar: An Ecumenical Dialogue', Bede McGregor and Thomas Norris (ed), *The Beauty of Christ*, Edinburgh, T & T Clark, 1994, 179.
[63] McGregor and Norris (ed), 1994, 179.

the only way to avoid the two opposed and incompatible extremes is that which relates the event of the Kenosis of the Son of God to what one can, by analogy, designate as the eternal 'event' of the divine processions. It is from the supra-temporal yet ever actual event that, as Christians, we must approach the mystery of the divine 'essence'. That essence is forever 'given' in the self-gift of the Father, 'rendered' in the thanksgiving of the Son, and 'represented' in its character as absolute love by the Holy Spirit.[64]

The framework of Balthasar's dialectic is set christologically by the outworking of the Trinity. Kenosis is not the incarnation but the divine processio within the Trinity. So the incarnation is the "exteriorisation of God" which "has its ontic condition of possibility in the eternal exteriorisation of God - that is his tripersonal self-gift" resulting in His self-expression.[65]

Only within the economy of the Trinity can the event of the incarnation occur without the limitation of the Godhead. This is important for the balance by which both the divine and human are able to retain their true natures as desired by Balthasar. Therefore he is at pains to make clear this

does not mean, however, that God's essence becomes itself (univocally) 'kenotic', such that a single concept could include both the divine foundation of the possibility of Kenosis, and the Kenosis itself. It is here that many of the mistakes of the more modern kenoticists take their rise. What it does mean - as Hilary in his way tried to show - is that divine 'power' is so ordered that it can make room for a possible self-exteriorisation, like that found in the Incarnation and the Cross, and can maintain this exteriorisation even to the utmost point. As between the form of God and the form of a servant there reigns, in the identity of the Person involved, an analogy of natures according to the principle *maior dissimilitudo in tanta similitudine*.[66]

Balthasar recognizes the importance of identity in telling the story of God and of Jesus Christ. However, he is also aware that identity is not simply a matter of sameness, idem identity, but that identity is found in the ipse, in the constancy of the self in the midst of apparent outward difference. Kenosis does not simply render God recognizable in Christ but asks what it means to be God and equally what it means to be human when one speaks of the second person of the Trinity becoming fully human in the

---

[64] Balthasar, 1990b, viii.
[65] Balthasar, 1990b, 28.
[66] Balthasar, 1990b, 29.

incarnation. According to Balthasar either,

> philosophy misconceives man, failing in Gnostic or Platonic guise, to take with full seriousness his earthly existence... Or, alternatively, ... forms man so exactly in God's image and likeness that God descends to man's image... Here God only fulfils himself and manages to satisfy his own desires by divesting himself of his essence and becoming man, in order, as man, 'divinely' to suffer and to die.[67]

Kenosis is therefore the identification of God in human form revealed in the incarnation.

One concern of Balthasar's kenotic theology is the meaning of the death and burial of Jesus Christ, as the second person of the Trinity. Balthasar does not believe that the story of Jesus in the passion can be understood simply through Jewish notions of martyrdom. Instead, if the passion is understood in the light of the Old Testament concept of "the 'suffering righteous man' who is subsequently exalted and rewarded" then all "'meaning' is inexorably reduced to the humble preference for the will of the Father, as loved for its own sake."[68] It is an act of sovereign grace and the Son is thus identified in relation to and by his obedience to the Father.

To this end Balthasar explores the concept of divine handing over,[69] in which God is the acting subject. This can be understood as "an act of judgment... 'He who is thus handed over is, in the true sense of the word, abandoned by God.'"[70] Balthasar suggests that the concept of handing over is not clear. However, though it speaks of transition and change resulting in boundaries being crossed nonetheless "God remains he who acts, and does so with inexorable, ineluctable character".[71] In short the "theology of delivering up can only be maintained in a Trinitarian fashion whereby the Father 'hands' over his Son." This he connects with Philippians 2 and the obedience of the Son.[72] It is possible to suggest that handing over is also a priestly notion, although Balathasar does not appear to recognise the

---

[67] Balthasar, 1990b, 66.

[68] Balthasar, 1990b, 106.

[69] According to W. H. Vanstone to hand over first, implies that being 'handed over' is 'to pass into good hands' (W. H. Vanstone, *The Stature of Waiting*, London, DLT, 1982, 6). Secondly, it occurs at the moment when Jesus changes from being the subject to the object in the passion narrative. (Vanstone, 1982, 20.) Thirdly, it is applied by Paul to the atoning action of God in Christ. (Gal 2.20; Vanstone, 1982, 14) and which Luther comments is indicative of the grace of God. (M. Luther, *A Commentary on St Paul's Epistle to the Galatians*, (Middleton Edition, 1575), London, James Clarke & Co. Ltd., 1953, 176-77).

[70] Balthasar, 1990b, 108.

[71] Balthasar, 1990b, 109.

[72] Balthasar, 1990b, 111.

possibility. But he does recognise that it is primarily an act of God and that "men can only play a subordinate role."[73]

However, there is a hiatus between Balthasar's understanding of kenosis and the doctrine of God and his ecclesiology.[74] The passion and resurrection story provides the dramatic context within which Balthasar's exploration of kenosis, as the *theologia crucis* is rooted. The powerfully experiential and mystical element in his thought emerges in his emphasis upon Jesus' descent to the dead. Here Balthasar's choice of dialogue partners is "at least idiosyncratic".[75] At this point Balthasar's theology is fundamentally speculative in attempting to go beyond the Biblical text[76] departing most significantly from Barth's particularism. Despite these reservations Balthasar stresses the drama of the cross and the importance of the actuality of the death of the Son. So the experience of death and Hades is indicative of the true solidarity of the incarnate Son of God with humanity in being dead.[77]

The death of the Son is an act of the sovereign God. However, "two affirmations must be made simultaneously: the absolute sovereignty of God, who in Jesus Christ alone set up this new and eternal covenant with humankind; and the obtaining of a consensual 'Yes' of humanity as represented at the cross".[78] What is hinted at here becomes problematic when Balthasar discusses the ecclesiological roles of Mary and Peter. Consequently Balthasar leaves open the possibility that humanity cooperates in its salvation, and so the relationship between divine sovereignty and grace remains imprecise.

Balthasar understands the resurrection as fundamentally a trinitarian event. It is the Father who raises the dead Son in an act which in turn is linked inextricably with the outpouring of the Spirit - which could itself be construed as a kenotic act. So,

> John gives this Trinitarian mystery its most concise expression, by coining, from the materials of the Old Testament, the phrase, 'The Word became flesh'. This formula allows us to understand the man Jesus - his life, death and resurrection - as the fulfilment of the living Word of God of the old covenant, shows the event of Jesus to be the definitive, superabundant consequence of the event of God himself.[79]

---

[73] Balthasar, 1990b, 112
[74] See: Chapter 5 below.
[75] McGregor and Norris, 1994, 67.
[76] John Riches, 'The Biblical Basis of Glory', Bede McGregor and Thomas Norris (ed), 1994, 68.
[77] Balthasar, 1990b, 175.
[78] Balthasar, 1990b, 133.
[79] Balthasar, 1990b, 203.

The passion narrative and the mystery of Easter are a dramatic presentation of the Trinity. As Graham Ward observes, this is very different from the traditional Lutheran doctrine in which kenosis is described in terms of the activity of the incarnate Son as a consequence of becoming incarnate. Instead kenosis

> is the disposition of love within the Trinitarian community. It is a community constituted by differences which desire the other... The circulation of divine desire is the *processio*. Obedience to that desire to abandon oneself is the nature of one's calling or *missio* - for the going out or *missio* is always the act of love towards the other.[80]

Consequently if "the sacrifice of the Cross is interpreted in a cultic context... then the Resurrection becomes the acceptance of the sacrifice by the Godhead."[81] The whole event is grounded in the possibility that the boundaries which define the divine-human encounter are crossed. This necessarily takes place within the Godhead as an act of intra-trinitarian love.

> God distances himself from himself: the intra-Trinitarian love is enacted... The inconceivable self-emptying of God in the events of Good Friday and Holy Saturday is no arbitrary expression of the nature of God: this is what the life of the Trinity is, translated into the world.[82]

Balthasar, like Barth, proposes kenosis as a critically realistic representation of the gospel narrative. The importance of which is that kenosis is not an informative proposition or truth claim about objective reality[83] but a dramatic account. In his account of the passion story, "Christ takes hold of our imaginative powers; we enter into a 'painterly world' which this discloses... [and] we become absorbed by it".[84] Balthasar's Christology is essentially participative; the participation of Jesus Christ within the Trinity and the participation of the believer within the "sacrificial love"[85] of Christ for the world. The focus upon the descent of Christ and his alienation from the Father is highly dramatic. Equally important is the resurrection, which follows the kenotic event of the descent, which Nichols says re-echoes the

---

[80] Graham Ward, 'Kenosis: Death, Discourse and Resurrection', Lucy Gardner, David Moss, Ben Quash, Graham Ward, *Balthasar At The End Of Modernity*, Edinburgh, T & T Clark, 1999, 45.

[81] Balthasar, 1990b, 205.

[82] Sykes, 1979, 177.

[83] Lindbeck, 1984, 16. (Quoted 7 above, n. 42.)

[84] Aidan Nichols, 'Introduction', Balthasar, 1990b, 6.

[85] Aidan Nichols, 'Introduction', Balthasar, 1990b, 6.

Incarnation by raising "the Son into visibility"[86] and is therefore, an act of externalization.

With his concept of theo-drama Balthasar introduces a different emphasis upon the mimetic nature of the narrative. Accordingly, Philippians 2 describes "different phases in the continuity of a single drama".[87] Balthasar presents kenosis as a drama, which unfolds in what appears to be a series of acts. Act One is the pre-existent Son, who is part of the Godhead. Act Two is the Incarnation. At its heart Balthasar's kenotic economy is the death of the incarnate Son in relation to his being 'truly God and truly man'. It is in this context that he focuses upon the descensus motif of Holy Saturday. However, it is arguable that Balthasar is over reliant upon the descent of Jesus to Hades. Act Three is the resurrection. Act Four is the consequences of the resurrection, which are not really explored. That this is a separate act and not another scene within the third act is because it marks the creation of the Church. For Balthasar, the "appearances of the Risen One always issues in mission."[88] This is itself to be understood kenotically in the outpouring or the sending of the Spirit upon the people of God.[89] For Balthasar the notion of kenosis is an account of the divine *processio* which results in *missio*, expressive of the movement from God to humanity.

Thus for Barth, kenosis provides a narrative within which God can be re-imagined to include the movement of his self-revelation in Jesus Christ, who is both 'truly God and truly man'. Whereas for Balthasar kenosis shapes the mimetic economy of the Easter drama such that the world of the biblical narrative and the actual world as the Church experiences it encounter one another. Crucial to the admissibility of the dramatic metaphor is the nature of the participation of the divine within the drama. For Balthasar, kenosis becomes the means by which the divine participation and therefore identity can be explored and represented in the drama.[90] Thus "in the Incarnation the triune God has not simply helped the world, but has disclosed himself in what is most deeply his own."[91]

Kenosis in the Theology of Jürgen Moltmann

The third dialogue partner is Jürgen Moltmann whose understanding of the *theologia crucis* emerges in dialogue with both Barth and Balthasar but

---

[86] Aidan Nichols, 'Introduction', Balthasar, 1990b, 8 – his italics. See: Philippians 2.6-11.
[87] Balthasar, 1990b, 24.
[88] Balthasar, 1990b, 254 – his italics.
[89] Balthasar, 1990b, 261.
[90] Ward, 1999, 46f.
[91] Balthasar, 1990, 29.

aspires to be even more radical in its trinitarianism.[92] Furthermore, if Barth's account of kenosis is a narrative governed by a trinitarian account of scripture and Balthasar's is a trinitarian drama, Moltmann's account is an attempt to engage with the divine human-encounter in the face of humanity's attempts at self-understanding not through the cross but through a *theologia gloria*. The importance of all three dialogue partners is to provide a multi-faceted and therefore nuanced understanding of kenosis linked by a common trinitarianism. The breadth of their understanding will enable the broadest understanding of kenosis as providing an analogy from which it will then be possible to develop an understanding of priesthood to which Moltmann's particular contribution is the re-imagining of power.

The need for the re-imagining of power is brought sharply to the fore in the shared experiences of the twentieth century that form another link between Barth, Balthasar and Moltmann.

[I]n the modern world, the misery of the modern age characterised by the names of Auschwitz and Hiroshima, and the conflicts which modern capitalism and the white man have produced. ...Yet even a theory of world-accepting Christianity, which saw Christianity as a religious culture, would not be able totally to conceal the alien nature of the crucified Christ.[93]

Most especially for Moltmann "the horrors of modern history make theistic belief impossible".[94] The experience of history has revealed that the traditional identity ascribed to God is impossible to maintain. Kenosis enables the articulation of the identity and the very nature of the divine and therefore humanity.[95] The theology of the crucified Jesus is about the image and therefore the identification of the invisible God[96] as one who participates fully in his creation. This is revealed through his engagement with the universal human experience of suffering. The representation of God in Christ upon the cross is a moment of liberation for humanity. The God who dies in Christ frees humanity both "from the concern for self-deification" and "the legalist concern to justify himself."

The theology of the cross necessarily must take seriously "the situation

---

[92] Jürgen Moltmann, *The Crucified God* (ET), London, SCM, 1974, 203. (See also: Jürgen Moltmann, 'God's Kenosis in the Creation and Consummation of the World', John Polkinghorne (ed.), *The Work of Love*, London, SPCK, 2001, 140-141.)
[93] Moltmann, 1974, 68.
[94] Richard J. Bauckham, *Moltmann: Messianic Theology in the Making*, Basingstoke, Marshall Morgan and Scott, 1987, 81.
[95] Moltmann, 1974, 3.
[96] Moltmann, 1974, 69, quoting Barth (*CD* II.2, 123) and Col 1.15.

of man in pursuit of his own interests, man who is really inhuman".[97] Furthermore "the theology of the 'crucified God' also leads to a corresponding anthropology."[98] When crossing the divine-human boundaries "it is not the ascent of man to God but the revelation of God in his self-emptying in the crucified Christ which opens up God's sphere of life to the development of man in him."[99] So I shall suggest that an understanding of *theologia crucis* necessarily undermines a traditional notion of priesthood as a *theologia gloriae*, according to which the priest if not deified is understood as fulfilling an intermediary role between God and humanity.

In representing the divine in relation to the cross, Moltmann seeks to develop Barth's emphasis upon the centrality of the event of God's self-revelation in Christ. Thus he approvingly quotes Barth's words that, "the crucified Christ is the 'image of the invisible God'."[100] Following Barth and Balthasar, he wishes to articulate an image of God who gives himself in risking all for his creation. He therefore adopts Luther's notion that "the cross is the test of everything which deserves to be called Christian."[101] It is in God's supreme revelation in the event of the cross that he finds hope. His is an eschatological and Spirit-directed theology in which he seeks to express the dialectic of the cross and resurrection, where he attempts to explore the possibility of kenosis within a trinitarian framework.

Immediately, like Barth, he is drawn into the particularism of christocentricism and rejects the modern phenomenon of 'Jesuology' or exemplarism in which Jesus is portrayed as the perfect and therefore universal man. For Moltmann such notions founder on the same rocks that threatened to wreck the Christology of the early church, namely "speculative idealism" lacking an "adequate interpretation of his death on the cross".[102] To speak of the crucified God refocuses the theological horizon on the trinitarian relationships rather than the soteriological. The traditional theological reflection is limited because it has "always considered the cross and resurrection of Jesus within the horizon of soteriology". It has failed to ask what for him is the crucial question, "'*What does the cross of Jesus mean for God himself?*'"[103] This is the fundamental question about the identity and therefore the portrayal of God in and for creation. It is at this point that Moltmann detects what he believes to be a real weakness in Barth's understanding of the cross in terms of his

---

[97] Moltmann, 1974, 69.
[98] Moltmann, 1974, 267.
[99] Moltmann, 1974, 275.
[100] Moltmann, 1974, 69.
[101] Moltmann, 1974, 7.
[102] Moltmann, 1974, 97.
[103] Moltmann, 1974, 201 – his italics.

doctrine of God. For Moltmann the problem is that in Barth the *diastasis* that separates God and humanity is too rigid, and so constrains any possible relationship between the two. The importance of this for my argument is that priesthood can only exist in the recognition of the distinctive natures of God and humanity. Any attempt to resolve this *diastasis* creates or requires some form of intermediary figure. But neither Christ occupies such a position[104] nor can a human being occupy it.[105]

He believes that despite the complexity of Barth's answer, his imagination is constrained by the traditional attributes of the immutable God, which Moltmann wishes to challenge. According to Barth, "it is God the Father who suffers in the offering and sending of His Son, in His abasement." The suffering "is not His own, but the alien suffering of the creature, of man, which He takes to Himself in Him." Here Barth wrestles with the implications of a theology of the cross for the very being of God. Despite these reservations he then proceeds to state that, "He does suffer it in the humiliation of His Son with a depth with which it was never suffered by any man - apart from the One who is His Son." This particular passage is prefaced by a reference to "a *particula veri* in the teaching of the early Patripassians".[106] Moltmann is aware of the pitfalls of such a stance and suggests his position is one of 'patricompassion'.[107] So that in trinitarian terms the Son

> suffers dying, [and] the Father suffers the death of the Son. The grief of the Father here is just as important as the death of the Son. The Fatherlessness of the Son is matched by the Sonlessness of the Father.[108]

According to Moltmann, Barth,

> has consistently drawn the harshness of the cross into his concept of God... Remarkably I see the critical limitation of Barth in the fact that he still thinks too *theo*logically, and that his approach is not sufficiently trinitarian.[109]

In other words Barth's thought is too consciously systematic in its approach and structure. In The Trinity and the Kingdom of God Moltmann states that he "finds Barth's 'modes of being' and Rahner's 'modes of subsistence' far

---

[104] See: Chapter 2 above.
[105] See: 92-96 above.
[106] *CD* IV.2, 357.
[107] The key to patricompassion is Moltmann's inclusion of the notion of compassion, so that patripassion is re-imagined in terms of the compassion of the Father for the Son.
[108] Moltmann, 1974, 243.
[109] Moltmann, 1974, 202 – his italics.

closer to German idealism than to biblical witness."[110] At the same time Balthasar is critical of Moltmann's understanding of kenosis on two counts. First it is "Hegelianising"[111] and secondly, it appears to suggest that "suffering man stands higher than the god who cannot suffer."[112] The point is that kenosis, as an account of the divine identity, an understanding which all three would share, begs a question about the possibility of a non-idealistic portrayal of that identity. One of the issues which will pre-occupy this thesis is what does it mean to understand priesthood in such a way that it is not an exercise in either speculative theology or idealism.

Moltmann recognises the contribution of Balthasar in making the doctrine of the Trinity central to the understanding of Jesus' death upon the cross. The result is that Moltmann can articulate kenosis as a trinitarian statement. But if "'The death of Jesus is a statement of God about himself'", is it possible to suggest that "the death of Jesus can be identified as the death of God? And in that case, who is God: the one who lets Jesus die or at the same time the Jesus who dies?"[113] Therefore the solution lies in:

> a trinitarian differentiation over the event on the cross. The Son suffers and dies on the cross. The Father suffers with him, but not in the same way. There is a trinitarian solution to the paradox that God is 'dead' on the cross and yet is not dead, once one abandons the simple concept of God.[114]

The cross for Moltmann is not an exterior but an interior mystery insofar as it is intratrinitarian.[115] Here he turns to Luther for whom

> the cross is not a symbol for the path of suffering that leads to fellowship with God, a reversal of the way of works that are well-pleasing to God; rather, as the cross of the outcast and forsaken Christ it is the visible revelation of God's being for man in the reality of his world.[116]

---

[110] John J. O'Donnell, 'The Doctrine of the Trinity in Recent German Theology', *The Heythrop Journal*, Vol 23, 1982, 165.
[111] Balthasar, 1990b, vii (Preface to the Second Edition).
[112] Balthasar, 1990b, 63.
[113] Moltmann, 1974, 202 While Moltmann accused Balthasar of taking the 'the ominous formula "the death of God" and developed the "paschal mystery" under the title: "The Death of God as the Source of Salvation, Revelation and Theology".' (Moltmann, 1997, 202.) Balthasar in turn suggests that Moltmann's theology is itself 'Hegelianising' (Balthasar, 1990b, vii.) and undermines the impassibility of the divine.
[114] Moltmann, 1974, 203.
[115] Moltmann, 1974, 204.
[116] Moltmann, 1974, 208.

It is also the occasion wherein God reveals himself "in the crucified Christ... contradicts the God-man who exalts himself, shatters his hybris, kills his gods and brings him back to his despised and abandoned humanness."[117] Moltmann proposes a kenotic pattern wherein God goes out of himself in his self-revelation at the incarnation in Jesus Christ, which in the event of the cross is concealed insofar as it occurs within the Godhead resulting in the exaltation of the resurrection.[118]

Like Luther, Moltmann believes that "God's being can be seen and known directly only in the cross of Christ and knowledge of God is therefore real and saving."[119] The cross becomes that by which God is identified and identifiable. It is, he suggests, a theology of the cross radically developed with due regard for the incarnation, with soteriological intent. The cross is soteriological not simply because sins are redeemed but rather because humanity is transformed through knowing God in Christ.

However, such a concept of God must necessarily question traditional doctrine. The problem is one of the inevitable clash with both metaphysics and theism, in seeking to represent the divine. As with Balthasar, a key point of departure questioned by the cross is what it means to speak of the death of Jesus Christ as the second person of the Trinity. Moltmann attempts this by explicitly rejecting the concept of God defined by the attributes of his impassibility and immutability as one who is over and above.[120] Like Dostoevsky he believes that, "a God who cannot suffer is poorer than any man. For a God who is incapable of suffering is a being who cannot be involved... So he is a loveless being."[121] Moltmann's defence against such pernicious metaphysics is the particularity of the cross.[122] On the other hand, Balthasar locates the answer precisely in the fact that God is impassable and immutable. But for both the solution lies in the event of the cross and the resurrection as an act of God as Trinity.[123]

If as Pannenberg says the "deity of the Father was itself called into question by the death of Jesus"[124] for Moltmann, as for Jüngel, the Father asserts himself in the act of resurrection. So that, "Jesus' death cannot be understood 'as the death of God', but only as death in God."[125] The cross

---

[117] Moltmann, 1974, 212.
[118] See: Chapter 4 below.
[119] Moltmann, 1974, 212.
[120] Eberhard Jüngel, *God as the Mystery of the World* (ET), Edinburgh, T & T Clark, 1983, 13, 198.
[121] Moltmann, 1974, 222.
[122] Moltmann, 1974, 214 – his italics.
[123] Moltmann, 1974, 206-07. (See also: Balthasar, 1990b, 136).
[124] *Syst.* I, 1991, 329.
[125] Moltmann, 1974, 207 – his italics.

can be nothing other than an act of God. Moltmann agrees that the Council of Nicea was correct to insist that God is not changeable, but continues that "this does not mean that he is not free to change himself."[126] Secondly, he suggests it is impossible for God to suffer but makes this a conditional rather than absolute statement, arguing that the nature of suffering is varied. To this end he proposes a notion of "active suffering," which is "the suffering of love, in which [a person] voluntarily opens himself to the possibility of being affected by another"[127] and therefore need not be inconsistent with the nature of God. Finally he asks, "can the salvation for which faith hopes be expressed significantly by means of general predicates of God from the *via negativa*, like unchangeableness, immortality and incorruptibility?"[128] The effect of his analysis is that he adopts a narrative-controlled pattern for the characterisation of God. The significance of this is that one aspect which is shared by all three of the dialogue partners in this chapter is that they seek to articulate a notion of kenosis that is governed by the need for a consistent characterisation of God within the narrative they wish to articulate. So too I shall argue that priesthood can only be understood within a consistent characterisation of the two chief characters – God and humanity.

But Moltmann goes beyond Luther, Barth, and Balthasar. Rejecting the classic notion of God defined negatively as unchanging, impassible, and a-temporal, he is simply in thrall to a different set of assumed characteristics. Instead he appears to have more in common with Bonhoeffer's notion that "Christ helps us, not by virtue of his omnipotence but by virtue of his weakness and suffering."[129] However, when Bonhoeffer suggests that the "God of Jesus Christ has nothing to do with God as we imagine him".[130] it is more an attempt to re-imagine the face of the cross. According to Moltmann:

> God is not unchangeable, if to be unchangeable means that he could not in the freedom of his love open himself to the changeable history with man and creation...God is not invulnerable, if this means that he could not open himself to the experience of the cross.[131]

God does not justify suffering but takes responsibility for it.[132] So it

---

[126] Moltmann, 1974, 229.
[127] Moltmann, 1974, 230.
[128] Moltmann, 1974, 230.
[129] Dietrich Bonhoeffer, *Letters and Papers From Prison* (ET), London, SCM, 1979, 360.
[130] Bonhoeffer, 1979, 391.
[131] Jürgen Moltmann, *The Future of Creation*, London, SCM, 1979, 93.
[132] Bauckham, 1987, 87.

is *essential* to Moltmann's trinitarian theology of the cross to be able to say that God *suffers*: not simply, as Chalcedonian Christology always maintained, that he suffers in the humanity of Jesus which is his own human nature, but that he suffers *in himself*.[133]

Moltmann thinks the Reformers were misled by the Patristic theologians for whom "the doctrine of the Trinity had its place in the praise and vision of God, and not in the economy of salvation."[134] However, what Moltmann fails to recognise is that precisely because the doctrine of the Trinity is concerned with the praise and vision of God it is essentially soteriological. So for Barth the doctrine of the Trinity is the basis of all dogmatics.

In common with Balthasar, Moltmann draws attention to the concept of 'handing over'(παραδίδωμι)in the passion narratives as evidence of the economic Trinity. According to Moltmann, in Pauline thought it expresses "the wrath and judgement of God and thus the lostness of man."[135] Further in Galatians 2.20

> the 'delivering up' formula also occurs with Christ as its subject... It is theologically important to note that the formula in Paul occurs with both Father and Son as subject, since it expresses a deep conformity between the will of the Father and the will of the Son in the event of the cross[.][136]

This re-echoes Luther's exegesis of the passage, which he sees as setting out "the true manner of justification"[137] as an act of God in Christ. The Father delivers up the Son who in turn offers himself to the Father in obedience to and for the atonement for mankind.[138] Moltmann suggests this confirms the intra-trinitarian event of kenotic divine self-giving. However, it is important to maintain two distinctions. First, Luther seems to propose a concept of *krypsis* in his *theologia crucis*, not kenosis.[139] Secondly, in Moltmann it is possible to detect the overtones of a substitutionary theology. It is curious that while certain strands of Protestant theology have emphasised substitutionary theology, especially with regard to atonement they have been highly uncomfortable with any notion that priesthood can or should be substitutionary, as undermining divine sovereignty.

---

[133] Bauckham, 1987, 100 – his italics.
[134] Moltmann, 1974, 237.
[135] Moltmann, 1974, 241-242.
[136] Moltmann, 1974, 243. A similar interchangeability of being both subject and object with regards to Jesus Christ occurs within Phil 2.5-11. (See: Chapter 4 below.)
[137] Luther, 1953, 172.
[138] Luther, 1953, 176.
[139] See: 42-46 above.

Moltmann believes that the traditional Christological doctrine of the two natures is an essentially static concept and consequently fails to do justice to the incarnation as an event. Similarly the failure of kenosis, as classically espoused, was precisely because it "was conceived within the framework of the distinction of the two natures of God and man." While kenosis was "still conceived within the framework of the distinction of the two natures" its strength was that it "attempted... to understand God's being in process."[140] For Moltmann "the elements of truth which are to be found in kenoticism... understand the event of the cross in God's being in both trinitarian and personal terms."[141] The kenotic concept of the cross can be understood only in "trinitarian terms as an event concerned with a relationship between persons in which these persons constitute themselves in relationship with each other". It is not "a divine human event but as a trinitarian event between the Son and the Father" which "overcomes the dichotomy between immanent and economic Trinity and that between the nature of God and his inner tri-unity."[142]

The Trinity ceases to be speculation about God. Instead it is a shorter version of the passion narrative and an account of salvation. It "is not the ascent of man to God but the revelation of God in his self-emptying in the crucified Christ which opens up God's sphere of life to the development of man in him."[143] By this action "God himself creates the conditions for communion with God through his self-humiliation in the death of the crucified Christ".[144] The cross is an event of the Godhead, in which boundaries are crossed whereby the divine is identified for humankind. The movement within the narrative is from God to humanity. Neither is there an "immanent Trinity supra-temporally 'behind' God's temporal, worldly history, so that he would be who he essentially is independently of history. This history is who he is."[145] There is a Hegelian influence upon Moltmann's concept of the Trinity as the key to understanding "the cross as the history of God".[146] Accordingly the event of the cross and the kenotic action of the Godhead in the Trinity is the means whereby God includes the temporal within his very being. This takes its shape through a combination of dialectical knowledge and analogy.[147]

Moltmann's methodology is different from both Barth and Balthasar.

---

[140] Moltmann, 1974, 206.
[141] Moltmann, 1974, 205.
[142] Moltmann, 1974, 245.
[143] Moltmann, 1974, 275.
[144] Moltmann, 1974, 275.
[145] Bauckham, 1987, 100.
[146] Moltmann, 1974, 254. For a fuller discussion see: Richard J. Bauckham, *The Theology of Jürgen Moltmann*, Edinburgh, T & T Clark, 1995, 154-155.
[147] Moltmann, 1974, 27.

Primarily his approach is less overtly narratival or dramatic, though he does recognise the need to maintain a consistent character of God. Secondly, he is less committed to the Chalcedonian Definition of Faith than Barth. Thirdly, in his rejection of the distinction between the economic and immanent Trinity he takes the overtly trinitarian concepts of Balthasar but develops them further. Fourthly, whereas Balthasar looks towards the significance of Jesus' descent to hell, Moltmann focuses upon Jesus' cry of dereliction from the cross[148] in which moment he sees the intra-trinitarian nature of the cross at its sharpest. In this he is nearer to Barth's particularism than Balthasar's idealism. Fifthly, in order to speak of the second person of the Trinity as 'truly God and truly man' it is necessary to go beyond the doctrine of the two natures. The cry from the cross is not the cry of the human Jesus to his divine Father; rather[149] the theology of the cross "must acknowledge the theological trial between God and God." Because the "cross of the Son divides God from God",[150] the importance of which lies in the implications of this statement for the divine-human relatedness. It is the crossing of the divine-human *diastasis* that lies at the heart of priesthood. For Protestants the problem is that this can only be achieved in the movement from God to humanity.

According to Barth kenosis is the account of the relationship between the divine and the human articulated in the narrative of the action of God in Christ. However, according to Balthasar kenosis is the dramatic representation of Jesus Christ as the exteriorisation of God in his self-representation and revelation to the world, culminating in his death and resurrection. While according to Moltmann, believing himself to be in direct descent from Paul and Luther,[151] salvation is not what God does for humanity but rather what God does with humanity such that "deliverance and liberation for godforsaken man lie in the figure of the God forsaken, crucified Christ".[152] The danger is that Moltmann, in his desire to include the death of Jesus Christ in the divine experience, actually ends up dissolving the differences between the immanent and economic Trinity. It was precisely this that Barth's literary narrative approach required him to resist. In the end Moltmann appears to stand theologically between the thoroughly Reformed Barth and the Roman Catholic Balthasar.

Conclusion

In this Chapter all three dialogue partners have contributed their individual

---

[148] Mk. 15.34.
[150] Moltmann, 1974, 151.
[150] Moltmann, 1974, 152.
[151] Moltmann, 1974, 3.
[152] Moltmann, 1974, 242.

elements to the understanding which will be significant in the emerging concept of priesthood. Karl Barth's contribution is twofold. First, there is his emphasis upon the particularism of the divine-human encounter in the person of Jesus Christ, known through Scripture. Secondly, and developing this, there is his emphasis upon a regulated narrative which maintains the consistent characterisation of the divine and the human which meets in Jesus, as classically defined by the Chalcedonian definition. This is important for the narration of a concept of priesthood in relation to the crossing of the divine-human boundaries. Hans Urs von Balthasar's contribution, while repeating some of Barth's concerns, represents the divine-human encounter as theo-drama. This is particularly important when discussing issues related to vocation. Jürgen Moltmann's contribution is perhaps more negative but significant nonetheless. This can be summed up as stemming from his desire to re-imagine the doctrine of God in the light of the *theologia crucis* and to challenge the traditional notion of the divine attributes. The result of this is to propose wholesale critique of the notion of power. The importance of this lies in the challenge it poses to the articulation of priesthood in terms of the power of the ordained.

The achievement of Barth, Balthasar and Moltmann was first the relocation of kenosis within a trinitarian framework as essentially a dialectical statement about the divine identity. Within a trinitarian setting and understood in terms of identity kenosis need not be self-contradictory. This is important for my thesis because it opens up the possibility that the analogy of kenosis and priesthood does not hinge upon the surrender of divinity by Jesus Christ at the Incarnation and the consequent divinization of human beings. There is no need for an intermediary being to bridge the gap. Instead it is concerned with the fluidity of identity such that God and humanity can encounter one another without the confusion of forms. Furthermore this encounter is the result of God's self-revelation in Jesus Christ such that he is both veiled and recognisable.

Secondly, for all three, kenosis provides a means for the critically realistic representation of the divine-human encounter. The weakness of the classic kenoticists of the nineteenth and early twentieth centuries was to believe it was possible to provide a naively realistic understanding of kenosis and the later Death of God theologians was to resort to an anti-realist account of kenosis as a propositional account of the Incarnation. However, for Barth, Balthasar and Moltmann kenosis provides a regulative principle governing "discourse, attitude and action."[153] The Protestant objections to the Catholic[154] concept of priesthood and the failure to reach

---

[153] Lindbeck, 1984, 18. Whereas the nineteenth century kenoticists fall within Lindbeck's first type Barth, Balthasar and Moltmann all appear to propose kenosis in a manner which falls within Lindbeck's fourth type, the regulative theory of doctrine.

[154] I am using 'Catholic' here not in a technical sense as that which is not Protestant.

any resolution between the divergent parties emerge precisely because it is discussed in propositional terms. For "a propositionalist, if a doctrine is once true, it is always true" and harmonization is impossible. The argument of this thesis is that it is this propositional concept of priesthood that is problematic rather than priesthood *per se*.

Thirdly, kenosis speaks of participation, which includes both God and humanity. Participation means that the divine-human encounter is possible without either party being absorbed into the other and thereby sacrificing its essential identity. Participation enforces identity. Participation and the nature of sacrifice are themselves key issues in the understanding of priesthood. Finally, therefore, the primary movement of kenosis is properly from God to humanity. Kenosis also offers a dialectic wherein the boundaries, which separate God and humanity, are crossed, but as an act of divine grace so that priesthood cannot therefore be propitiatory only responsive.

In the Chapter 3 I shall proceed to examine the Letter to the Philippians in which I shall argue that a key theme is that of identity which runs throughout the Epistle. Furthermore that it is the concept of identity which links the notions of kenosis and priesthood.

Chapter 4

Philippians as a Narrative Account of Identity in Kenosis

What has emerged thus far is that the divine-human encounter is grounded in God's sovereign grace. This is fundamental for any articulation of priesthood. Too often Protestants perceive that priesthood appears to suggest, if not wholly, at least partially a movement from humanity to God. Furthermore the *diastasis* which separates God and humanity has important implications for God's knowability and therefore his identity. Consequentially, in the representation of the divine to humanity, and humanity to God some notion of family resemblance, but not sameness is presupposed. Furthermore, once these conditions are met within the overall narrative, in which both God and humanity maintain their essential characters, participation and the crossing of boundaries as an event of grace are possible. Within this, kenosis becomes a means by which the story of God's reconciling actions can be represented critically realistically, though not propositionally. Kenosis also becomes that which identifies God such that he is recognizable.

Priesthood is concerned with crossing the divine-human boundary. However, because of the primacy of God's sovereign grace priesthood is therefore responsive, and secondary. The priesthood of the ordained therefore is not a necessary intermediary between God and humanity, neither semi-human nor semi-divine. It cannot permit any confusion of forms. But priesthood is concerned with the identity of humanity in relation to God. Priesthood is also concerned with the representation of the story of God's saving action in Jesus Christ and therefore his knowability.

The Letter to the Philippians, I shall argue, has a discernible narrative structure, concerned primarily with the identity and representation, first, of Jesus Christ in relation to God and, secondly, of Paul and the Philippians in relation to Christ Jesus.[1] It is in the dialectic of being distinct while

---

[1] This can be understood as an example of an Augustinian Trinitarian hermeneutic of love in which, 'the lover affirms the reality and the otherness of the beloved. Love does not seek to collapse the beloved into terms of itself; and, even though it may speak of losing itself in the beloved, such a loss always turns out to be a true finding. In the familiar paradox, one becomes fully oneself when losing oneself to another. In the fact

maintaining a discernible 'likeness' that identity is located. This is made possible by the right identification, first of Jesus Christ and secondly of Paul and the Philippians. As a result Paul and the Philippians participate in Jesus' mission and calling which is the mission and calling of God's people. In the epistle Paul's account proceeds from the *carmen Christi*, the source of the language of kenosis, and the response is articulated in priestly imagery. Therefore while a chronologically structured account of kenosis would begin with an exegesis of Philippians, I suggest that Paul's letter actually provides the framework in which the two concepts, kenosis and priesthood, each illuminate the meaning and nature of the other.

Some Introductory Remarks

Before entering upon a more detailed exegesis of the text it is necessary to outline three introductory remarks.

Assumptions about the Epistle to the Philippians

First it is necessary to identify four assumptions made about the text as it stands. First, that the author of the Epistle is Paul.[2] Secondly, that it is a unified text and not the result of later editing by someone other than Paul.[3] Thirdly, it is accepted that "the words used are the choice of the author of the text we now have."[4] Finally it is an ecclesiological document written to the whole Church (1.1) as a community of faith and as such therefore a public rather than private document.

---

of love, in short, both parties are simultaneously affirmed.' (N. T. Wright, *The New Testament and the People of God*, London, SPCK, 1993, 64.) This is derived d from Augustine. (*de Trinitate* VIII.14, 255). The Letter to the Philippians articulates the love between Paul and the Philippian Church as established in and shaped by the mutual experience of Jesus Christ, as the incarnate Word of God.

[2] For a good discussion of authorship see: Gerald W. Hawthorne, *Philippians*, Waco (Texas), Word, 1983, xxvii-xxix.

[3] A number of commentators have suggested that the letter as it stands is not a single piece but rather a compilation by a later editor of several letters by Paul. See: F. W. Beare, *A Commentary on the Epistle to the Philippians*, London, A & C Black, 1959, 1-5; J-F. Collange, *The Epistle of Saint Paul to the Philippians* (ET), London, Epworth Press, 1979, 4-12. However, the assumption of this essay is that it is a single unified text. (See: Jonas Holmstrand, *Markers and Meaning in Paul* (ET), Stockholm, Almqvist & Wiksell International, 1997, 94; also, G. D. Fee, *Paul's Letter to the Philippians*, Grand Rapids, Eerdmans, 1995, 22, P. T. O'Brien, *The Epistle to the Philippians*, Grand Rapids, Eerdemans, 1991, 18.)

[4] Fee, 1995, 193. See also: R. P. Martin, *A Hymn of Christ*, Downers Grove, Illinois, IVP, 1997, 59-60.

Narrative and the Text of Philippians

According to Anthony Thiselton a text remains little more than a potentially communicative document until it is actualized when the individual reader or reading community "perceives that the signs constitute an intelligible subsystem of some larger linguistic or semiotic code, and the process of interpretation begins."[5] An important aspect of the letter is that Paul writes to the Philippian community in order to address them directly despite his physical absence.[6] However the preservation of the letters within the process of the formation of the canon of the New Testament suggests that "his letters are now interpreted as an apostolic legacy to the whole Church."[7]

Fundamental to this reading of Paul's Letter to the Philippians will be the concept of narrative. According to Alasdair MacIntyre human actions are best understood in terms of story, or enacted narratives[8] which embody a worldview. A worldview normally seeks to answer four questions: 'Who are we?' - which the Bible answers - human beings made in the image of God. Secondly it asks, 'Where are we?' The answer for the Christian story is - in a good world created by God in whose image we ourselves are made. Thirdly it asks, 'What is wrong?' Humanity has rebelled against the creator. And finally, 'What is the solution?' The solution is that - "the creator has acted and will act within creation to deal with the evil that has resulted" from the rebellion of his creatures.[9] A worldview provides the framework through which the world is experienced and interpreted.

Stories operate as complex metaphors which serve to bring

> two sets of ideas close together, close enough for a spark to jump, but not too close, so that the spark in jumping illuminates for a moment the whole area around, changing perceptions as it does so.[10]

The problem is that of all forms of New Testament writing the epistle appears to be the least narratival in form. But Wright argues that even in his

---

[5] Anthony C. Thiselton, *New Horizons in Hermeneutics*, London, Harper Collins, 1992, 31.

[6] James D. G. Dunn, 'The Narrative Approach to Paul', Bruce W. Longenecker (ed.), *Narrative Dynamics in Paul*, Louisville, Westminster John Knox Press, 2002, 222).

[7] John Goldingay, *Models for the Interpretation of Scripture*, Paternoster, Carlisle, 1995, 130.

[8] Alasdair MacIntyre, *After Virtue* (2nd Ed), London, Duckworth, 1999, 215.

[9] N. T. Wright, *The New Testament and the People of God*, London, SPCK, 1993, 132. See also: J. Richard Middleton and Brian J. Walsh, *Truth is stranger than it used to be*, London, SPCK, 1995, 35.

[10] Wright, 1993, 40.

most overtly theological statements Paul's "are in fact expressions of the essentially Jewish story now redrawn around Jesus."[11] Furthermore that Paul's

> repeated use of the Old Testament is designed not as mere proof-texting, but, in part at least, to suggest new ways of reading well-known stories, and to suggest that they find a more natural climax in the Jesus story.[12]

Of course narrative is not a new concept.[13] Aristotle speaks of narrative taking the form of emplotment in the analysis of tragedy. Famously, according to Aristotle, "tragedy is an imitation of a complete, i.e. whole, action, possessing a certain magnitude... A whole is that which has a beginning, a middle and an end."[14] This is not a static notion but one of progression and movement through emplotment.

Furthermore it is the plot, which is thus ordered, and not necessarily the play or story, which may be re-ordered in order to be told to greater effect.[15] According to Thiselton, Ricoeur, drawing upon Aristotle, "identifies 'the decisive concept of plot' as that which having 'a particular directedness' allows the readers to be 'pulled forward' towards a conclusion".[16] However, reversals or acts of recognition do not mean that the conclusion is predictable.[17] This need not only apply to fiction but can also apply to other narrative forms. As a consequence

> as in Aristotle, isolated or seemingly random actions achieve coherence as part of a single, larger, action and the discontinuities of time, to which Augustine drew attention, assume a medium of 'human' time in which

---

[11] Wright, 1993, 79 – his italics.

[12] Wright, 1993, 79.

[13] I have previously drawn attention to Barth's employment of an Aristotelian narrative understanding (48 above). For Barth his imaginative narrative reading was in the context of the metanarrative provided by the Trinity (50 above) and the Chalcedonian Definition of Faith (51 above). Within his dialectical theology narrative provides a means of representing the story in a critically realistic form.

[14] Aristotle, *Poetics*, 1996, 13 [5.1] – his italics.

[15] Poetics, 1996, xxiii-xix.

[16] Thiselton, 1992, 356.

[17] One example is the detective story. (Anthony C. Thiselton, 'Communicative Action and Promise in Interdisciplinary, Biblical, and Theological Hermeneutics', in Roger Lundin, Clarence Walhout, Anthony Thiselton, *The Promise of Hermeneutics*, Grand Rapids, Eerdmans, 1999, 186.) For example *Tinker, Tailor, Soldier, Spy* is a detective story, in which apparently random events are linked by a unified plot, in which there are both reversals but also moments of recognition until finally Gerald the Mole is identified. Key concepts like motive serve both to identify him but are also confirmed in the naming of the character, as the only person who could occupy that space in the plot.

memory (past), attention (present) and hope (future) offer not the abstract intelligibility of logic, but the temporal logic of purposive life. 'The dynamic of emplotment is to me the key to the relation between time and narrative.'[18]

By means of emplotment, narrative creates order in what is otherwise an unstructured story. As I suggested in Chapter 2 Barth, Balthasar and to a lesser extent Moltmann utilize narrative in which God is a consistent character to uncover meaning in what would otherwise be a series of random events.

Narrative and the Structure of Philippians

The narrative structure of Philippians is doubly discernible. First the Epistle has an emplotted structure with a beginning, middle and an end. Secondly, identity provides a unifying theme throughout the Letter, of which priesthood is an important strand.

First I propose that the beginning of Paul's narrative is God's saving act in Christ (2.5-11). Thus the narrative movement is from God, who in an act of sovereign grace reveals himself to humanity. The basis of the shared past of Paul and the Philippians is the story of God's activity in Jesus Christ embodied in Paul's presence at Philippi. However, the immediate occasion of Paul's writing is his imprisonment (1.12-26). The middle of the narrative is the response of the Philippians by sending a gift to Paul as a token of their support (4.10-20). This is the consequence of their shared relationship in Jesus Christ. The present is concerned with the question, 'Who are you (presently)?' It is this Paul seeks to answer throughout the letter and which the Philippians have answered, in part at least, by their generosity to Paul. The final part, or the result, is that Paul and the Philippian Church are both striving to achieve a true identity in Christ (3.1-4.1) in which false (3.1-6) and true identity (3.7-11) lead in turn to a striving for identity which is still to come and which should resolve the internal dissension (4.2-4) that appears to be an issue at the time of writing.[19] The questions posed by Paul remain, as Karl Barth suggests, "The Word of God is the Word that God

---

[18] Anthony C. Thistleton, "Biblical studies and theoretical hermeneutics', John Barton (ed), *The Cambridge Companion to Biblical Interpretation*, Cambridge, CUP, 1998, 106.

[19] According some commentators the Epistle to the Philippians has no discernible plan (See: J. B. Lightfoot, *St Paul's Epistle to the Philippians* (New Edition), London, Macmillan, 1879, 68. See also Beare, 1959, 4, J. Calvin, *The Epistles of Paul the Apostle to the Galatians, Ephesians, Philippians and Colossians*, (tr T. H. L. Parker), Carlisle, Paternoster, 1996, 225.) Conversely other commentators do identify a discernible structure (See: Fee, 1995, 12, following Loveday Alexander, 'Hellenistic Letter-Forms and the Structure of Philippians', JSNT, 37, 1989, 87-101).

spoke, speaks and will speak in the midst of all men."[20]

Secondly Paul addresses the question of identity by means of five discernible issues which he raises with the Philippians as the recipients of the Epistle. First, there is Paul's identification with the Philippians (1.3-11); second, Paul's identification with Christ (1.12-26); third, to be Christian is self-identification with Christ (1.27-2.18);[21] fourth, there is the question of true and false identity (3.1-4.9) and finally, true identification is understood as participation in the other (4.10-20).

Finally, questions of identity are relatively common in Paul's writing. First, Paul's primary concern is Jesus and his identity. J. D. G. Dunn argues that the notion of Jesus as Lord is "the principal confession of faith for Jesus and his churches... [used] nearly 230 times."[22] This is most striking in Philippians 2.11 where it indicates the "climactic worship of all creation".[23] Likewise Paul's reference to 'the Lord Jesus Christ' (1 Cor. 8.6) is understood by N. T. Wright as a clear identification of Jesus in terms of "christological monotheism".[24]

Secondly, we know that a constant battle throughout Paul's ministry was his relationship with the Jewish Christians and most especially the 'Judaizers'.[25] Thirdly, circumcision raises questions about the identification of the people of God and his own identity. Paul twice, defending himself against Jewish Christians who opposed his Gentile mission, describes himself as being of the 'tribe of Benjamin'[26] but for him Israel can no longer be defined in terms of "ancestral privilege".[27] Rather for "Paul, Jesus stands in the place of Israel."[28] Israel is primarily God's people who are reconstituted as an act of sovereign divine grace in and through Jesus who is the Christ, the Messiah.[29] Fourthly there is Paul's own identification as an apostle.[30] However, given Paul's repeated reference to, and defense of his claims to be an apostle it would seem reasonable to suggest that it was for

---

[20] Karl Barth, *Evangelical Theology* (American Edn.), NY, Holt, Rinehart and Winston, 1963, 18.

[21] It is within this, in the *carmen Christi* (2.6-11), that Paul raises the identity of Jesus Christ in relation to God.

[22] J. D. G. Dunn, *Unity and Diversity in the New Testament*, London, SCM, 1977, 50.

[23] J. D. G. Dunn, *The Theology of Paul the Apostle*, Edinburgh, T & T Clark, 1998, 246.

[24] N. T. Wright, *The Climax of the Covenant*, Edinburgh, T & T Clark, 1991, 129.

[25] See: Acts 15 also Gal. 1.9;2.2; 2.12. Again the issue appears to be one of identity.

[26] Rom. 11.1; Phil. 3.5.

[27] Wright , 1991, 246.

[28] Wright , 1991, 40.

[29] Dunn, 1998, 506.

[30] 1 Cor. 9.1ff; 2 Cor. 11.1-6 Paul consistently describes himself as an apostle (Rom. 1.1; 1 Cor. 1.1; 2 Cor. 1.1; Gal 1.1). According to Dunn, Paul's sense of apostleship was something he 'was fiercely insistent on... from Galatians onwards.' (Dunn, 1998, 571-573.)

him an issue of his self-identity. Finally one characteristic way Paul speaks of the identity of the Christian community is by the use of the phrases ἐν Χριστῶ and εν κυρίω.[31]

However, "theology in Philippians first of all takes the form of story, [therefore] to isolate the theology from the story... would be to eliminate one of the primary theological contributions of the letter."[32]

Identity in the Epistle to the Philippians: Setting the Theme (1.1-2)

In the opening two verses of the Epistle, Paul goes beyond the requirements of a simple introduction.[33] Paul identifies himself (and Timothy) as δοῦλοι, slaves of Christ Jesus[34] a term suggesting ownership and therefore, by implication, identification with the owner. Furthermore Paul's use of δοῦλοι anticipates Philippians 2.7 where it is applied to Jesus Christ. Having identified himself, Paul then directs the letter to 'all the saints ἐν Χριστῶ (1.1) who live in Philippi. Their holiness and identification as a covenant people, like the Israelites, was "by virtue of their consecration" to God.[35] Paul sets the tone of the letter here that they "are to live as those who belong to Christ Jesus, as those whose lives are forever identified with Christ."[36]

Normally Paul's letters[37] are written to the whole community of faith and consequently the reference to ἐπισκόποις and διακόνοις has

---

[31] In Philippians these phrases are found on a total of nineteen occassions. Dunn suggests three broad categories of the usage of ἐν Χριστω by Paul are discernible. First, the objective 'referring to the redemptive act that has happened "in Christ" ' (Dunn, 1998, 397). Secondly a subjective usage 'where Paul speaks of believers as *being* "in Christ" ' (Dunn, 1998, 398). Thirdly an active usage in which 'both "in Christ" and "in the Lord" phrases occur where Paul has in view his own activity or is exhorting his readers to adopt a particular attitude or course of action.' (Dunn, 1998, 398.) In Philippians the phrases ἐν Χριστω and εν κυρίω are both found. (Dunn, 1998, 396-98; ἐν Χριστω occurs 10 times; εν κυρίω occurs 9 times; in the categories identified by Dunn; objective, 6 times [Phil 1.26; 2.5, 3.3, 9, 14; 4.19.]; subjective, 4 times [Phil 1.1; 2.1; 4.7, 21.]; active, 2 times [Phil 1.13; 4.13.]). Dunn suggests that Paul's usage is basic to his understanding for his 'perception of his whole life as a Christian, its source, identity and its responsibilities, could be summed up in these phrases.' (Dunn, 1998, 399.)
[32] Fee, 1995, 47.
[33] R. P. Martin, *Philippians*, London, Marshall Morgan and Scott, 1985, 60.
[34] See: Rom. 6.16-23; 1 Cor. 7.22-23.
[35] Lightfoot, 1879, 81. See also: *CD* IV.2, 518.
[36] Fee, 1995, 65.
[37] The exception is Philemon.

generated much albeit inconclusive debate.[38] However, two implications can be drawn from this reference. First it emphasises the ecclesial nature of the Epistle and secondly it suggests there is a recognisable group of people regarded as ἐπισκόποις and διακόνις.

Finally, having identified himself (and Timothy) and the Philippian believers in relation to Jesus Christ, Paul proceeds to speak of 'God our Father and the Lord Jesus Christ'(1.1). Unqualified use of the word καὶ implied that both are the source of 'grace' and 'peace'. Paul appears to identify the Son within the divine Godhead, suggesting that the "Son is truly God and works in co-operation with the Father and the Spirit for the redemption of the people of God."[39] In two extraordinary opening verses Paul has set the agenda of identity for himself, the Philippian Church and Jesus and therefore the divine-human relationship for the rest of the Epistle.

Paul's Identification with the Philippians (1.3-11)

Paul proceeds to identify himself with the Philippians by association. In a section most commentators regard as being one of 'thanksgiving and prayer'[40] Paul articulates his close identification with the people of Philippi.

1.3 I thank God in all my remembrance of you
1.4 in every prayer of mine
1.5 thankful for your partnership (κοινωνίᾳ)

In the New Testament a number of words with the common stem κοινων- are found,[41] which while they are usually translated into English "as 'fellowship' their primary referent is to participating in".[42] Likewise Paul says, 'I hold you in my heart, for you are all partakers (συγκοινωνούς)' (1.7) emphasising their being "'participants together' in the grace of God."[43] So Paul stresses his identification with them, prefacing his prayer with a mild oath, 'For God is my witness how I yearn for you all' (1.8). Finally, Paul introduces of the notion of being 'filled – πεπληρωμένοι' (1.11).

In the Septuagint πλήρωμα is used of God as the one who is present and who fills the world.[44] Πλήρωμα speaks of the presence of "the fullness of

---

[38] For a good summary of the debate see O'Brien, 1991, 47-50; also: Beare, 1959, 48-49; Lightfoot, 1879, 82; Martin, 1985, 61. See: Chapter 7 below.
[39] Fee, 1995, 71.
[40] Beare, 1959, 52; Martin, 1985, 52; Fee, 1995, 72.
[41] The four principal forms are: κοινωνός, a partner; κοινωνέω, to have a share in; κοινωνία, sharing or giving a share; κοινονικόσ, ready to give a share.
[42] Fee, 1995, 82 - his italics.
[43] Fee, 1995, 91.
[44] *TDNT*, VI, 288.

God dwelling in Christ... weaving together God, Christ, church, Christian living... into a dynamic soteriology of abundance."[45] This resonates with the forthcoming reference to emptying (2.7) and is suggestive of "a new location and content of selfhood"[46] so that humanity is identified anew in relation to the action of Jesus Christ in "*giving free access to God*".[47] It also resonates with the notion of sacrifice in relation to priesthood.[48]

But of course there is also a more prosaic understanding of 'filling' in Paul's mind, for he is also writing to acknowledge a gift sent by the people of Philippi to himself. Their being filled by God's generosity has spilt over into their identification with him.

Paul's Identification with Christ (1.12-26)

Here the emphasis changes[49] and Paul writes instead of his identification with Christ, that 'it has become known... my imprisonment is for Christ' (1.13). Most commentators acknowledge that Paul is writing from prison.[50] The RSV suggests that Paul's captors recognize he is imprisoned because of his identification with Christ.[51] However, in the text Paul does not use the word ὑπέρ ('for' or 'on behalf of'), rather he speaks of δεσμούς μου φανερούς ἐν Χριστῷ γενέσθαι (1.13) which suggests a desire to portray discipleship as "'participation in Christ's sufferings' (3.10)" and that the phrase would better be translated, "It has become clear... that I am in chains for Christ."[52] It is an act of self-identification[53] wherein Paul becomes recognizable by association with Jesus Christ.

Identification for Paul is a matter of vocation,[54] which is manifested in

---

[45] David Ford, *Self and Salvation*, Cambridge, CUP, 1999, 114. Ford is speaking of Ephesians, an Epistle whose authorship is probably not Pauline but what he says is also applicable to Philippians.

[46] Ford, 1999, 114.

[47] Ford, 1999, 115.

[48] See: Chapter 6 below.

[49] A transitional markers is an expression, for example; 'I wish you to know, brethren' (1.12) which makes 'clear that Paul now intends to inform the Philippians about something.' (Holmstrand, 1997, 98.)

[50] See: Markus Bockmuehl, *The Epistle to the Philippians*, London, A & C Black, 1997, 25-32. (Also: Calvin, 1996, 234; Lightfoot, 1879, 31; Martin, 1985, 71; J. L. Houlden, *Paul's Letters from Prison*, London, SCM, 1977, 23, 41; Fee, 1995, 34.)

[51] This would seem to suggest a notion of critical realism (See: Chapter 1 above) or tracking theory of representation whereby the resemblance is external and visible without privileged knowledge being required.

[52] O'Brien, 1991, 113.

[53] This reading accords with Dunn's concept of ἐν Χηριστῷ, in its active form (Dunn, 1999, 398).

[54] This idea is repeated throughout the section (1.14, 16, 17, 20).

his participation in the mission of Christ, 'fitting' the model of the trinitarian economy whereby the Son is sent by the Father in the power of the Spirit. Paul's desire to be identified with Christ is total, 'For me to live is Christ' (1.21). In David Ford's terms his selfhood is constituted in its representative association with Christ.[55] His self-valuation is in this identification. Paul's ambivalence is rooted in the duality of his being in the flesh and in Christ, a citizen of earth and of heaven (3.20).

Christian Living as Self-identification with Christ (1.27-2.18)

Paul now changes the emphasis to focus upon the nature of Christian identity, and in particular the identity of the Philippians themselves. This effectively occupies the next two chapters.[56]

For a number of commentators this section forms the core of the letter in the context of Paul encouraging the Philippians to "unity and courage in the face of opposition".[57] The point I wish to make is that it is the issue of unity rooted in their shared identity which is located 'in Christ' (2.5). Thus in the first subsection 1.27-30 Paul sets out his agenda in the opening verse when he says, 'let your manner of life be worthy of the gospel of Christ' (1.27).

Two points emerge from this section. First, salvation, is 'from God' (1.28) and therefore a sovereign act of grace. It is both his first word but also, by its position at the end of the verse, it is also the last word. Secondly, that suffering for another one, and so to suffer for Jesus, is a sign of favour.[58] Thus Paul can say 'not only believe in him but also suffer for his sake' (1.29). This needs to be understood in the light of 2.6-11. "They are to live 'on behalf of Christ' in the same way Christ himself lived - and died - on behalf of this fallen broken world."[59] Identification is made through the intentional repetition of the example of Christ by the Christian, in response to the self-identification of God in Christ with fallen humanity, and speaks therefore of an interchange.

In this section (2.1-11) the central passage falls into two sections 2.1-5

---

[55] Ford, 1999, 114. Lightfoot's paraphrase 'I live only to serve Him, only to commune with Him; I have no conception of life apart from Him.' is helpful (Lightfoot, 1879, 92). There are also overtones of Jesus' words in Mk. 8.34-38 (also Matt. 16.24-27; Lk. 9.23-26).

[56] At the heart of this section stands the *carmen Christi*. However, rather than attempt a reading of the passage, I propose to look at the *carmen Christi* in the context of the whole letter.

[57] O'Brien, 1991, 143. (See also: Martin, 1985, 80, Beare, 1959, 66; Houlden, 1977, 65, 85.)

[58] The word εχαρίσθη translated 'it was given' (29) as a variant upon the root χάρις 'grace'. This seems to refer back to 'salvation' (28).

[59] Fee, 1995, 172.

and 6-11. In the first part the words ἐν Χριστῷ occur twice.[60] This would seem to be a call to live as a Christlike people. It is in this context that Paul offers the christological hymn as an exploration of Christ's identity, which 6-11 is to be read in parenthesis as qualifying verses 1-5. It is a hiatus in the text for two reasons. First because of its poetic form and secondly, it is a statement about the identity of Christ in the midst of a passage about the nature of Christian living. It is about recognizing the example of Christ and his relationship with God. Therefore Christ's true identity is revealed, and thereby the possibility of God's participation in creation.

It is in the third section (2.12-18),[61] that Paul first introduces the language of priesthood when returning to the theme of the recognizable identity of the Philippians, embodied in Christian living. Significantly the passage begins with the call to 'work out your salvation' (2.12) which O'Brien suggests is "an exhortation to common action... to show forth the graces of Christ in their lives... as they fulfil their responsibilities to one another as well as to non-Christians."[62] The grammar of the text suggests 'work out your own salvation' is concerned with christlike 'obedience' (2.8). Once again it is a call to Christian living as an act of becoming recognizable 'in Christ' by word and deed. This seems to be underlined in the following verse when Paul reminds them that they are 'children of God', recognizable as bearing the image of the Father and that they are to 'shine (φαίνασθε) as lights (φωστῆρεσ) in the world' (2.15).[63] Barth reads this as an imperative, the Philippians are addressed as those who "possess, know, hear the Word of life"[64] and as such cannot keep such knowledge to themselves but become the means whereby others can cross the boundaries that mark the salvation of humanity. As such it is secondary to the prior act of divine grace and a priestly statement.

In the closing verses Paul speaks of his own life and ministry saying that he 'did not run in vain (κενὸν) or labour in vain (κενὸν)' (2.16). Repeating the imagery of the *carmen Christi* Paul's kenosis is the giving of himself to be filled by God in Christ. Paul has given himself to God and to his apostolic task, witnessed by the Philippians' community of faith. So Paul

---

[60] 2.1 (ἐν Χριστῷ Ἰεσοῦ, 2.5).

[61] 'Therefore my beloved' (2.12).

[62] O'Brien, 1991, 280.

[63] Phosteres according to Lightfoot 'is used almost exclusively of the heavenly bodies' (Lightfoot, 1879, 117). Lightfoot draws attention to the use of φαίνασθε, translated here as 'shine' but which is better translated 'appear' as it is in Matt. 2.7. This offers a possibly doubly nuanced meaning in Paul's mind. First, the Philippians are to live as visibly recognizable members of God's people. But it also has incarnational overtones by possible allusion to the story of the nativity and the star which shines, announcing the presence of the Word made flesh.

[64] Karl Barth, *The Epistle to the Philippians* (ET), London, SCM, 1962, 77.

speaks of himself being 'poured (σπένδομαι) as a libation upon the sacrificial (θυσία) offering (λειτουργία) of your faith' (2.17). The priestly nature of the language is reinforced by reference to cultic sacrifice. The "language of sacrifice is employed in a transferred sense... he is speaking of the willing yielding of his life to God."[65] The language of priesthood is critically realistic and the sacrificial is responsive to God's prior saving act.[66]

The word λειτουργία, used in the Septuagint to describe the "service of priests and Levites",[67] recurs at 2.30 referring to Epaphroditus' ministry to Paul. It is possible Paul has in mind that "Epaphroditus expended himself, risking his life and nearly dying for the sake of Christ's work, in order to serve Paul." That furthermore he does this "as a representative of the Philippian church".[68] Within this section (2.19-30) two themes are apparent. One is the use of priestly and sacrificial language. This is related to the second concept which is sending (2. 19; 23; 25; 28), specifically with reference to the activities of Timothy and Epaphroditus, which are to be understood in terms of vocation. Importantly both these concepts are linked in Paul's thought by kenosis.

True and False Identity (3.1-4.9)

In this section, beginning 'finally,'[69] Paul explores identity by a dialectic of false (3.1-6) and true identity (3.7-11).[70] In the light of this, reflecting the tension between non-Jewish Christian communities and Jewish Christians, he suggests that the people of God's covenant are those who are recognizable in relation to the story of God's saving activity 'in Christ'. Nonetheless, identity remains for Paul in some sense 'not yet' (3.12-21) and the dialectic unresolved.

Beare misses the point, commenting on 3.1-6 that "Paul seldom launches into such vicious invective".[71] Paul calls for attention by means of a series of short, sharp phrases.[72] The Philippians are to look out for 'the dogs', the 'evil-workers' and 'those who mutilate the flesh' (3.2). In the Greco-Roman world dogs were usually wild and regarded as dangerous. Jews

---

[65] O'Brien, 1991, 306.

[66] So elsewhere Paul speaks of the sacrifice to be offered which is 'your bodies' (Rom 12.1).

[67] O'Brien, 1991, 308.

[68] O'Brien, 1991, 309.

[69] See above: 76, n. 3.

[70] Stephen Sykes speaks of the 'formidable ambiguities' of Paul's own self-identity (*The Identity of Christianity*, Philadelphia, Fortress Press, 1984).

[71] Beare, 1959, 103.

[72] 'Look out (βλέπετε) for' (3.2.) repeated three times.

regarded dogs as unclean and the word was sometimes used to signify the Gentiles.[73] So in "an amazing reversal Paul asserts it is the Judaizers who are to be regarded as Gentiles... who stand outside the covenant".[74] The true covenant people are those identified with God's saving act ἐν Χριστῷ Ἰησοῦ (3.3) rather than any physical identification (mutilation) through circumcision.[75] Paul reiterates this with his own story (3.4ff) which is both witness to the strength of this false identification but also sets up the dialectic of the true identity of God's people.

In contrast Paul suggests that true identity (3.7-11) is to be found 'in Christ'. This section divides into two parts, each with their own inner metaphors. In the first part (3.7-8) the controlling metaphor is one of 'gain' and 'loss'. Here Paul returns to an idea that has already emerged.[76] The true value of 'loss' or 'gain' is clarified at the end of verse 8 in relation to the 'surpassing worth of knowing (γνώσεωσ) Christ Jesus my Lord'. Paul must have been aware of the significance of the word gnosis, as would the Philippians, but its usage here is controlled by the Old Testament and not Hellenistic philosophy. To 'know' signifies "'living in a close relationship with someone or something or somebody, such a relationship as to cause what might be called communion.'"[77] As Bockmuehl states, "Knowing Christ Jesus then, describes the fundamental reality of Paul's life"[78] so that by comparison all else is of no value.

In the second part of this passage Paul suggests that true value is in being identified with Christ. So in a complex verse Paul speaks of being 'found (εὑρισκῶ) in him... through faith in Christ' precisely because it is 'not... of my own' (3.9). Paul speaks of being incorporate in Christ[79] and links it to the following clause, 'the righteousness from God (ἐκ θεοῦ)'. This repeats by association 2.7 tracking the story of Jesus Christ who identified as 'being found (εὑρισκῶ) in human form'. So too Paul is 'found in Christ'. As Bockmuehl notes, "Christians are 'in Christ', but they in turn must be found in him".[80] What Paul understands to be 'in Christ' is underlined when he speaks of his wish to 'share (κοινωνίαν) in his sufferings'. As in 1.5, "κοινωνίαν is best understood in an active sense of 'participation'".[81]

"As Paul participates in Christ's sufferings, strengthened to do so

---

[73] Lightfoot, 1979, 143; Beare, 1959, 103; Martin, 1985, 124; Fee, 1995, 295.
[74] O'Brien, 1991, 355.
[75] Fee, 1995, 292.
[76] 1.21; also in the *carmen Christi* (2.6-11) with its implicit notions of loss and gain.
[77] T. C. Vriezen, quoted O'Brien, 1991, 388.
[78] Bockmuehl, 1997, 206.
[79] Hawthorne, 1983, 140.
[80] Bockmuehl, 1997, 208 – his italics.
[81] O'Brien, 1991, 405.

through the power of his resurrection"[82] so he is 'becoming like (συμμορφιζόμενοσ) him in his death' (3.10). This also echoes 2.6 (μορφῆ Θεοῦ) and 2.7 (μορφὴν δούλου). Paul is clearly seeking to locate the story of his own discipleship, and therefore the discipleship of the Philippians in the story of Christ's action as the embodiment of the grace of God.[83]

Finally Paul addresses the continuing pursuit of true identity (3.12-21). If false identity is mistaken identity, and true identity is ἐν Χριστῷ, Paul is quick to offer a third point of contrast with the previous two passages. The 'not yet' (3.12) is developed in the language of the passage which emphasises a sense of the story as incomplete.

[3.12] I press on
[3.13] straining forward to what
[3.14] I press on toward the goal

But lest this be understood in terms of Paul's own strivings it is counterbalanced in the same verses by:

[3.12] because Christ Jesus has made me his own.
[3.14] call of God in Christ Jesus.

Two points are significant for our purposes. First, there is Paul's use of a favourite athletic metaphor[84] which is implicitly teleological. Secondly, there is 'the upward call (κλήσεως) of God in Christ Jesus'. This is not wholly clear but it does have vocational overtones, which is primarily "the divine calling to salvation". It is "God himself who issues the call, while ἐν Χριστῷ' Ἰεσοῦ probably signifies that it is in the sphere of Christ Jesus himself that this summons is given."[85] For Paul the point is that he can only ever respond to what God has already done in Christ.[86]

As Paul has identified himself with Christ, so he calls upon the Philippians to 'join in imitating me' (3.17). So they too will identify themselves with him, for 'our commonwealth is' (3.20) in continued striving for full identification in Christ, which is essentially an eschatological hope of the sovereign reign of God. The focus of this sovereignty is Jesus Christ, the one spoken of (2.9-11) to whom every knee

---

[82] O'Brien, 1991, 406.
[83] Dunn, 1991, 223.
[84] See: Rom. 9. 16, 30-31; 1 Cor. 9.24; Gal. 2.2; Phil. 2.16. Also: 2 Tim. 2.5; 4.7-8; Heb. 12.1; Jas. 1.12. Balthasar argues it is also a dramatic metaphor (*TD* I, 154-155), but that does not seem to apply in this instance.
[85] O'Brien, 1991, 433.
[86] Fee, 1995, 346.

shall bow. The language[87] signals a return to the primary narrative,[88] the story of Christ, which is the story he calls the Philippians to inhabit with him. Here Paul applies it to the teleological and vocational lives of the Philippians. So, Jesus Christ

> 3.21 will change (μετασχηματίσει) our lowly (ταπεινώσεος - our humiliation) body to be like (σύμμορφον - to be conformed) his glorious body

First, there are deliberately mimetic linguistic overtones of 2.5-11 as well as clear differences. Secondly, the order in which the compounds of μορφῆ (2.6, 7a) and σχήματι (2.7b) occur are inverted here by Paul. Thirdly, ταπεινώσεος is here used adjectivally with reference to 'body' (σῶμα). Dunn suggests in Paul's usage soma is best understood as "the embodiment of the person" and that "it is precisely 'bodiness' (corporeality, corporateness) which enables individuals as bodies to interact with each other".[89] Fourthly, Paul speaks of God's will for his covenant people 'to be conformed (σύμμορφον) to his glorious body'.[90] Authorial intent is clear, Paul is calling the Philippians to be Christlike.[91] Nonetheless, the distinction (they are not identical) between Christ (God) and humanity is not dissolved, but identity (family likeness) is to be recognizable. In this verse Paul would appear to draw together elements of both tracking and fitting theories of representation. It is the vocation of the Philippians to be Christlike, identifiable ἐν κυρίῳ. This reiterates the movement of the narrative in which kenosis is God's graceful self-revelation to humanity and with which humanity responds by identifying itself with Christ.

4.1-3 serves a double purpose. It closes the preceding section with a double reference. First, the reference to 'crown (στέφανός)' which as Lightfoot[92] suggests alludes to the victor's crown sought by the athlete (3.14). Secondly, the injunction to 'stand firm thus in the Lord (ἐν κυρίῳ)' is localised and directed specifically to the two women Euodia and Syntyche who appear to be strong, but rival women who are the source of internal dissension within the Philippian community.[93] In effect Paul is

---

[87] For a discussion whether 3.20-21 is a hymn fragment see: O Brien, 1991, 467-72.
[88] That of God's saving act in Christ, 2.6-11.
[89] Dunn, 1998, 56.
[90] The only other parallel outside Philippians is where Paul says that God's covenant people are 'to be conformed (συμμόρφους) to the image of his Son' (Rom. 8.29).
[91] N T Wright, *The Resurrection of the Son of God*, London, SPCK, 2003, 226.
[92] Lightfoot, 1879, 157.
[93] See: Beare, 1959, 142; Martin, 1985, 152; Fee, 1995, 389.

asking them, through his 'true yokefellow',[94] to be united in Christ as their common mindset, by being conformed and recognizable by their way of living.

The final[95] section is not simply a concluding passage but makes explicit what has been implicit, the punch line, so to speak, which is the nature of true identification.

True Identification involves Participation in the Other (4.10-20)

I suggested earlier that the narrative emerges from Paul's account of God's saving act in Christ (2.5-11). However, the occasion of Paul's writing is his imprisonment (1.12-26). The middle section of the narrative concerns the sending of a gift to Paul (4.10-20) by the Philippians because of their shared relationship in Jesus Christ. The result is that both Paul and the Philippian Church are striving to achieve a true identity in Christ (3.1-21). In this section Paul acknowledges that the gift they have sent is not just a generous provision towards his physical needs, but an expression of their identification with Christ and with him and of their continuing "'partnership' with him in the gospel."[96] They thus form a relay of exchanges (4.15) in recognition of the gift of Christ they have themselves received from Paul.

Again Paul uses "the language of participation" and interchange;[97] it was 'kind of you to share (συγκοινωήσαντές - partnership) my trouble (τῇ θλίψει)' (4.14). However, "the gift was a sign that they identified with him in his ministry and further evidence of their participation in the apostolic task"[98] the root of which is their shared identity, in God through Christ, underlining their friendship.[99] This participatory identity of each with the other (ἐν Χριστῷ) is recognized in giving and receiving. As Paul 'gave' the Philippians the gospel (of which they are reminded in 2.6-11), they 'gave' by supporting Paul in his missionary activities beyond Philippi.

Paul then turns to the seemingly commercial metaphor of 'credit' and 'full payment', which a number of commentators have played down.[100] However, I suggest there is another reading, which makes the linguistic

---

[94] For discussion of the possible identity of who this may be see Lightfoot, 1879, 159; Fee, 1995, 393-94.

[95] In the preceding passage there appear to be two further false endings (4.4-7; 8-9). For a discussion of the significance of this see: Beare, 1959, 148, also: Holmstrand, 1997, 123.

[96] Fee, 1995, 426-27.

[97] Fee, 1995, 439.

[98] O'Brien, 1991, 530.

[99] Fee, 1995, 440.

[100] See: Lightfoot, 1879, 166; Beare, 1959, 155; Fee, 1995, 448.

transition at 4.18c less jarring.

According to Paul 'the gifts you sent [he understands to be] a fragrant offering (ὀσμὴν εὐωδίας), a sacrifice (θυσίαν) acceptable pleasing (εὐάρεστον) to God' (4.18). Here the metaphor is undeniably a priestly one couched in sacrificial language. This echoes a strand discernible throughout the letter (2.17-18; 3.8). The phrase ὀσμὴν εὐωδίας occurs frequently in the Old Testament in connection with the sacrificial cultic worship which on occasion is "transferred and applied to the house of Israel, whom the Lord promises to accept".[101] Furthermore the gift of money was probably costly to the Philippians and therefore a θυσίαν, which is εὐάρεστον to God. The spiritualizing of sacrifice, begun in the First Testament,[102] means that in the cult an acceptable sacrifice is no longer simply the prescribed animal or grain sacrifices, instead it is the totality of self-giving in response to God which this echoes.[103] Paul "views the Christian life as a whole in terms of a 'living sacrifice'."[104] So for Paul the use of a critically realistic priestly language is appropriate for his understanding of the Christian life.[105]

This combines with a return to the idea of πλήρωμα.[106] While Paul's immediate reference is to the generosity of the Philippians, behind this lies the generosity of God. For it is God who reveals his generosity 'his riches in glory in Christ Jesus' (4.19) in a counterpoint to the *carmen Christi* (2.7). The sacrifice offered is by God and yet the 'glory' of God is seen ἐν Χριστῷ Ἰεσοῦ (4.19). It is Jesus Christ who is given (Galatians 1.4, 2.20; Ephesians 5.2) for the redemption of mankind and who in turn is given the name above all names (2.9). The sacrifice does not result in loss but in even greater exaltation.

The Philippians recognized Paul's true identity through his giving of the gospel. So too the generosity of the Philippians to Paul identifies their genuineness to him. But over all and through all is the centrality of the recognition of the identity of Christ who above all is given for the world. Identity is rooted 'in Christ' and so being in the right relationship to God. The consequence of this is embodied in right living.[107] Right living is priestly, because it is offered to God as a paean of praise and thanksgiving. It is doubly sacrificial in that the offering of one's life to God is a kenotic event of emptying which itself mirrors the divine kenosis. It is a

---

[101] O'Brien, 1991, 541.
[102] LXX, Ps. 50.18-19. (Hawthorne, 1983, 207.)
[103] O'Brien, 1991, 542. (See Rom. 12.1,2; 14.18; 2 Cor. 5.9.)
[104] Bockmuehl, 1997, 266.
[105] Calvin, *Institutes of Christian Religion*, IV. 18. 16. (John T McNeill (ed), The Library of Christian Classics, Philadelphia, The Westminster Press, 1960.
[106] 4.18, 19.
[107] Jürgen Moltmann, *The Crucified God* (ET), London, SCM, 25.

representative identity which is both internal (2.5) but which is necessarily externalized through right living. But the consequences are the experience of God's generosity. In the light of this, what can Paul say except 'To our God and Father be glory for ever and ever. Amen' (20)? As Lightfoot notes, "It is no longer μου, for the reference is not now to himself [Paul] as distinguished from the Philippians, but as united with them."[108] It is in the reciprocity of this mutual participation that Paul locates their shared identity.[109]

The *Carmen Christi*

I have reserved Philippians 2.6-11, one of the most commented upon passages in Scripture,[110] for the conclusion of this Chapter, specifically to try and understand it in the context of the Epistle as a whole. What "is at stake is nothing less than our fundamental presumptions about divine and human nature, and the possibility, or otherwise, of their complete concurrence."[111] In other words the priestly concern is for the setting and crossing of boundaries between God and humanity. In this section I shall begin with a brief excursus prior to an exegesis of the text. This excursus will examine the plausibility of an Adamic Christology. In the subsequent exegesis I will suggest that the identity of Christ, and therefore the divine identity that Paul is speaking of in Philippians 2.6-11 is known through the self-revelation of the divine kenosis as an event of self-identification.

Adamic Christology and the Divine Identity

James Dunn argues that the key to the interpretation of Philippians 2.6-11 is found in Paul's concept of an Adamic Christology. Accordingly he suggests that in the first section (6a-7c) "its development is determined by a double contrast: first between 'form of God' and 'form of slave', ... and second between 'equality with God' and 'in likeness of men'". He argues this is best understood as an allusion to Gen 1-3; to the stories of the creation and fall of man."[112] So in Philippians Paul presents the story of God's saving action in Christ as a retelling of the Genesis story. Thus the 'form of God' (μορφῇ Θεοῦ) probably alludes to the notion of the image (εἰκών) of God believing that μορφῇ and εἰκών are used as near synonyms in the LXX. Therefore "'equality with God' probably alludes to Adam's temptation

---

[108] Lightfoot, 1879, 167.

[109] Moltmann, 1974, 19.

[110] Martin, 1997, has a 24 page bibliography on this particular passage alone.

[111] Sarah Coakley, 'Kenosis and Subversion', D. Hampson (ed), *Swallowing a Fishbone?*, London, SPCK, 1996, 88.

[112] J. D. G. Dunn, *Christology in the Making* (2nd Edn.), SCM, London, 1989, 115.

(Gen 3:5) and 'likeness of men' probably by way of contrast denotes the kind of man that all men now are."[113]

This is reinforced by the use of ἁρπαγμὸσ, with its notion of seizing, which echoes the story of the Fall. So "Christ faced the same archetypal choice that confronted Adam, but chose not as Adam had chosen".[114] Barth similarly understands Jesus as the 'second Adam' as not wishing "to be as God, but in Adam's nature acknowledges before God an Adamic being, the state and position of fallen man".[115] According to Barth, Jesus in his Incarnation retains his divine being, but he reinterprets emptying to be the revelation of a new dimension of the divine. But the key issue is the nature of Jewish monotheism and its implications regarding the identity of Jesus Christ. According to N. T. Wright, in Philippians 2.6-11, Paul identifies Jesus not as identical with the Father but yet "the one who became Jesus - must have been from all eternity 'equal with God' in the sense of being himself fully divine."[116] However, as Richard Bauckham observes "Wright is trying to have his cake and eat it".[117]

Bauckham is clear that for Jewish monotheism the key christological issue is the identification of Jesus in relation to God. The insurmountable problem in the use of the Adamic model is its reliance upon the notion of a Christology developing from the idea of intermediaries "who may or may not participate in divinity".[118] In Jewish monotheism God is God; man is man and there can be no intermediaries. So in the understanding I am seeking to develop priesthood cannot be understood as occupying an intermediary role between God and humanity. Like an Adamic Christology it is fundamentally flawed because it is essentially anthropomorphic, proceeding from the created to God. Richard Bauckham says such a Christology is primarily human rather than divine in identity. Thus with regard to Philippians 2.5-11, "Adam has proved a red herring in [the] study of this passage."[119]

Instead the New Testament proposes "a Christology of divine identity" since the "inclusion of Jesus in the unique divine identity had implications not only for who Jesus is but also for who God is."[120] The fundamental question is, "what, in the Jewish understanding of God, really counts as

---

[113] Dunn, 1989, 115-16.
[114] Dunn, 1989, 117.
[115] *CD* I.2, 157. Similarly Balthasar makes significant reference to an Adamic Christology e.g. *TD* II, 410-11.
[116] Wright, 1991, 94.
[117] Richard Bauckham, *God Crucified, Monotheism and Christology in the New Testament*, Carlisle, Paternoster, 1998, 57.
[118] Bauckham, 1998, 5.
[119] Bauckham, 1998, 57.
[120] Bauckham, 1998, viii.

'divine'"?[121] God emerges as having a unique identity. It is "by analogy with human personal identity, understood not as a mere ontological subject without characteristics but as including both character and personal story" that Bauckham understands the divine identity. So in the narratives of Israel's history, God acts to all intents and purposes, as "a character in the story".[122] God is revealed first to Israel as having a "consistent identity of the One who acts graciously towards his people and can be expected to do so."[123]

However, God is known in relationship not only to Israel, but to the whole of reality, "that he is Creator of all things and sovereign Ruler of all things."[124] Creation is the act of God alone. He neither used nor required any help. He has servants but they do not share in his rule. It was the exclusive worship of God alone that identified the Jews as quintessentially monotheistic.[125] Bauckham dismisses the idea of intermediaries, nonetheless in the Word and Wisdom of God it is possible to identify "personifications or hypostations of aspects of God" and "that the Word and the Wisdom of God are intrinsic to the unique divine identity".[126]

Crucially for priesthood what "Jewish monotheism could not accommodate were semi-divine figures, subordinate deities, divinity by delegation or participation."[127] Christologically Jesus is described as being exalted over 'all things'.[128] Secondly, in the New Testament Jesus is portrayed in his exalted state as being "seated with God on God's throne"[129] Accordingly, Jesus is "included in the unique identity of the one God"[130] Thirdly, Bauckham draws attention to the importance of name in reference to Jesus.[131] Fourthly, there is the recognition of Jesus in the worship of God.[132]

Bauckham proceeds to draw particular attention to two further aspects of the divine identity. First, 1 Corinthians 8.6[133] only makes sense as an

---

[121] Bauckham, 1998, 5.

[122] Bauckham, 1998, 7.

[123] Bauckham, 1998, 9.

[124] Bauckham, 1998, 10.

[125] According to the *Shema*, 'the Lord our God is one Lord;' or 'the Lord our God, the Lord is one.' (Deut. 6.4-6.)

[126] Bauckham, 1998, 20.

[127] Bauckham, 1998, 28.

[128] Jn. 3.35; 13.3; Acts 10.36; 1 Cor. 15.27-28; Eph. 1.22; Phil. 3.21. etc.

[129] Bauckham, 1998, 28.

[130] Bauckham, 1998, 33.

[131] Phil. 2.9; Heb. 1.4.

[132] Bauckham, 1998, 34.

[133] '[T]here is one God, the Father, from whom all things are and for whom we exist and one Lord, Jesus Christ through whom are all things and through whom we exist.' (1 Cor. 8.6.)

explicitly monotheistic statement. He argues that Paul includes "Jesus in the unique identity of the one God affirmed in the Shema" which "consists of the one God, the Father and the one Lord, his Messiah"[134] by including him in "the exclusively divine work of creation by giving him the role of instrumental cause."[135]

Secondly, there is the recognition that "the inclusion of the exalted Christ in the divine identity entails the inclusion of the crucified Christ in the divine identity."[136] It is precisely this which is the problem in Philippians 2 and which has undermined many attempts to articulate kenosis. The key to early Christological thought is the creative exegesis of the Old Testament, primarily the Torah but also in Deutero-Isaiah, providing the classic monotheistic sources of Second Temple Judaism. Accordingly Bauckham argues that:

> in the early Christian reading of Deutero-Isaiah, the witness, the humiliation, the death and exaltation of the Servant of the Lord are the way in which God reveals his deity to the world. The witness, the humiliation and exaltation of the Servant are the eschatological salvation event, the new Exodus.[137]

I have outlined Bauckham's argument in some detail, because the concept of identity provides the key for my reading of Philippians. In the same way it was the identity of God and therefore the status of the Son which lay behind the theology of Arius.[138] I have also drawn attention to the problem of the concept of the intermediary in relation to priesthood. Bauckham's suggested 'Christology of divine identity' echoes Barth's suggestion and is similarly reinforced by reference to Aristotle's key aspects of characterisation. In Philippians 2 both Christ and God are good characters, in the Aristotelian sense, because they fulfil their purposes. Christ is not grasping, but he is self-effacing and obedient, as the Son who is sent, and the Father who vindicates Christ in his exaltation acknowledges this. So, as Bauckham suggests, there is consistency of identity in God. Aristotle's requirement that a character must be appropriate, to be what they ought, corresponds to Bauckham's emphasis upon the creative exegesis of the Old Testament behind a Christology of identity. Likewise, only by the inclusion of the humiliation of the servant in the divine is it possible to develop ideas of the character of God who is in some sense 'like us' and not simply so 'other' as to be totally removed.

---

[134] Bauckham, 1998, 38.
[135] Bauckham, 1998, 39.
[136] Bauckham, 1998, 46.
[137] Bauckham, 1998, 49.
[138] See: 31-41 above.

Furthermore Aristotle considers both poetry and painting as types of representation. Therefore the person who looks "at a painting needs to recognize it as a depiction of a given object" and that this "act of recognition involves an exercise of our capacity for cognition".[139] Mimetic theory implies the priority of the thing or story that is being represented, whether according to a fitting or a tracking theory. So in Philippians 2.6-11 Paul tells the story of God in Christ by reference to allusion, metaphor and poetic representation in a non-realistic account but which is freed to span the gap between the human and the divine, without undermining the integrity of either.

Philippians 2.6-11

First, I shall set out the text in full highlighting a number of key words:

⁶ [Christ Jesus] who, though he was in the form (μορφῇ) of God, did not count equality with God a thing to be grasped (ἁρπαγμὸν),

⁷ but emptied (ἐκένωσεν) himself, taking the form (μορφὴν) of a servant, being born in the likeness (ὁμοιώματι) of men.

⁸ And being found in human form (σχήματι) he humbled (ἐταπείνωσεν) himself and became obedient unto death, even death on a cross.

⁹ Therefore God has highly exalted him and bestowed on him the name (ὄνομα) which is above every name.

¹⁰ that at the name (ὀνόματι) of Jesus every knee should bow, in heaven and on earth and under the earth,

¹¹ and every tongue confess that Jesus Christ is the Lord, to the glory of God the Father.

In the *carmen Christi* what emerges is the identification of Jesus Christ with the Godhead, in the language and the grammar of the narrative.[140] In the text I have highlighted seven key words. Each of these words has significance for any understanding of identity, and not simply within the framework of this passage. These seven words can be subdivided into two groups of words. One group (μορφῇ ὁμοιώματι, σχήματι, ὄνομα) are essentially words "associated with representation".[141] The second (ἁρπαγμὸν, ἐκένωσεν, ἐταπείνωσεν) group are all words which serve to

---

[139] *Poetics*, 1996, xii.
[140] Fee, 1995, 219.
[141] Graham Ward, 'Kenosis: Death, Discourse and Resurrection', Lucy Gardiner, Ben Quash, Graham Ward, *Balthasar at the End of Modernity*, Edinburgh, T & T Clark, 1999, 22.

qualify the identity revealed.

Ralph Martin is correct in his suggestion that it "would therefore be no exaggeration to say that μορφῆ Θεοῦ is the key-term of the entire hymn".[142] However, the key question remains, how are the words, 'the form of God' to be understood? It is precisely this question that kenoticism addresses.

Graham Ward argues that Philippians 2 is more than a theological statement but offers a poetic narrative, retelling the story of the action of God as experienced in Jesus. Ward's interpretation leans heavily upon the earlier work of J B Lightfoot, according to whom μορφῆ does not just mean "the external semblance only...but the characteristic attributes".[143] Therefore "μορφῆ is contrasted with the schema as that which is intrinsic and essential with that which is accidental and outward."[144] Thus, quoting F. F. Bruce, he says that the "implication is not that Christ, by becoming incarnate, exchanged the form of God for the form of a slave, but that he manifested the form of God in the form of a slave."[145] He here identifies the characteristic Pauline use of antithesis - God and slave in the use of the concept of μορφῆ.

Secondly, having explored the meaning of μορφῆ with regards to 'the form of God' and 'the form of a servant', he seeks to recognize the significance of the change of word to ὁμοιώμα. Drawing upon Lightfoot, Ward suggests, "*homoiōma* stands midway between *morphē* and *schēma*." Thus "*homoiōmata* can suggest both full identity with and difference from."[146] In a complex argument he sees the choice of this word as indicative of the progression of intention. But in the mimetic economy of the narrative action, at what point does likeness become representation?

Thirdly, Paul speaks of Jesus Christ 'being found in human form (σχήματι)'. According to Ward

> [s]*chēma* denotes the outward appearance, the accidents in the Aristotelian sense of human nature. But these appearances are not manifestations of the substance, rather they are signifiers distinct from but detailing the signified substance.[147]

The move from μορφῆ, through ὁμοίωμα to σχήματοσ expresses a deepening progression towards externality, secondariness and appearance - towards human externality which manifests the essential nature of being a

---

[142] Martin, 1997, 99.
[143] Lightfoot, 1879, 112.
[144] Lightfoot, 1879, 133.
[145] Ward, 1999, 22.
[146] Ward, 1999, 23 – his transliteration.
[147] Ward, 1999, 22 – his transliteration.

slave, toward a world in which what appears is not what is.[148]

In other words in the passage both fitting and tracking theories of representation are at play in the move from internal to external resemblance. Thus in the second part of the passage when Paul speaks of God having 'highly exalted him and bestowed on him 'the name (ὄνομα) which is above every name', there is

> a descent from a logic of identity into a world of shifting appearances and, with verse 9, there is a return to the logic of identity when the Father crowns the Son with his name; a name they share Lord, Yahweh.[149]

Indeed, in verse 10 the worship of the 'name of Jesus' reinforces the identification of Jesus as part of the Godhead. Kenosis is not the Incarnation as the limitation of the divine (voluntary or otherwise) in Jesus Christ. It is the taking of 'human form'. From the moment of Incarnation, death becomes inevitable as a universal human experience. Kenosis is also therefore about death - as non-being and absence; but is also about resurrection, as "renaming and a re-empowerment to speak".[150] If Incarnation and death are recognizably human, so resurrection is the acknowledgement of identification with the Godhead.

This has clear implications for the meaning of ἁρπαγμὸν, ἐκένωσεν, and ἐταπείνωσεν.[151] C. F. D. Moule seeks an understanding of μορφῆ by means of its relation to, or qualification by ἁρπαγμὸν. Moule's argument is that

> ἁρπαγμὸσ in verse 6 is an abstract noun meaning 'the act of snatching' and that οὐχ ἁρπαγμὸν ἡγήσατο τὸ εἶναι ἴσα Θηῷ thus means 'he did not regard equality with God as consisting in snatching'.[152]

The problem, he suggests, is that Latin paraphrasing influences exegetes. Either: *res rapienda* - something that is not yet possessed and therefore to be snatched as desirable and attractive, or *res rapta* - something snatched and already in one's possession which is not to be let go or surrendered. Moule rejects these as inappropriate, preferring *res retinenda* - a desirable thing which is to be clung to - which is how the word is used by non-

---

[148] Ward, 1999, 23.
[149] Ward, 1999, 23.
[150] Ward, 1999, 24.
[151] This second group of qualificatory words would seem to fall more naturally within the fitting theory of representation (See: 10 above).
[152] C. F. D. Moule, 'Further Reflexions on Philippians 2:5-11', W. W. Gasque and R. P. Martin (eds.), *Apostolic History and the Gospels*, Grand Rapids, Eerdmans, 1970, 266.

Christian authors of the same period. The problem is that this usage is rare and when used literally means robbery, which would not be appropriate in this context. He criticizes Martin's interpretation for seeking to be too literal in asking, what exactly was it that our Lord refused to plunder? Rather Moule understands it as not seizing or snatching as opposed to giving away.

The second word is ἐκένωσεν qualifying the identity which is revealed. Kittel believes the subject of "ἐκένωσεν is not the incarnate but the pre-existent Lord".[153] Martin proposes that there are four possible answers to the question, "Of what did Christ empty Himself...?" First, that he emptied himself of the divine nature, "of the glories, the prerogatives".[154] Secondly, that he emptied himself "of Deity".[155] Thirdly, emptying occurred as a general antithesis to the temptation of snatching. However, ultimately he believes that the "kenosis of Christ is His incarnation... It refers to Christ who voluntarily gave up His heavenly existence and limited Himself by becoming man."[156] Martin is clear that "[w]hatever may be the attraction... of the Kenosis principle... it seems clear on strictly linguistic grounds that verses 6 and 7 cannot mean the pre-existent Christ emptied Himself of the μορφῆ Θεοῦ and instead took the μορφῆ δούλου."[157] While Martin is correct in this last statement, however, his mistake is to understand kenosis as espoused by its nineteenth century proponents.

A further possibility is that ἑαυτόν ἐκένωσεν refers to "Christ making himself powerless in the sense of accepting the vocation which led to the real humiliation of his incarnation and finally his death on the cross."[158] Accordingly, the act of emptying is part of the divine economy of salvation. It is Christ's divinely ordained vocation, which is recognised elsewhere in the New Testament as being essentially priestly.[159]

The third word is ἐταπείνωσεν which qualifies the identity of the character of the one revealed. This word is used with reference to Jesus Christ but does it simply allude to the Incarnation? Bauckham suggests that Philippians 2.6-11 is a creative exegesis of Deutero-Isaiah[160] identifying

---

[153] *TDNT*. 3, 661.
[154] Martin, 1997, 165-66.
[155] Martin, 1997, 166.
[156] Martin, 1997, 178.
[157] Martin, 1997, 171.
[158] O'Brien, 1991, 217 – my italics.
[159] Heb. 4.14-16. Paul does not use explicitly priestly metaphors to describe Jesus' saving action he does speak of him offering himself. (Gal. 1.4; 2.20) and of his sacrifice (Rom. 3.25; 5.6-9; Col. 1.14; 1.20.)
[160] Bauckham has in mind Is. 52.13-53; 45.22-23.

Christ with God.[161] Isaiah tells that the Servant 'poured out [emptied] his soul to death' (Isaiah 53.12) having previously been described as appearing in an astonishing 'form' (Isaiah 52.14) and having 'no form or comeliness' (Isaiah 53.2) therefore he 'shall be exalted and lifted up' (Isaiah 52.13). In Isaiah 45 God speaks saying 'turn to me and be saved, all the ends of the earth. For I am God and there is no other' (Isaiah 45.22) and continues 'To me every knee shall bow, and every tongue shall swear.' (Isaiah 45.23)

Richard Bauckham argues that "Paul is reading Deutero-Isaiah to mean that the career of the Servant of the Lord, his suffering, humiliation, death and exaltation is the way the sovereignty of the one true God comes to be acknowledged by all the nations."[162] Thus when Paul says 'at the name of Jesus every knee should bow, in heaven and on earth and under the earth, and every tongue confess that Jesus Christ is the Lord, to the glory of God the Father' (Phil. 2.10-11) he is, by reference to Isaiah, clearly identifying Jesus Christ with the one God. The contrasts within the passage, servant/God, service/lordship, exaltation/humiliation are not essentially the divine-human conflict. Rather the contrast is an even more powerful one "for first-century Jewish theology with its controlling image of God as the universal emperor... Can the cross of Jesus Christ actually be included in the identity of this God?" The identification of Christ with God is above all a statement about who God is. "The God who is high can also be low, because God is not God in seeking his own advantage but in self-giving."[163]

Accordingly kenosis becomes "revelatory of the 'humility' of the divine nature".[164] What "is styled kenosis, is itself the height of πληρησες: the most divine thing is to give rather than to get." Thus kenosis, as applied to Jesus Christ as the one who has 'the form of God', cannot be a matter of loss.[165] Moule shows in his reading of ἁρπαγμὸν the possibility that kenosis is descriptive of the activity of Jesus Christ, without requiring him to cease to be identified with God. However, he underestimates the importance of the Isaiah narrative in the interpretation of the passage. For example, as recognized earlier, the text sees both Christ and God as the subject at times, as if to reinforce their common identity. In this narrative, Paul is engaging with a process, recognized by Bauckham, of which Hans-Georg Gadamer speaks suggesting that

> all interpretations of past literature arise from a dialogue between past and present. Our attempts to understand a work will depend on the questions

---

[161] This goes beyond Ward who argues that this passage simply stands "in the Jewish context of Isaiah's Suffering Servant" (Ward, 1999, 19).
[162] Bauckham, 1998, 59.
[163] Bauckham, 1998, 61.
[164] Coakley, 1996, 88.
[165] Moule, 1970, 273.

which our own cultural environment allows us to raise. At the same time, we seek to discover the questions which the work itself was trying to answer in its own dialogue with history... understanding [is] a 'fusion' of past and present: we cannot make our journey into the past without taking the present with us.[166]

So in Philippians Paul, through the creative use of the Old Testament inheritance, seeks to interpret the present in the light of his and the Philippians' shared experience of Jesus Christ. It is the story of Jesus Christ in Philippians 2.6-11 that provides a mimetic metanarrative of creation, the fall and redemption. The key to the metanarrative is the identification of Jesus with God. Kenosis therefore ceases to be simply a christological event. Instead it is an event of God in Trinity.[167] God, according to Paul, identified himself afresh in Jesus Christ. However, having told the story, Paul then asks the question what is the role of the Philippians, and therefore all who would seek to identify themselves εν Χριστῶ, in the narrative?

Philippians as a Mimetic Narrative of Priestly Identity

If there is a text for this study it is:

'Have this mind among yourselves, which you have in Christ Jesus' (2.5).

What I have proposed is a narrative reading in which kenosis and priesthood are united by the central issue of identity, lying at the heart of the Philippians 2.6-11. This underlines the proposed hermeneutic of love "[i]n love... the familiar paradox, one becomes fully oneself when losing oneself to another. In the fact of love, in short, both parties are simultaneously affirmed."[168]

Because it is rooted in a hermeneutic of love the identity being proposed is kenotic and relational. Representation, which encompasses elements of both fitting and tracking theories and participation, is based upon an understanding of identity as being 'recognizable'.[169] In the Epistle, Paul articulates a loving relationship between himself and the Philippian Church established in and shaped through the mutual experience of the love of God revealed in Jesus Christ. This is both a past event but also a present

---

[166] Raman Selden, Peter Widdowson, Peter Brooker, *A Reader's Guide to Contemporary Literary Theory* (4th Edn.), London, Prentice Hall, 1997, 55.

[167] I am not suggesting that Paul wrote a deliberately trinitarian account, but that the passage can only make sense when interpreted in the light of the Trinity

[168] See: 75, n. 1 above.

[169] Fitting and tracing theories of representation are both concerned with questions of recognition.

occurrence; being 'in Christ' (2.5) "designates... the reality, the place, the area in which the people addressed exist. They exist in the fellowship of Christ Jesus".[170]

Though fellowship (κοινόν) is not found in this verse it does recur throughout the Letter.[171] Κοινωνία here, and elsewhere, has connotations of participation and on occasions speaks of participation with regard to suffering.[172] The word πάθημα in secular Greek and in tragic usage denoted "that which befell a person and had to be accepted".[173] For Paul, it refers to the afflictions in which all Christians participate. While they do not share in the sufferings entailed in Christ's saving action upon the cross they do share in the birth pangs of the messianic age. But above all for Paul it is the story of Jesus Christ who is identified with God, revealing the possibility of participation between those who are apparently other but yet where there is a discernible oneness, ipse-identity.

The participation of Jesus Christ in humanity at the Incarnation is also vocational. For Paul, Jesus Christ's action as set out in the *carmen Christi* is essentially one of obedience to God.[174] This is his vocation. So too Paul, his fellow workers and the Philippians are people with a vocation[175] to be christlike[176] by being obedient people whose lives are 'handed over'[177] to God to be identified in him. It is this vocation which Paul identifies as priestly. As Christ gives himself for others, so Paul gives himself for Christ in the gospel.[178] Here Paul traces in his own ministry a resemblance to the kenosis of Christ but does so in explicitly priestly terms. Similarly Paul speaks of the ministry of Epaphroditus, an emissary from the Philippians, in priestly language as one who is prepared to sacrifice himself in serving him (2. 25, 30).

This marks the reciprocity of the relationship between Paul and the Philippians, so that as Paul poured himself out in bringing the gospel to them (2.17) so they in return gave sacrificially in support of him (4.18).

---

[170] Barth, 1962, 59 – his italics.

[171] In this I also include compound versions (Phil. 1.5; 1.7; 2.1; 3.9; 4.14).

[172] Phil. 1.9; 1.29; 3.10 also 1 Cor. 12.26; 2 Cor. 1.6,7; Col. 1.24.

[173] O'Brien, 1991, 405.

[174] There are echoes here of Gethsemane, where the Father's will and the obedience of the Son are one. (Mk. 14.36; Matt. 26.39.)

[175] Phil. 1.14-20; 2.19-30; 3.14.

[176] Phil. 2.5.

[177] Παραδίδωμι is not found in Philippians. However, Phil. 1.21; 3.7-8 have been connected by some commentators with Paul's thought as expressed Gal. 2.20, (see: Lightfoot, 1879, 92; Barth, 1962; 37; Hawthorne, 1983, 44; O'Brien, 1991, 121, 389; Fee, 1995, 141, 318; Bockmuehl, 1997, 87, 206.) See: 59 below (Balthasar) and see: 69 below (Moltmann).

[178] 'I am poured out (σπένδομαι) as a libation upon the sacrificial offering (λειτουργία) of your faith' (2.17).

Once again the language is priestly and couched in that of cultic sacrifice. This accords well with Paul's thought elsewhere, in which he reinterprets the cultic activity of sacrifice as the offering of oneself to God as, 'a living sacrifice, holy and acceptable to God'.[179] In this he is building upon the Old Testament understanding of sacrifice as the only possible response to the prior action of God towards his people.[180]

According to Dunn "Paul saw all ministry and service on behalf of the gospel as priestly".[181] Priesthood, however, is not cultically focused but the outworking of the hermeneutic of love, which is the discipleship of radical kenosis.[182] This is rooted in the community of faith to which they belong 'in Christ'. Though Paul does not use priestly metaphors to articulate the saving action of Christ (unlike the author of the Letter to the Hebrews) nonetheless he uses the language of giving[183] and of sacrifice.[184]

Kenosis provides an analogy for priesthood and the crossing of the boundaries between God and humanity. Kenosis is concerned with the divine-human engagement in which each participates with the other while maintaining their identity. The essential *diastasis* is not dissolved but retained. Secondly it provides an analogy for sacrifice. In kenosis the act of emptying is paradoxically also an event of filling in which the superabundance of God's graceful generosity is revealed. Kenosis is πλήρωμα and an act of identification, which is self-sacrificial in relation to God in Christ. Thirdly, priesthood enacts obedience which is responsive to God's prior sovereign grace such that "first he offereth and killeth his own reason, and the wisdom of the flesh; then giveth glory unto God... this is that daily sacrifice of the New Testament".[185]

Conclusion

In the mimetic economy of Philippians, the narrative of God's saving act in Jesus Christ represented by the *carmen Christi* precedes Paul's and the Philippians' shared responsive identification 'in Christ'. As shown in Chapter 3 kenosis is an event of the Godhead in which there is a move to the exteriorization of the divine in a fluidity of identity. Nonetheless identity is always maintained. The divine identity is the key to human identity, but because there is no confusion of forms being christlike in

---

[179] Rom. 12.1 cf. Ps. 51.17; Hos. 6.6.

[180] A. D. H. Mayes, *Deuteronomy*, Marshall Morgan and Scott, London, 1979, 58.

[181] Dunn, 1998, 547.

[182] Oliver Davies, *A Theology of Compassion*, London, SCM, 2001, 212.

[183] Gal. 1.4; 2.20; also Eph. 5.22, 25.

[184] Rom. 3.25; 5.6-9; Col. 1.14; 1.20; also: Eph. 1.7 2.13.

[185] M. Luther, *A Commentary on St Paul's Epistle To The Galatians*, London, James Clarke, 1953, 227.

human form involves the non-identical repetition of the original. In the same way Christ is identified in the Father. The vocation of Paul and the Philippians is to be recognizable 'in Christ'. This is the kenotic identity, in which Paul, the Philippians and Christ all participate enacted through obedient living which Paul describes using sacrificial and priestly language. What is evident is the greater use made by Paul of priestly language and metaphors than is usually acknowledged. Crucially in Philippians, notions of priesthood draw together the participation of the principal characters[186] in the narrative of their shared, yet distinct identities. Within the mimetic economy of Philippians representation is presented in ways suggestive both of the tracking and fitting theories that emerged in Chapter 3. Kenosis does not offer a propositional but regulative[187] account in which there is a dialectic of identity of likeness but not sameness. In the kenotic identity of Jesus Christ as 'truly God and truly man' the divine-human *diastasis* is crossed but not dissolved.[188] God is God, he is not constrained but he remains consistent in his identity and self-revelation to which humanity responds.

---

[186] The principal characters are Jesus Christ and God, Paul with Epaphroditus and Timothy, and the Philippians.
[187] George Lindbeck, *The Nature of Doctrine*, Philadelphia, The Westminster Press, 18. In this case regulation is provided by the Chalcedonian pattern.
[188] Nor conversely can there be any reductionism. (Moltmann, 1974, 160.)

Part II
Priesthood and the Grateful Human Response to the Divine Self-revelation

Chapter 5

Vocation and Priesthood

In Part I, I explored kenosis as the articulation of the divine identity revealed in Jesus Christ, the second person of the Trinity, as a divinely sovereign act and an event of grace. This culminated in Chapter 3 with an exegesis of Philippians in which, I proposed, kenosis and priesthood are united in a single narrative. These two strands, central to my thesis, combine in the Epistle through notions of mutual participation and representation, demonstrated by the interchange of gifts as the outworking of the respective vocations of the principal characters. The primary example of identification through mutual interchange is set out in the *carmen Christi* and is reflected or repeated, albeit non-identically, in the lives of Paul and the Philippian Church. Throughout Part I the emphasis was upon the divine-human encounter. While in Chapter 3 the narrative begins with God's act in Jesus Christ and concludes with the human response, in Part II the emphasis will be re-orientated and I shall examine the human-divine encounter and consequent relationship.

In Chapter 2 I demonstrated that Barth, Balthasar and Moltmann all employ the language of kenosis. Though each usage is distinct they all develop kenosis as the exteriorisation of the Trinity in the economy of salvation. In Chapter 3 true identity, which exists in the dialectic of what is and is to come, is revealed in the christlikeness of the community of faith. In the mimetic economy the divine revelation in Jesus Christ who is truly God and truly man, the original precedes, thereby identifying, the copy or likeness. As Oliver Davies says, listening "and speaking are the two pulsations of the Christian response" to God's prior act of sovereign grace in his self-revelation in Jesus Christ. For "speaking without listening is to fail to speak with the other, and listening without speaking is a failure to be drawn into the conversation". Furthermore the "contours of Christian faith follow the structure, form and content of the Christian revelation" which "is dialectical" and whose "content and substance" is located in "the kenosis of radical discipleship".[1]

In this Chapter I shall develop this conversation further in order to trace the relationship between the divine identity – kenotically revealed – and the

---

[1] Oliver Davies, *A Theology of Compassion*, London, SCM, 2001, 212.

kenosis of discipleship and vocation. Once again I shall develop this in conversation with Barth, Balthasar and Moltmann. However, since my previous discussion of the work of these three theologians two changes will be apparent. First, the differences between all three dialogue partners will become more marked when discussing anthropology, ecclesiology and vocation. Secondly, in this Chapter, I shall begin with an analysis of the theology of Balthasar and Moltmann. This is because I shall argue that both Balthasar and Moltmann are limited by their presuppositions.[2] In the light of which I shall proceed to examine the work of Karl Barth as offering a more coherently consistent and imaginative understanding of anthropology, ecclesiology and vocation within the structure of his theology overall. This coherence, consistency and imaginative development I shall suggest is a result of the foundational status he attributes to election and covenant, his particularism, his maintenance of the Chalcedonian pattern and the dialectical structure of his theology. Crucially for my thesis, I shall argue that by applying Barth's insights to 1 Peter 2.4-10 it is possible to suggest the basis for the development of a Protestant understanding of priesthood.

Vocation in the Theology of Hans Urs von Balthasar

Vocation forms a significant aspect of Balthasar's theology. Its origins lie in his theology of God as Trinity, in the concepts of *processio* and *missio*. In Part I, I proposed that kenosis attempts to explore the identity of God in Jesus Christ who is both God and man but such that both natures co-exist fully and without confusion. As a consequence I suggested that by analogy the priesthood of the ordained must exist within the integrity of its human identity in relation to God. I shall now develop this further in relation to Balthasar's understanding of anthropology, ecclesiology and vocation[3] and their interrelatedness. The question is whether he remains true to the 'structure, form and content of the Christian revelation' that he has established.

Drawing upon Hegel's typology of the poetic, Balthasar argues that life can be interpreted through the concept of theo-drama.[4] As a result of his indebtedness to Hegel, he is not as free from the failings of modernity as he

---

[2] In Balthasar's case his adherence to a conservative Roman Catholic ecclesiology whereas for Moltmann his dependence upon his Reformation inheritance.

[3] For the purposes of this study I shall pay particular, though not exclusive, attention to *Theo-Drama*.

[4] Ben Quash ('Drama and the Ends of Modernity', Lucy Gardiner, David Moss, Ben Quash, Graham Ward, *Balthasar at the End of Modernity*, Edinburgh, T & T Clark, 1999, 145.). There is also a full critique of Balthasar's use of Hegel in J. B. Quash, '"Between The Brutally Given, And The Brutely, Banally Free": von Balthasar's Theology of Drama in Dialogue with Hegel', Modern Theology, (13), 1997, 293-318.

Vocation and Priesthood

perhaps supposes.[5] Life is a series of actions between agents, and because the fundamental drama occurs in the encounter between God and the created world, it is theo-drama. It is therefore important to identify both the events of the drama and the characters.[6] Because of the need for characterisation within a dramatic narrative account, I shall focus upon the 'role' taken by the Church, as a character in the theo-drama (Ephesians is a favoured text), which is central to Balthasar's theology. The Church is the locus of the presence of Christ, in word and sacrament. For Balthasar the Church is a divinely established institution, manifested in human history. In this drama Peter and Mary model vocation as the response of faith to Christ and his saving act.

In Balthasar's trinitarian and dramatic theology the first question is not: 'What kind of being is Jesus Christ?' but 'Who is Jesus Christ?'[7] The same question also identifies the principal characters in the theo-drama. Therefore the second key question is: "How did Jesus understand his mission within the span of life granted him?"[8] He asks:

> Might not Jesus' consciousness of his mission have been that he had to abolish the world's estrangement from God in its entirety… in Pauline and Johannine terms, deal with the sin of the whole world?[9]

Similarly the other characters in the theo-drama can only be understood in terms of mission. That Jesus' identity can be understood in terms of authorial intent,[10] is consequent upon his trinitarian life and being. Emphasising the coincidence of mission and identity, Balthasar draws upon Aquinas who

> describes this identity by saying that in Christ the *processio* within the godhead, which constitutes the Son as the Father's dialogue partner, is identical, in God's going-out-from-himself toward the world, with the

---

[5] Gardiner *et. al.*, 1999, 159.

[6] See: 55 above.

[7] The question as I have posed it is not actually Balthasar's, who asks '*What* kind of being is man?' (*TD* I, 482 (his italics.) For a fuller discussion, see: *TD* I, 481-491, 591; *TD* II, 80). Therefore 'the mystery of the Kenosis whose first result is the incarnation…. not the language of "self-consciousness" but of mission.' Hans Urs von Balthasar, *Mysterium Paschale* (ET), Edinburgh, T & T Clark, 1990b, 90-91. (See also: the Introduction)

[8] *TD* III, 86.

[9] *TD* III, 110.

[10] Balthasar expresses authorial intent in a trinitarian context by reference to the concepts of *missio* and *processio*. (*TD* II, 91.)

missio, the sending of the Son to mankind.[11]

This identity is fundamentally kenotic and dramatic. The *Carmen Christi* provides an account of his collapse and rebirth, through which "he maintains his identity; and so... he embodies the absolute drama in his own person, in his personal mission."[12]

Therefore just as in the missionary imperative of the Incarnation the being of the Son is in the process of becoming, so too according to Balthasar's anthropology, humanity is in the process of becoming. Humanity's goal, reflecting the Incarnation, is: "a bodiliness in whose spirit the Spirit of God dwells... this is the human person arrived at the point to which Jesus wished to bring him."[13] Being in the image of God a human "is created different from the other beings and is placed in a particular 'relation' to God".[14] Furthermore the image of God can only be understood christologically.[15] Christ, in his kenosis, provides the basic analogy revealing what it is to be both fully divine and wholly human.[16] Despite humanity's fallenness the image remains, showing "some traits of this mystery."[17] Like Jesus Christ, humanity is defined in relation to God as Trinity and therefore by his place in the theo-drama, the stage upon which the infinite and triune God and the created and finite world encounter one another.

The central figure in the drama is Jesus Christ, in whom both God and man participate, and therefore encounter one another. It is the divine mission, embodied in the Incarnate Son, which lies at the heart of the emplotment of the theo-drama.[18] Two features emerge. First the divine drama of the two natures of Jesus "determines all anthropology."[19] Secondly, echoing Aristotelian narrative theory, "we see that the condition in which man finds himself can only be one 'scene' within a dramatic action; it points back to his origins and forward to his destination".[20] A human being

---

[11] *TD* I, 646.

[12] *TD* III, 162, 201.

[13] Hans Urs von Balthasar, *Explorations in Theology II, The Spouse of the Word* (ET), San Francisco, Ignatius Press, 1991, 354.

[14] *TD* II, 320.

[15] *TD* II, 407.

[16] *TD* III, 13.

[17] *TD* II, 345. Angelo Scola observes that for Balthasar 'man, the image of God, is simply the silhouette that finds its luminous figure only in Christ. God true to his original decree, reveals himself only in Christ, the authentic *ex-egesis* of God' (Angelo Scola, *Hans Urs von Balthasar, A Theological Style*, Edinburgh, 1995, 49 – his italics).

[18] Scola, 1995, 84.

[19] *TD* II, 407.

[20] *TD* II, 337.

cannot step out of the dramatic action in which he finds himself in order to reflect on which part he will play. He is part of the play without having been asked, and in fact he plays a role. But which role?[21]

At the very heart of his theo-dramatic anthropology is a question of soteriology from which emerges vocation. Jesus, in dying on the cross, "identifies himself with all that is anti-God" and it is in "the event of Christ's Resurrection" that liberation is possible and "the 'Old Adam'... is transcended in the 'New Adam'"[22] This is Jesus' vocation. Balthasar is correct that for the dramatic there must be movement between two agents but the weakness of the adamic understanding is that this appears to require a mediatory figure, who stands between the two parties.[23] The question is therefore: what does between mean in the context of drama? This becomes even more acute when Balthasar extends dramatic theory to articulate the human-divine encounter.

For Balthasar, the drama lies in the life and death struggle between the finite and the infinite, the divine and the human, a struggle in which vocation is the search for identity in this dialectic.[24] Balthasar's dramatic anthropology is one which is "drawn from the drama which God has already 'staged' with the world and with man, in which we find ourselves players."[25] It therefore revolves around the human-divine ('I'-'Thou') relationship[26] and "if we want to ask about man's 'essence', we can do so only in the midst of his dramatic performance of existence. There is no other anthropology but the dramatic."[27]

But this quote highlights a further issue, that of Balthasar's inherent idealism and non-particularity.[28] This is most apparent in his treatment of

---

[21] *TD* II, 341.

[22] *TD* II, 410.

[23] For Balthasar's use of an Adamic Christology, see: *TD* II, 325, 406, 409, 413, 414, 428; also Hans Urs von Balthasar (ET), *The Office of Peter and the Structure of the Church*, San Francisco, Ignatius Press, 1986, 184, 204.

[24] Balthasar - for whom identity can only exist in an 'I'-'thou' relationship with another, and supremely the other is the divine - therefore inverts the Hegelian understanding, outlined by Judith Butler (Judith Butler, *Subjects of Desire*, New York, Columbia University Press, 1999, 51).

[25] *TD* II, 9. Balthasar describes mankind, theologically, on the basis of a three act drama in which the first act, is the *status naturae integrae*, the second is the *status naturae lapsae*, and the last act, the *status naturae glorificatae* in which man is becoming 'God's partner' (*TD* II, 335).

[26] *TD* II, 54.

[27] *TD* II, 335.

[28] For example Balthasar's reference to 'man's "*essence*"' (my italics). According to Umberto Eco '[t]he problem is that man always talks in general while things are

Mary and Peter not simply as individual characters in the drama but as offering an ahistorical anthropological typology.[29] Balthasar speaks of the Marian and Petrine principles, which connect his anthropology and ecclesiology, developing it beyond the straightforwardly Christological. This development throws into sharp relief the difference between von Balthasar's methodology and that of Protestant theologians.

In order to establish Mary's role Balthasar sidesteps the biblically limited account by means of a threefold hermeneutical approach. First, much of his textual engagement utilises what is essentially an allegorical, and pre-modern approach rooted in a Patristic and Medieval understanding,[30] and which appears unrestrained[31] by any attempt to read the 'plain sense' of the passage.[32] Secondly, following the Fathers, Balthasar tends to use what might be described as a canonical reading of Scripture, interpreting the Old

---

singular.' (Umberto Eco, *Kant and the Platypus* (ET), London, Vintage, 2000, 23 – his italics.)

[29] Balthasar's theology of history is derived from the encounter between Christ the Son of the Father, as the eternal one who stands outside time but yet who in his kenosis descends 'into history' (Hans Urs von Balthasar, *A Theology of History* (ET), London, Sheed and Ward, 1964, 70) and the tension between the 'natural and the supernatural' (Balthasar, 1964, 116.) in which the Christian must exist, such that the 'meaning of history must emerge from the union of what God destines for it within its own interior line of development.' (Balthasar, 1964, 123.) According to Balthasar, Mariology 'is surely the supreme example of how the Holy Spirit interprets the Lord's life' (Balthasar, 1964, 104). In this Mary is the one who appears to offer a bridge between divine time and human or chronological time as the one through whom the divine enters history (Balthasar, 1964, 39, 56, 120.). 'Thus there is nothing in all the field of history more validly eloquent than the whole pattern of Mary's life' (Balthasar, 1964, 121).

[30] Three examples of Balthasar's creative handling of the text will serve: Ephesians 5.27 and the Immaculate Conception (Balthasar, 1986, 212.); Rev 12.1-6, in which 'Mary, in giving birth spiritually and physically to the Son, becomes the universal Mother of all believers, for the Church as a body is born of Christ and is herself Christ.' (Balthasar, 1991, 165.); referring to Mary's appearances in the annunciation, birth and the cross narratives that she is seen: 'being Mother and becoming a Bride (at the Cross and when the Church comes forth from Christ's side)' (*TD* III, 305).

[31] Henri de Lubac, *Catholicism* (ET), London, Burn and Oates, 1962, 81.

[32] According to Luther 'no allegory, or tropology or anagogy is valid, unless the same truth is explicitly stated in historical manner somewhere else.' (Quoted: Alister McGrath (ed), *The Christian Theology Reader*, Oxford, Blackwell, 1995, 55. See also: Richard Hooker, *The Laws of Ecclesiastical Polity*, V.lix. 2.) According to David Moss and Lucy Gardiner, while Balthasar claims that his Mariology is firmly rooted in the gospel accounts he is in danger of writing them out of his own text. (David Moss and Lucy Gardiner, 'Difference – the Immaculate Concept? The Laws Of Sexual Difference In The Theology Of Hans Urs von Balthasar', Modern Theology (14), 1998, 391-92.)

Testament by means of the New.[33] At the same time, like post-Enlightenment readers, he seeks universal timeless truths in his apparent willingness to over-ride the specificity of the text, whether in time, context or authorial intent.[34] Finally, in line with traditional Catholic practice, Balthasar reads Scripture in the light of tradition following the Tridentine method.[35] The Reformers cry of *sola scriptura*, that Scripture "containeth all things necessary to salvation"[36] did not seek to establish biblical literalism. The magisterial Reformers continued to interpret Scripture in the light of *traditio*, appealing to the Fathers and to the ecumenical creeds. Rather they sought to establish Scripture as the primary norm and basis for all doctrinal statements.[37]

One consequence of his hermeneutical approach is the roles allotted to Peter and Mary embodying the character of the Church within the theo-drama.[38] According to Balthasar, Peter signifies 'office' and 'objectivity'[39] whereas Mary signifies 'the feminine' and the 'subjective'.[40] This creates several problems. First, Balthasar does not explicitly define how he understands 'office' although he does attempt to make a distinction between 'office' and 'charism'.[41] While Balthasar does not deny the possibility of lay offices, the primary locus of office is hierarchical and clerical, 'for the building up of the body of Christ.'[42] What he proposes is a tiered structure not simply of the Church but seemingly of those who would identify themselves, in Paul's phrase, ἐν Χριστῷ. This seems to create something

---

[33] Balthasar on Eve and Mary; Eph 5.25-33. (See: Balthasar, 1986, 188. Gen 3.20; and *TD* III, 293: or Reading the Song of Songs as being about Mary; *TD* III, 309.) Walter Brueggemann comments that such an approach 'overrides and distorts the specificity of the text.' (Walter Brueggemann, *Theology of the Old Testament*, Minneapolis, Fortress Press, 1997, 85.)

[34] Quash, 1997, 308.

[35] 'All saving truths and rules of conduct… are contained in the written books and in the unwritten traditions, received from the mouth of Christ himself or the apostles themselves.' (The Fourth Session Of The Council of Trent (1546), quoted: Alister E. McGrath, *Reformation Thought* (2nd Edn), Oxford, Blackwell, 1993, 155.) Balthasar, like the Tridentine authors, understands Scripture and Tradition as having an equal authority for the Christian community whereas the Reformers regarded Tradition as standing under the authority of Scripture.

[36] The Thirty-Nine Articles, Article VI.

[37] Jaroslav Pelikan, *The Christian Tradition: The Reformation of Church and Dogma*, Chicago, Chicago University Press, 1985, vii.

[38] *TD* III, 352-355. (See: Scola, 1995, 98).

[39] *TD* III, 356-57.

[40] Balthasar, 1991, 161.

[41] Balthasar, 1991, 308, 313, 314.

[42] Eph 4.12.

of a fracture in the christological and trinitarian structure of his theology.[43] The clerical and hierarchical office is the guarantee whereby the faith is received and handed on in the succession established by Christ through Peter.[44] Commissioned by Jesus (Matt 16.18),

> Peter's (negative) infallibility and (positive) gift of teaching and being a shepherd make visible the indefectability of faith in Christ and of the deeply 'knowing' 'instinct' of following him... which belongs to the Church as a whole and has its home in the *sensus fidelium*.[45]

The objectivity of the Petrine Office stands in contradistinction to the subjectivity of the Marian faith. This is the believer's experience of faith, exemplified supremely in the Marian 'Yes'[46] as distinct from the "authority's official knowledge, which is imparted directly by Christ."[47] The Office, established through the hierarchy, is the ecclesial faith, which is given to humanity, and is the objective belief to which man must respond. The response is essentially Marian and subjective.

But most significantly, the idealism of Balthasar's concept of 'male' and 'female' and his applications of these to Peter and Mary (and by analogy to the hierarchy and laity of the Church) is purely speculative. "If man is the word that calls out [objective], woman is the answer [subjective] that comes to him".[48] One cannot underestimate the importance of the annunciation theme within Balthasar's thought. It is Mary's vocation to be the mother of the Redeemer,[49] the fulfilment of femininity in which she is overshadowed by the Holy Spirit.[50] Mary "is the model of the holy Church, spiritually bringing children to birth"[51] so the "maternal womb of Mary and of the Church are seen as strictly identical".[52] Thus the Church embodies subjective feminine characteristics which are receptive and passive, as

---

[43] Balthasar, 1990b, 56.

[44] Balthasar, 1991, 139. Cranmer makes a similar claim in the Introduction to the Ordinal.

[45] Balthasar, 1991, 310.

[46] Balthasar, 1986, 206. See: also Balthasar, 1991, 310 and Balthasar, 1992, 323, 338, 351-2, 357.

[47] *TD* III, 358.

[48] *TD* III, 284.

[49] *TD* III, 291.

[50] Balthasar, 1991, 161 and *TD* III, 285.

[51] *TD* III, 305. Aidan Nichols suggests Balthasar may be playing 'on the etymological fact that, in German, "word" (*Wort*) is masculine whereas "answer" (*Antwort*) is feminine' (Aidan Nichols, *No Bloodless Myth*, Edinburgh, T & T Clark, 2000, 109). However, this cannot be the case as in German '*Wort*' is not masculine, but neuter. (I am grateful to Dr Margaret Ives for pointing this out.)

[52] *TD* III, 327. (Quoting: Ireneaus).

Vocation and Priesthood 115

exemplified in Mary. Office, exemplified by Peter, is masculine, giving, communicating and impregnating.[53]

Balthasar's notions of 'objective/subjective'[54] and 'male/female' in relation to Peter and Mary are unsatisfactory. As Mary Daly says, women "are not symbols; they are people, and each person is a unique subject."[55] Balthasar's idealism removes them as flesh and blood[56] and they are re-interpreted as 'types'.[57] The insubstantial description of Mary's nature reflects Balthasar's theology of history. So the positioning of Mary as one who stands between God and man is as problematic as the 'when' that connects time and eternity. Mary becomes an intermediary, neither wholly divine[58] nor yet quite recognisably human.[59] This confuses the role of Christ, who is both eternal and historic, who stands not simply between, but with God and man.[60] Balthasar compounds the insubstantial nature of Mary as the one who stands between by emphasising her immaculateness. Rejecting Augustine's anti-Pelagianism, which "sees sin present everywhere"[61] Balthasar argues that Mary's immaculateness is necessary to her role as the bearer of the Son of God. This requires that she "stands outside the fallen world".[62] The effect is to diminish Mary's genuine

---

[53] Balthasar, 1986, 183 See also: Balthasar, 1991, 158. For a critique of this active/passive conceptualisation of male/female: see: Ann Loades, 'The Virgin Mary and the Feminist Quest', Janet Martin Soskice (ed), *After Eve*, London, Collins, 1990, 156-178. Furthermore there has not been space to explore the conflicting sexual images of Mary as bride and mother in relation to her virgin status, which Balthasar acknowledges. (*TD* III, 309.)

[54] Quash suggests that Balthasar's 'ecclesiology which attributes a dimension of "objective" holiness to the Church' (Quash, 1997, 303.) is a consequence of his dependence upon Hegel's dramatic typology for his dramatic theology.

[55] Mary Daly, *The Church and the Second Sex*, London, Geoffrey Chapman, 1968, 119.

[56] Nicola Slee, 'Parables and Women's Experience', Modern Churchman (26), 1984, 21). See also: Angela West, *Deadly Innocence*, London, Cassell, 1995, 212.

[57] Moss and Gardiner, 1998, 386. Elsewhere Ben Quash says that this 'enables Balthasar in his ecclesiology to structure atemporally what is a phenomenon that ought to have an irreducibly temporal aspect, namely the Church itself.' (Quash, 1999, 160.)

[58] *TD* III, 310, 312.

[59] Accordingly 'if Mary is to be the true Mother of the Redeemer, she must genuinely belong to the race of Adam, which stands in need of redemption, at the same time, if she is to be his Mother she needs to be entirely holy, "immaculate".' (*TD* III, 319.)

[60] Lucy Gardiner, David Moss, 'Something like Time; Something like the Sexes – an essay in reception' Gardiner et. al., 1999, 108, the section subtitled *Mary the atemporal 'between'*. See also: Moss and Gardiner, 1998, 389.

[61] Balthasar, 1991, 178.

[62] Hans Urs von Balthasar, *The Christian State of Life*, San Francisco, Ignatius Press, 1983, 201. However, he appears to contradict this statement elsewhere. (Balthasar, 1992, 290.)

humanity,[63] because she is distinct from the rest of humanity who "have gone into an alien place far from God."[64]

However, the contrast between the receptive and passive female and the giving, communicating and impregnating male is unsustainable. The roots of this attitude are to be found in the analogy of 'male is to female as form is to matter'. Thus the man impregnates the woman who receives and nurtures the seed. But such a theory "has been untenable without considerable qualification since the beginning of embryology from the early nineteenth century onwards".[65] Balthasar's attempt to make a clear distinction between male and female as the basis for ecclesiology ignores the "significant similarities and overlaps" between the sexes.[66]

The Petrine and Marian principles proposed by Balthasar result in a false imagining[67] of the narrative in which he fails to maintain a consistency of 'structure, form and content of the Christian revelation' previously established in trinitarian kenosis.[68] First, in Balthasar's mimetic economy, both Mary and Peter are *typoi* of being the Church, and therefore being Christian.[69] The model to be imitated is idealised, abstract and impersonal. By contrast in Philippians Paul offers himself as a 'prototype'[70] which is repeatable and can be lived by others.[71] For Paul this is essentially charismatic[72] whereas according to Sarah Coakley for Balthasar "the Virgin *replaces* the (ineffectual?) Spirit"[73] undermining his trinitarianism by the

---

[63] Ann Loades, *Searching for Lost Coins*, London, SPCK, 1987, 80.

[64] Balthasar, 1991, 180. In his phraseology there are overtones of Barth, and the notion of Jesus Christ whose mission is to go 'into a far country' (*CD* IV.1 157-210.), except that into this space Balthasar introduces Mary as the locus of the activity of God the Father in the power of the Spirit.

[65] Loades, 1987, 81.

[66] Elaine Graham, 'Gender, Personhood and Theology', SJT (48), 1995, 345.

[67] Eberhard Jüngel is highly critical of the form of exaggerated Mariology asking: 'What are we to make of the fact that in the *Dogmatic Constitution concerning the Church* [upheld by Balthasar as a vital aspect of the Church, Balthasar, 1986, 202-204] Mary can be described as "cause of salvation" and… Mediatrix… How do we reconcile talking of Mary as mediatrix with the declaration that Christ is the one (single) mediator?' (Eberhard Jüngel, *Justification* (ET), Edinburgh, T & T Clark, 2001, 170-171.) '[W]e can honour Mary as the model of a believer. But there is no question of the believer, or of course of Mary, being a cause of salvation' (Jüngel, 2001, 179).

[68] See: 72 above.

[69] *TD* III, 333.

[70] Phil. 3.17. Balthasar recognises that Paul is offering himself and not an office to be imitated. (Balthasar, 1991, 116.)

[71] Phil. 3.17 'fellow imitators' – συμμιμηταί.

[72] Edward Schillebeeckx, *The Church with a Human Face* (ET), London, SCM, 1985, 74 – 123.

[73] Sarah Coakley, 'Creaturehood before God', Theology (XLIII), 1990, 346 – her italics. This may also be suggestive of the perceived role of the Spirit within any possible

weakness of his pneumatology.[74] Furthermore it is impossible to imitate an office, only the office holder and is indicative of an institutional ecclesiology.[75] There is an uncertainty in the narrative he wishes to relate concerning the relationship between *typos* and office and therefore the role of the pneumatological.[76]

Secondly, as *typos*, Mary is important for Balthasar's theo-dramatic scheme "because her existence lies between the various states of human nature."[77] Peter's dramatic character is established as a "member of the Marian Church"[78] in which he 'stands between'[79] as "a bridge between the real rock, Christ... and the rock of the Church"[80] and as the one to whom the keys are given (Matt 16.18).[81] Thus *communio* in and through Peter (and his successors) guarantees the apostolicity of the Church.[82] It is through the elevation of the roles of Peter and Mary that the Church is effectively a 'character' in the theo-drama. Again this undermines the pneumatalogical in Balthasar's ecclesiology.

Balthasar correctly recognises the importance of movement in drama, but a weakness is his emphasis upon the mediatory, focused in the one who 'stands between'. Effectively he resolves the dialectic of Peter and Mary as human characters in the human-divine drama by seeking to establish them

---

trinitarian hierarchy. (Coakley, 1990, 344-45.) Once again Balthasar is not innovating but following a pre-existent strand in Western Medieval thought.

[74] John Webster, 'The Self-Organizing Power Of The Gospel of Christ: Episcopacy And Community Formation', *Word and Church*, Edinburgh, T & T Clark, 2001, 198. Consequently 'human acts of ministry threaten to assume his [Jesus Christ's] role' and result in the gifts of the Spirit being understood as 'manipulable possessions rather than as events of relation.' (Webster, 2001, 199.)

[75] See: Avery Dulles, *Models of the Church*, Dublin, Gill and Macmillan, 1983. According to Balthasar the 'answer lies in the creation of the Church as an "institution" ' and that every 'institutional aspect of the Church was prepared by Jesus during his public ministry.' (*TD* III, 354, see also: 325, 423, 430, 448.) Of course Balthasar's ecclesiology is not so simplistic. Balthasar also draws heavily upon the notion of the Church as Sacrament (*TD* III, 429, 432.), a model particularly favoured by Henri de de Lubac. (Lubac, 1962, 28.) Balthasar repeats the notion of office discerned by Ernst Troeltsch in which the episcopate (office) 'was substituted for the earlier faith in the Exalted Christ and the Spirit'. (E. Troeltsch, *The Social Teaching of the Christian Churches*, London, 1931, 92, quoted Stephen Sykes, *The Identity of Christianity*, Philadelphia, Fortress Press, 1984, 63.)

[76] See: 'Charis and Charisma', Balthasar, 1991, 301 – 314.

[77] *TD* III, 318.

[78] Balthasar, 1986, 210.

[79] Balthasar, 1986, 149. So Balthasar suggests that Peter is called Simon Peter to indicate the duality of his character.

[80] Balthasar, 1986, 280.

[81] Balthasar, 1986, 210; Balthasar, 1991, 112.

[82] Balthasar, 1986, 164.

as at best not truly human and possibly quasi-divine figures. Consequently the Church, because it is Petrine and Marian, then emerges as a composite divinely instituted, idealised and therefore flawed 'character' in the theo-drama. A pneumatic notion of the Church has a more coherent unity, particularly within a fundamentally trinitarian theological structure. Another important consequence of Balthasar's ecclesiology and anthropology in relation to both Peter and Mary is that it establishes a mediatory role between humanity and God. Initially this is focussed in Peter and Mary who are required to sacrifice their true humanity in order to fulfil their ahistorical and idealised roles. But this also applies to the Church, as the divinely instituted mediator of the faith through the ordained priesthood in the line of Peter. There is within this economy sacrifice as loss with the implication that humanity, albeit through these ahistorical figures or the priestly office, cooperates in its salvation.

Anthropologically, in the theo-drama, existence and therefore identity is invested in role. The *dramatis personae* are those who become characters by virtue of their roles in the action. Role becomes a means of identifying the elusive 'I'. Mission is that which unites the 'I' and the 'role' by externalising the relationship as a result of which they become God's "fellow-agent."[83] Personhood includes the dramatic notions of 'mask' and 'role', which unite both the 'I' and the social role.[84] Mission is vocational, moving the individual from the impersonal role to the "genuinely dramatic role... of life" in the "unique 'name'... of the individual addressed by God".[85]

Humanity becomes, through participation in the divine mission, God's partner.[86] As the Son is named in his mission, so too being chosen and being named by God is the way the individual "becomes a unique person."[87] In this way the "individual is transformed by being addressed by God, being called and sent forth"[88] to fulfil her divinely given role. Identity and vocation are consequent upon mission. Calling and naming is unique to each individual except for Mary and Peter, when it is also prototypical, which would seem to confirm their segregation from humanity as a whole.

In the "acting area opened by Christ" humanity is given the 'role' of becoming a 'co-actor' "in the theo-drama" affirming "the election, vocation and mission which God in sovereign freedom offers him"[89] whereby the

---

[83] Nichols, 2000, 41.
[84] *TD* I, 517-18.
[85] *TD* I, 645.
[86] *TD* II, 335.
[87] *TD* II, 402.
[88] *TD* II, 414.
[89] *TD* III, 263.

individual becomes a person.[90] This has overtones of Philippians 3 in which identity is 'not yet' but in the process of becoming.[91] The person is the one who imitates Christ by their presence in the theo-drama ἐν Χριστῷ except that unlike Christ "there is no identity between their (eternal) election and their (temporal) vocation and mission."[92] This is a crucial distinction. Election, vocation and mission are the means by which man is identified as being ἐν Χριστῷ. But this is a mimetic representation of Christ's total identity with his (eternal) mission, vocation and election. It is precisely this distinction which appears to be blurred with regards to Peter and Mary's election, vocation and mission as a consequence of their mediatorial status.

A person is one who is "positively endowed with missions ('charisms') that make them persons of profile and quality *within the prototypical mission of Jesus.*"[93] Balthasar's theo-dramatic interpretation of vocation is one of narrative participation. Theologically election, vocation and mission "are always pure grace."[94] Consequentially the man "who is called becomes himself by serving and sharing in God's work in Jesus Christ."[95]

Two factors have emerged in this discussion of Balthasar's anthropology, ecclesiology and vocation. On the one hand the hierarchical nature implicit in his anthropology, in relation to Mary and Peter and made explicit in his ecclesiology, results in a priestly testimony, in which the ordained, in the line of Peter, represent objective faith and stand in a particular relationship over and above the non-ordained. As Nichol's recognises, according to Balthasar, the Church "in her Christic foundation"[96] is a sacrament in its divinely given hierarchy. This exists in the complex hierarchy which extends from the divine (including Christ) through Mary, Peter and the λαος; between the laity and the ordained; between male and female.[97] In this he traces a different form and content to the trinitarian structure of his kenotic theology of the divine identity. In his anthropology and ecclesiology there appears to be a confusion of identities. This confusion has implications for the nature of the priesthood. Furthermore allied with Mary's immaculateness and Peter's and the Church's infallibility, not only are their characters sacrificed, but the sacrifice effectively enables them to participate as agents in the crossing of the human-divine *diastasis*. In this the institution of the Church grounded in the persons of Mary and Peter encroaches upon the role of the Holy Spirit.

---

[90] *TD* III, 207.
[91] Phil 3.12-21. (See: 88 above.)
[92] *TD* III, 263.
[93] *TD* III, 231 (my italics).
[94] *TD* III, 269.
[95] *TD* III, 269.
[96] Nichols, 2000, 124.
[97] *TD* III, 430.

The Church, Mary and Peter all appear to fulfil a mediatory role in the theo-drama, standing between humanity and God. Implicit within this is a notion that humanity can co-operate in its own salvation. He thus repeats the traditional priestly testimony, of the intermediary through whom access to God is made possible and which is rejected by Protestant theology.

On the other hand Balthasar is consistent in his articulation of vocation with the kenotic narrative he sets out elsewhere.[98] Vocation is the participation of the person within the theo-drama so that not only do they hear God's Word, but in turn they are able to speak, to respond. Vocation is responsive to the prior sovereign act of God revealed in the theo-drama of salvation. Vocation does not distinguish, theoretically at least, between the ordained and the non-ordained. Thus Balthasar provides a warning of the consequences of the failure to maintain an appropriate characterisation of all the parties in the narrative. But he also provides an understanding of vocation, which is missiological, an event of grace and therefore responsive.

Vocation in the Theology of Jürgen Moltmann

Moltmann's theology highlights the problems with vocation and priesthood for Reformed theology.[99] There is an outward similarity in theological procedure with Balthasar since both begin with God as Trinity. Anthropologically Moltmann, like Balthasar, takes his cue from the notion of the *imago Dei* as revealed in Christ through the *missio dei*. This is significant in Moltmann's ecclesiology and his notion of vocation. According to Moltmann, the identity of God is revealed through the cross,[100] an interior mystery, which is trinitarian.[101] Kenosis is that by which God is recognisable bridging "the ontological gap between God and his creatures".[102] This is the image of God, revealed in the kenotic identity of Jesus Christ,[103] which forms the basis of Moltmann's anthropology.[104]

A second strand in Moltmann's anthropology is his political agenda expressed as human rights,[105] conflating modernity's project and theology's task. This introduces an overtly phenomenological element to his

---

[98] See: Chapter 3 above.
[99] Jürgen Moltmann, *The Church in the Power of the Spirit* (ET), London, SCM, 1977, 245f.
[100] See: 62 above.
[101] Moltmann, *The Crucified God* (ET), London, SCM, 1974, 204.
[102] Douglas B. Farrow, 'In The End Is The Beginning: A Review Of Jürgen Moltmann's Systematic Contributions', *Modern Theology* (14), 1998, 425-447, 438.
[103] Jürgen Moltmann, *On Human Dignity* (ET), SCM, London, 1984, 22.
[104] Moltmann, 1974, 70, 96, 212.
[105] Moltmann, 1984, 20.

theological anthropology. Like Balthasar, though for different reasons, he privileges the universal over the particular, weakening the characterisation of the person in the narrative as a whole. Nonetheless his account of anthropology remains grounded in the divine-human encounter. Moltmann suggests that in the Old Testament the basic categories by which humanity encounters God are liberation, covenant and the claim of God. In the New Testament "the liberation of human beings from sin, law, and death through the coming, the sacrifice, and the resurrection of Jesus Christ "[106] makes possible "the realisation of their human destiny as the image of God in the world."[107] As Christ is the image of God, so men and women are to be the image of Christ[108] as the one who is 'truly man'. What he outlines might be described as a christologically sacrificial and priestly anthropology, though Moltmann would balk at the use of such language.[109]

According to Moltmann Christology is "the dominant theme of ecclesiology."[110] Therefore if

> the church sees itself to be sent in the same framework as the Father's sending of the Son and the Holy Spirit, then it sees itself in the framework of God's history.[111]

Unlike Balthasar, for Moltmann the Church is neither an institution nor a sacrament providing a "representation of the history of Christ".[112] Following the classic Protestant line, Moltmann's ecclesiology proceeds from the doctrine of justification so that the Church is the community of those who are justified by faith.[113] Neither does Moltmann's ecclesiology fall into Balthasar's failure to acknowledge the role of the Spirit. In his quest for an ecumenical doctrine of the Church,[114] Moltmann draws upon the Orthodox tradition, to restore the pneumatological alongside the

---

[106] Moltmann, 1984, 21.
[107] Moltmann, 1984, 22.
[108] Moltmann, 1984, 21-22.
[109] Moltmann, 1977, 173-74. He continues to develop this theme, not explicitly in terms of priesthood but of political theology suggesting that domination 'suppresses and exploits, isolates and leads through isolation to lack of relationship; and that means death.' (Moltmann, 1977, 175. See also: *Christianity in the Process of Economic Life: Symbiosis,* Moltmann, 1977, 168-176.)
[110] Moltmann, 1977, 6.
[111] Moltmann, 1977, 11.
[112] Moltmann, 1977, 26.
[113] Moltmann, 1977, 35. If Moltmann understands the Church as the community of the elect, Barth, while remaining within the Reformed tradition, regards the Church as the elect community. (See: 134 below.)
[114] Moltmann, 1977, xv.

christological.[115] The Church is shaped by Christ and empowered by the Spirit, but remains a human community and fallen, while retaining a sense of being in the 'image of God'[116] and therefore trinitarian in shape. The mission of the Church re-echoes the trinitarian mission[117] in which the Trinity is not a closed circle, symbolic of perfection, because the "triune God is the God who is open to man, open to the world and open to time."[118] Moltmann attributes this openness to the Spirit.[119] The Church which "lives in the 'today' of Christ's messianic mission and presence"[120] is also concerned for the divine *doxa*. But the *theologia crucis* dictates that the glorification of the Father is fellowship "with Christ in the Spirit [which] is the fellowship of Christ's sufferings and the fellowship of his death." This is "at the same time the fellowship of his resurrection through newness of life".[121]

It is in the light of a theology of glory, focused upon the cross, that Moltmann speaks of the "priestly ministry in the church", which, "must take its bearings from the one who was crucified". This "corresponds in the deepest sense to the glory of the one who became man, the God who humbled himself and whose love reached the point of suffering death."[122] It is therefore the locus where the identification of man as being in the 'image of God' becomes possible.[123]

However,

> there can really be no fundamental division between the general priesthood of all believers and the particular priestly ministry... It is a question for the whole fellowship how it realizes the 'priestly ministry', about which Dietrich Bonhoeffer said that 'participation in the sufferings of God in secular life' makes the Christian.[124]

---

[115] Moltmann, 1977, 36.

[116] This contrasts sharply with Balthasar's notion of the church as a divinely given and infallible institution.

[117] Accordingly the '*missio ad intra* is the foundation of the *missio ad extra*. Thus theological reflection moves inevitably from the contemplation of the sending of Jesus from the Father to God himself.' (Moltmann, 1977, 54.)

[118] Moltmann, 1977, 56.

[119] Moltmann, 1977, 55.

[120] Moltmann, 1977, 48.

[121] Moltmann, 1977, 59. Moltmann has in mind Phil 3.10-11.

[122] Moltmann, 1977, 85. Moltmann has in mind here Phil 2 6-11.

[123] Moltmann suggests that the statement that 'Jesus is the Lord' as a result of his resurrection is open to misunderstanding and again re-echoing Phil 2.9,10 the 'real statement is the reverse: "The Lord is Jesus."' (Moltmann, 1977, 102.)

[124] Moltmann, 1977, 97. According to Moltmann says, 'When the New Testament uses the word "priest" it does not mean any special priestly class.' (Moltmann, 1977, 301.)

Moltmann seeks to develop an understanding of priesthood which is universal and not defined by reference to office.[125] He wishes to describe priesthood by reference to *theologia crucis* as the identifying mark of the Christian. Priesthood is a sacrificial event of kenotic identification. Once again, Moltmann is indebted to Luther when he states that "God's being can be seen and known directly only in the cross of Christ"[126] and is essentially kenotic.[127] It is not kenotic through the surrender of self and loss of identity[128] but rather it is the very opposite. It is "the power of ... God's

---

[125] This can be seen in Moltmann's indebtedness to the work of both Luther and Bonhoeffer concerning vocation. In *Theology of Hope* the final subheading is 'The Calling of Christians in Society', (Jürgen Moltmann, *Theology of Hope* (ET), SCM, London, 1967, 329.) which was precisely what Luther addressed in his writing about vocation. According to Luther 'priests and bishops are neither different from other Christians nor superior to them... except that they are charged with the administration of the word of God and the sacraments, which is their work and office... A cobbler, a smith, a peasant – each has the office and work of his trade, and yet they are all alike consecrated priests and bishops. Further, everyone must benefit and serve every other by means of his own work or office so that in this way many kinds of work may be done for the bodily and spiritual welfare of the community, just as the members of the body serve one another [1 Cor. 12.14-26].' (*To The Christian Nobility of the German Nation Concerning the Reform of the Christian State*, (1520), Luther, *Works* 36, 127-130.) The key text for Luther is I Cor. 12 [.12-13]: priesthood is a vocation like any other in the city of God.

Two consequences of Luther's thought are, first, that there is no Christian hierarchy, (Luther, *Works*, 28, 40.) Secondly, therefore, does he conflate election and vocation into one single concept? In fact Luther wishes to distinguish between call and calling. The call or election is to faith that is open and available to all. This is the primary event. However, calling, or vocation, as living the Christian life on a daily basis in terms of marriage, work, and community, while still universal, is secondary.

A second significant influence upon Moltmann's thinking was the Lutheran, Dietrich Bonhoeffer, who 'fought passionately against' withdrawn piety. (Moltmann, 1977, 283.) It is possible to discern in Bonhoeffer three aspects of call and calling. First, there is the absoluteness of discipleship. For Bonhoeffer the 'gulf between a voluntary offer to follow and genuine discipleship is clear.' (Dietrich Bonhoeffer, *The Cost of Discipleship* (ET), London, SCM, 1976, 51.) Discipleship is fundamentally sacrificial and therefore an aspect of the *theologia crucis*. Secondly, vocation is a necessary aspect of a Christian anthropology, which is Christological. Thus, according to Bonhoeffer the 'form of Jesus Christ takes form in man. Man does not take on an independent form of his own' (Bonhoeffer, *Ethics* (ET), London, SCM, 1985, 63.) Once again Bonhoeffer looks to Phil 1.21 as the source of the identity of man *in Christ*. (Bonhoeffer, 1985, 62.) Thirdly, vocation is 'religionless'. (Dietrich Bonhoeffer, *Letters and Papers from Prison* (ET), London, SCM, 1979, 280f.) Vocation is therefore no longer the property of the Church and cannot be described in terms of office.

[126] Moltmann, 1974, 212.

[127] Moltmann, 1974, 214.

[128] Moltmann, 1974, 214.

potentiality."[129] The divine kenosis, as portrayed in the *theologia crucis*, results not in death or loss but in resurrection and renaming. The crucified Christ becomes the ground of a "new creation, in which death is swallowed up in the victory of life"[130] Like Bonhoeffer, Moltmann wishes to redraw the 'image of God', which has rather been previously mis-identified.[131] But to re-imagine the image of God means to reconsider what it means to speak of humanity as being in His image.[132] A *theologia crucis* redefines priesthood as being in the image of 'Jesus Christ and him crucified'.[133] As a result it contests the *theologia gloriae*, expressive of God in terms of his glorious attributes. Priesthood is vocationally an act of following, responsive to the sovereignly divine initiative of grace. Priesthood is the living witness "from Christ's self-giving and in self-giving for the reconciliation of the world."[134] The sacrifice is of itself, but as in kenosis this does not imply loss but rather re-identification.

The "church of Christ" is the "church under the cross",[135] lived in the experience of the resurrection of Jesus Christ,[136] proclaiming hope and liberation. It is liberation from a false image of God. It liberates from bondage to an institutional 'office' of priests, by recognising that all Christians are a priestly people.[137] The "presence of the Spirit" marks the inauguration of the new creation.[138] Messianic living, or living the new creation, is for the future. However, it is not "life in constant deferment, but life in anticipation"[139] ushered in and therefore present.[140] Anticipation includes the "messianic mediation of what is to come... bound up with representation and self-giving" and is "a fragmentary taking possession" of what is yet to come.[141] The calling of the Church in the power of the Spirit anticipates what is to come.[142]

---

[129] Moltmann, 1974, 215.
[130] Moltmann, 1974, 217.
[131] Bonhoeffer, 1979, 361.
[132] Moltmann would define priesthood in terms of the *theologia crucis*, and not the *theologia gloriae*.
[133] 1 Cor. 2.2.
[134] Moltmann, 1977, 97.
[135] Moltmann, 1977, 97.
[136] Moltmann, 1977, 99.
[137] Following Bonhoeffer Moltmann envisages that 'religionless' Christianity is liberated from a priesthood shaped by a *theologia gloriae* by instead taking its image from a *theologia crucis*.
[138] Moltmann, 1977, 193. (See also: Moltmann, 1974, 217.)
[139] Moltmann, 1977, 193.
[140] Moltmann understands anticipation as 'not yet a fulfilment... [but] part possession of what is still to come.' (Moltmann, 1977, 193.)
[141] Moltmann, 1977, 194.
[142] Moltmann, 1977, 225.

The importance of liberation and anticipation is re-echoed in baptism which "is efficacious *ex verbo vocante*".[143] It is the word of promise that calls to faith, making "clear the believer's Christian identity".[144] Moltmann understands baptism as identificatory and vocational[145] by which the person called is liberated, not for the Church but empowered and equipped by the Spirit for service. The person called ceases to be the object of religious activity but becomes a subject, the one who is active in the life of the church.[146]

Here the Protestant-Catholic divide between the thought of Moltmann and Balthasar concerning ministry is laid bare. First, they employ different hermeneutical methodologies. Secondly, whereas Balthasar emphasises office, the key for Moltmann is charismatic.[147] These differences emerge from their anthropologies, which are both essentially participative, though for different reasons. Balthasar's anthropology is grounded in the participation of the person in the theo-drama but the importance he attaches to the notion of 'standing between' introduces a distinctive mediatory element particularly in relation to the Marian or Petrine Principle and the priestly office in the Church. The participatory nature of Moltmann's anthropology is grounded in the image of God and more directly trinitarian. However, despite these differences, Moltmann and Balthasar have some similarity of intent if not of method, but for different reasons neither successfully manages to get behind modernity.[148]

Moltmann, like Balthasar, wishes to establish the mutual participation of the human and the divine. Moltmann suggests that at the Lord's Supper the saying, 'This is my body... given for you' identifies both the presence and promise of Christ to his people.[149] This is an act of kenotic identification and self-giving. But identity cannot be formless and therefore nameless. As God is given form and named in Jesus Christ, so too Christians who live messianic lives cannot be 'formless'. They must take their identity from the one whose identity is given.[150] Just as the identity of

---

[143] Moltmann, 1977, 240.

[144] Moltmann, 1977, 241. See: Phil. 2.5; 3.12, 14; 4.1,7, 21. See: Chapter 4 above.

[145] Moltmann, 1977, 242.

[146] Moltmann, 1977, 242.

[147] Moltmann emphasises the importance of the Spirit as the power of the church whereas Balthasar stresses the importance of 'office' through which the Pneumatic is channelled by his exploration of the dialectic of the Marian and Petrine principles, and the contrasts of male and female.

[148] Balthasar is dependent upon Hegel's typology as a framework for his theo-dramatic theory; Moltmann's anthropology depends on the assumption of the 'rights' of man.

[149] Moltmann, 1977, 255.

[150] Phil. 2.6-11. Moltmann notes one 'can "lose face" but one cannot live without a face. "Let your manner of life be worthy of – or, in accordance with – the gospel of Christ",

God in Christ is given kenotically, so too it "is only the person who finds himself" in Christ, in the triune history of God, "who can give himself."[151]

According to Moltmann, identity resides in memory[152] and the eucharist is the enacted memory of the death of Christ, a present celebration which also anticipates the future consummation. In this context vocation exists analogically through participation in this narrative identity.[153] As for Luther, the key text is 1 Corinthians 7.[154] Calling takes place in the context of ordinary life and is always orientated towards the world.[155] Like Balthasar, Moltmann acknowledges vocation, but unlike Balthasar, Moltmann explicitly rejects the possibility that different statuses exist in the Christian community,[156] rejecting both office and hierarchy as contrary to the pneumatic oneness of the church.[157] The importance of ministries and structures are as signs of the nature and purpose of the church,[158] in the light of the trinitarian mission of God. They are kenotic and anti-hierarchical mirroring Christ's self-giving as "the point of departure for the conquest of godless and inhuman conditions of rule and oppression".[159] Whereas Balthasar's concept of office leads him to articulate a priestly testimony, conversely Moltmann voices a counter-testimony in which the priesthood of the ordained is denied.

Individual vocation proceeds "from the calling of the community as a whole"[160] to be a kingdom people, priestly in their self-offering and in their intercession for others.[161] This narrative identity is given so they are to "live from the Spirit, in which they experience identity, finding their place and

---

demands Paul (Phil 1.27)… a conduct of life which receives its messianic quality from Christ's gospel' once again referring to the Philippian narrative. (Moltmann, 1977, 276.)

[151] Moltmann, 1977, 285f. It is the centrality of the cross in discipleship and therefore call to which I wish to draw attention in the thinking of Moltmann so repeating the emphasis of *The Crucified Christ*.

[152] Moltmann, 1977, 281. In this Moltmann is indebted to Augustine, *Confessions*.

[153] What he proposes therefore, is a narrative reading according to which life can be understood only as having a beginning (or beginnings), is lived here and now (the middle) but which has a future orientation (or goal) yet to be achieved but which can be anticipated. According to Moltmann therefore, 'the Spirit is not to be apprehended in the ministries of the church, but the church, with its manifold ministries and tasks, is to be conceived in the movement and presence of the Spirit.' (Moltmann, 1977, 289.) Thus this is not an *anologia entis* but *analogia fidei*.

[154] Moltmann, 1977, 296.
[155] Moltmann, 1983, 70 – his italics.
[156] Moltmann, 1977, 324.
[157] Moltmann, 1977, 343.
[158] Moltmann, 1977, 290.
[159] Moltmann, 1977, 292.
[160] Moltmann, 1977, 300.
[161] Moltmann, 1977, 301.

Vocation and Priesthood

their charge in the history of God's kingdom".[162] The 'priesthood of all believers' is commissioning for service or ministry but it does not 'separate'[163] because the Spirit unites "giving everyone his own place and his particular charge."[164] Necessarily therefore all "can become charismatic through a person's call, if only they are used in Christ."[165]

Moltmann abandons all notions of office in the twofold sense that Balthasar speaks of hierarchy and apostolic succession. In defining ministry in terms of the *bene esse* of the Church, Moltmann's is the functional Reformed counter-testimony to office.[166] Ministerial vocation is understood charismatically, 'for building up the body of Christ'[167] and not institutionally.

Apostolic Succession[168] does not establish authority but ensures continuity of narrative identity. The apostolic role, as eyewitness, is unrepeatable. What is repeatable, however, is the proclamation of the gospel.[169] For a Reformed theologian the fundamental norm of the narrative is Biblical. However, the principle of *sola scriptura* is rarely absolute.[170] Moltmann reads the narrative in terms of the Trinity ensuring that the pneumatological is not subordinated to the christological.[171] This mirrors the concept of trinitarian procession, and here Moltmann echoes Balthasar.[172] Where they part company is in their respective understandings

---

[162] Moltmann, 1977, 302.

[163] Moltmann, 1977, 303.

[164] Moltmann, 1977, 307. Moltmann is critical of Ignatius of Antioch (Moltmann, 1977, 305) suggesting, one consequence of a monarchical ministry is that the 'community would then no longer be considering itself charismatically gifted and alive but would be delegating its own commission to the single holder of a central office' (Moltmann, 1977, 307). Emphasising the priesthood of all believers, the importance of call and calling for Moltmann, accords with his 'emphasis on radical change and discontinuity' (Richard Clutterbuck, 'Jürgen Moltamnn As A Doctrinal Theologian: The Nature Of Doctrine And The Possibilities For Its Development', *SJT*, 48, 1995, 494).

[165] Moltmann, 1977, 297.

[166] *Officium*, is often understood to refer to work. Reformed Protestant scholars will sometimes speak of the *officium Christi* as a synonym of the *munus Christi*. It is used to speak of the 'work of Christ', his redemptive mission. Any definition of ministry which is functional will be based upon its fundamental tasks.

[167] Eph 4.12.

[168] Moltmann, 1977, 311.

[169] Moltmann, 1977, 312.

[170] Traditionally, this would be by reference to the declarations of the ecumenical councils.

[171] Richard Bauckham, *The Theology of Jürgen Moltmann*, Edinburgh, T & T Clark, 1996, 6.

[172] 1 Cor. 15.3 see also: Jn 17.18, 20.21; Matt 28.19.

of the basis of the unity of the church,[173] which is the work of the Spirit and not grounded in the Petrine office.[174] The Church should be kenotic, thereby reflecting the image of God as 'love' and not the picture of God 'as almighty'.[175]

Finally, election or the call to be 'in Christ' is ontological and primary.[176] Whereas "*callings*, however, are historic, changing, changeable, temporally limited, and are therefore to be shaped in the process of being accepted in terms of call, of hope and of love"[177] and equated with roles or functions and relationships. The Christian "seeks to live" to his call because it is "this that gives him identity and continuity – even, and indeed precisely, where he expends himself in non-identity... in surrendering himself to the work of mission". Christians are to be assessed as "to whether and how far they afford possibilities for the incarnation of faith".[178] Priesthood is a reflection of the priesthood of Christ, among God's covenant people, and the incarnation of that faith. The priestly sacrifice is not to cooperate in order to effect salvation but obedience to God through conformity to the divine narrative, which is "'creative discipleship' and 'creative love'."[179] Obedience is shown by its faithfulness to its origins revealed in its being "directed towards the kingdom of God, without deviation."[180]

Ecclesiologically the priesthood of all believers gives expression to "the common human identity of rulers and ruled alike."[181] There can be no hierarchy within humanity. The source of human identity is not simply anthropological but divinely given in the incarnate Christ.[182] Humanity is 'called' to selflessness and sacrifice, re-echoing the priestly life of Christ.[183] Vocation is participation in the activity of the divine. Call remains an ontological event, which results in function. All who are called must respond outwardly. Their calling or vocation is to live their lives engaged in the world while participating in the divine mission.

---

[173] The emphasis upon Petrine office and succession effectively means that Jesus 'resurrection plays no part at all in the justificatory complex of ecclesiastical authority.' (Moltmann, 1981, 201.)
[174] Moltmann, 1981, 202 – his italics.
[175] Moltmann, 1981, 202.
[176] Moltmann, 1967, 333, citing various texts – Rom 8.29; 11.29; I Cor 1.9, 26; Phil 3.14; Eph 4.11f; Heb 6.4ff.
[177] Moltmann, 1967, 333 – his italics.
[178] Moltmann, 1967, 333-34.
[179] Moltmann, 1967, 334.
[180] Moltmann, 1977, 312.
[181] Moltmann, 1984, 24. Part of his objection to office is phenomenological, a reaction against the way he perceives ministry and priesthood in the experience of the Church.
[182] Moltmann, 1984, 31.
[183] Moltmann, 1984, 32.

Previously I suggested that Balthasar failed to trace a consistency of form and trinitarian structure both ecclesiologically and anthropologically because of the role he accords to Peter and Mary. Consequently the priestly testimony he articulates is hierarchical. Likewise the examination of Moltmann's ecclesiology, anthropology and theology of vocation has revealed an inconsistency of structure, form and content. Whereas Moltmann, unlike Balthasar, is careful to emphasise the Christological and pneumatological nature of ecclesiology, his anthropology falls prey to post-enlightenment influences, notably the language of human rights, and while he seeks to maintain the importance of the *imago Dei* there is a much more consciously phenomenological approach. By doing this he gives equal weighting in his account to the empirical account of humanity observed. This results in a priestly counter-testimony of universal priesthood.

I shall now examine anthropology, ecclesiology and vocation in the theology of Karl Barth. Though Barth largely predates both Balthasar and Moltmann I shall suggest that he is more rigorous in the application of his overall structure. As a result Barth's account traces more consistently the form, content and of his trinitarian structure. The importance of this for priesthood will be that it permits no blurring of the human or divine identities. However, Barth does not appear to acknowledge the priesthood of the ordained. But what will emerge is the consistent application of the concepts of covenant and election. It is this consistent form and structure that provides the possibility of a dialectical understanding of priesthood as both testimony and counter-testimony, initially examined with regard to the whole people of God (1 Peter 2.4-10).

Vocation in the Theology of Karl Barth

The theological anthropology of Karl Barth is more positive than might be expected from a Reformed theologian[184] and it is rooted in Christology.[185] Unlike Moltmann's anthropology it is not phenomenological. Its starting point is Jesus Christ, the one who is both fully human and yet also wholly divine, setting the Chalcedonian pattern of its structure.[186] Furthermore, because Jesus Christ is God's Word to us, which is a word of grace, people exist as beings who look each other in the eye.[187] This encounter is twofold. First it is between persons (as human

---

[184] Colin Gunton, 'The Triune God and the freedom of the creature', Stephen W. Sykes (ed.), *Karl Barth: Centenary Essays*, Cambridge, CUP, 1989, 53. See: *CD* IV.1, 177.

[185] *CD* III.2, 132.

[186] George Hunsinger, *How to Read Karl Barth*, Oxford, OUP, 1991, 283.

[187] *CD* III.2, 250. Barth restates this proposition negatively when he suggests that, 'it is not human if he really thinks he can be self-sufficient... In this very likeness to God he becomes inhuman.' (*CD* III.2, 263.)

beings) and God (as other) in Jesus Christ.[188] Secondly it is between a man\woman and his\her fellows. In both there must be "mutual speech and hearing."[189] The Word of God, which addresses us, is supremely an address from another. It is not a subjective interpretation of the self but an objective voice by which God reveals himself.

To encounter Jesus as the One who is the true man is to be confronted with the dialectic of the Chalcedonian Definition,[190] encountering One who is both "our true and absolute Counterpart; ... who is like us for all that he is so unlike in the full majesty of God".[191] Barth's anthropology is descriptive, not of humanity as a state of being but as an event or act of becoming. This is revealed in his understanding of sin and underscored in his attitude to sexuality.[192]

---

[188] *CD* III.2, 135.

[189] *CD* III.2, 252.

[190] *CD* III.2, 53.

[191] *CD* III.2, 135.

[192] Barth states that 'we cannot say man without having to say male or female and also male and female. Man exists in this differentiation'. Here Barth avoids the trap which ensnares Balthasar recognising there is 'no abstractly human but only concretely masculine or feminine being' (*CD* III.2, 286). Indeed he proceeds to warn against generalisations based upon psychological presumptions about the nature of being male and female, 'because real men and real women are far too complex and contradictory to be summed up in portrayals of this nature.' (*CD* III.2, 287.) Barth's discussion of male and female underlines the rootedness of his anthropology as a part of the doctrine of creation. This 'man created good by God must have a partner like himself, and must be a partner to a being like himself' (*CD* III.2, 291). Previously Barth read Gen 2.18 alongside and Gen 1.27, 'that God did not create man alone, as a single human being, but in the unequal duality of male and female.' (*CD* III.1, 288.) Man is complete in his duality, as male and female, but remains incomplete in being human as either male or female. While Barth's reading of Genesis may be creative, it avoids Balthasar's idealism and abstraction, which results in sweeping generalisations. Barth's methodology requires that 'It is not the general which comes first, but the particular. The general does not exist without the particular and cannot therefore be prior to the particular' (*CD* II.1, 602). Unlike Balthasar, whose own use of male and female is derived from tradition and somewhat detached from Scripture. As George Hunsinger argues, 'Barth strove to take his bearings from the particularities of the biblical witness, especially its narrative portions.' (Hunsinger, 1991, 33.) This Hunsinger helpfully discusses in terms of unity, differentiation and asymmetry (which he contrasts to hierarchy - Balthasar's theology is more hierarchical, especially in his discussion of male and female, the church and orders). According to Hunsinger, the Chalcedonian pattern 'is a pattern of unity (without separation or division), differentiation (without confusion or change), and asymmetry (the unqualified conceptual precedence of the divine over the human nature of Jesus Christ).' (Hunsinger, 1991, 85.) Barth understands this analogy, as he understands the analogical nature of his anthropology, in terms of an *analogia fidei*. Accordingly, he understands 'the correspondence between the existence of God and the existence of the

At the start of Church Dogmatics III.2 what is apparent is the force of his dialectical thinking when discussing the significance of sin. Sin is self-contradiction when we try to make ourselves what we are not intended to be.[193] Barth says sin is neither the last nor the first word about humanity. Man "is the object of divine grace... he is not merely a sinner... he is God's creature and as such real before God."[194] Humanity is only real in relationship to God. Reality is in God. Sin, which cannot be created by God, is unreality.[195] This is twofold. First, sin is counter to the sovereign divine intention. But secondly, this reveals the "impossible possibility"[196] wherein that which is not created by God can not exist independently and therefore is inherently self-contradictory. Sin exists in this unresolvable dialectic. The key is God's electing purpose revealed in Jesus in whom humanity is itself elected;[197] man's true nature is he who "lives with God as his covenant partner."[198] Sin is when man as God's covenant-partner breaks the covenant. "Real man can deny and obscure his reality."[199] Humanity's sinfulness may be the "distortion or corruption of his being" but "it is not the same as its annihilation."[200]

As God's covenant-partner, humanity "is the object of God's favour... the object of divine grace."[201] In the encounter of humanity, as God's covenant partner with the divine, what is experienced, what is heard, and what is received, is the word of grace. Thus Barth establishes the thrust of God's sovereign activity and the prevenience of grace. This theological anthropology has a twofold thrust. On the one hand it is a theology of

---

human person' or specifically here the relationship of male and female as being human and the nature of the divine, 'as something that only discloses itself in faith in the God who affirms all human beings in the man Jesus.' (Wolfe Kröpke, 'The humanity of the human person in Karl Barth's anthropology', J. B. Webster (ed), *The Cambridge Companion to Karl Barth*, Cambridge, 2000, CUP, 167.)

[193] *CD* III.2, 28.

[194] *CD* III.2, 31.

[195] According to Barth sin 'has the character of that which God did not will to create'; sin may blind man to God but 'God is not blind to him.' (*CD* III.2, 33. See also: *CD* III.2, 51-52.)

[196] *CD* III.3, 351. (See also: Eberhard Jüngel, *Karl Barth, a Theological Legacy* (ET), Philadelphia, The Westminster Press, 1986, 61.)

[197] *CD* III.2, 142. For Barth this reveals the will of God, which is 'that the Yes which He as the Creator has spoken to His creation should prevail... [sin] He did not will and therefore did not create, to which He gave no being, which can exist only as non-being' (*CD* III.2, 143).

[198] *CD* III.2, 203.

[199] *CD* III.2, 205.

[200] *CD* III.2, 27.

[201] *CD* III.2, 31.

gratitude[202] and is therefore responsive.

God comes to man – this is the objective basis of man's being. But God is the Creator and

> man is His creature. Hence there is a supreme disparity between the coming of God and the going of man, between the objective and the subjective basis of human being. The grace of God and the gratitude of man, the Word of God and the response of man, the knowledge and the act of God and those of man, take place on two very different levels…[203]

On the other Barth seeks to maintain narrative consistency in the characterisation of humanity in relation to God.[204] Human beings as sinners may be consistently self-contradictory[205] but God is consistently gracious in his nature and therefore his being[206] across time and location.[207] Herein lies another distinction between God and creation. God and Christ as the second person of the Trinity stand outside and above time in eternity. The man Jesus "has his lifetime: the time bounded at one end by His birth and at the other by His death."[208] This repeats the pattern of the Chalcedonian Definition, that Jesus in his given time is "not only God and therefore different from us, but also man and therefore like us."[209] As a covenant partner and a recipient of God's grace "I have God (or rather God has me), I need no more. I have space and therefore time."[210]

Gratitude is the recognition that what is received is beyond one's own achievement, honours the benefactor and "implies obligation".[211] Gratitude is the mark of the one who is God's covenant-partner and the recognition

---

[202] Following Barth I tend to use the word 'gratitude' when speaking of the human response to God. However, as Barth himself acknowledges: 'Praising God shows that thanks for his benefits cannot be concealed or unexpressed' (Karl Barth, *The Christian Life* (ET), Edinburgh, T & T Clark, 1981, 87)

[203] *CD* III.2, 187.

[204] For Barth the consistency of God is revealed in the doctrine of election, 'the decision by which He institutes, maintains and directs this covenant'. (*CD* II.2, 9.) The only possible response to such a God is one of gratitude.

[205] *CD* III.2, 26.

[206] *CD* III.2, 281. Earlier, discussing the self-contradictory nature of sin Barth is explicit stating that 'even and precisely in becoming man God remained true to Himself, true to His mercy to creation,' and this is therefore 'the secret of the sinlessness of Jesus and therefore of the maintenance of human nature in Him.' (*CD* III.2, 52.)

[207] In Barth's discussion of time and history what is apparent is God's constancy. See: *CD* III.2, § 47.

[208] *CD* III.2, 440.

[209] *CD* III.2, 516.

[210] *CD* III.2, 530.

[211] *CD* III.2, 167.

"that he belongs to God, that God is for him, and for him in the person of the man Jesus."[212] We shall need to return to this when we look at vocation.

Balthasar regards the Church as divinely instituted.[213] Barth's understanding is more existential.[214] Balthasar necessarily takes issue with Barth's ecclesiology suggesting that he "was forced to stress the relativity of the Church",[215] as a fundamentally human rather than divine institution. Barth, however, remains within the narrative constraints he has set himself. The "whole community of God – Israel and the Church – is elected"[216] as God's people. But this community is a "human fellowship"[217] and essentially "provisional"[218] in character. Thus he is able to hold together Israel and the Church as the elect community, once again repeating the Chalcedonian pattern, as he does in his anthropology.[219] For Barth

> the Church is the gathering of Jews and Gentiles called on the ground of its election…(grounded in the election of the one Jesus Christ)… The object of election is neither Israel for itself nor the Church itself, but both together in their unity.[220]

In Israel and the Church, God in Jesus Christ elects "an obdurate people".[221] The Church is the community chosen by God "for communion with Himself in His eternal election of grace… All this happens wholly for our benefit".[222] Like humanity the Church is thus a community, which exists to praise its divine creator.[223]

---

[212] *CD* III.2, 265.

[213] *TD* III, 354.

[214] According to *The Barmen Declaration*, the 'Christian church is the congregation of brothers and sisters in which Jesus Christ acts presently as the Lord in Word and sacrament, through the Holy Spirit. As the church of forgiven sinners, it has to bear witness in the midst of a sinful world' (Alister E. McGrath (ed), *The Christian Theology Reader*, Oxford, Blackwell, 1995, 278.)

[215] Hans Urs von Balthasar, *The Theology of Karl Barth* (ET), New York, 1962, Holt, Rinehart and Winston, 202.

[216] *CD* II.2, 205.

[217] *CD* II.2, 206.

[218] *CD* II.2, 196.

[219] *CD* II.2, 200.

[220] *CD* II.2, 199.

[221] *CD* II.2, 206.

[222] *CD* II.2, 211.

[223] Interestingly, Israel's unbelief is supremely their resistance to being elected in Jesus Christ, such that they 'put themselves in the wrong, but not God's offering of His Son and the ordering of human affairs accomplished by it.' (*CD* II.2, 209) This repeats

Community is another important word for Barth's ecclesiology suggestive of the dynamic nature of the Church, where Balthasar's institutionalism is more static. The Church as "the community (the environment of the man Jesus) is the centre of communication between Jesus and the world"[224] and this has similarities to Balthasar's understanding of the Church as the mother which brings to birth the faith of the community.[225] But as result of the Chalcedonian bi-polarity, the Church includes both unity and diversity. It is and it is not.[226] It exists in a dialectic tension rather than the propositional certainty of Balthasar's institutional understanding. Instead the Church is a herald, a community of proclamation, a witnessing community by virtue of its post-resurrection existence.[227]

Barth addresses the Church in relation to the Holy Spirit. While Balthasar's ecclesiology is, pneumatically deficient[228] and Moltmann's charismatically driven, Barth manages to avoid the polarity of both.[229] The Holy Spirit is the life source of the Church as a Christian community.[230] The activity of the Holy Spirit establishes the Church as the presence of Christ.[231] The ontological reality of the Church is analogous to the reality of the presence of God in Jesus through the power of the Holy Spirit.[232] This is a return to a theological anthropology of gratitude and a mimetic retelling of Philippians 2.[233] The identity of the Church "does not belong to itself, but to Him; it does not live of itself, but can only follow the movement of His life".[234] But this is no abstract, idealised notion of the Church because it is

---

Barth's understanding of sin as self-contradictory when we try to make ourselves what we are not intended to be. (*CD* III.2, 26.)

[224] *CD* II.2, 239.

[225] *CD* II.2, 233. However for Barth this is because the Church is the environment of Jesus Christ, who is the Word of God, and not through a third party, like Mary, as Balthasar suggests.

[226] *CD* II.2, 260.

[227] *CD* II.2, 240, 267. Avery Dulles suggests that Barth's understanding of the Church 'is [as] essentially a herald of Christ's Lordship' (Dulles, 1976, 73).

[228] See: 116, n. 73.

[229] §62, 'The Holy Spirit and the Gathering of the Christian Community'. In the chapter heading he speaks of the Holy Spirit as 'the awakening power in which Jesus Christ has formed and continually renews His body, i.e., His own earthly-historical form of existence, the one holy catholic and apostolic Church' (*CD* IV.1, 643).

[230] *CD* IV.1, 647.

[231] *CD* IV.1, 661.

[232] *CD* IV.1, 661.

[233] *CD* IV.1, 661.

[234] *CD* IV.2, 662.

the *body* of Christ, it is necessarily visible, it cannot be invisible.[235]

The Church is the community of the covenant.[236] This community is not simply the gathered faithful, but the elect. The emphasis is upon the believing community of which they are a part and only secondly the individual Christian.[237] This is the visible community of two natures (divine and human) that Barth describes as one,[238] holy,[239] catholic[240] and apostolic,[241] all gifts of the Holy Spirit[242] and a sign that it is the visible body of Christ. Following the Chalcedonian pattern the two natures are united while remaining distinct and unconfused. The Church remains a human 'body', historical, temporal and finite. It is this finitude which ultimately prevents the Church being confused with the divine.[243] The Church's (churches) failure to live to its true nature is sinful and therefore self-contradictory.[244]

A central motif of Barth's anthropology is encounter, whereas for Balthasar it is the divine drama. To be with means encounter[245] between the 'I' and the 'thou', whether the 'thou' is human or divine. It is only in this double encounter that real man exists, wherein there "is mutual speech and hearing."[246] Encounter is an event of speech.[247] That is why the Doctrine of the Word is so crucial, for it is in His Word that God declares and reveals Himself, opening Himself to possible encounter.[248] The "Word of God is obviously not only a communication but a challenge, not only an indicative but as such an imperative, because it is the Word of His grace."[249] According to Barth vocation is praise as

> the precise creaturely counterpart to the grace of God... and man's casting of his trust upon God is nothing other or less, but also nothing

---

[235] *CD* IV.2, 652-653. Thus again as one Church 'the visible and the invisible Church are not two Churches' they are necessarily one. (*CD* IV.1, 669.)
[236] *CD* IV.1, 698.
[237] *CD* IV.1, 705.
[238] *CD* IV.1, 668.
[239] *CD* IV.1, 685.
[240] *CD* IV.1 702.
[241] *CD* IV.1, 712.
[242] For example discussing the holiness of the Church see: *CD* IV.1, 693.
[243] *CD* IV.1, 725.
[244] For example discussing the catholicity of the Church, *CD* IV.1, 708.
[245] *CD* III.2, 247.
[246] *CD* III.2, 252. Or as I began this Chapter by reference to Oliver Davies (see: 107 above, n. 1).
[247] *CD* III.3, 253.
[248] *CD* III.2, 255.
[249] *CD* III.2, 165.

more, than the being of man as his act in gratitude.[250]

Vocation is both an act of grace, by which God calls,[251] but also a human response. It is gratitude lived. Just as being human is a process, always becoming - as indeed is the Church - so too is vocation.[252] Vocation assumes a narrative form. The person "is called and becomes a Christian as he is illuminated",[253] as that person daily inhabits the story of Jesus Christ. The goal of vocation is "not a special Christian existence but the existence of the Christian as such."[254] Once again Philippians 2.6-11 provides the metanarrative.

> Vocation is... the action of Jesus Christ who in His time lived and died as the Lord humbled to be a servant and the servant exalted to be Lord, but who is risen again and therefore lives eternally... His action in time, itself a temporal event.[255]

Consequently, it necessitates a new form of existence to which the Christian is called "not an angelic, let alone divine form. But it is one which is divinely fashioned."[256] Vocation is therefore a question of identity.[257]

Barth refers to Philippians 2.5, and the charge to be christlike when he asks what identifies the Christian. Christians, he suggests, exist in "proximity to Him and therefore in analogy to what he is."[258] Barth proceeds to describe the Christian by means of *analogia fidei*.[259] Vocation is therefore the incarnation of the real man as he hears and responds to the divine Word, so ceasing to follow himself and instead following Christ.[260] In this way he becomes his true self as intended by God. The Chalcedonian pattern dictates that the Christian may indeed be 'christlike' but never identical with Christ.[261] The relationship of the Christian follower to the

---

[250] *CD* III.2, 166.
[251] *CD* IV. 3ii, 507.
[252] *CD* IV. 3ii, 507.
[253] *CD* IV.3ii, 508.
[254] *CD* IV.3ii, 524.
[255] *CD* IV.3ii, 497.
[256] *CD* IV.3ii, 530.
[257] *CD* IV.1, 497.
[258] *CD* IV.3ii, 530.
[259] To be truly human 'is to be with God.' (*CD* III.2, 139.) Thus 'the real man... is the creature of God' (*CD* III.2, 202).
[260] *CD* IV.3ii, 535-36.
[261] *CD* IV.3ii, 539. This is crucial for Barth for whom God's constancy is key. In the narrative of his theology God is a good character, because he is consistent. Thus 'the incarnation [of the second person of the Trinity] is as such the confirmation of the distinctive reality of creation' and therefore man as a created being. However, the

Lord is asymmetrical; both retain their integrity. Each encounters and can participate in the other's world, but each remains distinct. The encounter is one of kenotic re-identification. Kenosis is not a negative event of self-emptying, the loss of selfhood and therefore identity, but an act of obedience and conformity to God's electing will.[262] In this there is both testimony in the kenotic re-identification of the self but also a sacrificial counter-testimony in the subjective response to God's prior electing grace.

Following the Chalcedonian pattern there are two elements to Christian living. One, that "Christ should live in the Christian by the Holy Spirit is the purpose of vocation." Secondly, "the purpose of the vocation of the Christian is that he should live in Christ by the Holy Spirit."[263] As the Spirit breathes life into the Church, so He energises the Christian. Vocation is a narrative event whereby the Christian inhabits the divine story[264] living within the divine purpose.[265] Finally, humanity is historical and temporal and has a 'given time'.[266] Vocation is the living of particular life given with particular purpose in accord with the Word of God.[267]

Vocation is an act of gratitude, in response to the call to be God's covenant-partner. The nature of the Church as the covenant community defined in the encounter with God can be summed up in five words: integrity, mutual self-involvement, encounter, fellowship and witness. First, vocation establishes the integrity of the human person before God. In it our own identity is manifested, but so too is Christ's.[268] Secondly, it involves a mutual self-involvement by which we receive our vocation in the encounter with God through the Word.[269] Furthermore, this is always in the process of becoming a new people, the "called instead of the uncalled."[270] Thirdly, vocation is fellowship activated by the encounter with the Holy Spirit. Not only are we in Christ, but Christ is in us.[271] Fourthly it is the human response to the fact that as Christ has placed himself at the disposal of humankind, so the Christian is the one who places him or herself at Christ's disposal in an asymmetrical act of grateful response to the divine sovereignty of Christ's saving grace. Finally, vocation is witness. The

---

incarnation 'does not mean any curtailment or compromising of the immutable divine nature' (*CD* II.1, 515).

[262] *CD* II.1, 516.
[263] *CD* IV.3ii, 594.
[264] *CD* IV.3ii, 548.
[265] *CD* IV.3ii, 572.
[266] *CD* III.2 (§47.2, Given Time).
[267] *CD* IV.3ii, 573-74.
[268] Hunsinger, 1991, 156.
[269] *CD* III.2, 257.
[270] *CD* IV.3, 516.
[271] *CD* IV.3, 555.

Christian life does not consist in the reception of benefits, but rather in the reception of a task. And the special vocation of the Christian is to share in the living self-witness of the Crucified. This is the priestly testimony of bearing witness to the redeeming sacrifice of the cross and a counter-testimony in that it is only ever a witness and representation of the story.[272]

As I have suggested, within the form and trinitarian structure of their theologies there is inconsistency both in Balthasar's anthropology and ecclesiology and Moltmann's anthropology. However, Barth's anthropology, ecclesiology and theology of vocation maintains a greater consistency of form and structure. This consistency is a result of a number of factors not least his particularism, the centrality he accords to the Chalcedonian pattern and the importance he attaches to the essential dialectic of the human-divine encounter. As a consequence God is always the one who by his sovereign grace initiates; humanity responds. Within this structure the foundational metanarrative is the account of election and covenant, by which humanity is identitified in relation to God. The concern for my thesis is Barth's lack of interest in questions concerning priesthood. However, this is consistent within the traditionally received structure, form and content of Reformed theologies of anthropology, ecclesiology and vocation. The question is whether this tradition is consistent with the Biblical account.

In the next section I shall develop the key ideas that have emerged from Barth's undertsanding of anthropology, ecclesiology and vocation, in the light of the interweaving of priesthood, covenant and election in 1 Peter 2.4-10, in the context of God's prior grace. Protestants frequently cite this passage, as exemplifying a counter-testimony to the priesthood of the ordained,[273] emphasising instead the priesthood of all believers. However, I shall argue that the traditional Protestant assumptions concerning priesthood are less secure than has perhaps been presumed.[274]

Election, Priesthood and Covenant in 1 Peter 2.4-10

The writer of 1 Peter addresses "the nature of the community which he outlines in terms and conceptions drawn from the Old Testament, from intertestamental Judaism and from primitive Christian tradition."[275] 1 Peter 2.4-10 is a deliberately mimetic testimony and counter-testimony of the

---

[272] See: James D. G. Dunn, 'What Makes a Good Exposition?', ET, (114), 2003, 155 where he discusses the 'expositor as priest'.
[273] John Webster, *Holiness*, London, SCM, 2003, 46, 52.
[274] Paul J. Achtemeier, *1 Peter*, Minneapolis, Augsburg Fortress, 1996, 156.
[275] Ernest Best, *1 Peter*, London, Oliphants, 1977, 99.

priestly identity of the Church that is both allusive and imitative.[276] The priestly counter-testimony retells the narrative of Israel's covenant identity in the light of the emerging Christian tradition.[277] This embodies an associative or tracking notion of representation and a fitting theory of internal resemblance. Covenant identity is understood as extending but yet maintaining a recognisable likeness based upon election and covenant between Israel (in the First Testament) and the Christian community.[278] Furthermore there is the suggestion of a link between humanity as God's covenant-partner and priesthood in this narrative. This emerges through the interplay of three ideas; election, priesthood and covenant.[279]

---

[276] The writer's description of the new community 'shows by its language that the church has taken over the role of Israel' (Achtemeier, 1996, 152). This encompasses elements of both tracking and fitting theories or representation.

[277] Ellen Juhl Christiansen suggests that 'collective identity... answers the questions, "Where do we come from?" and "Where are we going to?", with reference to a common tradition' (Ellen Juhl Christiansen, *The Covenant in Judaism and Paul*, Leiden, E J Brill, 1995, 1). She suggests that the answer suggested by Paul, and I would add the author of 1 Peter and other New Testament writers, builds upon the foundations of and therefore take its reference from Israel's Scriptures (otherwise known as the Old Testament or First Testament). She suggests that their concern for interpreting validity by referring to the 'eternal covenant' reflects a topical interest in the Old Testament traditions of belonging in general and covenantal boundaries in particular. (Christiansen, 1985, 25.) Accordingly it 'is significant that, when Israel sees itself as a people bound together in what is termed God's covenant, and when further a future, fuller realisation of the covenant is expected by the people, Israel's identity consists of a common history and tradition, of shared values, norms and rituals, but also the common life and the common goal of the people.' (Christiansen, 1995, 27-28.) The writer of 1 Peter seeks to establish that covenant identity 'means there are different boundaries, and different values for setting these boundaries.' (Christiansen, 1995, 271.) She concludes that there are three recognisable types of corporate identity. First 'where covenant identity is defined primarily in national terms' (Christiansen, 1995, 322). Secondly, 'where identity is defined in more narrow categories such as priestly purity, purity rites...[or] to adopt the lifestyle of the community.' (Christiansen, 1995, 322.) Thirdly, (see: Chapter 3 above) that 'for Paul Christian identity depends on the community's faith in Christ, on how visible [the community is] in Christo-centric symbols'. This is not covenantal in traditional First Testament terms, however, the 'redefinition of [the] covenant as a vertical relationship with God... [in which] christological and pneumatological principles are employed for the sake of defining what [constitutes] a true relationship with God in Christ and the Spirit.' (Christiansen, 1995, 323.)

[278] Rather than suggesting that the Church is a wholly new event the writer of 1 Peter re-identifies the people of the covenant, as Paul re-identifies the people of God in Phil. 3. (See: 87 above.)

[279] *CD* II.2, 445. Barth reads this as the re-founding or renaming of Israel in relation to God's action in Jesus Christ.

At the start of the letter the writer addresses the recipients as 'exiles... chosen and destined by God the Father and sanctified by the Spirit for obedience to Jesus Christ and for sprinkling with his blood'.[280] The motif of election recurs at 2.4. The writer speaks initially of Jesus Christ as 'chosen (ἐκλεκτὸν) and precious'. The words serve as both a metaphor for the building but are also distinctly theological, alluding to Isaiah 28.16.[281] Thus at "the heart of Peter's interpretation... is the election of Jesus Christ as God's instrument of salvation". Subsequently this notion of being "chosen" is applied to the "election of the believing community".[282] One "of the objects of 2.4-10 is to remind readers that they belong to the same people of God"[283] as the people of the First Testament. They too are included within God's elect. Furthermore "[e]lection and sanctification... are inseparably

---

[280] I Pet. 1.1, 2. The opening verses raise a number of interesting points. The writer's refers to the recipients as 'ἐκλεκτοῖς παρεπιδήμοισ διασπορᾶς' which would seem to suggest 'a natural transfer of one of the titles of Israel to the Church' (Peter H. Davids, *The First Epistle of Peter*, Grand Rapids, Eerdmans, 1990, 46). The RSV word 'chosen' translates πρόγνωσιν, 'foreknowledge' and refers to God's knowledge as 'part of His eternal counsel' (E. G. Selwyn, *The First Epistle of St Peter*, London, Macmillan & Co, 1946, 118.) and is understood by commentators as referring to the concept of the divine election of the people of God. (Michaels, 1988, 10; Davids, 1990, 48.) Secondly, 'ῥαντισμὸν αἵματοσ Ἰεσοῦ Χριστοῦ' has both priestly overtones, recalling as it does, 'the Jewish sacrificial system' but applied to 'Christ's redemptive death' (Michaels, 1988, 12.) and speaks of covenant ratification. This is alluded to in Heb 9.19f and 12.24 which itself draws upon Exod. 24.3-8. F. J. A. Hort draws four conclusions from this allusion to sprinkling. First 'it takes its whole meaning from the conception of the new order of things introduced by the Messiah's appearing, Death, and Resurrection as a New Covenant between God and man'. Secondly, 'sprinkling presupposed a shedding; the consecration of the New Covenant presupposed the antecedent sacrifice of the cross... at the Father's will.' Thirdly, the admittance of non-Jewish converts to covenant membership 'was a consecration of themselves in a Divine communion, an initiation into newness of life to be governed by willing fulfilment of the New Covenant.' Finally 'reception into the Christian covenant implied acceptance of an authoritative standard of righteousness contained in the Gospel'. Furthermore, 'each element of the transaction recorded in Exodus had its counterpart.' (F. J. A. Hort, *The First Epistle of St Peter I.1-II.17*, London, Macmillan & Co., 1898, 24.) It does undoubtedly signify that the writer wishes to convey to his listeners that they too have been 'properly brought into a covenant relationship with God... one based on the blood of Christ himself.' (Davids, 1990, 49.)
[281] See: 2.6.
[282] C.f. 2.9, see: J. Ramsey Michaels, *1 Peter*, Waco, Word Books, 1988, 99.
[283] Best, 1977, 105.

Vocation and Priesthood 141

linked."[284] God's people is to be a holy people 'a royal priesthood'[285] consequent upon the "utterly gratuitous"[286] nature of their divine calling.

The second motif to emerge, therefore is priesthood (2.5). This is the vocation of the Church as God's elect and covenant people. Alluding to the temple, the Church as 'the house of God' is 'a spiritual house'.[287] But it is not a physical building but "a living 'house' in which God lives."[288] The Christian community is 'a holy priesthood' of this reconstituted Temple. The word used for priesthood is only found in Exodus 19.6 and again 1 Peter 2.9.[289] Commenting on Exodus 19.3-6 Barth observes that as a priestly nation Israel "should fulfil a mediatorial ministry... proving itself to be the possession... of King Yahweh in this way, to be His holy people, separated from the peoples for the peoples."[290] The task of the priesthood, "as the parallel with 2.9b suggests, includes a witness to all humanity."[291] The vocation of the covenant people is to be a priestly people. It is therefore also a priestly testimony in which God's saving act is announced as a result of which the divine-human boundary can be crossed. In the First Testament the priestly vocation was to offer sacrifices. The writer of 1 Peter knows this but immediately qualifies the sacrifices, which are to be spiritual.[292] In a

---

[284] Webster, 2003, 59.

[285] 1 Pet. 2.9 (c.f. 2.5)

[286] Webster, 2003, 60.

[287] 'οἶκος πνευματικὸς εἰς ἱεράτευμα ἅγιον ἀνενέγκαι πνευματικὰς τηυσίας εὐπροσδέκτους τηεῷ διὰ Ἰεσοῦ Χριστοῦ' (1 Peter 2.5,) According to Selwyn οἶκος πνευματικὸς does not refer to the domestic household but 'God's true temple' (Selwyn, 1946, 160). Some Protestant commentators have found the conjunction of οἶκος πνευματικὸς and εἰς ἱεράτευμα problematic because of its inherently 'sacerdotal' (Selwyn, 1946, 160.) implications. However, the consensus accepts that it is a reference to the Temple (Michaels, 1988, 100; Davids, 1990, 87.)

[288] Davids, 1990, 87. He suggests that the 'concept of a nonphysical church replacing the material Temple in Jerusalem is widespread in Christian writings (Mark 14.58; 15.29; John 2.19, 4,21; 23-24; Acts 7.48; 17.24).'

[289] Only here and in one other place does the First Testament speak of the priesthood of all Israel. (Best, 1977, 102: Is 61.6.) Hort suggests that a better reading of the text is οἶκος πνευματικὸς ἱεράτευμα ἅγιον omitting εἰς which would follow the Syrian text and 'make the two phrases exactly symmetrical, and also in accordance with v 9' reading 'a spiritual house for a holy act of priesthood' (Hort, 1898, 109).

[290] *CD* IV.1, 424.

[291] Achtemeier, 1996, 156.

[292] They are to 'offer spiritual sacrifices'. Some commentators have looked to the Qumran Community as those who had withdrawn from the Temple cultus but who retained a strong emphasis upon the place of 'non-material sacrifices' (Best, 1977, 102.) as a possible source of understanding. However, J Ramsey Michaels is probably correct when he suggests that 'the priestly activities of the "house" are as metaphorical as the house itself' (Michaels, 1988, 101). In the First Testament there are references in which sacrifice is intended metaphorically (Hos. 6.6; Mic. 6.6-8; Ps. 50.13, 14; 51.17; 141.2).

phrase echoing Philippians 4.18 the sacrifice, is to be 'acceptable to God'.[293] In the First Testament such wording usually occurs in connection with the sacrificial cultic worship but on occasion it is "transferred and applied to the house of Israel, whom the Lord promises to accept"[294] and which forms a non-material sacrifice.[295] Importantly, however, there is an implicit notion of 'spiritual sacrifices', which are 'acceptable to God' which are the outward sign of praise for His saving grace.[296] In this priestly testimony the sacrifices do not effect salvation but celebrate God's prior sovereign grace.

The priestly testimony introduces the third motif of covenant, covenant identity and the continuity between church as the community elect 'in Christ' and Israel as God's covenant people.[297] Here the writer articulates a counter-testimony drawing upon three First Testament texts[298] suggesting a progression from Christology to Ecclesiology. This commences with Temple imagery, and through the relationship between 'the living Stone' and the 'living stones' the metaphor is underlined by the translation of ἐπ' αὐτῷ 'in him' rather than 'in it'. This serves a double function. First, it identifies the Christian community as God's 'covenant partner'. Secondly,

---

Furthermore, as Michaels suggests this would also appear to echo Paul's thought, in which sacrifice is a metaphor for an all –out personal commitment to do the will of God' (i.e. Rom. 12.1, Michaels, 1988, 101).

[293] Writing to the Philippians (4.18), Paul understands their gift to be 'a fragrant offering, a sacrifice (θυσίαν) acceptable and pleasing to God'. Hort observes the two passages use 'strikingly similar language' (Hort, 1898, 111).

[294] O'Brien, 1991, 541.

[295] O'Brien, 1991, 541. O'Brien quotes: Ps. 51.17; also Qumran 1QS 8.7-9; 9.3-5; 10.6.

[296] This would clearly accord with Barth's concept of election, covenant, grace, and to which gratitude is the fundamental response of vocation.

[297] Discussing 1 Peter and a 'Judaizing' tendency among some early Jewish Christians Michaels speaks of the writer addressing 'a shared self-understanding' (Michaels, 1988, l-li), what Christiansen speaks of as the 'redefinition of [the] covenant' (See: 160, n. 283 below).

[298] Is. 28.16 (LXX); Ps. 118.22; Is. 8.14-15. The quotation of Is. 28.16 interestingly begins with the same variant as that quoted by Paul. (i.e. Rom. 9.33). For a discussion of the dependency of the early Christian writers upon one another and the resultant intertextuality see: Thomas L Brodie, 'Towards Tracing the Gospels' Literary Indebtedness to the Epistles', Dennis R. MacDonald (ed), *Mimesis and Intertextuality in Antiquity and Christianity*, Harrisburg PA, Trinity Press International, 2001, 104-116. Also there is a full discussion of the relation between and possible dependency of Paul upon Peter and *vice versa* in Selwyn, 1946, 268-277. However, Peter's focus is a positive one. The cornerstone is 'chosen and precious' whereas according to Paul the stone 'will make people stumble' (Rom 9.33). The author wishes to stress that Jesus Christ is 'the unique base upon which the church is built' (c.f. 1 Cor. 3.11; Michaels, 1988, 103).

it can be read in terms of the Chalcedonian pattern.[299] Like Paul, writing to the Philippians it contrasts true and false identity,[300] in a series of quotations from the First Testament, of which Psalm 118.22 is the linchpin,[301] from which the author develops the building and stone metaphor. The evidence of the other Second Testament writers suggests that this Psalm featured significantly in the teaching and self-understanding of the primitive Church.[302] By placing it in the mouth of Jesus, the synoptic writers suggest it can be read as a crypto-messianic claim,[303] set in the context of his activity in the Temple and the prelude to the events of Easter.

Accordingly, stumbling is a consequence of unbelief and not synonymous with it. It "is the opposite of divine vindication, the negative equivalent of the honour reserved for Christian believers of not being 'put to shame'".[304] If God's covenant people are to be defined in relation to Jesus Christ it is an act of self-contradiction. The use of an emphatic 'but you'[305] points up the distinctiveness of the people of the covenant. Again the allusion is to a series of First Testament texts[306] encapsulating the three motifs of covenant, election and priesthood. The writer addresses his listeners, as a chosen people and God's own people who are a royal priesthood.[307] They are the priesthood of the Divine King, of whose holy

---

[299] The first reference to 'the living stone' is a reference to Jesus Christ, as risen living Lord. In the second reference, they as the community are 'like living stones'. Thus there is both unity and differentiation. Christ is the same as they are (truly man) while retaining his divinity (truly God) but they are 'like' in the image of, but different.

[300] See: 102-106 above. In 1 Peter 2.4-10 the contrast is different: true identity is in becoming 'like living stones', whereas those who 'reject' 'the living stone' 'stumble' and 'fall'. However, those who identify themselves in relation to the 'living stone' are called (a chosen race) to 'declare the wonderful deeds of him who called you', the continuing living of their renewed identity. Christiansen suggests that, with the resurrection, for Paul there is a fundamental change in the way in which God is identified and therefore encountered. (Christiansen, 1995, 213) This is exactly what happens in the *carmen Christi* in Philippians where God is re-identified in the Christ event.

[301] Is. 28.16; Ps. 118.22; Is. 8.14-15, see: Selwyn, 1946, 269, though Selwyn's suggestion that 2.6-10 is constituted from an early Christian hymn would seem to be conjecture with little supporting evidence (Selwyn, 1946, 268-81).

[302] Acts 4.11, Peter's self-defence before the Sanhedrin.

[303] Matt. 21.42; Mk. 12.10-11; Lk. 20.17 At the climax of the parable of the vineyard, which is a retelling of a parable told by Isaiah (5.1-7). See: Tom Wright, *Jesus and the Victory of God*, London, SPCK, 1996, 178, 497-501, 566.

[304] 2.6b-7. (Michaels, 1988, 106.)

[305] 2.9.

[306] Exod. 19.5-6; Is. 43.20-21; Hos. 1.9, 10; 2.23.

[307] Royal does not have to be a noun (e.g. Selwyn, 1946, 165-66; J. H. Elliott, *The Elect and the Holy: An Exegetical Examination of 1 Peter 2.4-10 and the Phrase Basíleion ieráteuma*, Novum Testamentum Supplement, Leiden, Brill, 1966, 149-54) but can be

nation they are citizens. Their priestly identity is consequent upon their election and being the people of the covenant. In the priestly tradition they stand close to God. But this is a corporate, not individual picture. Their testimony is 'to declare the wonderful deeds of him who called' them 'out of darkness into his marvellous light.'[308] The counter-testimony is the sacrificial offering of their gratitude in response to the grace they have received.[309]

There remain four final points to be made. First, I have proposed that central to the intention of this passage is the notion of covenant identity, suggesting a corporate identity answering the questions, 'Where do we come from?' and 'Where are we going to?', by reference to a common tradition.[310] While the early Christian community did not adhere to "the symbols of the Jewish worldview",[311] nonetheless they provided a "rich source of metaphor through which they lent depth to their beliefs".[312] Tom Wright suggests there are four symbols, the Temple, the Land, the Torah, and racial identity which bring the Jewish worldview "into a visible and tangible reality".[313] I suggest that all four images are found in 1 Peter 2.4-10.[314] These are all images indicative of the presence of YHWH.[315] What the writer does is to re-identify these symbols in relation to the community, which now exists 'in Christ' and which according to the Second Testament writers represents the redefined covenant people of God by tracking externally but also by internal resemblance.

Secondly, one consequence of the Christian community being included within a redrawn covenant identity is that it too receives Israel's calling. Its vocation as God's own people is to be a 'holy priesthood, a holy nation'. The priestly activity is therefore one of incarnate gratitude that "the "covenant of God with man"[316] is fulfilled in Christ and so God makes common cause with his covenant people.

Thirdly, in this passage there is a discernible narrative, in the course of which there is both reversal and recognition.[317] This tells of a 'descent from

---

an adjective (Davids, 1990, 91).

[308] 2.9b.

[309] C.f. Hos. 1.10, 2.23.

[310] Christiansen, 1995, 1.

[311] N. T. Wright, *The New Testament and the People of God*, London, SPCK, 1993, 365.

[312] Wright, 1993, 366.

[313] Wright, 1993, 224-25.

[314] Thus there are references to the Temple (2.4-5, 6), to the (promised) Land (2.9), the Torah (2.8), Jewish ethnicity (implicit in whole text).

[315] Wright, 1993, 224-25.

[316] *CD* IV.3ii, 542. Barth speaks of this in terms of Christ's prophetic office and work. However, in the language of the paragraph 'reconciling' and 'intervening' are also priestly attributes.

[317] In 2.4 there is the reversal of the 'living stone, rejected by men' but which is actually

a logic of identity into a world of shifting appearances' in which the order of things is inverted and by which re-identification is made culminating in 'a return to the logic of identity'.[318] The result is the identification of "the Gentile Christian readers as if they were Jews".[319] They are indeed God's elect, the King's priestly people, the people of the covenant.

Finally, the passage contains an inherent dialectic. On the one hand, the writer affirms the identity of God's elect, the covenant and priestly people. On the other, this identity is cancelled. However, identity is reconstituted, but no longer in relation to racial identity, the Torah, the Land, and the Temple. The potency of the symbols remains, but refocused through Jesus Christ and reapplied to his followers, embodying both testimony and counter-testimony.

Conclusion

When applied to 1 Peter 2.4-10 Barth's understanding of humanity, as God's covenant partner, begins to cast light upon the possibility of a Protestant concept of priesthood. In this passage there is a notion of corporate vocation of those who are in Christ to be a priestly people so extending the covenant identity of Israel. In this it is possible to distinguish both the particularism of Jesus Christ and the Chalcedonian pattern of the two, co-equal natures, Israel and the Church. The mimetic narrative of 1 Peter 2.4-10 has structural overtones with the *carmen Christi*, insofar as there is an instability of identity which is overcome, resulting in renaming. Thirdly, the event of renaming and re-identification maintains a dialectic. The writer reconstitutes election, covenant and priesthood, in relation to Jesus Christ rather than the nation of Israel. The concepts remain the same but are differently identified. At the heart of the accounts of Barth, Balthasar and Moltmann is the *theologia crucis* understood trinitarianly, which redefines God and also humanity in relationship to him. However, as Barth stresses, the divine-human *diastasis* remains unchanged. The crossing of the boundaries, according to Barth, is a consequence of the event of

---

'chosen and precious' in God's sight. And again 2.7, 'The very stone which the builders rejected has become the head of the corner'. Here the misidentification of Jesus Christ who was rejected and crucified, is revealed as actually being God's grace and saving presence. Likewise there is genuine recognition when Peter addresses his gentile audience as 'a spiritual house to be a holy priesthood' (2.5) and again, 'a chosen race, a royal priesthood, a holy nation, God's own people'. (2.9) And again that once they 'were no people but now you are God's people' (2.10).

[318] Graham Ward, 1999, 23 (see: 98 above). However, the same pattern is also present, albeit in a double form in 1 Pet 2.4-10 as I shall demonstrate. Similarly Peter H. Davids suggests that 1 Pet. 2.1-10 is concerned with 'Christian identity' (Davids, 1990, 79-93.).

[319] Michaels, 1988, 107.

God's Word by which humanity is addressed and, through Jesus Christ, crucified and risen, is recreated a covenant partner. This is a priestly event, from God to humanity whereby "God not man is always the Lord."[320] Humanity is the object of divine sovereignty and grace and can only respond with praise.

In the next Chapter I shall therefore continue to develop an account of priesthood, with reference to these notions of particularism, the Chalcedonian pattern and the dialectic of testimony and counter-testimony. Secondly, I shall argue that sacrifice (an essential component of priesthood) is an event of gratitude in response to the prior act of divine grace. Therefore that both priesthood and sacrifice have been wrongly identified as propitiatory. Thirdly I shall demonstrate that priesthood exists in a critically realistic form. Fourthly I shall suggest that the priesthood of the ordained can only be understood if it maintains a form of representation based upon the previous three points signifying both internal resemblance and external tracking in which its dialectic and Chalcedonian identity is maintained. As humanity is identified in relation to God so priesthood is identifiable in relation to Jesus Christ and his saving act. But such identification by means of a family likeness does not presuppose that the priesthood of Christ and the priesthood of the ordained are identical. In so doing I shall seek to maintain a consistency of structure, form and content.

---

[320] *CD* II.1, 45.

Chapter 6

Covenant, Sacrifice and Priesthood

In Part II the emphasis has been upon the human-divine encounter and the importance of maintaining the necessary divine-human *diastasis* by paying careful attention to an appropriate human identity. What emerged from Chapter 5 was the possibility of formulating a Protestant understanding of priesthood defined by reference to five key boundary markers. These are first, that man is God's covenant partner; second, the particularism of being in Christ; third, the Chalcedonian pattern and fourth, the maintenance of a necessary dialectic of testimony and counter-testimony and fifth, the emphasis upon vocation as the grateful human response to divinely sovereign grace. I concluded the Chapter with a study of priesthood in 1 Peter 2, the importance of which lies in its status for Protestant accounts of priesthood. In analysing the text I argued that what emerges is a notion of priesthood which is corporate. This does not mean that every Christian is a priest, but that the Church as the community of faith fulfils a priestly role as "a witness to all humanity"[1] of God's saving grace. Furthermore, within the Petrine text there is evidence of a dialectic of a priestly testimony and counter-testimony, resulting in a reconstitution, renaming and re-identification of priesthood in the light of God's prior sovereign act of grace in Jesus Christ. It is this rewriting of the understanding of a dialectic of priesthood that I shall now explore more fully.

In this Chapter I shall explore four aspects of priesthood. Following the examination of 1 Peter 2, and wishing to establish a Protestant understanding of priesthood, in the first two sections I will examine the dialectic of the priestly identity in the Bible. First, I shall briefly examine the priestly testimony and counter-testimony of the First Testament. Secondly, I shall examine the priestly testimony and counter-testimony of Jesus Christ according to Hebrews. This will demonstrate that there is a dialectic of priesthood within Scripture. Thirdly, I shall explore the nature of sacrifice as an event of responsive gratitude in relation to the priesthood of the ordained. The importance of this is that it does not require priesthood to be propitiatory, and therefore maintains appropriate characterisation and the human-divine *diastasis*. Fourthly, I shall explore the priesthood of Jesus

---

[1] Paul J. Achtemeier, *1 Peter*, Minneapolis, Augsburg Fortress, 1996, 156.

Christ and the relationship between sacrifice and priesthood in the revelation of the divine *pro nobis*.

The Priestly Testimony and Counter-testimony of the First Testament

In order to develop the dialectical account of priesthood in the Bible I shall explore three particular aspects of priesthood in the First Testament. First, I shall sketch the nature of the priestly testimony, secondly, I shall consider the relationship of priesthood and covenant and, finally, I shall outline the priestly counter-testimony in the First Testament.

The Priestly Testimony

Classically Protestantism "has had a profound aversion to cult, regarding cultic activity as primitive, magical, and manipulative".[2] This aversion has been most apparent in its attitude to the concept of priesthood, and especially the priesthood of the ordained. Julius Wellhausen[3] believed that priesthood constrains God's sovereignty.[4] If Wellhausen is correct then it

---

[2] Walter Brueggemann, *Theology of the Old Testament*, Minneapolis, Augsburg Fortress, 1997, 650. For Brueggemann the term 'counter-testimony' is the cross-examining Israel's core testimony. Brueggemann's dialectic enables him to read the theological stance of the Old Testament as a series of claims asserted for Yahweh, the God of Israel. Its 'truth claims' are arrived at 'through incessant engagement' (Breuggemann, 1997, xvi). While I shall use Brueggemann's notions of testimony and counter-testimony my concern is whether priesthood can only be described dialectically. This then raises two possibilities. First, whether through the dialectical process it is possible to redefine priesthood anew in a final synthesis or alternatively, whether divergent understandings co-exist in a creative tension.

[3] Julius Wellhausen (1844-1918) was one of the fathers of critical study of the First Testament and proponent of the four-document (J, E, D, P) hypothesis which transformed First Testament studies.

[4] According to Wellhausen the impact of the Priestly tradition ('P') was that the 'Creator of heaven and earth becomes the manager of a petty scheme for salvation; the living God descends from his throne to make way for the law. The law thrusts itself in everywhere; it commands and blocks up access to heaven; it regulates and sets limits to the understanding of the divine working on earth. As far as it can, it takes the soul out of religion and spoils morality. It demands a service of God which, though revealed, may well with truth be called a self-chosen and unnatural one, the sense and use of which are apparent neither to the understanding nor the heart. The labour is done for the sake of the exercise; it does no one any good and rejoices neither God nor man. It has no inner aim after which it spontaneously strives and which it hopes to attain by itself, but only an outward one, namely the reward attached to it, which might as well be attached to other and possibly even more curious conditions.' (Julius Wellhausen, *Prolegomena to the History of Israel* (ET), Edinburgh: A & C Black, 1885 [reprint Atlanta, Scholars Press, 1994], 509. Quoted, Joseph Blenkinsopp, *Sage, Priest, Prophet*, Louisville,

would be impossible to make any equation between the covenant as the sign of God's electing grace,[5] and 'a petty scheme for salvation... which it hopes to attain by itself' in which priestly activity was understood as being meretricious.[6] It is important to attempt, albeit very briefly, a discussion of the priestly testimony in the First Testament.

Deborah Rooke proposes that within P the cultic and the covenantal together serve to define Israel's identity. They provide "a great sense of God's holiness and power, and a corresponding sense of human sinfulness and unholiness, which somehow have to be reconciled with each other if the cultic community is to be meaningful".[7] Rooke's particular concern is the role of the High priesthood, which she says is never "portrayed as anything more than a cultic or sacral office".[8] Furthermore the instructions for the establishment of priesthood and its regulation show it to have been imparted

> by Yahweh to Moses, who is the appointed mediator between the deity and the community... presumably because any material which comes via Moses is regarded as having the stamp of divine authority... part of the divine ordering of the community.[9]

According to Richard D. Nelson the 'pivotal' role of the priests in Israel was as boundary setters.[10] He identifies two key groups of boundaries: clean/unclean and holy/profane. That "which is clean... may be thought of as that which is in its proper place within the boundaries established by God".[11] The unclean is that which is out of place. To be "holy... was to be

---

Westminster John Knox Press, 1995, 66.): see also: J. B. Lightfoot, 'Christian Ministry', in Saint *Paul's Epistle to the Philippians* (Revised Edn), London, Macmillan, 1879, 181).

[5] See: 129-138 above and the discussion of 'Vocation in the Theology of Karl Barth'.

[6] According to Wellhausen, following Luther, the notion of priesthood as 'standing between' God and man and a channel of grace distinct from that open to fellow human beings is not acceptable. (*To The Christian Nobility of the German Nation Concerning the Reform of the Christian State*, 1520: James Atkinson (ed), *Luther's Works* (Vol. 44, American Edn), Fortress Press, Philadelphia, 1966.) Luther understands priesthood, like merit, as as the antithesis of the Pauline doctrine of justification by faith alone. (Jaroslav Pelikan, *Reformation of Church and Dogma (1300-1700)*, Chicago, Chicago University Press, 1985, 145.)

[7] Deborah Rooke, *Zadok's Heirs*, Oxford, OUP, 2000, 14.

[8] Rooke, 2000, 34.

[9] Rooke, 2000, 16. (See: Brueggemann, 1997, 662.)

[10] Richard D. Nelson, *Raising Up a Faithful Priest*, Louisville, Westminster/John Knox Press, 1993, 20.

[11] Nelson, 1993, 21.

in the realm of the divine."[12] Profanity, however, was simply the normal state "of human existence".[13] Further, for "the priestly mind, the order of creation was linked directly to the world of the tabernacle/temple."[14] He also underlines the importance of identity and the delineation of boundaries "for Israel in times of peril."[15] Finally the "paradox of the priestly role was that sacrifice and ritual compelled the priest to cross these same boundaries for the welfare and safety of the whole people."[16] The emphasis upon purity is reinforced in the priestly writings by the three strands identified by Rooke.[17] Purity is understood as "holiness and therefore access to God."[18] A genealogically legitimated priesthood is demonstrably a distinctive group within the community, which acts as the identifiable guardians of purity, thereby institutionalising access to God.

Rooke also explores the association between the monarchy and priesthood in Israel.[19] Such a connection indicates the potential for a theology of priesthood, which takes its roots from a *theologia gloria*. While in ancient Israel the monarchy has a sacral role the priesthood is not monarchical. In the Pre-Exilic and Post-Exilic periods the role of the priesthood is limited by the presence of a number of local shrines. The emergence of the monarchy did not mean that the Temple had "exclusive claims to the nation's religious allegiance that would enhance the status of the Temple officers".[20] Even subsequently this does not change significantly.[21] Therefore "for all its significance the high priesthood is in some areas at least secondary to other structures in the community."[22]

---

[12] Nelson, 1993, 26. Thus the story of the fall (Gen. 3) is a story of the consequence of being in the right or wrong place.

[13] Nelson, 1993, 25.

[14] Nelson, 1993, 37.

[15] Nelson, 1993, 37.

[16] Nelson, 1993, 37.

[17] They are: the legislative, the narrative and the genealogical. (Rooke, 2000, 15.)

[18] L. William Countryman, *The Language of Ordination*, Philadelphia, Trinity Press International, 1992, 17.

[19] Rooke does this by reference to some elements of the high priest's vesture notably the twelve stoned breastplate (Exod. 28.15-30) and the royal pectoral; the turban (Exod. 28.37, 39) as indicators of royal prerogative. (See: Ezek. 21.26; gold plate Exod. 28.36 - diadem or crown.) (Rooke, 2000, 19.) She suggests there is a very close relationship between the priest and the community (Lev 4.3), 'reminiscent of that between monarch and people' insofar as 'the king was the embodiment of the people he ruled.' (Rooke, 2000, 23. See: 1 Kgs. 14.15-16; 2 Kgs. 13.2—3; 20.1-6; 21.10-12; 23.26-7.)

[20] Rooke, 2000, 121.

[21] Rooke, 2000, 238. Even as late as the Maccabean Period, although its leaders, Jonathan and Simon Maccabee, were of priestly descent they rose to prominence as military leaders. (Rooke, 2000, 326.)

[22] Rooke, 2000, 16.

Covenant, Sacrifice and Priesthood 151

While Rooke's concern is for the emergence of the High Priesthood "as the chief cultic minister in a community",[23] Brueggemann believes that the concern of the priesthood and the cult is the mediation of the divine presence, "nothing less and nothing other",[24] and Israel, "as Yahweh's covenant partner, is expected to order its life in ways that are appropriate to this relationship."[25] Priesthood and the cult "mediates Yahweh's 'real presence'"[26] in relation to which "Israel worked out its peculiar identity and sustained its odd life in the world."[27] Israel's identity is that which distinguishes it from and therefore renders it recognisable to other people. The cult serves to make the presence of Yahweh "graciously accessible and available to Israel"[28] and to understand its cultic activity as meretricious is to misrepresent its purpose.

One aspect of P is that it demonstrates the importance of the priesthood within the life of Israel, in legitimating of the cultus and its practices in defining Israel's identity. However, Israel's identity is not simply defined cultically; rather the cult is the embodiment of its covenant relationship with Yahweh.

Priesthood and Covenant

Walther Eichrodt sought to explore the emergence of the religion of Israel through the fundamental concept of covenant.[29] According to Eichrodt the First Testament writings suggest a dialectical contrast between the attempt

---

[23] Rooke, 2000, 39.
[24] Brueggemann, 1997, 663.
[25] Brueggemann, 1997, 419.
[26] Brueggemann, 1997, 650.
[27] Brueggemann, 1997, 653.
[28] Brueggemann, 1997, 663.
[29] According to Walter Brueggemann, 'Eichrodt's greatness... is that his one idea was *covenantal relatedness.*' (Brueggemann, 1997, 28 – his italics.) First, according to Eichrodt, covenant is based upon '*the factual nature of the divine revelation.*' (Walther Eichrodt, *The Theology of the Old Testament* (vol 1, ET), London, SCM, 1961, 37 – his italics.). Secondly, it is evidence of a clear divine will: 'In this way it provides life with a goal and a history with a meaning' (Eichrodt, 1961, 38.). Thirdly, it relates to a concept akin to the Kingdom of God (Eichrodt, 1961, 40.) providing a 'unifying bond' (Eichrodt, 1961, 39). Fourthly, as suggested, therefore, 'In the covenant, God assumes the existence of a remarkable *interior attitude to history*' (Eichrodt, 1961, 41 – his italics). This is based upon a narrative reading of history. Finally, therefore, this denies any notion of natural or naturalistic religion. (Eichrodt, 1961, 44.)

to render the divine recognisable by using anthropomorphic language[30] and the priestly testimony emphasising the otherness of God,[31] stressing God's sovereign will and activity in reaching out to humanity.[32] The First Testament account attempts to hold together these two divergent witnesses to the divine nature.[33] This dialectic is repeated in Eichrodt's contrast of the roles of priests and prophets within the covenant community. Whereas the priests provided the official functionaries, the prophets' role was essentially charismatic.[34] The "dominant note in P is his feeling for the statutory, the consistent, the eternally binding, corresponding to his towering vision of the transcendent, eternal God."[35]

Priesthood, drawn in relation to the covenant, recognises the importance of form and structure for the identity of the community[36] as divinely given.[37] The emphasis is firmly upon the divine grace; to which mankind can only respond.[38] The emergence of the Temple and the temple cult is concerned for the divine presence.[39] On the one hand the institutionalisation of the priesthood, implicit in Eichrodt's analysis, can lead to the perception of the divine as distant and impersonal.[40] On the other hand, the presence of the priesthood was a constant reminder of the abiding presence of God in the community while maintaining the divine/human *diastasis*.[41] The covenant community required prophets and priests,[42] as well as the Torah, the Monarchy, and the Sage to mediate the presence of the divine.

However, it is necessary to explore the tension between the presence of

---

[30] Eichrodt, 1961, 216.
[31] Eichrodt, 1961, 217.
[32] Eichrodt, 1961, 58.
[33] Eichrodt, 1961, 287 – his italics.
[34] Eichrodt, 1961, 395 – his italics. Thus it is possible to suggest that Balthasar's emphasis upon the objective nature of the Petrine faith and his understanding of apostolic succession in relation to the ministry of the ordained repeats this notion of a priestly testimony.
[35] Eichrodt, 1961, 58.
[36] Eichrodt, 1961, 404.
[37] Eichrodt, 1961, 404.
[38] Eichrodt, 1961, 422.
[39] Eichrodt, 1961, 409.
[40] Eichrodt, 1961, 434.
[41] Eichrodt, 1961, 433. 'In actual fact, the priesthood undertook a function just as important for the life of Israel as that fulfilled by the prophets... While the prophet's vision was constantly fixed on the struggle between the Kingdom of God and the kingdom of this world... a priestly outlook effectively championed the concern over revealed religion with that sole and absolute divine sovereignty, which not only has existed from all eternity, but also holds sway here and now over the world and mankind, even where the latter has turned away from God.' (Eichrodt, 1961, 435.)
[42] Eichrodt, 1961, 436.

Yahweh mediated through the Temple by the priesthood and a clearly discernible anti-clericalism within the prophetic tradition. Thus there is a dialectic tension between the priestly and cultic testimony as a guardian of the covenantal relationship of Israel and Yahweh and the frailty of the priesthood and the consequent counter-testimony of its failure to fulfil its calling.

Central to any account of the covenant history of Israel is the fall of Jerusalem and the resultant exile. Tom Wright argues that in the Jewish worldview the Temple is one of four key symbols indicative of their covenant identity.[43] However, this does not imply a simple spatial limitation by identifying God's presence in relation to the Temple, so that its destruction was indicative of the Divine absence. While the authors of the First Testament seem to have little anxiety about the anthropomorphic representation of God,[44] nonetheless He is sovereign and remains 'other' than[45] His creation. The Temple, as part of the created world, is a sign of the divine presence but not necessarily the divine presence.[46] Just as God cannot be physically represented,[47] He may be represented verbally by reference to other familiar forms. Words can signify the divine. Similarly the Temple is indicative of the presence of the divine. The Temple is central to Israel's sense of identity[48] but this identification was not unambiguous.[49]

This ambiguity throws into relief the prophetic counter-testimony. It is possible to summarise the role of the priest thus: to "*facilitate* the carrying out of ritual"; to emphasise the sacrificial event as the mediating agent

---

[43] According to Tom Wright the four primary symbols are 'Temple, Torah, Land, and ethnic identity' (N. T. Wright, *The New Testament and the People of God*, London, SPCK, 1993, 365).

[44] Eberhard Jüngel, ('Anthropomorphism: a fundamental problem in modern hermeneutics', *Theological Essays* (ET), Edinburgh, T & T Clark, 1989, 72-94.) quotes Kierkegaard's aphorism that 'People rant so much against anthropomorphism and forget that Christ's birth is the most significant anthropomorphism.' (Quoted: Jüngel, 1989, 88.)

[45] I.e. 2 Sam. 7.5-7, Nathan's voicing of Yahweh's resistance to David's plan to build the Temple, or Ps. 50.9-15 in which the Psalmist reminds Israel that it is the cult which depends upon Yahweh and not *vice versa*.

[46] Brueggemann, 1997, 675.

[47] Exod. 20.4, 23; 34.17; Lev. 19.4; 26.1; Deut. 4.15-19; 5.8; 27.15.

[48] Wright, 1993, 224-25.

[49] Wright suggests that at the time of Jesus this ambiguity revolved around the objections to Hasmonean priesthood. Although the Temple was rebuilt by Herod, who because he was not of the line of David and Solomon was not a true king, nonetheless it 'remained, *de facto* at least, the focal point of national, cultural and religious life.' (Wright, 1993, 226.)

within the sacrificial system; divination; and as teacher.[50] But the record of the priesthood in the First Testament reveals evidence of anti-priestly rhetoric including charges of veniality, drunkenness, negligence and ignorance, and even murder.[51] Consequently the priesthood which, like the Temple, should be indicative of the presence of the divine, by its failure signifies the perceived absence of the divine.

Counter-testimony in the First Testament against the Priests

Alongside the priestly testimony of the First Testament there is also a broad counter-testimony against both the cult and the priestly role. According to the Prophets the cult had become "a place of self indulgence"[52] instead of a place where God was encountered through worship. The counter-testimony is the recorded failure of the priesthood and the cult to mediate the presence of the divine. The dialectic of priesthood exists in the priesthood, which signifies the divine presence, but yet it does not guarantee the divine presence. This cannot be resolved into a higher synthesis but it opens the way to a clearer understanding of priesthood. I shall therefore briefly examine two particular strands of the priestly counter-testimony in the First Testament: the apparent failure of the priesthood to live up to its calling and the priestly counter-testimony of Melchizedek.

The First Testament unsparingly records the failures and shortcomings of the Temple cultus and priesthood. Blenkinsopp suggests the pseudonymous Malachi understood the priesthood as a sign of Israel's covenant relationship with Yahweh.[53] Its failure to fulfil this calling results in a savage attack accusing it of offering false and therefore defective sacrifices[54] and neglecting to give true instruction to Israel, God's covenant people.[55] Malachi is not alone in his criticism.[56]

> For thou hast no delight in sacrifice; were I to give a burnt offering, thou

---

[50] Blenkinsopp, 1995, 80-81 – his italics. This included the 'maintenance, transmission, teaching of the laws' (Deut. 31.9-13, 24-26: Blenkinsopp, 1995, 82).

[51] Veniality: Mic. 3.11; Jer. 6.13; 8.10: drunkenness: Is. 28.7; Jer. 13.13: negligence and ignorance: Zeph. 3.4; Jer. 14.18; Ezek. 22.26: murder: Hos. 6.9.

[52] Brueggemann, 1997, 678.

[53] That Malachi, may have been 'a dissident member of the Jerusalem temple clergy' (Blenkinsopp, 1995, 89f).

[54] Mal. 1.6-8, 10, 12-13.

[55] Mal. 2.1-9.

[56] So for example, Hosea proclaims: 'For I desire steadfast love and not sacrifice, the knowledge of God, rather than burnt offerings' (Hos. 6.6). See also: Ps. 40.6; Prov. 21.3; Is. 1.11; 56.6-8; Jer. 6. 20, 21; 7.21-23; 17.21-27; 33.16-22; Ezek. 20.27-33; [39.17-20 – God is the one who provides the sacrifice]; Hos. 3.4; 8.11-13; 9.4; [Zeph. 1.7-8 - again God is the one who provides the sacrifice].

wouldst not be pleased he sacrifice acceptable to God is a broken spirit; a broken and contrite heart, O God, thou wilt not despise.[57]

This is no outright rejection of the cult and the attendant priesthood. Instead the cult is subverted by this counter-testimony.[58] While the cult and its sacrificial practices remain a significant and distinctive aspect of Israel's life and identity, the problem is that the sacrifices no longer facilitate the true relationship between God and His covenant people. Instead they have become self-indulgent and an end in themselves. There appears, as a consequence, to be a connection between sacrifice and external identity, defined in terms of obedience to God. Negatively stated, disobedience is the denial of one's covenant identity,[59] rendering the person, or the community 'unrecognisable'. The counter-testimony is not simply criticism of the improper conduct of the cult, rather the cultus can only be understood in relation to the life of the community as the people of the covenant.[60]

The divine 'absence' is therefore part of the counter-testimony becoming another way in which "the community is given new life" as Yahweh's covenant partner in his "inclination toward Israel."[61] The covenant may be broken by humanity but it cannot be "reversed or removed or destroyed as the omnipotent work of the grace of God."[62] The fall of Jerusalem and the destruction of the Temple may speak of the divine 'absence' but the covenant is part of God's permanent elective purpose for Israel.[63] It is the "construal of Israel as Yahweh's partner" that Brueggemann argues is the theme of Israel's narrative life. Israel is loved into existence, commanded to be obedient and when it is not, it is scattered into exile. It is in this moment

---

[57] Ps. 51.16, 17.

[58] Similarly the author of 1 Peter in his mimetic account of the Church in terms of covenant identity subverts the prior use of such language and thereby introduces a new meaning and a new frame of reference. Jeremiah addresses a similar problem in the danger that the cultic sacrificial practices become 'a stumbling block' (Jer 6.21). Stephen Sykes argues there is a distinction within theology between the internal and external exemplified in 'the Judeao-Christian tradition of the heart. It is the tradition of inwardness... which makes it impossible to identify Christianity merely with its external features, whether myths, teaching, rites, or social embodiment.' (Stephen Sykes, *The Identity of Christianity*, Philadelphia, Fortress Press, 1984, 213.) I have preferred the notions of testimony and counter-testimony because while they include both they could be understood as being the equivalent of the external and internal. Furthermore, both testimony and counter-testimony require that each (while perhaps priviledging either the external or internal) includes within it both intentionality and expression.

[59] This is precisely the point that Barth makes in his anthropology. (see: 131 above.)

[60] Frances M Young, *Sacrifice and the Death of Christ*, London, SPCK, 1975, 33.

[61] Brueggemann, 1997, 442. (See also: *CD* III.2, 31-34.)

[62] *CD* IV.1, 481.

[63] Blenkinsopp, 1995, 108.

of the seeming absence of the divine that Israel is once again the recipient of Yahweh's turning to them so that they are gathered back into obedience and hope. In this Brueggemann discerns a general pattern consisting of sovereignty and fidelity, disobedience and judgement, rescue and rehabilitation.[64]

A second, seemingly slight strand of the priestly counter-testimony in the First Testament is the story of the mysterious Melchizedek, 'king of

---

[64] Brueggemann, 1997, 447. Brueggemann proceeds to offer four examples:
(1) Deut. 32.1-43.
vv. 1-6   introduction
vv. 7-14   appeal to the mighty acts of Yahweh
vv. 15-18   indictment
vv. 19-29   sentence
vv. 30-38   assurance
vv. 39-42   confirmation of the poet's words of hope
v. 43   praise
(2) Hos. 2.2-23.
vv. 2-13   indictment and sentence
vv. 14-15   invitation
vv. 16-20   renewed covenant
vv. 21-23   restored creation
(3) Ezek. 16.1-63.
vv. 1-14   Yahweh's initiatory goodness
vv. 15-52   indictment and sentence
vv. 53-63   forgiveness and restoration
It is not the institution itself but rather the chosenness of the Davidic dynasty that is its significance. Once again here as elsewhere there is evidence of the pattern discerned by Brueggemann of sovereignty and fidelity, disobedience and judgment, rescue and rehabilitation.
(4) Ps. 106.1-48.
vv. 1-5   introduction
vv. 6-12   rebellion and rescue
vv. 13-39   rebellion
vv. 40-43   judgement
vv. 44-46   rescue
v. 47   petition
v. 48   doxology
What is particularly interesting is that a similar pattern (excepting the middle pairing of disobedience and judgement) is also discernible in Philippians 2.
(5) Phil. 2.6-7.
v. 6   sovereignty
vv. 7-8   fidelity
v. 9   rescue
vv. 10-11   rehabilitation

Salem... priest of God Most High.'[65] Whereas Mosaic law stipulated, "the high priest had to be able to trace a line of physical descent back to Aaron on his father's side" as well as being a pure bred Israelite,[66] Melchizedek has no recognizable lineage standing outside the "established line of succession to the Levitical high priesthood."[67] Lane suggests the counter-testimony articulates a priesthood that "will be qualitatively different" from that of the existing Temple cultus. Melchizedek could therefore be interpreted to be a "heavenly high priest".[68]

Psalm 110 suggests that another possible difference between Melchizedek and the Jerusalem priesthood is the desire to prevent any attempt to separate "ecclesiastical power from the secular".[69] Possibly this mysterious kingly and priestly figure who blesses Abram and to whom Abram responds with due homage,[70] despite his apparently non-Israelite origins, bridges in his person the sovereign and priestly functions. Although the role ascribed to Melchizedek is by no means clear, and the references slender in the extreme, his role might be to "connect Abraham with the location of the Davidic throne" so that he serves as a "prototype and precursor of the Davidic dynasty."[71] It is not the institution itself but rather the chosenness of the Davidic dynasty that is significant. Once again,[72] there is evidence of the pattern of sovereignty and fidelity, disobedience and judgment, rescue and rehabilitation. The Psalmist does not repudiate priesthood. Rather as the concept of the Davidic dynasty offers the ideal of the monarchy in the person of David, so too Melchizedek offers an idealized priesthood.[73] Both base their claims on historic figures but they are not simply retrospective; for both embody future, eschatological hopes.[74]

Neither the Psalmist nor the Prophet contends that sacrifice is inherently wrong. The priestly testimony is the mediated presence of God made

---

[65] Gen. 14.18. The other reference to Melchizedek in the First Testament is Ps. 110.4, 'one of the most difficult Psalms' (A. A. Anderson, *Psalms* (Vol 2), London, Marshall Morgan and Scott, 1977b, 767).

[66] William L. Lane, *Hebrews 1-8*, Waco, Word Books, 1991, cxxxi.

[67] Lane, 1991, cxxxi.

[68] Margaret Barker, *The Gate of Heaven*, London, SPCK, 1991, 62. Barker is reliant upon the evidence from the Dead Sea Scrolls in her interpretation.

[69] Anderson, 1977b, 771.

[70] Gerhard von Rad, *Genesis* (ET, Rev Edn.), London, SCM, 1972, 180.

[71] von Rad, 1972, 180.

[72] This is perhaps implicit in Ps. 110 but is rather more explicit in Ps. 132, where there are distinct echoes of the former Psalm, especially vv. 11-12.

[73] John Dunnill, *Covenant and Sacrifice in the Letter to the Hebrews*, Cambridge, CUP, 1992, 165.

[74] Robert Davidson, *The Vitality of Worship*, Grand Rapids, Eerdmans, 1998, 367. The Psalm imagines the 'ideal' God-appointed priesthood that is yet to come.

graciously available. It fails if it either ceases to mediate the presence of God or if the divine presence is not a gift of grace. Rather the counter-testimony of the Psalmist and the Prophet challenges the externality of the sacrifice and whether it is to be construed as propitiatory. It still proclaims a sacrifice, but one which is the vocational sacrifice of the 'self'.[75] So Barth speaks of the Word of God as being above all a word of grace, so that to be "summoned is to be called out of oneself and beyond oneself",[76] in recognition of which the only possible response is the praise of the creature to the Creator.

Like the First Testament writers, Barth is not afraid to use cultic language as part of his counter-testimony. Any sacrifice[77] offered by humanity cannot be propitiatory, because "the sacrifice of Jesus Christ had been offered once for all and could not be repeated."[78] The Christian's "whole life" is an event of "appropriate worship"[79] offered in grateful response to God's grace. In the context of Christian living sacrifice "means surrender, it means an unconditional gift" offered to God. As an acceptable sacrifice "it is not a human action whereby the will of God is fulfilled" but "a 'demonstration' demanded by God for His glory."[80]

The Testimony and Counter-testimony of the Priesthood of Jesus in the Letter to the Hebrews

I have argued that priesthood, according to the testimony and counter-testimony of the First Testament, exists within a dialectic of covenantal identity embracing both its external, cultic and the internal, obedient sameness and difference through both tracking and fitting theories of representation. A key concern is the relationship between divine sovereignty and the priestly tradition. In this second section I propose to explore further the dialectic of priestly tradition in the testimony and counter-testimony of the priesthood of Jesus in the Letter to the Hebrews. Here the writer explores sacrifice and priesthood in a creative exposition of Jesus Christ's saving act upon the cross.[81] The importance of this for Protestant theology is twofold: first the maintenance of the divine

---

[75] Ps. 50.16-17; Hos. 6.6.
[76] *CD* III.2, 166.
[77] Rom. 12.1, also Rom. 15.6; Phil. 2.17.
[78] *CD* IV.2, 640.
[79] *CD* IV.2, 640.
[80] Karl Barth, *The Epistle to the Romans* (ET, 6th Edn), Oxford, OUP, 1957, 431.
[81] F. F. Bruce states that priesthood 'and sacrifice are inseparable entities.' (F F Bruce, *The Epistle to the Hebrews*, Grand Rapids, Eerdemans, 1979, liv.) The importance of this statement lies in the impeccable credentials of F. F. Bruce as a Protestant biblical scholar.

sovereignty; secondly, the creation of a dialectic which embraces both real and metaphorical usage of the notion of priesthood.

Unlike the First Testament in which priestly testimony and counter-testimony originate separately, the author of Hebrews sets them side by side as a deliberate literary device. As a result, in the mimetic economy of Hebrews it is possible to discern continuity and discontinuity leading to an inevitable reconstitution key to which are the concepts of sacrifice, atonement and priesthood. However, there is no final synthesis but rather priesthood remains in a creative tension denying ultimate closure or definition.

Barnabas Lindars says it is "a mistake to look for a leading idea as the key to the whole".[82] Instead he identifies a literary device whereby the author brackets the body of the text between the ascription of Jesus as the 'pioneer of their salvation',[83] suggesting that the argument proceeds "from the known to the unknown and back to the known at the end."[84] Lindars asks what prompts the author to explore Israelite atonement ritual and cultic ritual given the lack of reference to the Jerusalem Temple. He believes that the answer can be found in the text "by looking back to 13.7-16."[85] The author urges his listeners to imitate the faith of 'those who spoke to you the word of God'.[86] He argues that this imitation demonstrates "the exemplary quality of their life is the fruit of the faith which they maintained."[87] Lindars emphasizes that in Hebrews, faith

> does not mean the content of the Christian confession, i.e., what I believe, but the quality of faithful living in accordance with the Christian confession, i.e., what I do as a believer.[88]

Lindars believes that the intended recipients of the letter are a group of Jewish Christians[89] who would recognise the cultic and priestly frame of reference. So for example, in Hebrews 9

---

[82] Barnabas Lindars, *The Theology of the Letter to the Hebrews*, Cambridge, CUP, 1991, 26.

[83] Heb. 2.10, 'pioneer and perfecter of our faith' (Heb 12.2.).

[84] Lindars, 1991, 27. There are here overtones of the pattern, identified by Brueggeman, of sovereignty and fidelity, disobedience and judgement, rescue and rehabilitation. (See: 156, n. 64.) See also: B. F. Westcott, *The Epistle to the Hebrews*, London, MacMillan & Co, 1889, xxxviii; Bruce, 1979, xxx; Lane, 1991a, lv-lviii.

[85] Lindars, 1991, 8.

[86] Heb. 13.7.

[87] Lindars, 1991, 8.

[88] Lindars, 1991, 8-9.

[89] Lindars, 1991, 17.

the strange teachings are the details of atonement sacrifice which were there set out. If so, the whole point at issue is a felt need on the part of the readers to resort to Jewish customs in order to come to terms with their sense of sin against God and the need for atonement. Thus the central argument of the letter is precisely a compelling case for the complete and abiding efficacy of Jesus' death as an atoning sacrifice.[90]

Priestly Testimony in Hebrews

The key issue identified by Lindars is why "is it that the readers have lost confidence in the power of the sacrifice of Christ ...?"[91] The author addresses this by offering practical ways the community can continue to live the faith that they were taught. Lindars argues that the writer feels it is necessary to address what it means to be recognisably 'in Christ' and the problem of the incipient loss of identity, in order to prevent them lapsing into their former Jewish identity.[92]

The sacrificial and priestly testimony in the Letter to the Hebrews "has three principal strands."[93] The first is the "real priesthood of the Messiah".[94] Secondly, there is the "eschatological concept of the inauguration of the new covenant."[95] This is what gives perpetual efficacy to Christ's sacrifice, opening a renewed era of salvation in which fresh sacrifices for sin are no longer required. Consequently although "Hebrews casts doubt on the efficacy of the old covenant... its criticism does not amount to a dismissal."[96] It is the covenant inaugurated and sealed by the blood of Jesus Christ, which, even more than the former covenant, reveals the goodness of God.[97] The third strand is the Day of Atonement, "which provides the essential requirements for an atoning sacrifice."[98]

The writer of the Letter to the Hebrews does not regard the notion of Jesus' priesthood as an interesting metaphor; it is "meant seriously. Jesus really is a high priest."[99] The author presents creatively an account of the death of Jesus Christ *pro nobis* within the Jewish cultic metanarrative of the

---

[90] Lindars, 1991, 10.

[91] Lindars, 1991, 12.

[92] What is apparent is a certain similarity with the Letter to the Philippians and the question of the covenant identity of God's people. (See: Chapter 4 above.)

[93] Lindars, 1991, 71.

[94] Lindars, 1991, 72. (See: Heb 5.1-10.)

[95] Lindars, 1991, 72.

[96] Dunnill, 1992, 229.

[97] Dunnill, 1992, 230.

[98] Lindars, 1991, 72.

[99] Lindars, 1991, 58. 'Thus, Hebrews is conscious that he is giving a new exposition of the sacrifice of Christ ... a creative, new development ... that "Christ died for our sins according to the scriptures" (1 Cor. 15.3).' (Lindars, 1991, 60.)

Day of Atonement.[100] So too the conservative Reformed theologian Louis Berkhof is adamant that "Jesus is a real priest."[101] Thus the root of Jesus' priesthood lies in his atoning work.

The dialectic of the metaphorical, but yet real, priesthood of Jesus is maintained even within the literary structure of the text, for example, in the chiasmic form of Hebrews 5.1-10.[102] In verses 1-4 the office of the high priest is characterised and its qualifications set out. The author then demonstrates how "Christ satisfied the qualifications (5-8) and fulfils the office (9, 10)."[103]

The author adopts a chiasmic structure again in Hebrews 9, which on the one hand, contrasts the recognizable elements of Christ's priesthood in relation to the high priests of Jerusalem, while on the other, he highlights its dissimilarities.[104] The writer compares and contrasts the efficacy of Jesus Christ's high priesthood and that of the Jerusalem cultus proposing that the "superiority of Christ's cultic action" is twofold. First there is the uniqueness of the heavenly, compared to the earthly sanctuary. Secondly there is the "uniqueness of the sacrifice which he presented."[105] Christ, as high priest, is both the one who makes the sacrifice and sacrifice. In effect the author presents his argument dialectically. As Lindars recognizes,

> atonement has certain requirements and these must be seen to be fulfilled

---

[100] Lane, 1991, cxxiv.

[101] Louis Berkhof, *Systematic Theology*, Edinburgh, Banner of Truth, 1984, 366.

[102] Given the nature of the Letter to the Hebrews and its clearly constructed literary structure, albeit one which is widely debated. (For a sense of the breadth of the discussion of Hebrews and its genre see: Lane, 1991a, lxix-xcviii.) It would seem that the author's repeated use of chiasmic structure (Heb. 1.1-4; 3.3-3; 5.1-10; [7.1-10]; 9.1-10; 10.9, 33-34; 12.6; 13.2, 4, 10-16) is not simply accidental. One effect of this particular literary device by which the order of the initial statement is reversed in the second part is implicitly a form of a dialectic of stating and restating.

[103] Westcott, 1889, 121. (See: Lane, 1991a, 111.) Lindars helpfully sets it out in full:
a a priest is commissioned to 'deal gently' with sinners (1-2)
  b his ministry is on behalf of all people, including himself (3)
    c it is a divinely called status (4)
    c´ Thus Jesus was divinely called (5-6)
  b´ Jesus shared our sufferings and learnt the meaning of human obedience (7-8)
a´ Jesus thus became the means of salvation to all in His priestly capacity (9-10)
(Lindars, 1991, 61).

[104] William L. Lane, *Hebrews 9-13*, Dallas, Word Books, 1991b, 237.
a 'δια the greater and more perfect σκηνῆ'
  b 'not made with hands, that is to say, not of ordinary building...' (11b)
  b´ 'not by means of the blood of goats and calves'
a´ 'but by means of his own blood' (12b)

[105] Lane, 1991b, 237.

in Jesus. It would be pointless to make such an elaborate proof of His priesthood, unless it was necessary for Him to perform a priestly task.[106]

The author does this by reference to the ceremonial of the Day of Atonement. Just as the animal 'without blemish' is the proper sacrifice, so it "becomes apparent that the sinlessness of Jesus, which has been mentioned several times, previously in other connections, qualified Him for the role of sacrificial victim."[107] Secondly, the blood in its liminality of life and death belongs to God. Consequently the

> sacrifice is holy, because it has been made over into the sphere of God's holiness, and the blood, which is special and belongs exclusively to God, is available to convey holiness, and therefore cleansing, to people and objects with which it is brought into contact.[108]

Not only is Jesus' priesthood real but (and this is fundamental to the authorial intent) it is uniquely efficacious. The experience of the Jerusalem high priesthood is presented and then restated in order to explicate Christ's atoning act. In the process priesthood is reconstituted anew by means of an act of "non-identical repetition".[109]

Counter-testimony against the Priestly in Hebrews

Having affirmed that priesthood has reached its apotheosis in Jesus Christ, the writer of the Letter to the Hebrews appears also to propose its cancellation. Thus while the priesthood of Jesus Christ is affirmed as genuine, nonetheless it is "introduced as a metaphor" in Hebrews 2.17.[110] The metaphorical reference to priesthood is repeated when the writer calls upon those whom he is addressing to, 'consider Jesus, the apostle and high priest of our confession.'[111] The first thing to note is that this verse is set in a tightly composed passage in which the author seeks to compare Jesus and Moses, demonstrating that Jesus combines within himself the roles of Moses and Aaron "in a infinitely loftier form."[112] The double titles of 'apostle' and 'high priest' "simply sum up the presentation of Jesus in 1.1-2.18 as the one through whom God proclaimed the definitive word of

---

[106] Lindars, 1991, 91.
[107] Lindars, 1991, 93. This is a traditional idea, see also 1 Pet 2.19.
[108] Lindars, 1991, 93.
[109] John Milbank, 'Stories of Sacrifice', *Modern Theology* (12), 1996, 44.
[110] Lindars, 1991, 58.
[111] Heb. 3.1.
[112] Westcott, 1889, 74.

salvation and made propitiation for the sins of the people."[113] Should, however, this phrase be best understood more elliptically?

Luther suggested that Jesus was called an 'apostle' because "he was sent into the world by the Father".[114] As we have seen, the concept of *missio* forms a key strand in Balthasar's Christology. So here, and in the Johannine prologue where Jesus is 'sent from God',[115] *missio* is the key which "expresses both the trinitarian and soteriological dimensions"[116] of Jesus Christ. As Balthasar recognizes, this is a vocational notion, which presupposes a calling and a sending of one, by another.[117] Hence only in the light of an understanding of his mission is it possible to attempt to answer the question, 'Who is Jesus Christ?'[118]

In the opening verses of Hebrews,[119] the writer sought to establish the divine identity of Jesus Christ. And it is a question of identity, which lies at the heart of the counter-testimony that the writer presents. First, the writer understands Jesus' priesthood as being 'after the order of Melchizedek.'[120] Secondly, there is a connection between the priesthood of Jesus and the First Testament counter-testimony.[121]

The first strand is provided by the mysterious First Testament figure of Melchizedek, whose priesthood contrasts sharply with that of Aaron and his successors.[122] Whereas the Aaronic priesthood was a genealogically determined line of succession, the priesthood of Melchizedek was quite distinct. First, as the Psalmist suggests, the one who is 'like Melchizedek' is similarly one who "owes his appointment to God rather than the law of physical descent."[123] Secondly, the Psalmist announces such a priest will be 'a priest forever'.[124] In "the early Christian Church the Psalm was interpreted christologically"[125] and understood messianically.[126] Thus God

---

[113] Lane, 1991, 75.

[114] James Atkinson (ed), *Luther: Early Theological Works*, (The Library of Christian Classics) London, SCM, 1962, 69.

[115] Jn. 1.6.

[116] *TD* III, 151.

[117] *TD* III, 154.

[118] *TD* III, 155.

[119] Heb. 1.1-4, containing a similar ideas to Phil 2.6-11, culminating in the naming of Jesus Christ.

[120] Heb. 5.6, 10; 6.20, 7.11, 17.

[121] Heb. 10.5-6; c.f. Ps. 40.6-8. (LXX).

[122] See: earlier discussion of Melchizadek, 156-7 above. Also: Dunnill, 1992, 166; Lindars, 1991, 76.

[123] Lane, 1991a, cxxxi.

[124] Lane, 1991a, cxxxi. (Cf. Ps. 110.4.)

[125] Anderson, 1977b, 767. (See: Mk. 12.35-37; Matt. 22.41-46; Lk. 20.41-44.)

[126] Morna Hooker, *The Gospel According to St Mark*, London, A & C Black, 1997, 290-92.

gives directly the priesthood of Jesus which is part of no human order. Thirdly, it is not finitely limited but transcends historical time marking the encounter of human καιρός with the eternal and the divine. The counter-testimony of Jesus' divinely appointed priesthood revealed in the efficaciousness of its ability to reconcile God and human beings is 'once and for all'.[127]

Quoting Jeremiah's prophecy of the establishment of a new covenant,[128] which will be unlike the 'old' covenant, Hebrews promises "the establishment of a definitive relationship with God that is described as qualitatively 'new.'"[129] By stressing "the imperfect and provisional character of 'that first' covenant"[130] it similarly contrasts the priesthood of Jesus Christ as being 'after the order of Melchizedek'; eternal and divinely given as distinct from the Aaronic priesthood.

The second strand of Jesus' priestly role according to Hebrews alludes explicitly to the First Testament counter-testimony.[131]

> Consequently, when Christ came into the world, he said, 'Sacrifices and offerings thou hast not desired, but a body hast thou prepared for me; in burnt offerings and sin offerings thou hast taken no pleasure. Then I said, "Lo, I have come to do thy will, O God," as it is written of me in the roll of the book.'[132]

By placing the words of Psalm 40.6-8, in Jesus Christ's mouth the writer suggests that he does not simply articulate, but embodies the priestly counter-testimony of the First Testament. According to Westcott, the words of the Psalmist are not merely the recognition of the inherent powerlessness of sacrifices themselves but look forward to "a perfect sacrifice (death) of one who has served perfectly."[133] But this presupposes a concept of sacrifice in which sacrifice equates to loss (death) by yielding up to the divine that which will facilitate appeasement. I propose that, understood

---

[127] Heb. 9.25-28 develops the theme of Jesus' 'once for all' sacrifice (and therefore priesthood) a theme alluded to by Cranmer in the Book of Common Prayer, The Order For The Administration of The Lord's Supper or Holy Communion, in the prayer of thanksgiving or consecration.

[128] Heb. 8.8-12 c.f. Jer. 31.31-34; Heb. 10.16 c.f. Jer. 31.33-34. That the writer feels it necessary to quote it twice would seem to underline the importance of it within his argument.

[129] Lane, 1991a, 209.

[130] Lane, 1991a, 208.

[131] This is also implicit in the contrast between Jesus' priesthood with that of the Aaronic priesthood.

[132] Heb. 10.5-7, referring to Ps. 40.6-8.

[133] Westcott, 1889, 309.

kenotically, sacrifice is when the one who sacrifices is able to offer *"everything* for the sake of its *return* ... as the same but different."[134] What Christ offers "is the sacrifice of obedience."[135]

In conclusion, the argument of Hebrews is structured dialectically. On the one hand, the testimony of the letter is not only to the historical reality but also the essential superiority of the priesthood of Jesus Christ.[136] On the other, Jesus' priesthood is the embodiment of the priestly counter-testimony of the First Testament.[137] Importantly the writer of the Letter to the Hebrews does not seek to reject the priestly and sacrificial testimony of the First Testament. Instead by engaging the readers' familiarity with the concept, he proposes that the person and atoning event of Jesus Christ are above all *the* genuinely priestly event. Jesus' priesthood provides an analogy for the event of his reconciliation of both God and humanity.

Analogy proposes that there is a resemblance between otherwise distinct beings or objects discernible in the similarity of their attributes.[138] Fitting and tracking theories,[139] of representation and content determination, are concerned not primarily with *what* they point to but *how*.[140] According to fitting theories, a sign points to that which it resembles and may be said either to 'mirror' or to 'model' "structural relationships among the elements represented."[141] In other words, they have some shared features and likeness is a consequence of interpretative judgment. For tracking theories, however, "if representation is a matter of the nonaccidental or nonarbitrary covariance of signs and that to which they point, then it is not a matter of interpretation at all".[142] In this case the content or meaning is beyond our control and objectively determined.

Jesus Christ, the Word of God, models priesthood in its fullness. His is the once for all priestly testimony of reconciliation.[143] In an *analogia fidei* Jesus Christ is the one who gives meaning to all notions of priesthood. But he is also the priestly counter-testimony, tracking priesthood which presents itself as the sacrifice of praise and thanksgiving, which celebrates humanity

---

[134] Milbank, 1996, 51 – his italics.

[135] Timothy Gorringe, *God's Just Vengeance*, Cambridge, CUP, 1996, 78.

[136] I.e. Heb. 9.1-14.

[137] Heb. 10.1-18 is a mimetic retelling of the cultic event of the Day of Atonement but one in which the focus is the superiority of Christ's sacrifice and his priesthood.

[138] But not necessarily its fundamental definition. (Rowan Williams, *Arius*, SCM, 2001, 218.)

[139] See: 10 above.

[140] Donna M. Summerfield, 'Fitting versus tracking: Wittgenstein on represenation', in Hans Sluga, David G. Stern (ed), *The Cambridge Companion to Wittgenstein*, Cambridge, CUP, 1999, 102.

[141] Summerfield, 1999, 102.

[142] Summerfield, 1999, 113.

[143] Heb. 9.24-28.

as God's covenant partner.

In the narrative I have outlined there is both reversal and recognition. As a result the apparent uncertainty of identity and seemingly shifting appearances is resolved in re-identification and renaming.[144] If, as F. F. Bruce suggests, priesthood "and sacrifice are inseparable entities"[145] then necessarily the redefinition of priesthood will also require the possibility that sacrifice must also be redefined.

The Testimony and Counter-testimony of Sacrifice

I have proposed that, according to both the First Testament and the Letter to the Hebrews, priesthood is to be understood dialectically. Central to both is the relatedness of priesthood and sacrifice,[146] imaginatively brought together in the Letter to the Hebrews, in a creative exposition of the identity of Jesus Christ. Next I shall examine sacrifice before exploring the priestly nature of the event of Jesus Christ's atoning action in the following section.

Two definitions of the word 'sacrifice' are commonly advanced. That it simply means to make holy;[147] or that 'sacrifice' is derived from that which is "made both accursed and holy".[148] John Dunnill suggests, following structural anthropologists and their emphasis upon the arbitrary nature of signs, a threefold understanding of sacrifice. First, that sacrifice is to

---

[144] Heb. 1.4.

[145] Bruce, 1979, liv.

[146] John Dunnill proposes a reading of Hebrews guided by structuralism and the findings of anthropology. 'Hebrews does not decry sacrifice, but offers a "better" and final rite.' So that, the 'cultus is essentially a system of actions mediating between humanity and God, so "understanding" it must involve entering into the assumptions and thought-patterns intrinsic to that relationship'. (Dunnill, 1992, 47.) Dunnill adopts a narrative understanding assuming that meaning is 'a function of relationship within a pattern'. (Dunnill, 1992, 49.) Hebrews, he suggests, appeals to a '*bricolage* of random events into significant wholes, on the "meaning-world" which is composed of the text's inner-relations.' (Dunnill, 1992, 50.) This serves to establish the identity of the Hebrews as the people of the Covenant. The author of Hebrews appropriates the language of the Jerusalem cultus and its priesthood, mimetically re-interpreting it to articulate the story of God's saving act in Christ. Hence 'the letter to the Hebrews exhibits signs of a liminal-sacral world-view, most obviously in relation to elements of Israel's cultus – the new covenant being presented in imagery drawn from the old ... Hebrews alone attempts a systematic interpretation of Christian salvation as fulfilment of the Old Testament sacrificial cultus.' (Dunnill, 1992, 115.) However, in his adherence to a structuralist reading he fails to acknowledge the intent of the writer, as discernible from the internal evidence of the text. Whereas for Barnabas Lindars it is this which, taken alongside the use made of cultic thought patterns, is key to the understanding of Hebrews. (Lindars, 1991, 8-12.)

[147] Ian Bradley, *The Power of Sacrifice*, London, DLT, 1995, 22f.

[148] *TD* IV, 302.

"represent in miniature"[149] the distinction of order and chaos by ensuring that the pure and the impure are kept in their proper place. Sacrificial ritual provides a means of possible movement between one state and another by means of separation and aggregation. Secondly, it is a symbolic action, which structures and defines *"system-affirming events*, whose precise purpose will be contextually established by the needs of any particular system."[150] Thirdly, there is a basic "three-fold form of symbolic action: entry into sacred/significant space; a highly charged action there; and exit now transformed."[151] As a result of this, there is "a *communication* of sacred power."[152] This threefold understanding would lend itself to either of the two definitions of sacrifice.

A fourth and essentially kenotic understanding, is proposed by John Milbank, in which identity is both affirmed but necessarily redefined so that the essential metanarrative is symbolically confirmed. In this complex crossing of boundaries from the sacred to the secular and the secular to the sacred, transformation is made possible. Milbank criticizes what he calls a "pernicious 'sacrificial'" in which the individual or the community is required to give "up one thing for the sake of something greater".[153] The focus of this critique is the definition of sacrifice as loss, whether voluntary or otherwise.

The problem with pernicious sacrifice can be demonstrated with regards both to the priesthood of Jesus Christ and human priesthood. In the saving work of Jesus Christ what does Jesus sacrifice (lose) in the priestly transaction? If it were either his divinity or his humanity he would cease to be himself, and become another. Conversely what can humanity offer to God? Following Anselm, if God is that than which nothing greater be conceived? God is neither incomplete nor can he be propitiated.

Instead Milbank[154] proposes a concept of sacrifice as "a genuine religious sacrifice of *everything* for the sake of its *return* (repetition, *mimesis*) as the same but different."[155] Milbank says that, biblically, sacrifice is essentially

---

[149] Dunnill, 1992, 72.

[150] Dunnill, 1992, 75 – his italics.

[151] Dunnill, 1992, 76, following Hubert and Mauss, (*Sacrifice*, 1898).

[152] Dunnill, 1992, 76 – his italics.

[153] Milbank, 1996, 51.

[154] Milbank draws upon the work of J. Wellhausen, W. Robertson Smith, J. G. Frazer and H. Hubert with M. Mauss who composed 'great "stories of sacrifice"' (Milbank, 1996, 30.) which undergird much twentieth century thought on the subject. He then proceeds to analyse the work of René Girard and Jacques Lacan and the introduction of notions of mimesis within the sacrificial economy. Nonetheless Milbank concludes that their work remains influenced by 'the thought and thematics akin to those of nineteenth-century positivism.' (Milbank, 1996, 50.) This is evident in the presumption that the logic of sacrifice necessarily implies some form of ritualistic violence at its root.

[155] Milbank, 1996, 51 – his italics.

kenotic. Giving

> is not loss but a self-emptying *in order* to be, and sacrificial response is, in return, a total giving back which is the only possible mode of continuing to participate in Being.[156]

I have outlined Milbank's argument because it also points forward to the theme of atonement in which

> God offers himself to us, but not in a dying that is a loss, nor a dying which institutes a debt to be paid back. Instead it is a dying whose loss is overtaken by giving, a mode of being for which a present 'remaining' consists in a total act of extrusion.[157]

There are parallels here with Barth's[158] understanding of atonement as the divine *pro nobis*. One similarity is Barth's understanding of kenosis.[159] According to Barth, the kenotic identity of the Son reveals that "God gives himself"[160] to be known in the humanity of Jesus Christ "which means God's self-humiliation and self alienation".[161] But "God is man"[162] for Barth in Jesus Christ. This deceptively simple statement encompasses two methodological presumptions. First, there is the underlying Chalcedonian

---

[156] Milbank, 1996, 52 – his italics. A biblical example is the feeding of the five thousand (Mk. 6.32-44; c.f. Matt. 14.13-21; Lk. 9.10-17; Jn. 6.5-13.) a small gift of food is handed over to Jesus which becomes the means wherein the crowd is fed. Even so there is more left over than comprised the original gift. The handing over, far from being loss, becomes a means of receiving back far more than was given. There is no ritualistic violence involved. See: Chapter 8 below where I discuss the priesthood and the eucharist.

[157] Milbank, 1996, 54.

[158] Milbank would not be happy with this proposal believing that humanity participates in its salvation insofar as 'incarnation cannot be by the absorbing of divinity into humanity, but only the assumption of humanity into divinity.' The problem Milbank suggests is that the 'more he [Jesus] is identified with God, the more he becomes abstract'. For Milbank the gospels 'can be read not as the story of Jesus, but as the story of the (re)foundation of a new city, a new kind of human community' (John Milbank, 'The Name of Jesus', *The Word Made Strange*, Oxford, Blackwell, 1998, 150). His critique of Barth, and particularly his understanding of atonement, is that his theology remains 'somewhat liberal' (Milbank, 1998, 167.) in its individualism. Nonetheless, they both wish to understand sacrifice as a positive event whereby the giver is also supremely the recipient.

[159] See: Chapter 3 above.

[160] *CD* II.1, 53.

[161] *CD* II.1, 55.

[162] *CD* II.1, 151.

Covenant, Sacrifice and Priesthood

pattern,[163] which results in a necessary dialectic where the two natures coexist in perpetual and irresolvable tension, in Jesus Christ. Jesus Christ stands between God and man, by standing before both[164] fulfilling a priestly role.[165] Secondly, the kenosis of Jesus Christ is a positive not a negative assertion. It is "kenosis by addition"; but the addition of the human is not the same as its divinization. The resulting unity is firmly based upon appropriate "'differentiation', [and] 'a strictly dialectical union'".[166] The result, to utilize Milbank's phraseology, is not 'pernicious' but one in which *everything* is risked but it is *returned*, transformed.

However, Barth and Milbank are not speaking with a single voice. While they both wish to refute the notion that sacrifice must *necessarily* involve loss and negation, significantly they disagree over the reciprocity entailed by sacrifice. For Barth sacrifice marks the responsive gratitude of humanity to God's prior saving act. But no sacrifice can effect humanity's cooperation in its salvation. However, John Milbank says that by superseding the existing sacrificial structures of the earthly city, which were based upon loss and giving up, Christ "has *inaugurated* a new kind of efficacious sacrifice of praise, self-sharing and probable attendant suffering". Milbank says, following Hebrews 13.13-16, that the sacrifices offered are an efficacious "mode of atonement", and "voluntarily embraced... in the course of our self-sharing and offering of praise."[167] But such an interpretation undermines the notion that grace is the result of divine sovereignty and instead proposes a form of Pelegianism. It is this which lies at the very heart of the Protestant objection to the priesthood of the ordained.[168]

Milbank's reading is posited upon the understanding that the writer "puts us in the place of the animals once sacrificed for atonement."[169] However,

---

[163] Thus the 'crucified Jesus Christ, [is] very God and very man' (*CD* II.1, 153).

[164] *CD* II.1, 151-155.

[165] *CD* II.1, 156. See: the following section.

[166] Bruce McCormack, *Karl Barth's Critically Realistic Dialectical Theology*, Oxford, OUP, 1997, 361.

[167] Milbank, 1998, 151 – my italics. Milbank's choice of *inaugurated*, which is preceded by quoting Heb. 13.13-16 echoes the Letter to the Hebrews which designates Jesus as the 'pioneer of their salvation perfect through suffering' (2.10) which repeats at 12.2.

[168] See: 1, n.3 above.

[169] Milbank, 1998, 152. Gavin Hyman in his critique of the work of John Milbank suggests that one of the problems is that 'in the particular guise of John Milbank, the theologian speaks with an authority that is almost divine.' (Gavin Hyman, *The Predicament of Postmodern Theology*, Louisville, Westminster John Knox Press, 2001, 79). Furthermore it is 'his tendency to make the sweeping statement, the gigantic claim' (Hayman, 2001, 108) which leads ultimately to a speculative theology. (Hayman, 2001, 90).

the controlling image within the passage[170] is the comparison between the Church as God's covenant people and Israel during the period after the Exodus, but prior to the settlement in the Promised Land. More particularly, the imagery is that of the golden calf, when God "chose to demonstrate his presence... outside the camp."[171] There are two implications of this. The first is concerned with covenant identity. Traditionally the passage has been read as an exhortation to the Hebrews to put the Judaist ritual of atonement behind them.[172] Instead in the cross[173] there has been an event of re-identification, by which "what was formerly unhallowed was now sacred".[174] But secondly, because the Letter to the Hebrews re-interprets the priestly and the sacrificial as having been brought to its perfect consummation in and through Jesus Christ, the going out is a *reciprocal response* "descriptive of the Christian celebration of worship as the response of praise to the experience of salvation."[175] It is the priesthood of Christ which removes the barriers between the divine and the human so that "the community enjoys unlimited opportunity to offer God their praise."[176] Such sacrifices are efficacious as sacramental statements; the outward embodiment of an inner truth.

While sacrifice is fundamentally reciprocal, at issue is the nature of the reciprocity in the light of divine sovereignty and the precedence of grace. Because Milbank misunderstands the nature of the reciprocity the divine-human *diastasis* is undermined. This raises questions about the nature of the covenantal relationship of God and Israel in which there is a clear association between repentance, restitution, sacrifice and future obedience to the law.[177] However, Balthasar suggests that such reciprocity serves on the one hand to emphasize the *diastasis* between heaven and earth[178] and, on the other, it is indicative of the divine *pro nobis*, of the fact that "the dwelling of God is with men".[179] The divine-human reciprocity is revealed in the interplay between heaven and earth within which framework the history of the world takes place such that each remains distinct.[180]

Another aspect of the reciprocity is the articulation of the relationship in

---

[170] Westcott, 1889, 442; Bruce, 1979, 402f; Lane, 1991b, 544.

[171] Lane, 1991b, 543.

[172] Westcott, 1889, 442.

[173] Golgotha, the place of crucifixion is outside the city. (cf. Heb. 13.12.)

[174] Bruce, 1979, 403.

[175] Lane, 1991b, 459. (See also: Heb. 12.28.)

[176] Lane, 1991b, 459.

[177] E. P. Sanders, *Jesus and Judaism*, London, SCM, 1985, 207.

[178] *TD* V, 411.

[179] *TD* V, 411. (Quoting: Rev. 21.3; Lev. 26.11; Ezek. 37.27.)

[180] Balthasar quotes the Chalcedon Definition 'unconfused and unseparated' (*TD*. V, 412).

the framework of the worldview of the sacrificial cultus. In Israel the sacrificial "system functioned as a regular pointer back to the great acts of redemption such as the exodus, and equally as a pointer forward to the great redemption still come."[181] It operates as an institutionalized enactment of the worldview whereby God as a result of his covenant with Israel "would restore the fortunes of his people creating them as his true redeemed humanity".[182] Sacrifice is a dramatic enactment of "the movement of judgment and salvation, exile and restoration, death and resurrection for which Israel longed."[183] Essentially it is a mimetic event of narrative repetition. While the narrative is grounded in a unique historical origin and therefore unrepeatable, its attributes are repeatable and therefore to be repeated.[184] The persistent identity of the historic event and its enactment resides "purely on the 'surface'" whereby there is exhibited "a certain pattern and coherence."[185]

This 'characterisation' is significant for covenant identity. The reciprocity of ritual activity identifies the community by establishing boundaries and defining membership.[186] It provides a theology of separation - on the one hand of Israel and its neighbours and, on the other, between God and the created order.[187] Dunnill says that the rationale behind the priestly code is one whereby "holiness is equated with separation and essentially protective."[188] It is repeatedly stated "that it is the *priests* who 'make atonement' for sins".[189]

But what does it mean to speak of the priests as those who '*make atonement*'? It does not imply that the priests "usurp God's function; rather the holiness of God is such that the priesthood is established as a barrier endowed with sufficient holiness to communicate God's 'covering' of

---

[181] Wright, 1993, 274.

[182] Wright, 1993, 275. (See also: Gorringe, 1996, 263.)

[183] Wright, 1996, 277.

[184] Milbank, 1998, 159.

[185] Milbank, 1998, 157. This is therefore necessarily a matter of identity, of being recognisably a particular group indicative of a fitting theory of representation. (See: 10.)

[186] In 'Leviticus [this] means wholeness, completeness, as the sign of Israel's being (holy) "set apart". Israel is treated as a priestly nation which must, therefore, like its priests above all, be uncontaminated by the relativities and confusions of ordinary life. So the nation's boundaries must be strictly defined' (Dunnill, 1992, 83).

[187] Dunnill, 1992, 84.

[188] Dunnill, 1992, 85 – his italics. See: Ps. 24:3f. Consequently 'there is a tendency for expiation – offerings made to God to set right a relationship broken by sin – to be confused with aversion – offerings to be made to demons to ward them off. This is a transition with serious consequences for Israel and its understanding of God.' (Dunnill, 1992, 85.)

[189] See: Lev. 4:20, 26, 31, 35; 5: 6, 10, 13, 16, 18; 6: 7, – but notably omitted at 4; 12, 21.

sin."[190] In other words the priests *make atonement* by delineating the *diastasis* between God, who is holy, and secular humanity. Boundaries are established to retain things in their proper place. Priests are system-affirming and facilitate, by symbolic action, the transformation of the community and its members as a result of the presence of the divine.[191]

The complexity of the sacrificial cultus can be seen in the significance of 'blood' in relation both to covenant and sacrifice. Dunnill refers to the possibilities that blood within sacrificial rites is both symbolic of death while it also speaks of a 'life power'. Balthasar suggests the "blood event of the cultic sacrifices" are indicative of a true seriousness, which is revealed in the "commitment of one's entire bodily existence"[192] to the cause. Blood as a concept includes life and death and the possibility of transition from one to the other. However, Balthasar argues that "it is irrelevant" whether blood is intended to convey notions of life or death.[193] But it is precisely this liminality which links it with the divine "power of life and death".[194] Balthasar does not recognize this because he is, at best, ambivalent about the sacrificial blood cultus of the First Testament.[195] Two further elements are discernible in the use of blood in ritual. First, in the atonement ritual blood signifies hallowing or purification whereby creation is cleansed and restored. Secondly, blood was indicative that the "movement of the ritual was from the holy of holies into the world"[196] and revelatory of the divine *pro nobis*.[197]

To return to the sacrificial and priestly counter-testimony, the absence of blood might be interpreted as a rejection of the sacrificial cult. But an examination of the texts[198] challenges such a sweeping assumption. The injunction, 'Bring no more vain offerings'[199] is a protest against the multiplicity of sacrifices offered in times of crisis which are implicitly perceived to be propitiatory.[200] What is repudiated is any understanding that sacrifice enacts a mechanical relationship between God and His covenant

---

[190] Dunnill, 1992, 87-88.

[191] Colin E. Gunton *The Actuality of Atonement*, Edinburgh, T & T Clark, 1988, 118. Sacrifice thus serves the double purpose of on the one hand crossing the boundaries such that life can be reordered, and on the other in the process it enacts the worldview.

[192] Hans Urs von Balthasar, *The Glory of the Lord VI, The Theology of the Old Covenant* (ET), Edinburgh, T & T Clark, 1991, 391.

[193] Balthasar, 1991, 391.

[194] Dunnill, 1992, 102.

[195] Balthasar, 1991, 391.

[196] Margaret Barker, *On Earth as It Is in Heaven*, Edinburgh, T & T Clark, 1995, 45.

[197] Is. 26.21; Mic. 1.3.

[198] Ps. 40.6; Prov. 21.3; Is 1.11; 56.6-8; Jer. 6. 20, 21; 7.21-23; 17.21-27; 33.16-22; Ezek. 20.27-33; Hos. 3.4; 6.6; 8.11-13; 9.4.

[199] Is. 1.13.

[200] See: 2 Sam. 24. 24f; Amos 5. 21-4; Ps 51.16-17.

people. Neither can the counter-testimony be understood as a prelude to the total rejection of the sacrificial; instead what is required is sacrificial living as the true response to the Divine sovereignty[201] rather than simple ritual purity. Metaphorically, the blood shed is the life laid down before God as the prelude to taking up a renewed life lived in accordance with the Divine will. The sacrifice is even more acute because it is self-risking rather than the offering of an external sacrificial token.

Sacrifice is the grateful response of the person or the community to the covenantal action of God. Ultimately, obedient "sacrifice was a symbol of faith and loyalty" and an "occasion for joy".[202] It was the outward sign by which the whole community and individuals demonstrated their covenantal commitment. Sacrifice makes holy. That which was previously not holy can be covered by the divine holiness, but this is not consequential upon the surrender of one thing in order to obtain something greater.[203] Rather it is an event of kenotic re-identification in which giving results in receiving back the same but transformed. Sacrifice is therefore a positive event. But, remaining within a Protestant understanding of grace, it is supremely the work of the sovereign God in Jesus Christ for us and, therefore, following the pattern of Chalcedon, only asymmetrically repeatable. Humanity's sacrifice is necessarily responsive to the divine initiative.

The Testimony and Counter-testimony of the Divine *pro nobis* in Jesus Christ

In this Chapter I have explored the dialectic of priesthood through the testimony and counter-testimony of the First Testament and secondly the application of this priestly dialectic in Hebrews to the event of Jesus Christ. One consequence of such a kenotic renaming of priesthood as existing within a dialectic structure is the implications for the understanding of sacrifice. Returning to the earlier discussion of kenosis there is a 'descent from a logic of identity into a world of shifting appearances'[204] which results ultimately not in loss or negation but renaming. It is in this world of shifting appearances I shall seek to explore the doctrine of atonement.

In my exploration of the divine *pro nobis* I shall explore the relationship between sacrifice, priesthood and the person and work of Jesus Christ with particular reference to Karl Barth's doctrine of atonement, but also drawing

---

[201] Is. 1.16-17.
[202] Nelson, 1993, 81. (For the former see: Ps. 4.5; 66.13-15. For the latter see: Ps. 27.6; 107.22.)
[203] Milbank, 1996, 51.
[204] Quoted, 98, n. 149 above. (Graham Ward, 'Kenosis: Death, Discourse and Resurrection', Lucy Gardiner, Ben Quash, Graham Ward, *Balthasar at the End of Modernity*, Edinburgh, T & T Clark, 1999, 23.)

upon the theologies of Balthasar and Moltmann, thereby continuing the existing dialogue.[205] Barth has a clear understanding of gratitude in relation to grace. It is the concept of gratitude which enables him to propose a concept of sacrifice, recognizing both the primacy of divine sovereignty and the precedence of grace, and the reciprocity of sacrifice. The importance of this is the possibility of an asymmetrical repetition of priesthood by humanity *ad deum*.

The Reformed tradition acknowledges Jesus Christ under the three titles, prophet, priest and king.[206] Calvin defines priesthood as "the office and prerogative of presenting oneself before the face of God to obtain grace, and of offering sacrifice". The purpose of Christ's priestly office is that "he is our mediator, who reconciles us to the Father."[207] As a christological title 'Christ' is indicative of "the Anointed... one who has received a certain office in the framework of God's Covenant with his people."[208] Thus the concept of priesthood is explicitly associated with the relationship of God and humanity, properly understood as his covenant partner. Secondly, "Jesus Christ is the reality of all priesthood."[209]

It is the embodiment of this priestly counter-testimony by Jesus Christ that provides an important element in Karl Barth's Christology and the doctrine of reconciliation.[210] Despite this there is a certain reserve in Barth's willingness to explore more fully the doctrine of reconciliation by reference to the cultic imagery of the high priesthood of Christ.[211]

---

[205] See: Chapters 3, 5 above.

[206] 'What force then has the name Christ? – By this epithet his office is even better expressed. For it signifies that he is anointed by his Father to be King, Priest and Prophet.' (Question 34, Calvin's Catechism of the Church of Geneva, 1545, quoted by Karl Barth, *The Faith of the Church* (ET), London, Fontana Books, 1960, 51.) See also: *CD* IV.1, 124-125. Barth rescues the *munus triplex* from simply expounding the 'work' of Christ by combining it with the states of Christ within a narratively constructed discussion in *CD* IV.1, notably, as regards His priestly office. (§58. 3, 4; §59. 1, 2.)

[207] Quoted by Barth, 1960, 57, Questions 38, 43.

[208] Barth, 1960, 52.

[209] Barth, 1960, 58.

[210] Phil Butin draws attention to the influence of both the 'Geneva and Heidelburg Catechisms' on Barth's Christology. In particular 'their use of the **munus triplex**.... had a profound influence impact upon the shape of the Church Dogmatics, Volume IV: The Doctrine of Reconciliation.' (Phil Butin, 'Two Early Reformed Catechisms, The Threefold Office, And The Shape Of Karl Barth's Christology', *SJT* (44), 1991, 195 – his highlighting. See also: the 'architectural plan' offered by Butin, 1991, 201. See also: Eberhard Jüngel. (*Karl Barth, A Theological Legacy* (ET), Philadelphia, The Westminster Press, 48-49.)

[211] The doctrine of reconciliation, developed through Church Dogmatics, is initially signalled in *CD* I.2. There Barth discusses the relationship of 'Jesus Christ to the Old Testament covenant' and the varied 'human "instruments"' which foster and maintain

The doctrinal context for Barth's exploration of Jesus' high-priesthood is "in the event of the reconciliation of man with God as the fulfilment of the covenant". Writing of 'Jesus Christ the Mediator' he proposes Jesus Christ as "a middle point"[212] between God's sovereign saving grace and humanity, which is reconciled. Thus humanity and God can be identified. But crucially, because of Barth's structural dependency upon the Chalcedonian pattern and dialectical argumentation, humanity and God remain distinct entities, not to be confused. Jesus Christ includes in himself both "the reconciling God and the reconciled man" as the "Mediator between God and man". Jesus Christ is the one who mediates God and man, whereby man "*participates* in His [God's] grace."[213] In Jesus Christ "we have to do wholly with God and wholly with man".[214] Barth proposes an event of God's participatory mediation[215] in Jesus Christ. This is no abstract dogma but rooted in the temporal reality of Jesus Christ and the totality of his person and work.[216] There can be no "ahistorical relationship"[217] between God and humanity. Rather it is an event possible only in Jesus Christ for which humanity lives in perpetual gratitude.[218]

This highlights both the strength and weakness of Barth's thought as revealed in the threefold designation of Christ as 'very God, very man and very God-man'. It could be suggested that implicit in this, and in the notion of 'Jesus Christ the Mediator', is the possibility that he could be understood as an intermediary figure that was neither truly human nor truly divine.

---

the covenant, namely Moses, Abraham, David, Solomon, the Isaianic servant of God, kings and priests and prophets. This builds with a number of references in the index of II.1 to Jesus Christ as priest. But often the references are oblique and in the context of the 'knowability of God' which is precisely the priestly role of Christ which ultimately encompasses his saving act whereby he 'has entered into our place... has borne the punishment which was rightly ours' (*CD* II.1, 152). Barth suggests a priestly and substitutionary understanding of Jesus' expiation of man's separation from God such that God's accusation of man is abandoned and the former enmity is annulled, by his obedience. This is a result of his 'obedience' which 'cost Him His humiliation to our station,, His blood, His suffering' (*CD* II.1, 153). It is worth noting at this juncture the kenotic nature of Barth's narrative. The doctrine of reconciliation reaches its fullest exposition in *CD* IV.1.

[212] *CD* IV.1, 122.

[213] *CD* IV.1, 123 – my italics.

[214] *CD* IV.1, 126.

[215] *CD* IV.1, 127.

[216] *CD* IV.1, 245. Accordingly Barth rejects of any abstraction of the person of Christ as essentially 'empty'. (*CD* IV.1, 127.) Interestingly the Canons of Chalcedon reject as invalid all ordinations *in abstracto*. (Canon 6, J. Stevenson (ed), *Creeds, Councils, and Controversies*, London, SPCK, 1973, 326.)

[217] Hunsinger, 1991, 30.

[218] *CD* IV.1, 128.

Barth seeks to counter any suggestion of this by stating that the designation of Jesus Christ as the God-man is "only the viewing of this history in its unity and completeness".[219] This underlines his commitment to a notion of Jesus Christ's participatory mediation[220] which is developed by reference to his priesthood. In Barth's theology, Christology[221] is also a question of Pneumatology. It is the means by which the grace of Jesus Christ is appropriated through "the apprehension of the reconciliation of the world with God made in Him".[222] The work of Christ is itself "ultimately grounded in the being and work of the Holy Spirit."[223] The consequence is that ultimately the Christian is not only the recipient of God's grace, but is also joined to Christ in the exercise of the *munus triplex*.[224]

Barth discusses the priesthood of Jesus Christ in the context of the doctrine of reconciliation. One strand is his concept of substitutionary atonement; of God who is *pro nobis*. Introducing the fourfold "for us", he suggests that this describes "His activity as our Representative and Substitute."[225] Within the event of the reconciliation of God and man "'Jesus Christ for us' means that this one true man Jesus Christ has taken the place of us men".[226] This is fundamentally a priestly act. Barth defined Jesus' high-priestly office "that in Him and by Him we are not outside but inside."[227] In priestly terms, the outcome of this is that humanity is restored to its proper place; in Barth's terminology man is restored as God's

---

[219] *CD* IV.1, 136.

[220] 'Participatory mediation' is a phrase of my own devising. According to Barth the 'He himself, His existence, is this reconciliation. He Himself is the Mediator and pledge of the covenant. He is the Mediator of it in that He fulfils it – from God to man and from man to God. He is the pledge of it in that in His existence He confirms and maintains and reveals it as an authentic witness – attesting Himself, that in its fulfillment it presents and shines out and avails and is effective in Him. This is the new thing in the third christological aspect. Jesus Christ is the actuality of the atonement' (*CD* IV.1, 136). In Jesus Christ therefore God and man can encounter one another but without either party having to lose its essential identity. I shall return to this idea in the concluding section of this chapter.

[221] Barth, 1962, 46.

[222] *CD* IV.1, 147.

[223] 'He is *conceptus de Spiritu sancto*.' (*CD* IV.1 148.) Some scholars, like Pannenberg, have been critical of the coherence of Barth's theology with regard to the Spirit and its tendency to subsume pneumatology within Christology. (*Syst*. III, 5.) See also: Rowan Williams, 'Word and Spirit', Rowan Williams, *On Christian Theology*, Oxford, Blackwell, 2000, 118.

[224] Butin, 1991, 211.

[225] *CD* IV.1, 230.

[226] *CD* IV.1, 230. The 'first part of the doctrine of reconciliation as the doctrine of substitution.' (*CD* IV.1, 273.)

[227] *CD* II.1, 156.

covenant partner. He develops the idea using "forensic imagery" or juridical language.[228] But he acknowledges that, following Hebrews, he could just as satisfactorily have used "cultic language".[229]

Barth himself does not do so for two reasons. First he suggests there is the difficulty of the concepts articulated by cultic language in a form "which is now rather remote from us."[230] According to Barth the language, like the cultus, is obsolete, superseded by Christ's once for all sacrifice. Second that "we are able to see the matter better and more distinctly" using his chosen 'forensic imagery'.[231] But when has Barth ever been deterred from expounding a concept because it is complex? Barth's reluctance may simply stem from the traditional concerns of Protestant theology about the cultus, priesthood and the desire to ensure beyond any possible doubt the precedence of divine grace in the divine /human economy.[232]

In the hands of less subtle Protestant theologians' substitutionary atonement can become a prejudged means of systematizing the saving work of Christ[233] which leads to a rigid emphasis upon a substitutionary interpretation of the atonement,[234] understood in strictly juridical terms.[235] However, the language favours priestly concepts, not least because "his special work is to offer gifts and sacrifices for sins".[236]

---

[228] *CD* IV.1, 274.

[229] *CD* IV.1, 274.

[230] *CD* IV.1, 275. See also: Dunnill, 1992, 6; Lindars, 1991, 3.

[231] *CD* IV.1, 275.

[232] Wolfhart Pannenberg, commenting upon the use made of the *munus triplex* and, particularly, the 'priestly office', argues that primarily 'this idea has typological significance. It expresses the fulfilment and consummation of the old covenant in the history of Jesus by uniting the three most important offices of God's people in one person. Thus the idea has more poetic than dogmatic value.' (*Syst.* II, 446.)

[233] See: Louis Berkhof, *Systematic Theology*, Edinburgh, Banner of Truth, 1981, 361-66.

[234] Berkhof, 1981, 373-83.

[235] Timothy Gorringe argues that while the 'New Testament can certainly be read as supporting satisfaction theory... it does not have to be in this way, and that there is much which points in other directions.' (Gorringe, 1996, 81.) Rather Gorringe reads the New Testament account as a counter-testimony (my word) or texts of protest, in which sacrifice and atonement are (in Paul) the work of God 'effected by reconciliation, which in turn demands the "sacrifice" of obedience, which works itself out in community life.' (Gorringe, 1996, 77.)

[236] Berkoff, 1981, 361. The understanding of the atonement in terms of penal substitution is still significant for Reformed Protestantism. The fourth clause of the Evangelical Alliance Statement of Faith states that the 'substitutionary sacrifice of the incarnate Son of God [is] the sole and all-sufficient ground of redemption'. The theory of penal substitution is thus presented in accordance with George Lindbeck's analysis of doctrine as 'informative propositions or truth claims about objective realities.' (George Lindbeck, *The Nature of Doctrine*, London, SPCK, 1984, 47.) For example, this is very

Unsurprisingly, Balthasar is less anxious about the concept of the priesthood of Jesus Christ acknowledging that the "main features of atonement in the New Testament" are implicitly priestly. Thus

> the idea arises that he is both the (sacrificial) 'Lamb' who is 'given up' (Jn. 1.29) and the sacrificial Priest who surrenders himself (Heb. 2.14ff); he is both at the same time (Heb. 9.14). In virtue of this identity, he supersedes the whole sphere of previous ritual sacrifice.[237]

The action of Jesus Christ in the atonement is to be understood *pro nobis*;[238] a ransom cultically presented in terms of 'propitiation'[239] and is "something to do with God's covenant 'righteousness'".[240] But surprisingly Balthasar does not proceed to develop the significance of such language and imagery.

Balthasar's account of atonement is guided by two controlling motifs. The first, drives much of his theology, and is the absolute centrality of the Trinity.[241] The second motif is the dramatic. Thus he sees Luther's Christological concept of atonement, presented in terms of substitution and rooted in the Chalcedonian tradition, as "high drama"[242] but ultimately confused. The confusion, he suggests, is within the characterisation of man "who is both sinner and righteous"[243] and in the person of Christ who is 'truly God and truly man'.[244]

Balthasar offers another possibility, in which the action of Jesus Christ, as the second person of the Trinity, is understood eucharistically. Accordingly "God the Father, in the Holy Spirit, creates the Son's Eucharist." Consequently only "the Eucharist really completes the Incarnation."[245] This is the "deepest mystery of the Trinity in its salvation-

---

much the understanding espoused in the work of James Packer. (See: J I Packer 'On Penal Substitution', quoted, A. E. McGrath [ed], *The Christian Theology Reader*, Blackwells, Oxford, 1995, 204-6.; J. I. Packer, *Knowing God*, Hodder and Stoughton, London 1975, 199-202. J. I. Packer, 'Sacrifice and Satisfaction', *Collected Shorter Writings of J. I. Packer* (Vol 1), Paternoster, Carlisle, 1998, 125-136.)

[237] *TD* IV, 241.
[238] *TD* IV, 241.
[239] *TD* IV, 242.
[240] *TD* IV, 243. He acknowledges four of the five 'main features' to be to some extent priestly actions.
[241] 'What is lacking is the link with the Son's trinitarian *missio*, his "sending" by the Father on the basis of his *processio*.' Thus he criticises Anslem's presentation of atonement for being insufficiently trinitarian. (*TD* IV, 261.)
[242] *TD* IV, 290.
[243] *TD* IV, 290.
[244] *TD* IV, 290.
[245] *TD* IV, 348.

historical reality", whereby "God is confronted by God".[246] In cultic terms "the Son is the High Priest offering himself for the world." Balthasar quotes Helmut Thielicke "God himself is the offerer, sacrificing himself for man."[247] But Balthasar's problem remains his unwillingness to maintain a sufficient emphasis upon divine sovereignty and the precedence of grace.[248]

Balthasar, like Barth, wishes to pursue the notion of God, who, in his righteousness, acts in the atonement *pro nobis*. For Balthasar, the importance of this is as the "basis for the incomparable dramatic interplay"[249] between, on the one hand, God in Christ and on the other, analogically between God and mankind. The drama of Jesus Christ's death *pro nobis* is ultimately "the singular, unique and unrepeatable destiny of Jesus",[250] the "hour" towards which his life is directed.[251] Despite this, it is apparent that his priestly understanding of God's saving act in Jesus Christ is implicit. The weakness of his thinking lies in his attempt to develop a theology of the priesthood of Christ, as revealed in the events of the cross, and in the response of the Church.

Nor is it surprising that Moltmann eschews priestly language. But even he is unable to avoid priestly imagery. Echoing a classic priestly formula he speaks of Jesus as "'God's representative', who stands for God before men and for men before God."[252] He believes that the event of the resurrection has a double significance for understanding the meaning of the cross. First God has "identified himself, his judgment and his kingdom with the crucified Jesus."[253] Secondly, the resurrection is a statement of "the righteousness of God."[254] This occurs within the Godhead, thus gaining its special meaning.[255] Nonetheless Moltmann rejects a penal or substitutionary understanding of the crucifixion and death of Jesus. He asserts that if one understands the cross through the resurrection it cannot be a historic event in which history is finished; rather it is one, which looks ahead to the recreation of mankind who lives "in the midst of history".[256]

Nonetheless Moltmann understands Jesus' death as *pro nobis*.[257] He considers it possible that the death of Christ upon the cross was understood

---

[246] *TD* IV, 348.

[247] *TD* IV, 349.

[248] See: the discussion of Balthasar's Mariological theology, 111-118 above.

[249] *TD* IV, 373.

[250] Angelo Scola, *Hans Urs von Balthasar, A Theological Style* (ET), Edinburgh, T & T Clark, 1995, 70.

[251] *TD* IV, 231-40.

[252] Jürgen Moltmann, *The Crucified God* (ET), London, SCM, 1974, 180.

[253] Moltmann, 1974, 169.

[254] Moltmann, 1974, 174.

[255] Moltmann, 1974, 182.

[256] Moltmann, 1974, 164.

[257] Moltmann, 1974, 181.

by Paul to include the possibility of either (or even both?) "personal representation or in the cultic sense of expiation 'for our sins'".[258] However, his understanding of Christ's death as 'expiatory' introduces a degree of definition to the event of the cross, as does Balthasar by his preference for a 'propitiatory' understanding that Barth on the whole avoids. Barth understands the event of the cross as being simply *pro nobis*. Once again, the key issue is sacrifice. Moltmann is adamant that it is essentially a consequence of the resurrection, as the sign of God's satisfaction revealed in the vindication of the crucified one. Referring to 1 Corinthians 15.3b-4, Moltmann draws attention to the fact that the cross and resurrection are to be understood together. Thus

> his suffering and death must be understood to be the suffering and death of the Christ of God. Only in the light of his resurrection from the dead does his death gain that special, unique saving significance which it cannot achieve otherwise, even in the light of the life he lived.[259]

This is a key insight, which is absent from Balthasar and underplayed by Barth. The mimetic economy of Moltmann's concept of atonement draws upon Philippians whereby "the resurrection expresses the significance of his cross."[260] Despite his reference to the cross as expiatory it is possible to detect that sacrifice is not understood in terms of loss but rather as vindication and therefore renewing.[261] However, in emphasising the resurrection as the key to the event of the cross, Moltmann potentially weakens the reality of the Son's dying. His death on the cross *pro nobis* "makes relevant his resurrection 'before us'."[262]

There is here a seeming confusion in Moltmann's thinking. He seems to understand the event of the cross as being expiatory. But his wish to emphasise the significance of the resurrection leads him to suggest that,

> the early Jewish-Christian idea of the dying Christ as an expiatory offering for our sins, which has constantly been repeated throughout the tradition in varied forms, cannot demonstrate an intrinsic theological

---

[258] Moltmann, 1974, 181.

[259] Moltmann, 1974, 182.

[260] Moltmann, 1974, 182. There are echoes here of Phil. 2.6-11, in which the one who has the 'form of God' humbles himself being 'obedient unto death, even death on a cross' as a consequence of which God 'highly' exalts him so that 'every tongue confess that Jesus Christ is Lord'.

[261] This is essentially implicit in Moltmann's thought but we shall it is developed independently by John Milbank. (See: 166 above.)

[262] Moltmann, 1974, 183.

connection with the kerygma of the resurrection.[263]

He suggests it is "very difficult to harmonize the resurrection of Jesus with these interpretations of his death and to harmonize these interpretations of his death with his resurrection from the dead." Expiation for sin he says "always has a retrospective character."[264] But Moltmann fails to ask the key question, which proceeds from Christ's death 'for us': what is the purpose of Christ's atoning act? Balthasar and Barth would each answer this differently but with the same intent. For Barth, Christ dies in order that humanity might fulfil her calling to be God's 'covenant partner'. Whereas Balthasar addresses this question in terms of humanity as full character and so becoming a person within the theo-drama of Christ's saving act. Both of these answers are concerned with the future, the life of discipleship.

But Moltmann cannot abandon the expiatory nature of the cross.[265] What he emphasizes is the need to read history eschatologically, which reverses the sense of time.[266] Balthasar similarly detects an aspect of atonement that is related to the theology of time.[267] Balthasar understands the priesthood of Jesus Christ as propitiatory and chronologically focused, whereby the priesthood of Jesus mediates God's time with the time in the created world. Accordingly it is possible for the καιρός; the time, the season, Jesus' hour to encounter the divine χρόνος.[268]

Barth's exploration of the doctrine of reconciliation as *Deus pro nobis* states that "Jesus Christ took our place as Judge."[269] Or in cultic terms, Jesus Christ "is the Priest who represented us."[270] In his priestly role, Christ

> has penetrated to that place where every man is in his inner being supremely by and for himself. This sanctuary belongs to Him and not to man. He has to do what has to be done there.[271]

The second forensic statement that "Jesus Christ was and is for us in that

---

[263] Moltmann, 1974, 183.
[264] Moltmann, 1974, 183.
[265] Moltman 1974, 183.
[266] Moltmann, 1974, 184. *The Crucified God* is a significant Christological statement by Moltmann. However, it is not his latest word. Nonetheless significantly he remains true to his essential argument. (*The Way of Jesus Christ* (ET), London, SCM, 1990, 183-195.)
[267] *TD* III, 241.
[268] *TD* III, 113-115.
[269] *CD* IV.1, 275. (c.f., 273, 231.)
[270] *CD* IV.1, 275.
[271] *CD* IV.1, 232.

He took the place of us sinners"[272] can be restated in priestly language as he "gave himself".[273] This is an overtly sacrificial statement of Jesus Christ's role as the One who is elect. In "taking our place as Judge He takes the place which belongs to Him, which is His own from all eternity."[274] Again rephrased in cultic terms, in Jesus Christ is

> the one person electing God and the one elect man is as the rejecting God, the God who judges sin in the flesh, in His own person the one rejected man, the Lamb which bears the sin of the world that the world should no longer have to bear it, or be able to bear it, that it should be radically and totally taken away from it.[275]

Thirdly, "Jesus Christ was and is for us in that He suffered and was crucified and died."[276] Or cultically expressed, he was "offered up as a sacrifice to take away our sins".[277] Jesus Christ, as priest, is both the one who sacrifices and the sacrificial offering. As the counter-testimony to the priesthood presented in the First Testament, the priesthood of Jesus is the atonement whereas the former merely represents atonement.[278]

Finally, juridically stated, "Jesus Christ was and is for us in that He has done this before God and has therefore done right."[279] Restated cultically, "in our place He has made a perfect sacrifice... by offering Himself has substituted a perfect sacrifice for all the sacrifices offered by men."[280]

Both the models that Barth offers, the forensic and the cultic, are fundamentally articulations of *Deus pro nobis*. This relates to Barth's anthropology, according to which man exists primarily as God's 'covenant partner'. This has two consequences for his thought. The first is his emphasis upon the substitutionary and therefore representative nature of Christ's atoning act[281] focused through the passion.[282] The second emphasis, as we shall see, is the event of kenotic re-identification in which Christ's sacrifice results in receiving back the same but transformed. This is revealed initially in the resurrection and consequently in the transformation of the lives of those who call themselves Christians.

---

[272] *CD* IV.1, 235. (c.f., 273, 277.)
[273] *CD* IV.1, 277.
[274] *CD* IV.1, 236.
[275] *CD* IV.1, 277.
[276] *CD* IV.1, 244. (c.f., 273, 277.)
[277] *CD* IV.1, 277.
[278] *CD* IV.1, 278.
[279] *CD* IV.1, 244. (c.f., 273, 281.)
[280] *CD* IV.1, 281.
[281] *CD* IV.1, 222, 230.
[282] *CD* IV.1, 259-273.

One would assume, given his preference for the forensic model, that Barth would simply restate the traditional Reformed notion of penal substitution. But he is more subtle in his thinking.

> [W]e must be careful that the strict 'for us' that we have to do with here does not become a 'with us' which unites our existence with that of Jesus Christ, in which He is simply the author and initiator of what has to be fulfilled in and through us on the same level, in His discipleship and fellowship with Him, as though the redemptive happening which has to be proclaimed and believed under His name were something that embraces both Him and us... Discipleship, the being of the Christian with Him rests on the presupposition and can be carried through only on the presupposition that Jesus Christ is in Himself 'for us' – without our being with Him – on the contrary without any fulfilment of our being either with Him or after Him... He is for us Himself quite independently of how we answer the question that is put to us... The event of redemption took place then and there in Him, and therefore 'for us.'[283]

We should do well to note the allusion to Hebrews in the description of Jesus Christ as 'the pioneer of their salvation'.[284] Hebrews is a key text whose narrative drives Barth's reflection and to which he finally turns in the significant exegesis which forms the climax of the section.[285] Secondly, it is 'for us', or 'in the place of' and therefore substitutionary. Thirdly, it is a statement of God's sovereign grace revealed in Jesus Christ. Therefore any human response is simply one of gratitude. But this act of substitution is not simply penal, though it embraces this as one aspect of what occurs. Rather the "decisive thing in the suffering and death of Jesus Christ" is that "it has come to pass in His own person".[286]

In *Church Dogmatics* IV.1 he speaks of 'Jesus Christ the Lord as Servant' in whom "we have to do with very God".[287] The second emphasis within this first aspect of Barth's doctrine of reconciliation is the 'Lord as Servant' who fulfils the priestly office as reflected in his *status exaninitionis*.[288] Jesus Christ is "altogether man just as he is altogether God – altogether man in virtue of His true Godhead whose glory consists in His

---

[283] *CD* IV.1, 229.

[284] '*author and initiator*' c.f. Heb. 2.10 in which the Greek, ἀρχηγὸν can be rendered pioneer, founder, author or originator.

[285] *CD* IV.1, 273-283.

[286] *CD* IV.1, 253.

[287] *CD* IV.1, 128.

[288] *CD* IV.1, 132. Furthermore *status exaninitionis* (state of self-emptying) is a kenotic term.

humiliation. That is how He is the reconciler between God and man"[289] – a classic statement of the Chalcedonian definition. There is thus an implicit – and, at times explicit - kenotic setting of the priestly office within Barth's thought. This takes form in the emphasis upon Jesus Christ's obedience[290] and self-giving,[291] his humiliation,[292] and his dying.[293] So that the climax of his discussion of the fourth part, the sinlessness of Christ, "that he has done this before God and has therefore done right" is set out by explicit referral to the mimetic economy of Philippians 2.6-11.[294]

Both substitution and kenosis, which form key elements in Barth's account of the first aspect of the doctrine of reconciliation, are concerned with identity as that which can be recognised and therefore named. On the one hand, the priesthood of Jesus Christ presents a counter-testimony to the cultic priesthood of the First Testament. On the other, it is also a testimony to the power of the cult. So too Jesus Christ, the 'Lord as Servant' who is the Son of God in a 'Far Country' and therefore the 'Judge Judged in Our Place' is also both testimony and counter-testimony to God. Jesus Christ is to be identified as "*vere Deus vere homo*"[295] but this can only be recognised kenotically[296] by humanity. Jesus Christ does not cast off "His Godhead but (as the One who loves in His sovereign freedom) activates and proves it by the fact he gives Himself to the limitation and suffering of the human creature".[297] Similarly his activity as man's representative and substitute is recognised by the Father. In this "suffering and dying of God Himself in His Son, there took place the reconciliation with God".[298] In him man becomes recognisable in his true form such that "the covenant which God

---

[289] *CD* IV.1, 130. This is implicit in his discussion of 'The Way of the Son of God into the Far Country' where he reiterates this earlier statement when he suggests 'the *forma Dei* consists in the grace in which God Himself assumes and makes his own the *forma servi*.' (*CD* IV.1, 188.) Indeed the references to *forma Dei* and *forma servi* are taken from Phil 2.6-11.
[290] *CD* IV.1, 223, 257.
[291] *CD* IV.1, 223.
[292] *CD* IV.1, 244.
[293] *CD* IV.1, 250.
[294] *CD* IV.1, 259: See: *CD* IV.1, 134.
[295] *CD* IV.1, 133.
[296] Barth has already signalled this in *CD*. II.1 § 26 'The Knowability of God' in which he discusses 'the basis on which God is known.' (*CD* II.1, 63.) This is grounded primarily in 'His own readiness to be known' (*CD* II.1, 66.) which is confirmed in that 'He gives Himself to be known' (*CD* II.1, 69). This is an act of grace which is presented in 'Jesus Christ who is God's revelation' (*CD* II.1, 74). It is Jesus Christ who is truly God and truly man (*CD* II.1, 151.) and therefore in his incarnate form is knowable. Becoming human is no diminution of the Godhead.
[297] *CD* IV.1, 134.
[298] *CD* IV.1, 250.

has faithfully kept and man has broken is renewed and restored."[299]

This opens an intriguing possibility. Is it possible to extend, by analogy, the concept of the high-priesthood of Jesus Christ to his followers? Is this part of the Christian testimony, and if so what form should it take? I believe that Barth's own ideas make this is possible. One advantage of Barth's approach is his greater narrative consistency, compared to Balthasar and Moltmann. Secondly, although his doctrine of atonement is implicitly substitutionary, it is ambiguous in that it is not explicitly expiatory or propitiatory, unlike Balthasar and Moltmann.[300] Thirdly, it is rooted in identity as being recognizably 'in Christ' or Christ-like. Finally, the advantage of Barth's approach is his methodology. This, I have argued, arises from the importance of election and covenant in relation to God who is *pro nobis*, the understanding of kenosis in relation to the divine identity, and the maintaining of the divine-human *diastasis* and the consequent dialectic of the Chalcedonian pattern. These will provide the parameters for delineating a Protestant doctrine of priesthood.

Conclusion

It is important now to draw together the emerging strands of my argument. In Part I we saw that the fundamental direction of the divine-human narrative was from God to man. Kenosis is not the loss or renunciation of the divine identity, but the self-revelation of God, in Jesus Christ, who is recognisable as truly God and truly man.[301] Theology "is a wordy business... [However i]t is not about language... [But i]t is about God."[302] Kenosis therefore provided the analogy for the divine-human encounter in which "the truth of God's self-revealing" was "safeguarded" without compromise.[303] This has significant implications for priesthood. First, salvation is affected by an act of divine sovereign grace. Priesthood cannot occupy an intermediary role. Secondly, priesthood, like kenosis, proposes fluidity of form but without loss of identity. Thirdly the language of priesthood, like kenosis, is critically realistic. As a result three significant words: identity, representation and participation emerged. Both kenosis and priesthood are concerned with the identity and therefore the representation of the divine and the human such that each is recognizable. Both kenosis and priesthood are concerned with the divine-human interchange through

---

[299] *CD* IV.1, 251.

[300] Balthasar tends to favour notion of 'propitiation' (180) whereas Moltmann tends to speak of 'expiation' (181) when discussing atonement.

[301] See: Chapters 2 and 3 above.

[302] Trevor Hart, 'Speaking God's of Love: Analogy, Reference and Revelation', in Trevor Hart, *Regarding Karl Barth*, Carlisle, Paternoster, 1999, 173.

[303] Hart, 1999, 185.

mutual participation, but without any confusion of form. The study of Philippians demonstrated the interrelatedness of notions of identity, kenosis, representation and priesthood.

In Part II the focus has been upon human identity in relation to God. In Chapter 4, it became apparent that there were inconsistencies in the form and structure of the ecclesiologist and anthropologies proposed by Balthasar and Moltmann. Whereas Moltmann redresses the pneumatic inconsistency of Balthasar's ecclesiology, Balthasar is consistent in his understanding of vocation within a theo-dramatic context. While Balthasar's ecclesiology provided a distinctive priestly testimony, unsurprisingly Moltmann's account underscores the traditional Reformed counter-testimony to priesthood. However, overall Barth's account of ecclesiology, anthropology and vocation maintained a greater consistency. This, I suggested was a result of the dialectical structure of his theology, his particularise and his emphasis upon the Chalcedonian pattern. This enables him to maintain the priority of the divinely sovereign nature of grace to which humanity can only respond. I then applied Barth's insights to 1 Peter 2.4-10 in order to examine the relationship between priesthood, covenant and election confirming a dialectic of a priestly testimony and counter-testimony.

In this Chapter I have demonstrated the dialectic of the priestly testimony and counter-testimony. Because my concern is a Protestant understanding, I have initially sought this through the Bible. Secondly, that sacrifices, like kenosis, results not in loss but renaming. Finally I explored Barth's account of atonement as the divine pro nobis and his reluctance to articulate this using priestly language. What emerged from this brief study of atonement was the presence of both a priestly testimony and the counter-testimony.

What I have demonstrated is that priesthood must be spoken of dialectically and not univocally. Crucially, for any Protestant account of priesthood this critically realistic dialectic is in Scripture. Furthermore the dialectic of the priesthood of Jesus Christ and God's covenant people, repeating the Chalcedonian pattern, are neither identical nor to be confused. The priesthood of Christ is atoning and *pro nobis* whereas the priesthood of God's people is one of responsive praise *ad Deum* for the prior act of divinely sovereign grace. Consequently the two forms of priesthood remain unconfused. Secondly, priesthood and sacrifice are intimately connected. Sacrifice like priesthood is kenotic. However, neither is negative. As the priesthood of the ordained is neither propitiatory nor expiatory so sacrifice is not a matter of loss or self-negation in order to achieve a greater good. Instead sacrifice, priesthood and kenosis result in renaming and restoration. Thirdly, priesthood is christological. Priesthood is only experienced concretely in and through Jesus Christ, the second person of the Trinity. It is from this that both the priesthood of all believers and the priesthood of the ordained are both derived.[304] The priesthood of Christ and that of man share a common identity but are not identical. Priesthood is embodied in Jesus Christ but participated in by humanity.

It remains to define how priesthood can be understood in terms of the ordained ministry.

---

[304] This can perhaps be pictured in terms of a family tree whereby the priesthood of Jesus Christ occupies the position of the parent whereas the priesthood of all believers and the priesthood of the ordained are the sibling offspring. As such they share a family likeness but they are not identical.

PART III

Priesthood: The Imaginative and Human Retelling of God's Story

Chapter 7

Narrative and Imagination

In Chapter 6 I demonstrated that priesthood exists in a dialectic of testimony and counter-testimony. I suggested that there were three aspects to priesthood. First, that priesthood cannot be understood as being naively realistic representative. Secondly, priesthood and sacrifice are kenotic, not perniciously so but instead result in renaming and restoration. Thirdly, priesthood is christological repeating by reflecting the Chalcedonian pattern established in Jesus Christ, who is truly God, and man such that the two natures remain distinct and unconfused. The priesthood of Christ and that of man share a common identity but are not identical. Priesthood is embodied in Jesus Christ but participated in by humanity.

In this Chapter I shall propose that the priesthood of the ordained cannot be understood propositionally. Instead I shall argue that the priesthood of the ordained is fundamentally imaginative and can exist only within a necessary narrative framework maintained through adherence to emplotment and characterisation.[1] In the first section I shall demonstrate the sterility of the traditionally univocal, historically grounded debate concerning the priesthood of the ordained. This I shall demonstrate by reference to the discussions concerning the nature of the priesthood of the ordained in English theology at the end of the nineteenth and the start of the twentieth centuries.

Different Conceptions of Priesthood and Sacrifice

In December 1899 a conference, attended by fifteen eminent Victorian Churchmen was held at Christ Church, Oxford to discuss the nature of the priesthood of the ordained. The chairman was William Sanday.[2] To his left

---

[1] 'We must not conclude from the diversity of present opinion… that there is no correct interpretation.' (Kevin Vanhoozer, *Is There a Meaning in This Text?*, Leicester, Apollos Press, 1998, 303).

[2] W. Sanday (ed.), *Different Conceptions of Priesthood and Sacrifice*, London, Longmans, Green and Co, 1900. Participants were invited who were representative of 'the whole of English Christianity' deliberately including a 'group of High Churchman, a group of Nonconformists and an intermediate group of Churchmen who would not be called "High".'(Sanday, 1900, vii). Those present throughout were Rev William Sanday

sat the Nonconformist and Protestant Anglicans, and to his right, facing them across the table, sat the Catholic Anglicans.[3] One central concern, shared by all the participants, was the nature of sacrifice in relation to the priesthood.

The origins of the debate can probably be traced to J. B. Lightfoot's essay, 'The Christian Ministry,' offering a scholarly study of the origins of the nature of the ordained ministry[4] published thirty years previously.[5] At the heart of his thesis was a concern for the nature of priesthood and sacrifice. The evidence of the New Testament and the Fathers persuaded Lightfoot that Christianity "interposes no sacrificial tribe or class between God and man". He was also acutely aware "that no society of men could hold together, without officers, without rules".[6] Lightfoot did not deny the need for order but believed that Christian ministry could not appropriately be identified as 'priestly.'

(Chair), Father Puller, Dr R. C. Moberly, Canon C. Gore, Canon Scott Holland, the Rev C. G. Lang, Archdeacon Wilson, Dr J. C. Ryle, Canon E. R. Bernard, Rev A C Headlam (replacing Prof H. C. G. Moule), Dr Salmond (Scottish Presbyterian), Dr Davison (Wesleyan), Dr A. M. Fairburn, Mr Arnold Thomas, Dr P. T. Forsyth (Congregationalists).

[3] Though the seating plan is not given the text permits the reconstruction of the conference, which is illuminating. As the Chair Sanday ('a moderate English liberal protestant'. Stephen W. Sykes, *The Integrity of Anglicanism*, London, Mowbrays, 1978, 26.) sat at the head of the table and to his left sat the distinctly Protestant group consisting of: Archdeacon Wilson, Dr J. C. Ryle, Canon E. R. Bernard, Dr Salmond (Scottish Presbyterian), Dr Davison (Wesleyan), Dr A. M. Fairburn, Mr Arnold Thomas, Dr P. T. Forsyth (Congregationalists). On his right sat the Catholic group consisting of: Father Puller, Dr R. C. Moberly, Canon C. Gore, Canon Scott Holland, the Rev C. G. Lang, Rev A. C. Headlam. Sanday locates his own sympathies with the right-hand group. (Sanday, 1900, 153, 156 [Rev Arnold Thomas], 160 [Rev A. C. Headlam])

[4] Lightfoot argued that he was attempting a scholarly assessment of Cranmer's statement that: 'It is evident unto all men diligently reading the Holy Scripture and ancient authors that from the Apostles' time there have been these orders of Ministers in Christ's Church, Bishops, Priests, and Deacons.' (J. B. Lightfoot, 'The Christian Ministry', *Saint Paul's Epistle to the Philippians* (3rd Edn), London, Macmillan and Co., 1881, x.) The essay is an *excursus* upon Phil 1.1 which refers to ἐπισκόποις καὶ διακόνοισ, but the reaction of his readers suggested that they did not read the essay in quite the scholarly light he had intended. For example Charles Gore, having praised Lightfoot's skills as an interpreter of Paul and the Fathers, continues suggesting that 'it has been found an effective instrument in defence of "Congregational principles"... [and] the great ambiguity of the position which it takes up.' (*The Church and the Ministry* (4th Edn, Rev.) London, Longmans, Green and Co., 1900, 321.)

[5] 1868.

[6] Lightfoot, 1879, 181.

Edwin Hatch developed Lightfoot's ideas[7] believing he too stood firmly within the Anglican tradition.[8] His first stated concern was "the organisation of the Christian Churches" and not the Christian faith.[9] Hatch asserted that the origin of the ordained ministry was essentially philanthropic. The presiding minister was the one who "received" the offerings of the faithful, "dedicated them to God, and uttered over them, in the name of the assembly, words of thanksgiving and benediction."[10] This administrative role was encapsulated in the "title which clung to him… ἐπίσκοπος".[11] Drawing upon Justin Martyr he suggested that "each church was complete in itself," the presbyter having "no official part" and the normal Eucharistic president being the bishop.[12] Ordination was simply the "appointment and admission to office" and as such no different from comparable civic appointments.[13] Furthermore, the imposition of hands did not, nor was it intended to confer "special and exclusive spiritual powers."[14] According to Hatch, the supremacy of the bishop "was not peculiarity of function but priority of rank"[15] and the real distinction "was not between clergy and laity, but between baptized and unbaptized".[16]

Gore refuted Hatch, believing that what he had written was in "direct violation of the evidence."[17] He also argued that Lightfoot's essay was "misleading" in matters of "great importance", confusing "means and unessentials"[18] in its apparent denial that the form of the ministry was of the *esse* of the Church. Lightfoot had asked whether "an unordained Christian at the last resort could celebrate the Eucharist?" Such a form of ministry, Gore suggested, put itself outside the community of the covenant.[19] Gore's

---

[7] Edwin Hatch, *The Organization of the Christian Churches* (2nd Edn Revised), London, Rivingtons, 1882.
[8] Hatch cites *Laws* (Preface to the Second Edition, x.)
[9] Hatch, 1882, 23.
[10] Hatch, 1882, 40.
[11] Hatch, 1882, 41.
[12] Hatch, 1882, 79.
[13] Hatch, 1882, 132.
[14] Hatch, 1882, 136.
[15] Hatch, 1882, 110.
[16] Hatch, 1882, 111.
[17] C. Gore, *The Church and the Ministry* (4th Edn, Rev), London, Longmans, Green and Co, 1900, 48. Hatch, in the 'Preface to The Second Edition' welcomes Gore's criticism which he then rejects as based upon 'unproved assumptions' (Hatch, 1882, xii.) However, in a footnote he cites Gore's book as *The Church and the Ministry: A Review of the Rev E. Hatch's Bampton Lectures* (Rivington's, 1882).
[18] Gore, 1900, 322 – his italics. Indeed in his book Lightfoot's treatise warranted a whole appendix, albeit brief, to refute its basic premise.
[19] Gore, 1900, 325.

objection was to Lightfoot's suggestion that the ordained 'priesthood' was not validated by its apostolic succession, embodied in office.

In 1896 Pope Leo XIII had issued *Apostolicae curae*, which declared that "Ordinations carried out according to the Anglican rite have been and are absolutely null and void."[20] The crux of the problem concerned whether the orders conferred by the Edwardian ordinal "possessed the nature and effect of a sacrament".[21] It was suggested that this failure was one of "matter and form".[22] The first problem was the failure of the intention to ordain to a "Sacred Order of Priesthood" which exists with the power of "consecrating and offering the true body and blood of the Lord".[23] The second problem was that the sacrifice for which the priesthood was ordained was not only absent but had been "deliberately removed and struck out"[24] and was consequently "destructive of the sacrament."[25]

R. William Franklin argues that *Apostolicae Curae*, undoubtedly the most significant of the four works cited was not based upon "historical continuity alone, rather validity was a matter of sacramentology."[26] However, Lightfoot and Hatch's arguments touched a nerve, judging by the response evoked among some English theologians. Furthermore, given the time that had lapsed since the Edwardian Ordinal was issued it would seem that something must have precipitated the issuing of the encyclical.[27]

Gore was not alone in his reaction. The most significant and lasting exploration of the nature of the priesthood of the ordained by an English theologian was by R. C. Moberly.[28] Moberly's concern was the nature of

---

[20] R. William Franklin (ed), *Anglican Orders, Essays on the Centenary of Apostolicae curae*, London, Mowbray, 1996, 136.

[21] Franklin, 1996, 127.

[22] Franklin, 1996, 133 – authors' italics.

[23] Franklin, 1996, 133 – authors' italics, quoting from the statement of the Council of Trent.

[24] Franklin, 1996, 134.

[25] Franklin, 1996, 135.

[26] R. William Franklin, 'The Opening of the Vatican Archives and the ARCIC Process', Franklin, 1996, 18.

[27] There are two problems with *Apostolicae Curae*. First, as suggested, that almost 350 of years after the publication of the Edwardian Ordinal passed before the declaration that Anglican Orders are 'null and void' Secondly, *Apostolicae Curae* refers simply to the 'new rite for conferring Holy Orders... introduced under Edward VI'. However, Cranmer introduced two ordinals. The first (1550) was largely modeled upon the Sarum Pontifical whereas the second (1552) no longer included provision for the giving of the patten and chalice to the newly ordained. (See: G. J. Cumming, *A History of Anglican Liturgy* (2nd Edn), London, Macmillan, 1982; Paul Bradshaw, 'Ordinals', Stephen Sykes and John Booty (ed), *The Study of Anglicanism*, London/Minneapolis, SPCK/Fortress, 1993, 143-153.)

[28] R. C. Moberly, *Ministerial Priesthood*, 1897

Narrative and Imagination 195

sacrifice, in relation to the priesthood of the ordained. He argued from the ordinal[29] that Lightfoot and Hatch, like Hooker, misunderstood the meaning of sacrifice. His accusation was that they have "made the capital mistake of taking the Mosaic use of the words" suggesting priests are "a class really intervening, as indispensable intermediaries between Christians and their God."[30] In other words he accused them of offering a naively realistic understanding of the language of priesthood. Moberly believes that the ordained ministry is summatively representative of the whole body of believers. It is "not so much that they do it, in the stead, or for the sake, of the whole; but rather that the whole does it through them." In this way their action "is identified upon earth with the heavenly offering of atonement of Christ" but is not intended to be supplementary.[31]

Moberly qualified the previous statement, suggesting that although the ordained are representative of the body, it did not follow that "the authority of the ministers to minister is derived from or is conferred by, the mere will or act of the Body."[32] Neither the body as a whole, nor its individual members were "*de jure* a minister"[33] and cannot confer ministerial authority. Moberly's dominant image was the 'body of Christ'[34] but he appears to understand this analogy in a naively realistic way, precisely the hermeneutical concern over which he took issue with Lightfoot.[35] He therefore maintained the notion of a priesthood, which is directly appointed by God through the necessary episcopal succession without reference to the Church as a whole.[36]

At the Oxford Conference, pressed by A. M. Fairburn, Moberly explained his understanding of "Christian sacrifice"[37] in terms of penitence.

---

[29] R. C. Moberly, *Ministerial Priesthood* (2nd Edn), London, John Murray, 1919, 220-300.
[30] Moberly, 1919, 241.
[31] Moberly, 1919, 242.
[32] Moberly, 1919, 69.
[33] Moberly, 1919, 69.
[34] Moberly, 1919, 66-73.
[35] So for example, Moberly presses, almost to the point of literalism, the image of the eye. According to Moberly if the eye either is blinded or removed from the body no other organ can replace that role nor is the 'sight-capacity... conferred upon the eye at the will or by act of the body.' (Moberly, 1919, 69.)
[36] Moberly, 1919, 106.
[37] Sanday, 1900, 124. The first session, exploring the 'Presuppositions of New Testament Doctrine' included the 'Definition of Sacrifice and Priesthood' (Sanday, 1900, 62.) After the opening five minute statements by those involved, Fairburn stated that he 'should like Canon Moberly to explain certain statements concerning the priesthood of Christ' (Sanday, 1900, 94). However, Cosmo Gordon Lang caused the question to be deferred until the second afternoon.

Atonement was not simply retributivist but penitential.[38] Through his life and death Christ brings about the reconciliation of God and man, not only by the offering of his perfect obedience but also by his perfect penitence. The combination of these two attributes overcomes the divine/human *diastasis* by Christ's sympathetic identification on the one hand with humanity and on the other with God. Atonement is of God but man is instrumental because "his penitence" serves as "the re-identification of the sinful consciousness with holiness."[39] But immediately Moberly is exposed to the charge that his understanding fails to acknowledge the priority of divine sovereignty in its definition of sacrifice and is therefore implicitly Pelagian.

This brief examination of a late nineteenth and early twentieth century debate concerning the ordained ministry[40] highlights three concrete examples of points raised by my thesis. First the naively realistic emphasis upon the historicity of the Apostolic Succession as that which validates the priesthood[41] of the ordained effectively unchurches the majority of the Reformed tradition. This emphasis follows from an understanding of priesthood and episcopacy in terms of office, which in turn emphasises the distinction between lay and ordained resulting in a hierarchical structure both ministerially within and also between churches.[42]

Second is the importance of the meaning of sacrifice. The understanding of sacrifice articulated by the participants in the Oxford Conference differed hugely. The problem is not the diversity but the assumption that sacrifice

---

[38] Moberly's argument is more fully developed in *Atonement and Personality* (1901). However, it is here (Sanday, 1900, 125-126.) that perhaps for the first time Moberly deploys the parable of the mother's self-identification with the sin of her child. Timothy Gorringe draws attention to the original idea for the parable in the work of John McLeod Campbell, *The Nature of Atonement*, 1856. (See: Timothy Gorringe, *God's Just Vengeance*, Cambridge, CUP, 1996, 209.)

[39] Moberly, Sanday, 1900, 125.

[40] Other examples that continue the debate would include: H. B. Swete (ed), *Essays On The Early History Of The Church And The Ministry* (2nd Edn), London, Macmillan and Co., London, 1921, and K. E. Kirk (ed.), *The Apostolic Ministry*, London, Hodder and Stoughton, 1946.

[41] According to John Webster '[f]orms cannot guarantee authenticity' (John Webster, 'The Self-Organising Power Of The Gospel of Christ: Episcopacy And Community Formation', *Word and Church*, Edinburgh, T & T Clark, 2001, 208) and that the traditional historical basis of Apostolic succession is 'naive' (Webster, 2001, 210). However, he believes Apostolicity is concerned with 'identity and authenticity, with the "Christianness" of the church's teaching and mission.' (Webster, 2001, 210.)

[42] As *Apostolicae Curae* unchurched the Church of England so too Gore, Moberly, Swete and Kirk tend to unchurch those churches whose ordained ministry they deemed to be 'defective'. More recently Balthasar's emphasis upon the notion of the Apostolic nature of the office repeats this.

must be understood propositionally and therefore univocally.[43] For the Protestant participants at the Conference, Moberly's understanding was wholly unacceptable because it failed to maintain the divine sovereignty and therefore the precedence of grace. My suggestion is that imagination offers the "capacity to represent an object [in this case sacrifice] without its being present",[44] that it is not to be understood as a statement of naïve realism, but analogically and dialectically.[45]

Third, if sacrifice cannot be understood propositionally then neither can priesthood. Priesthood exists in a dialectic of testimony and counter-testimony.[46] Both parties acknowledged that priesthood and sacrifice are intimately related. This repeats the dialectic of the Chalcedonian pattern whereby boundaries are crossed, and the divine and the human encounter one another but without either negating its essential self by becoming that which it is not. This notion of priesthood refers to the priesthood of Christ[47] in a dialectic of ambiguity combining elements of both tracking and fitting theories[48] wherein 'likeness' is discernible but there is no final synthesis resulting in 'sameness'. Consequently priesthood becomes an act of imagination.

The Dialectical Imagination

The example of the English debate about priesthood demonstrated the severe limitations of representation understood in terms of naïve realism when discussing priesthood. In the debate both the Catholic and Protestant attempts to articulate priesthood univocally share a common "positivist philosophy of history" according to which once the facts are revealed it is possible to know "what really happened."[49] Either one interpretation must withdraw because it is wrong, proven so by the evident correctness of the alternative understanding. Or they must remain irreconcilable because of their claim that their historical account is objectively true.[50] However,

---

[43] George Lindbeck, *The Nature of Doctrine*, Philadelphia, Westminster Press, 1984, 47.
[44] Umberto Eco, *Kant and the Platypus* (ET), London, Vintage, 2000, 81.
[45] Eberhard Jüngel discussing metaphor, truth and religious language says 'in order to be true…a text has to say more than what is actual' (Eberhard Jüngel, 'Metaphorical Truth' in *Theological Essays* I (ET), Edinburgh, T & T Clark, 1989, 17).
[46] See: Chapter 6 above.
[47] See: Chapter 6 above in which I argue that Christ's priesthood embodies both testimony and countertestimony.
[48] See: Chapter 1 above.
[49] Karl Möller, 'Renewing Historical Criticism', Craig Bartholomew, Colin Greene, Karl Möller (ed), *Renewing Biblical Interpretation*, Carlisle, Paternoster, 2000, 151. So Stephen Sykes suggests that Gore looked to historical argument as evidence for the veracity of dogmatic statements (Sykes, 1978, 22.).
[50] Roy Porter, *Enlightenment*, London, Penguin Books, 2000, 233.

Gerard Loughlin argues, that history and fiction resemble one another insofar as "both are narrative works... made by people." History-writing, though not fictional, is never scientifically objective but "always proceeds from somewhere" raising questions about the very nature of representation never being simply "a reduplication of past reality, but a present construction."[51] In short, in tracing past events, historians tell plotted stories.[52]

This is important for the attempt to provide a Protestant re-evaluation of the priesthood of the ordained ministry. Protestant foundationalism understands reality as "mind independent objects" from which it follows "that there is one true complete description of these brute facts."[53] However, the attempt "to produce an objective account of 'the facts as they really are'" is illusory.[54] The issue is one of hermeneutics. Protestant foundationalism, according to which objective authority is grounded in the claim of biblical inerrancy, is comparable to "the Catholic doctrine of the immaculate conception of Mary."[55] Ultimately they fail to take seriously the true nature of humanity. For the Protestant foundationalist this is most acute in the "scandalous humanity" of the Word of God, which is replaced in the attempt to capture the revelatory nature of Scripture in "its literal propositional truth".[56] The approach, epitomised by the two parties at the Oxford Conference, stressed either the objective foundationalism of history or the biblical texts, which it applied to priesthood and has proven itself fruitless and ultimately mistaken.[57]

Previously I discussed the importance of imagination by reference to Garrett Green[58] who argues that the Enlightenment and modernity stress history and critical reason, regarding the imagination as "the source of speculation, fantasy and illusion... the organ of fiction".[59] Also previously I

---

[51] Gerard Loughlin, *Telling God's Story*, Cambridge, CUP, 1999, 149.
[52] Loughlin, 1999, 150.
[53] Möller, 2000, 151, quoting F. W. Dobbs-Allsopp, 'Rethinking Historical Criticism', Biblical Interpretation: A Journal of Contemporary Approaches (7), 1999.
[54] Möller, 2000, 151.
[55] Trevor Hart, *Regarding Karl Barth*, Carlisle, Paternoster, 1999, 43. (See: 130-38 above.)
[56] Hart, 1999, 39.
[57] Stanley Grenz, 'Articulating the Christian Belief-Mosaic', John G. Stackhouse Jnr. (Ed), *Evangelical Futures*, Grand Rapids, Baker Books, 2000, 109. Grenz speaks of 'foundationalism' and 'grounding the entire edifice of human knowledge on something unquestionably certain.' (Grenz, 2000, 110.) Foundational certainty of knowledge can be provided by various sources including history or 'the blind acceptance of Christian doctrine' by appeal to tradition by the Catholic or the Bible by the Protestant. (Grenz, 2000, 111-12.)
[58] See: 26 above.
[59] Garrett Green, *Theology, Hermeneutics and Imagination*, Cambridge, CUP, 2000, 14.

have criticized Balthasar's ecclesiology because of the role he accords to Peter and Mary, resulting in a priestly testimony grounded in a historically validated office. Also I suggested that Moltmann's priestly counter-testimony was a consequence of his phenomenological, and therefore empiricist, influenced theology. Both, I suggested, failed to maintain a consistent theological form and trinitarian structure. Conversely I proposed that Barth is able to maintain greater theological consistency [60] resulting from the rigor of the boundaries[61] by which he defines his theology and which by their very existence allow scope for the imaginative thought without resulting in fantasy or speculation.

Discussing his hermeneutical methodology, Barth regards the Enlightenment emphasis upon the supremacy of historical criticism in reading the Bible as the abrogation of the interpretive task.[62] It is not that historical investigation or criticism is inappropriate, but that it is only part of the task, which ultimately is the imaginative inhabitation of the text by the reader.[63] What is immediately apparent is the dialectical nature of Barth's proposal,[64] at the heart of which, is the priestly task of conveying the presence of the divine in the midst of the secular.[65] But it also repeats the Chalcedonian pattern in which the divine and the human each participate in the other but without any confusion of forms. There is in Barth an imaginative and "dialectical relationship of... veiling and unveiling."[66] Revelation means "giving signs" therefore "revelation means sacrament" which must be "in a form adapted to our creaturely knowledge."[67] The "Word comes to expression in human words" but it "is not a second form of 'incarnation'",[68] always expressed by analogy.

---

[60] See: 126, 135 above. Though Moltmann avoids the hierarchical problems apparent in Balthasar's ecclesiology his theology is orientated to praxis as a major methodological principle. (See: Richard Bauckham, *The Theology of Jürgen Moltmann*, Edinburgh, T & T Clark, 1996.)

[61] These are: men and women as God's covenant partner, particularism, the Chalcedonian pattern, the maintenance of dialectic and the maintaining of divinely sovereign grace. (See: 107, 135, 143 above.)

[62] Karl Barth, *The Epistle to the Romans* (6th Edn, ET), London, OUP, 1957, 6.

[63] Barth, 1957, 8.

[64] Barth, 1957, 8. See: Bruce L. McCormack, *Karl Barth's Critically Realistic Dialectical Theology*, Oxford, OUP, 1997, 142-147.

[65] Graham Ward, *Barth, Derrida and the Language of Theology*, Cambridge, CUP, 1998, 21.

[66] Green, 2000, 146.

[67] *CD* II.1, 52. See also: Karl Barth, 'The Task of the Ministry', *The Word of God and the Word of Man* (ET), London, Hodder and Stoughton, 1935.

[68] Bruce McCormack, 'Article Review: Graham Ward's *Barth, Derrida And The Language of Theology*', *JTS* (49), 1996, 107.

The error of the participants at the Oxford Conference, the debate concerning priesthood and the classic expositions of kenoticism during the later nineteenth century is the same.[69] At its root it is a suspicion of the imaginative as self-deceiving[70] in an age in which "science has served as the paradigm for knowledge, truth and morality."[71] Instead I shall argue that "realistic imagination... is of or about something... a way of being related to facts... of knowing facts through images."[72] The failing of both sides in the nineteenth century, and repeated in the subsequent debates concerning priesthood, has been the assumption that "Christian faith must either side with the absolutist past or abandon its claim to witness to a unique truth." So Protestant foundationalism typically identifies "biblical revelation with reality itself," and therefore that "orthodox Christian doctrine" provides an "objective description of that reality."[73]

However, if we attend to "the paradigmatic drama of the Bible, we catch a vision" in which "God has revealed himself to our imagination".[74] Echoing the accounts of, on the one hand, Philippians,[75] and on the other, sacrifice as a non-pernicious[76] event, biblical interpretation is open ended, always containing a "surplus of meaning".[77] According to the traditional Protestant account, priesthood articulates an essential misunderstanding rooted in a form of bad imagining.[78] But if we reject that naïve realism and turn instead to metaphor as "based upon an analogy between something known and something to be elucidated"[79] we must reject any univocal claims and actively call for interpretation, which requires "the active engagement of the imagination."[80]

J. B. Lightfoot argued that "Christianity stands apart from all the older religions",[81] and by implication from the religion of the Jewish people, as recorded in the First Testament, not requiring a priestly or mediatory caste

---

[69] Interestingly both Charles Gore and P. T. Forsyth were actively engaged in all three examples cited.
[70] Green, 2000, 192.
[71] Green, 2000, 194.
[72] Francesca Aran Murphy, *Christ The Form Of Beauty*, Edinburgh, T & T Clark, 1995, 7.
[73] Green, 2000, 197. This Green calls 'foundationalist objectivism' (Green, 2000, 198) or what I have called naïve realism.
[74] Green, 2000, 204.
[75] See: 83, 91, 103 above.
[76] See: 166-173 above.
[77] Green, 2000, 173, referring to the work of Paul Ricoeur.
[78] Green, 2000, 171.
[79] Green, 2000, 174.
[80] Green, 2000, 175.
[81] Lightfoot, 1879, 182.

since such a provision had "served its temporary purpose",[82] an understanding which is repeated by Jürgen Moltmann.[83] In so doing they both articulate a naively realistic understanding of the language of priesthood. However, in the First Testament, as I have demonstrated, priesthood is not presented univocally but dialectically.[84]

Likewise the writer of the Letter to the Hebrews presents an image of priesthood, specifically in relation to Jesus Christ, caught in creative dialectical tension. On the one hand, Jesus Christ is the true priest, who expiates the sin of mankind and so mediates the reconciliation of God and man, 'once for all.'[85] On the other, Jesus is the embodiment of the priestly counter-testimony of the First Testament standing outside the priestly line of succession. Jesus' priesthood is real in its salvific efficacy, but it is also metaphorical.[86] Jesus is not a member of the priestly caste.[87]

Metaphor "is the application of a noun which properly applies to something else."[88] Thus the writer to the Hebrews calls Jesus a 'priest' just as one might speak of a ship 'standing' at anchor, where standing is both similar and dissimilar to the person who is 'standing' at a bus stop. Metaphorical language need not simply be figurative, but can add new meaning[89] enriching the original. Discussing metaphor, truth and religious language Eberhard Jüngel says "in order to be true…a text has to say more than what is actual".[90] Metaphor is dialectical, encompassing the familiar and the strange.[91] Metaphor also fulfils a priestly function signifying transference,[92] so that horizons are expanded,[93] mediating between the familiar and the unfamiliar,[94] by crossing boundaries.[95] Jüngel's chief

---

[82] Lightfoot, 1879, 183. For criticism of supersessionism as anti-cultic see: Walter Breuggemann, *Theology Of The Old Testament*, Minneapolis, Fortress Press, 1997, 651.

[83] Jürgen Moltmann, *The Church in the Power of the Spirit*, London (ET), SCM, 1977, 301.

[84] See: Chapter 6 above.

[85] Heb. 9.24-28.

[86] Gunton, 1988, 122. Gunton draws attention to the inherently dialectical structure, 'it is and is not', of metaphor.

[87] C.f. Zechariah (Lk. 1. 5, 8-9); Annas and Caiaphas (Lk. 3.2; Acts. 4.6) also Mk. 11.27-33; Lk. 22.2.

[88] Aristotle, *Poetics* (ET), London, Penguin Books, 1996, 9.3

[89] Gunton, 1988, 28. This draws attention to is the connection between metaphor and identity, and the recognisability of that which is being signified or described.

[90] Eberhard Jüngel, 'Metaphorical Truth' in *Theological Essays* I (ET), Edinburgh, T & T Clark, 1989, 17.

[91] Jüngel, 1989, 57, 68.

[92] Jüngel, 1989, 35.

[93] Jüngel, 1989, 40.

[94] Jüngel, 1989, 43.

[95] Metaphor affords 'access to a new dimension of being' (Jüngel, 1989, 61).

concern is the problem of speaking meaningfully of God, believing that metaphor enables speech about God while "at the same time we speak of the fundamental difference between God and the world."[96] So the concern of priesthood is the recognition of the essential *diastasis* between God and humanity. Metaphor brings "together two horizons"[97] but without any loss or merging of identity. If metaphor acts in what might be described as a priestly capacity then it would be singularly appropriate if priesthood could be understood metaphorically. We might say

> Jesus was not actually a priest. In actuality he was 'truly God and truly man', the second person of the Trinity. But in truth? Was he actually in truth only what he was in actuality? Is it only words which describe the actual Jesus Christ that tell the truth to the hearer of this prediction which is accomplished in these words, whereas the word which normally signifies one who provides for the crossing of the boundaries which divide God and man tells the hearer an untruth when taken in its literal sense?[98]

Jüngel believes that metaphors "are the articulation of discoveries"[99] making it possible to express something of the "unexplored and the unexperienced" by expressing "the possibility of innovation".[100] Analogy is a special case of metaphor as transferred but understandable or recognisable naming.[101] However, analogy exceeds simple rhetoric in that "the same word can be used for different things without becoming meaningless".[102] Jüngel draws attention to how Aristotle places analogous speech at the midpoint between equivocity and univocity[103] in which "different things named

---

[96] Jüngel, 1989, 58.

[97] John Webster, 'Introduction', Jüngel, 1989, 5.

[98] I have substituted a statement about Jesus' priesthood for Jüngel's discussion of metaphor. In the original Jüngel discusses the statement: Achilles was a lion, but that of course 'Achilles was not actually a lion. In actuality he was a brave warrior. But in truth? Was he actually in truth only what he was in actuality? Is it only words which describe the actual Achilles that tell the truth to the hearer of this prediction which is accomplished in these words, whereas the word which normally signifies wild animal tells the hearer an untruth when taken in its literal sense?' (Jüngel, 1989, 24.)

[99] Jüngel, 1989, 51.

[100] Jüngel, 1989, 52, n 87. See also: Eberhard Jüngel, *God the Mystery of the World* (ET, Edinburgh, T & T Clark, 1983. The original German edition was written after 'Metaphorical Truth' but translated first), 289-293.

[101] Jüngel, 1983, 267. Analogy because its name is therefore a form of recognition or identification.

[102] Jüngel, 1983, 268.

[103] Jüngel, 1983, 268.

by the same word are addressed not in the same but in a similar sense." This similarity is grounded in a mutual relatedness to

> *one identical thing*, on the basis of which the varying usage of the word is justified as similar usage. This one thing to which the various things called by the same word are related is then the hermeneutical first thing… in relation to which other things can also be named.[104]

The fundamental analogy is Christological because God became man in Christ, without which "God's unknownness" is obtrusive.[105] The Incarnation identifies God in the man Jesus Christ so that the "concrete difference between God and man"[106] is revealed. Thus God is thinkable because he can be posited in human language. But this is also priestly because the analogy permits the boundaries defining the divine-human *diastasis* to be crossed. Analogy, as well as being imaginative, is also dialectical suggesting 'this' is like 'that', while both remain distinct.

Jüngel's analysis suggests a very different meaning of the language of priesthood in comparison to Lightfoot's propositional understanding. This can be confirmed by its application to Philippians 2.5-11. The *carmen Christi* is the controlling text upon which the whole of the Letter to the Philippians hangs.[107] Following Jüngel, the *carmen Christi* says more than the actual gospel account, telling the truth extraordinarily concisely. Its concern is who is Jesus and what is he like? This in turn is located in the Epistle, which explores the identities of Paul and his Philippian audience, who are to be Christ like. The hymn is "a language event. Because what happens in it is that God relates himself to the world and to man and thus is expressed in language"[108] so that the necessary *diastasis* of God and humanity is overcome but not dissolved. The dialectic is maintained, there is no synthesis. Humanity is invited to respond by being God's covenant partner. Similarly priesthood is a language event expressing the divine-human relationship.

Imagination is therefore not to be simply equated with the fictive. But in order for this to be the case it, the imaginative, must be appropriately regulated. The regulative process is essentially a hermeneutical framework,

---

[104] Jüngel, 1983, 269. Jüngel identifies this as an analogy of relation or attribution in which 'B, C, and D all relate in varying ways to A on the basis of which they are commonly named.' (Jüngel, 1983, 270) This corresponds to a fitting theory of representation. (See: 10-11 above.)

[105] Jüngel, 1983, 277.

[106] Jüngel, 1983, 288.

[107] See Chapter 4 above.

[108] Jüngel, 1983, 289 – his italics.

for example, the "thick description"[109] proposed by Kevin Vanhoozer. Thick description is concerned with what the text "is about rather than to what purportedly lies behind it"[110] requiring "more than one interpretive approach."[111] Therefore Vanhoozer defines literal meaning "as 'the sense of the literary act.'" It is "less a matter of identifying objects in the world than in specifying communicative acts." The ultimate communicative act is located in the doctrine of God whereby "Jesus (the Word become flesh) 'exegetes' the Father (John 1.18)".[112] Vanhoozer therefore stresses the trinitarian nature of God as underlying all language and its essentially communicative nature. Not only is God "first and foremost a communicative agent" as evidenced in that it is the Word made flesh which is incarnate, but that his very being is a self-communicative act which "enacts the covenant of discourse: speaker (Father), Word (Son), and reception (Spirit) are all interrelated."[113]

Secondly, communication is for a purpose.[114] What

> is handed on from one person, group, culture and generation to the next is not just words and ideas, important though these will always be, but a set of vital practices and roles that must constantly be improvised upon in order to meet the demands of particular environments.[115]

I wish to argue that the designation of the 'ordained ministry' as 'priestly' is not just words and ideas but carries its own meaning.[116] The debate concerning priesthood, a part of which I outlined earlier,[117] was a hermeneutical debate concerning the meaning of the words associated with priesthood. However, the meaning of priesthood does not just reside in the

---

[109] Vanhoozer, 1998, 285. Vanhoozer acknowledges his indebtedness for the term 'thick description' to Clifford Geertz (see: Vanhoozer, 1998, 284, n. 13)

[110] Vanhoozer, 1998, 291-92.

[111] Vanhoozer, 1998, 302.

[112] Vanhoozer, 1998, 304. See: *CD* IV.1, 177. Vanhoozer recognises this correlation with Barth but also with Balthasar. (Kevin Vanhoozer, 'The Voice and the Actor,', John G. Stackhouse Jnr., *Evangelical Futures*, Grand Rapids, Baker Books, 2000, 72.)

[113] Vanhoozer, 1998, 456.

[114] Thus, for example Philippians addresses a specific communication to the Philippians. (See: 75 above.)

[115] Trevor Hart, 'Imagining Evangelical Theology', John G. Stackhouse Jnr. (Ed), *Evangelical Futures*, Grand Rapids, Baker Books, 2000, 194 – my italics.

[116] Richard Hooker is not entirely correct when he suggests 'whether we call it [the ordained ministry] a Priesthood, a Presbytership or a Ministry it skilleth not' (*Laws*, V. lxxviii.3). The effect of his indifference is that he thereby fails to consider the potential riches offered for the understanding of the Christian life and ministry offered by the word 'priest'.

[117] See: 186-192 above.

words. Priesthood also describes a set of vital practices and roles. It is possible to argue that the debate about the priesthood between Lightfoot and Moberly fundamentally concerns the nature of the relationship between the internal or doctrinal understanding of priesthood and the external roles and practices of the ministry.[118] It is the very nature of these roles and practices that have caused Protestants to balk at the concept of priesthood as traditionally understood. I have suggested that the traditional understanding of the priesthood of the ordained is presented as a series of "informative propositions or truth claims about objective realities."[119] The ecclesiology, articulated by Balthasar and some of the participants in the Oxford Conference, sought to demonstrate that the priesthood of ordained was a historically validated office given by Christ through the apostles. Conversely opponents of this view sought to propose an alternative historical account based upon the biblical account and the supposed absence of a priestly testimony in the Second Testament. Whereas, I have suggested that the biblical account is not as straightforward as is sometimes supposed by some Protestant exegetes, but essentially dialectical.[120] Both accounts I have suggested are flawed. The flaws are fundamentally to do with identification and appropriate characterisation of both God in relation to humanity or humanity in relation to God and the place of any intermediary; the role often ascribed to the priest.

Analogously, kenosis asks similar questions concerning identity. Clearly kenosis as the renunciation of the divine attributes is impossible. At best one is left with a semi-divine figure or at worst one who is simply human.[121] Instead I suggested that kenosis offers four essential pointers towards the nature of priesthood. First, that kenosis and priesthood propose a dialectical statement about the divine and human identities in which there is fluidity but not confusion. Second, kenosis and priesthood provide a means of representing the story of the divine-human encounter that is regulative. Third, kenosis and priesthood are both concerned with divine-human participation but without any loss of identity and cannot therefore be negative. Fourth, as kenosis proceeds from God to humanity, so the priesthood of the ordained is responsive from humanity to God, and cannot therefore be propitiatory.[122] The priesthood of the ordained narrates the story of the human response to the prior event of divine grace thereby "render[ing] a 'debt of recognition'"[123] or gratitude.

---

[118] See: Stephen Sykes, *The Identity of Christianity*, Philadelphia, Fortress Press, 1984, 46-50.
[119] Lindbeck, 1984, 16.
[120] See: Chapter 6 above.
[121] See: Chapter 2 above.
[122] See: Chapter 3 above.
[123] Loughlin, 1999, 151.

Therefore what I wish to escape is the understanding of the priesthood of the ordained as confined to just words and ideas and instead to consider the vital practices and roles. As Trevor Hart suggests, it is the encounter between on the one hand, words and ideas and on the other, roles and practices that requires imaginative performance, which is an interpretive act.[124] This presupposes a narrative understanding in which the story is incomplete. The plot and characterisation call for a continual dialectic between the priesthood of Christ, and the priesthood of the ordained. This dialectic repeats the Chalcedonian pattern, whereby Jesus Christ, is 'truly God and truly man' without confusion and without synthesis. So the priesthood of the Church and the ordained is like but not identical to that of Christ. The Christian priesthood is not to be confused with the priesthood of Christ. Nonetheless it takes its form from Christ, in whom it is recognizable, but not identical with. The priesthood of the ordained is secondary so its sacrificial nature is asymmetrically relational to the prior event of God in Christ. This is an act of divine sovereignty demonstrative of the primacy of grace and to which the corresponding sacrificial activity of the Church is always doxological and responsive.

It is in this imaginative encounter that I believe it is possible to begin to offer a Protestant re-evaluation of the priesthood of the ordained ministry and which I shall develop in the next Chapter.

---

[124] Trevor Hart quotes Flannery O'Connor, 'When you can state the theme of a story, when you can separate it from the story itself, then you can be sure the story is not a very good one.' (Hart, 2000, 194.) This is a version of the point made earlier (Chapter 4 above) concerning Philippians where Paul calls upon the recipients of the letter to be Christlike, to enact their identity 'in Christ' (Phil. 2.5).

Chapter 8

Priesthood and the Ordained

Protestant theology has accepted the concept of priesthood when applied to the Church as God's covenant people or to Jesus Christ's saving act. What is problematic for Protestant theology is the appropriateness of notions of priesthood in relation to the ordained ministry. However, I suggest that this reservation is misplaced and indicative of the failure to maintain a consistency of structure, form and content. By means of analogy it is possible that the same word can include relatively different meanings while sharing a common root. It is important that any articulation of priesthood is recognisable when understood distinctively with reference to all believers, Christ and the ordained.

In proposing a Protestant re-evaluation of the priesthood of the ordained ministry I have argued that the meaning of priesthood is not simply located in the words but in an imaginative engagement with roles and practices. Indeed I have argued that it is precisely when the meaning of priesthood is located in a set of words understood naively realistically that the traditional Catholic and Protestant understandings are irreconcilable. However, in dialogue with Scripture, Barth, Balthasar and Moltmann, I have established a number of characteristics or boundary markers, which provide a framework within which it is possible to speak of a Protestant understanding of the priesthood of the ordained. Briefly these are the necessary maintenance of the precedence of divinely sovereign grace, the particularism of the biblical account, the Chalcedonian pattern and the dialectic of testimony and counter-testimony in the Scriptural account of priesthood. Furthermore, these four characteristics also apply to kenosis not as negation but that which renders the divine recognisable. The priesthood of the ordained can only be understood if it maintains a form of representation based upon the previous four points signifying both internal resemblance and external tracking. Furthermore, that priesthood is identifiable in relation to Jesus Christ and his saving act. However, the existence of a family likeness does not mean that the priesthood of Christ and of the ordained is identical. In developing my argument I shall seek to maintain a consistency of structure, form and content.

In this Chapter I shall demonstrate three foundations for a Protestant re-evaluation of the priesthood of the ordained ministry. First I shall explore the understanding of priesthood as analogy. Secondly, I shall argue that priesthood is representative. Thirdly, I shall argue that the priesthood of the ordained is concerned with the externalisation of representation and participation in the human-divine encounter. In the light of the above I shall demonstrate that notions of priesthood can appropriately and fruitfully be used to describe but also to explore the roles and practices with which the ordained ministry is engaged. In order to do this I shall return to the dialogue with Philippians as a text, which through its concern for identity draws together the themes of kenosis and priesthood.

Priesthood and Analogy

To speak of priesthood in terms of analogy is to say it is neither a univocal concept,[1] nor is the meaning of priesthood equivocal or indefinable. Wittgenstein's analogy of language as a 'game' provides a helpful tool for understanding, as seen in Richard Hooker's discussion of the word 'priest.' Hooker preferred the designation 'presbyter' over 'priest' because of the inherent difficulty in the meaning of the word in the light of its First and Second Testament usage. Nonetheless, he does not reject 'priest' as an inappropriate designation of the ordained.[2] Importantly, he recognises the connection between priesthood and sacrifice, noting that the same word can embody variant meanings, which are defined by usage.[3] To speak of priesthood by analogy requires that the words used are both imaginative and maintain the necessary dialectic of similarity and difference.

Analogy and the Dialectical

Wittgenstein's later exploration of the nature of language and meaning begins with a quote from Augustine[4] who suggested that "words label things, and that sentences describe states of affairs".[5] It is this seemingly simple notion of language as naming that Wittgenstein challenges, recognising that language is a communicative action within a social

---

[1] See: Chapter 6 above.
[2] *Laws*, V. lxxviii.3.
[3] *Laws*, V. lxxviii.3
[4] *PI*. 1, n. 1. Wittgenstein uses the quote from Augustine in order to distance himself from as expressing his own position as outlined in *Tractatus Logico Philosophicus*, 1922. (See: 4 above.)
[5] Fergus Kerr, *Theology after Wittgenstein* (2nd Edn), London, SPCK, 1997, 57.

setting.[6] A "language-*game*" articulates the belief "that the speaking of a language is a part of an activity, or a form of life."[7] Meaning is not simply resident in the individual words, but in "the practical exchanges that constitute the public world which we inhabit together."[8] Language is to be understood in terms of relatedness (family likeness)[9] which he illustrates by reference to those activities which are called games. Chess, snap, football and golf are all 'games' as dissimilar as they are alike. What they have in common, he suggests, are shared "family resemblances."[10] Furthermore a game is a human construct whose only reality exists in the playing of it. What is significant are the conventions by which usage is governed, for example the giving of a gift. Wittgenstein asks, "Why can't my right hand give my left hand money?"[11] But, giving a gift is not simply passing an object from hand to hand. "Something can't be a gift without the giver and receiver sharing a concept of gift, and they can't have that without the institution of gift giving."[12]

Hooker recognises there is a dichotomy between on the one hand; 'priest' as labelling univocally one whose role is defined sacerdotally and on the other, a plurality of meaning as conventionally used, but without sacerdotal intention to describe all 'clergy'. While the latter popular usage is less defined there is a discernible 'family resemblance'. Such a concept of likeness does not require simple or univocal meaning for words but a sufficiency of similarity to enable recognition. This Wittgenstein demonstrates by the particularism and realism of simple examples; buying five red apples, a builder building, games and buying cheese.[13] The point is that language, although imprecise, works.[14]

For Barth language is also a central concern.[15] Like Wittgenstein, Barth recognized knowledge is bound to language, which exists within "a historical community."[16] Language is priestly because it is communicative, crossing the borders between oneself and another. But language is also

---

[6] Thus from *PI* 2-21 he explores language within this context.

[7] *PI*. 23 – his italics.

[8] Kerr, 1997, 58.

[9] *PI*. 65.

[10] *PI*. 67.

[11] *PI*. 268.

[12] David Bloor, 'The question of linguistic idealism revisited', in Hans Sluga, David G Stern, *The Cambridge Companion to Wittgenstein*, Cambridge, CUP, 1999, 366.

[13] *PI*. 1, 2, 8-10, 15, 17, 19-21, 66, 142.

[14] Robert J. Foglin, 'Wittgenstein's critique of philosophy', in Hans Sluga, David G. Stern, *The Cambridge Companion to Wittgenstein*, Cambridge, CUP, 1999, 51.

[15] As 'a theological discipline, dogmatics is the scientific test to which the Christian Church puts herself regarding the language about God which is peculiar to her.' (*CD* I.1, 1.)

[16] Kerr, 1997, 76.

particular, in that it recognises the other which is both similar and dissimilar. According to Barth it "is not the general which comes first but the particular. The general does not exist without the particular and therefore cannot be prior to the particular."[17] God's power cannot be discussed as a general statement of eternal truth but only in the context of a narrative account in a particular historic occasion. Biblical narratives are "not about ideas or universals... but about unique and unrepeatable events".[18] In his dialectic there is an implicit awareness of the importance of 'family resemblance.' This has a twofold consequence. First Barth understands language about God as neither literal[19] nor expressive[20] but analogical, and therefore imaginative. As McCormack recognises, the failure of Balthasar's reading of Barth was his belief that Barth's turn to analogy coincided with the abandonment of dialectic. Whereas in reality the "*analogia fidei* is itself an inherently dialectical concept."[21] Secondly the "authoritative and referential aspect of the narratives was not so much the literal details as the underlying patterns and structures."[22] Interpretation is not "the mere deciphering of words as though they were runes".[23] Instead it is "creative... dialectical" and therefore imaginative because the "Word ought to be expressed in the words."[24] The fundamental dialectic, which governs everything, is the divine-human *diastasis*, which shapes every encounter between God and creation and is repeated in the inerrancy of the Word of God and the fallibility of the words of God spoken or written by humanity. The asymmetry of the divine-human relationship is repeated.

Applied to priesthood it is necessary to maintain the asymmetry of the divine-human encounter. In this there is a fundamental resemblance and therefore analogy. The priest may speak the Word of God but only in words. Priests signify the crossing of the boundaries, which separate God and humanity, but they do not cross them in their own name. The same regulative processes that govern all divine-human encounters must also govern the imaginative account of priesthood. The imaginative use of analogy permits creative representation in which the identity and therefore the differences between the participants are maintained.

---

[17] *CD* II.1, 602.

[18] George Hunsinger, *How to Read Karl Barth*, Oxford, OUP, 1993, 47.

[19] Hunsinger, 1993, 43. Hunsinger's account of literalism equates to my concept of naïve realism. See: Chapter 1 above.

[20] Hunsinger, 1993, 44. Hunsinger's account of expressivism is similar though not identical with anti-realistic modes of representation. See: Chapter 1 above.

[21] Bruce L. McCormack, *Karl Barth's Critically Realistic Dialectical Theology*, Oxford, OUP, 1997, 16.

[22] Hunsinger,1993, 48. This corresponds to an analogy of relation.

[23] Karl Barth, *The Epistle to The Romans* (6th Edn, ET), London, OUP, 1957 7.

[24] Barth, 1957, 8.

The Particularism of Priesthood in the Bible

The imagination is not unbounded, but exists within a series of defining parameters. An example of this is the particularity of the biblical stories. All too often theology fails to treat the particularity of the text seriously preferring instead to speak of the essence or essential intentions.[25] Traditionally Protestant theology has argued that priesthood is largely absent from the Second Testament.[26] However, what is evident in the Second Testament is Paul's deliberate choice of priestly and sacrificial language when speaking of the Christian vocation and life.

Paul employs priestly and cultic imagery in relation to his own ministry, the discipleship of the Philippians and elsewhere in his writings.[27] However, there is an ambiguity in Paul's language. One word he uses, λειτουργία can refer to either 'public' or 'cultic' service.[28] Given the infrequency with which λειτουργία, and other cultic words occur in the Second Testament[29] their inclusion by Paul reflects a significant authorial choice. But he employs cultic imagery on other occasions, for example, calling upon the Romans to present their 'bodies as a living sacrifice (θυσίαν), holy and acceptable (εὐάρεστον) to God, which is your spiritual worship (λατρείαν).'[30] This echoes the priestly counter-testimony of the First Testament in which genuine sacrifice is of a life lived in obedience to the divine. The result is a kenotic re-identification of the person in relation to God in Christ.[31]

The ending of the cultus of the First Testament "through Christ and his death upon the cross means that there is no priestly caste" may be true, but to conclude that therefore such "words are not suitable for the functions of Christian ministers"[32] fails to take seriously the nature of the language in its narrative setting. Paul uses priestly language and imagery precisely because it is appropriate to some aspects of the Christian ministry. Even though his usage tends towards a priestly counter-testimony rather than testimony

---

[25] One example is Balthasar's largely speculative Mariology (see: 111-118 above).

[26] Jürgen Moltmann, *The Church in the Power of the Spirit* (ET), London, SCM, 1977, 301.

[27] For example Phil. 2.17; 2.30; 4.18; Rom. 12.1; 15.16; 2 Cor. 2.14-16; 9.12.

[28] B. F. Westcott, *The Epistle to the Hebrews*, London, Macmillan and Co., 1889, 230-231.

[29] Peter T. O'Brien, *The Epistle to the Philippians*, Grand Rapids, Eerdmans, 1991, 308, 360f. For example θυσία (sacrifice), εὐαρεστέω (to please) and λατρεία (worship).

[30] '[W]hich is your reasonable service.' Compare Rom 12.1 and Phil 4.18 'the gifts you sent [he understands to be] a fragrant offering (ὀσμὴν εὐοδίας), a sacrifice (θυσίαν) acceptable and pleasing (εὐάρεστον) to God'. Also: Philippians 1.20. (James D. G. Dunn, *Romans 9-16*, Dallas, Word Books, 1988, 709.)

[31] See: 154-158 above.

[32] O'Brien, 1991, 308.

there remains sufficient 'family resemblance' to justify his choice of language.[33] Paul re-interprets the concept of priesthood, liberating it from any fixity of meaning and preventing any premature closure in the light of the Christ event. Instead its meaning is given dialectically and imaginatively. So in Romans 15.16 Paul chooses to use priestly language and the cultic imagery of Christian ministry thereby transforming it.[34] Consequently Paul says 'more than what is actual'[35] providing a 'thick description' of priesthood. Indeed his missionary and evangelistic ministry is articulated as priestly, enabling boundaries to be crossed, sacrifices offered and right order to be restored.[36] The priestly counter-testimony[37] is such that the Gentiles are included within God's covenant people.[38]

Paul's use of priestly language is often explicitly sacrificial. The ambiguous use of such imagery enables the inclusion of non-cultic activity as a result of which boundaries, for example, clean/unclean and holy/profane[39] are crossed and communities and individuals transformed in relation to God, thereby creatively repeating the priestly testimony of the First Testament. One such example is 2 Corinthians 9.12, in which Paul describes the work of making a collection to support the saints in Jerusalem as a διακονία τῆσ λειτουργίας.[40] Paul interprets the generosity of the Macedonian church as demonstrative of their giving 'themselves to the Lord'.[41] The same pattern was observed when writing to the Philippians, whose generosity is imitative of God's grace in Christ.[42] Furthermore in this verse there is discernible a pattern of divine sovereignty and grace which results in the rescue and rehabilitation of God's people.[43] Consequently the pattern of kenosis, of *descensus* followed by *ascensus*[44] revealed in Christ is mirrored by the Macedonians whose poverty is transformed into hitherto

---

[33] 1 Pet. 2.4-10 and covenant identity in relation to Israel and the Church (see: 138-145 above.)

[34] Dunn, 1988b, 860.

[35] That 'in order to be true...a text has to say more than what is actual' (Eberhard Jüngel, 'Metaphorical Truth', in *Theological Essays* I (ET), Edinburgh, T & T Clark, 1989, 17).

[36] The author of 1 Peter proposes 'a priesthood whose chief function is to evangelize' (Paul J. Achtemeier, *1 Peter*, Minneapolis, Fortress Press, 1996, 152).

[37] Is. 56.6-8.

[38] See: 87 above, also Rom. 9.25-26.

[39] See: Priestly Testimony, 148 above.

[40] 2 Cor. 8.1-9.15 concerns the collection for the saints in Jerusalem by Paul and his co-workers.

[41] 2 Cor. 8.5.

[42] Phil 2.5 c.f. 3.21..

[43] See: 156, n. 64 above.

[44] See: 61-62 above.

unknown wealth. Paul thereby equates sacrificial giving with receiving.[45] The anticipated generosity of the Corinthians will be their response to the prior grace of God and their anticipated liberality 'the rendering (διακονία) of this service (λειτουργίας)'[46]

That Barrett translates ὅτι ἡ διακονία τῆσ λειτουργίας, 'the execution of this act of public service'[47] is indicative of the unwillingness to acknowledge the far greater usage of priestly language in the Second Testament than is usually recognised. If we compare this passage with Philippians 4.10-20, two points are apparent. First there is a notion of interchange and the participatory involvement of the Philippians with Paul in his apostolic task. Secondly, while apparently pervaded by commercial analogy, the imagery in this passage is priestly.[48] The generosity of the Philippians is understood "on the basis of the salvation procured by Christ's sacrificial death to offer sacrifices" an idea which Paul develops as the "total response to the living God which is called for in Rom 12.1."[49] This provides a 'thick description' with 2 Corinthians, as according with Paul's ideas as expressed elsewhere.

Paul's use of priestly language is deliberate, and has sacrificial overtones, as the response to God's divinely sovereign act of prevenient grace in Jesus Christ. Sacrifice is no longer limited to the realm of the liturgical but encompasses the whole of life, re-ordered through Jesus Christ in relation to God. Furthermore Paul's use of priestly language implies a notion of vocation. As Balthasar recognises, vocation understood in terms of role is analogous to the divine Trinitarian mission in which personhood occurs through living within the unique call of God. Vocation transforms people when they inhabit the role allotted to them by God in the theological narrative by naming and identifying themselves in relation to

---

[45] 2 Cor. 9.6-8.

[46] 2 Cor. 9.12. Paul Barnett argues that to understand this verse in 'cultic terms' is literalistic and 'improbable' (Paul Barnett, *The Second Epistle to the Corinthians*, Grand Rapids, Eerdmans, 1997, 444.) and that Paul's infrequent use of priestly language should be 'seen as allusive and metaphorical and not systematic and theological' (Barnett, 1997, 444, n 46). However, Paul's use of priestly language is more frequent than is usually acknowledged. Furthermore he is relatively consistent in its application to Christian ministry and service. While he may intend it to be both 'allusive and metaphorical' nonetheless there 'can be little doubt... that the religious connotation of these terms [διακονία and λειτουργία] is paramount... The offering is a benefaction to God and its conveyance is a priestly service, intimating sacrifice' (Jerry W. McCant, *2 Corinthians*, Sheffield, Sheffield Academic Press, 1999, 97).

[47] C. K. Barrett, *The Second Epistle to the Corinthians*, London, A & C Black, 1973, 239.

[48] See: 90 above.

[49] O'Brien, 1991, 542.

God.[50] Moltmann, however, distinguishes between the call to be Christian and vocation as the calling to a specific task. Vocation is therefore less concerned with the ontological, but with role and function, understood in relation to the extent to which they are the incarnation of faith and therefore participatory in the divine mission.[51] Barth believes that vocation exists through the double relatedness of men and women primarily in relation to God but also in relation to one another. The primary relationship between God and man is one founded upon divine grace to which the only possible response is praise. Vocation is gratitude lived.[52] This seems to me to be nearer in understanding to my reading of Paul.

For Paul vocation, and therefore identity, is responsive to the prior act of God's sovereign self-revelation in Christ.[53] Further, there is a second strand in Barth's understanding, which is also present in the thought of Balthasar. Vocation is rooted in an act of kenotic re-identification of the person, in relation to God in Christ. By inhabiting their true role in the divine narrative people attain their true God-given identity. The person risks all, but receives back more.[54] As Paul says, in Philippians 3.8, true identity is to be found 'in Christ,' and all else is σκύβαλον, and therefore no loss. 'What will it profit a man, if he gains the whole world and forfeits his life?'[55] Paul's apparent loss[56] is actually a blessing. Barth is thus able to retain both the particularity and richness of the biblical account.

Vocation is no pernicious sacrifice but genuine gain. Commenting upon Philippians 1.21, Barth suggests that the "decisive commentary... is Gal. 2.20, 'I live, yet *no* longer I (οὐκέτι ἐγώ), *Christ lives* in me'."[57] In Galatians 2.20 the old person has been 'crucified (συνεσταύρωμαι) with Christ'.[58] By participating in his death Paul has the "marks stamped upon him to show he belongs to this Lord".[59] This is a statement of vocation; the kenotic self-identification of the disciple with Jesus Christ, mirroring Christ's own vocation. Christ's vocation is not just that he is given up

---

[50] See: 118-120 above.
[51] See: 126 -127 above.
[52] See: 135 above.
[53] See: 103 above.
[54] See: 167 above.
[55] Matt. 16.26, c.f. Phil. 3.8.
[56] Phil. 3.5,6.
[57] Karl Barth, *The Epistle to the Philippians* (ET), London, SCM, 1962, 37 - his italics. One might also point to other passages where Paul articulates similar ideas i.e. Rom. 8.13; 14.8 2 Cor. 5.17.
[58] A similar notion to συνεσταύρωμαι (crucified with, Gal. 2.20) as participation is repeated in Phil. 3.21 (σύνμμορφον, conformed with).
[59] *CD* III.2, 622.

(παραδίδωμι) but that he gives himself up to die *pro nobis*.[60] Vocation is giving oneself up to God and thereby discovering one's true self. Christ becomes the form[61] of the true self in an event of non-identical repetition[62] by which they are to be recognisable while remaining distinct and unconfused. Vocation is the sacrifice in which ultimately all is offered, but in return life is given by an act of unmerited divine grace. Vocation is the living of a resurrection life.

Thus I have argued first that dialectic, like analogy,[63] both similarity and dissimilarity of identity is maintained. Furthermore, that Paul's use of priestly language and imagery in relation to his own ministry and that of others draws upon a notion of priestly counter-testimony. Finally, Paul has a high doctrine of sacrifice as exemplified in vocation. The key to this is through kenotic identification. This is both responsive to what God has done in Christ and non-pernicious, thereby demonstrating the divine propensity to grace, whereby "what is *styled* kenosis, is itself the height of *plerosis*."[64] In this context the application of priesthood as an appropriate designation of ministry is justifiable and appropriate. I shall illustrate this by reference to Paul's concept of exemplarism with particular reference to the Letter to the Philippians.

Exemplarism and Interchange

For Paul exemplarism[65] stands within the asymmetrical interchange between Christ and human beings which articulates their response to God's prior saving act. In the Letter to the Philippians Paul encourages his

---

[60] 'I have been crucified with Christ; it is no longer I who live, but Christ who lives in me; and I now live in the flesh I live by faith in the Son of God, who loved me and gave (*paradontos*) himself for me.' (Gal. 2.20.)

[61] M. Luther, *A Commentary on St Paul's Epistle to the Galatians*, (Middleton Edition, 1575), London, James Clarke & Co Ltd, 1953, 168.

[62] See: 35, n 93 above and the concept of the mirror image as non-identical repetition in which representation is being 'like' but 'not the same as'. William Thompson asks of women 'who pray with Paul, "I live, no longer I, but Christ lives in me" (Gal. 2.20), as surely as we men are "*imagines Christi*", in the analogous way in which we understand this... But how can we affirm this without denying the theological relevance of Jesus' sex and gender identity?' (William M. Thompson, 'Women And "Conformity to Christ's Image": The Challenge Of Avoiding Docetism And Affirming Inclusivism', *SJT* (48), 1995, 23.)

[63] See: 198 above.

[64] C. F. D. Moule, 'Further Reflexions on Philippians 2:5-11', W. W. Gasque and R. P. Martin (eds), *Apostolic History and the Gospels*, Grand Rapids, Eerdmans, 1970, 273. See: 98 above.

[65] By exemplarism it is important to be clear that I do not intend the understanding of the atonement, articulated in the work of Abelard and more recently Hastings Rashdall.

audience to let the manner of their lives 'be worthy of the gospel of Christ'[66] which is repeated in 2.5 and which underlies 3.17.[67] The language of vocation is the call to live a recognisably Christian life, as a result of "God's sovereign initiative and human responsibility for living... [which] go hand in hand".[68] Christ does not by his life and death morally convict the sinner so that they change. Rather because God in Christ died for them and thereby atoned for their sin, their future lives are lived in and under the example of Christ in the power of the Spirit.[69] This ethical injunction is not a matter of conforming to "an uncompromising moral ideal"[70] but a "question of what kind of person"[71] one should be before God and the world. The presence of God is revealed in the love of Christ and therefore Christians are imitative of His love, externalising that they live 'in Christ.'

The "characteristic Pauline formula 'in Christ'" is that "old distinctions are done away, and all are one."[72] According to Morna Hooker, the statement in Galatians 3.13 of Christ becoming 'a curse for us' raises a fundamental question concerning "the logic of Paul's thought".[73] Hooker suggests that

> the experience of Gal iii. 13 is not a simple exchange. It is not that Christ is cursed and we are blessed. Rather he enters into our experience, and then we enter into his, by sharing in his resurrection.[74]

This is not an isolated statement but recurs throughout the Pauline corpus.[75] In Philippians 2 "we have an account of what Christ became through the incarnation... followed by a description of what happened to Christ at his exaltation." But on this occasion the "interchange of experience takes place

---

[66] Phil. 1.27.

[67] 'Brethren, join in imitating [συμμιμηταί] me' (Phil 3.17). Bengel understands Paul inviting the Philippians to be 'fellow imitators with me of someone else, that is Christ.' (Quoted, O'Brien, 1991, 445.)

[68] Andrew T. Lincoln, *Ephesians*, Dallas, Word Books, 1990, 235, commenting upon Eph. 4.1 with which he draws parallels to Phil. 1.27; Col. 1.10; 1 Thess. 2.12.

[69] Phil. 2.5-11.

[70] Stanley Hauerwas, 'Clerical Character', *Christian Existence Today*, Grand Rapids, Brazo Press, 201, 133.

[71] Hauerwas, 2001, 135.

[72] Morna Hooker, 'Interchange in Christ', *JTS* (22), 1971, 351.

[73] Hooker, 1971, 350.

[74] Hooker, 1971, 352.

[75] In the article Hooker examines Rom. 8.3, 14f; Gal. 3.13; 4.4-7; 2 Cor. 5.21; 8.9 culminating in Phil. 2.5-11; 3.17-21. The weakness of Hooker's argument is its assumption that the *carmen Christi* necessarily develops from an Adamic Christology. (See: 92-96 above.)

within Christ himself."[76] However, in Philippians 3 this is re-interpreted by means of notions of interchange and exemplarism as identity 'in Christ.' Hooker recognises the particular choice of language in Philippians 3.21[77] noting that, "more important even than the language is the theme."[78] In these verses "the meaning of Christ's exaltation for the believer is worked out: in Christ the Christian participates in the reversal of status, which took place when God raised him."[79] What she appears to identify is a pattern of asymmetrical interchange and repetition, more fully developed in the Chalcedonian Definition of Faith.

Paul calls upon the Philippians to live lives recognisably[80] imitative of Christ, visibly Christ like.[81] Philippians 2.6-11 is no abstract doctrinal statement, but a fundamental assertion of what it means to live 'in Christ.'[82] This affirms the asymmetry of the imitation of Christ. The mimetic economy is one of non-identical repetition. The Christ like person is recognisably similar, by analogy to, but not the same as Christ. Identification is possible through 'family resemblance' but without the loss of personal identity. What Paul proposes is narrative identity, which is only possible in the commitment to its performance through daily living;[83] it is a question of appropriate characterisation within the narrative. As a result the person is called to engage with the appropriate and necessary practices and roles. It "is not simply a question of following a good example: he *must* think and behave like this, because the behaviour of Christ is the ground of his redemption".[84]

The fact that humanity exists only in the one nature distinguishes Christ and his human imitator. Men and women take their characterisation from Christ, even though Chalcedonian orthodoxy identified both the human and the divine natures in him, without either of which he would cease to be himself. Nonetheless the person who imitates Christ is bound by the inherent dialectic of the Chalcedonian pattern, which cannot result in any final synthesis. This is the dialectic of the divine-human encounter in Jesus Christ in which there is unity ('without separation or division') but yet distinction ('without confusion or change') and asymmetry (such that the divine always has precedence over the human).

---

[76] Hooker, 1971, 355.

[77] Hooker, 1971, 357.

[78] Hooker, 1971, 357. It is the language and the theme together that yields 'thick description'.

[79] Hooker, 1971, 357.

[80] See: 84-86 above.

[81] Phil. 1.27; 2.5.

[82] Hooker, 1971, 361.

[83] Stephen Barton, 'New Testament Interpretation as Performance', *SJT* (52), 1999, 179.

[84] Hooker, 1971, 361. This seems like traditional exemplarism.

The Pauline concept of interchange in Christ can not result in the divinisation of the human – to do so would be self-contradictory.[85] Instead it is a fundamentally participative interchange which anticipates the Chalcedonian pattern. This enables God and man to encounter one another in the unique historical figure of Jesus Christ.[86] This interchange is a 'priestly' act by Christ wherein the boundaries of the divine-human *diastasis* are crossed but not removed. The gift of grace in the divine *pro nobis* means "we too are present, genuinely participating in what he has done."[87] The initiative, however, remains firmly with God to which humanity can only respond.

Above all the priestly testimony of Christ is evident in his 'once for all'[88] salvific death and resurrection. But because the priesthood of Christ is an analogy for his atoning action by his death and resurrection he also embodies the priestly counter-testimony, through the sacrifice of obedient living.[89] It is this counter-testimony and testimony that is reflected rather like mirror writing in the priesthood of the ordained. What is important is not the literal notion of inversion or reversal but the moment of reflection when the object viewed through the mirror makes sense. Or this might be described as an example of *analogia fidei* wherein priesthood as a human event or activity is always secondary, only becoming meaningful in the light of the prior priesthood of Christ. The imitation of Christ is repetitious, but as with the image in the mirror it is only ever a virtual copy; like, but not identical to the original. The dialectic of the divine-human encounter in Jesus Christ is retained in which there is unity, 'without separation or division,' distinction, 'without confusion or change,' and asymmetry between the human and the divine. In other words, as Jesus Christ in the incarnation retains his essential divinity, so that in becoming man he does not cease to be himself, so too a person may imitate Christ but not so that they 'become divine' and contradict themselves.

Humanity can neither effect its own salvation nor can the Christian offer atonement for others. Pauline exemplarism is neither salvific nor atoning, but responsive to the primary event of divine sovereignty revealed through grace. The imitation of Christ is the visible sign of the divine-human interchange. Within such a mimetic economy praise is embodied by living

---

[85] Rather it is a matter, in Barthian terms of being God's 'covenant partner' or, as Balthasar might suggest, fulfilling one's role in the theo-drama and thereby becoming a person, a co-actor in the drama. and as being the person God intends, and therefore standing in the right relationship with God or 'atoned'.

[86] See: 169, n. 164 above and the discussion of *CD* II.1, 155.

[87] *CD* II.1, 156. Barth looks to Heb 4.14f for support.

[88] Heb. 9.26-28.

[89] Heb. 10.5-7; cf. Ps. 40.6-8. For a fuller discussion of the priestly testimony and countertestimony of Jesus Christ see: 160-166 above. Also: Phil. 3.21 (See: 105 above.)

in response to the divine grace.[90] This is a priestly act because it is concerned with crossing the boundary, which separates present reality from future possibility in Christ. To imitate Christ is an act of kenotic re-identification in which the person submerges him/herself 'in Christ', but this results in no loss of identity but rather the renewal of identity established through discernible 'family resemblance' in which distinctiveness is not only possible but maintained. If Christ's priesthood bridges the divine-human *diastasis* then Christian priesthood, while it cannot repeat Christ's saving act, does point to the reality of this event, and its availability to all.

In summary, what has emerged is the possibility and the appropriateness of priestly language as analogous of the Christian life and the ordained ministry. Priesthood cannot be dismissed either as belonging to a former dispensation or as the prerogative of Jesus Christ or as belonging to the whole Church. Priesthood remains all of these but the presence of a family likeness, retaining its sacrificial overtones without undermining the sovereignty of God and the precedence of grace, can also include the ordained ministry. What remains therefore is the imaginative interpretation of such a concept of the priesthood of the ordained in relation to those practices and roles, which identify the Christian community.

A Representative Priesthood

The task remains to establish the compatibility of priestly and sacrificial language about reference to Christian ministry with a Protestant doctrine of God. A fundamental foundation for a Protestant re-evaluation of the priesthood of the ordained ministry is the Bible. In the previous section it was suggested that the analogical nature of the biblical language of priesthood meant that it was represented critically realistically within a dialectic of testimony and counter-testimony. In this section I shall further develop the representative nature of the priesthood of the ordained, returning to the particularity of the account in Philippians. Finally, I shall explore the relationship between the eucharist, as the representation of the gospel, and the role of the ordained as those who articulate the crossing of the divine-human *diastasis* within a participative encounter in which the identities of the participants are maintained, unconfused.

The Particular and the General

The concept of *analogia fidei* in Barth's thought "refers most fundamentally"[91] to "the act of divine Self-revelation and the [responsive]

---

[90] Hauerwas, 2001, 143.
[91] McCormack, 1997, 16.

human act of faith".[92] Its basis therefore is the "highly concrete event: the event of revelation."[93] Discussing the 'constancy and omnipotence of God',[94] Barth states that "God confirms Himself as the creator of the world by having a special history with it in His work of reconciliation and revelation."[95] This event is "the history of Jesus Christ"[96] wherein the knowledge of God "has its source in the revelation of God".[97] Constancy and omnipotence are not attributes, philosophically deducible from the idea of God, but are revealed in the Scriptural narrative. Particularism reinforces the divine sovereignty and therefore the primacy of grace. What he proposes is the 'scripture principle.'[98]

The 'scripture principle' appears to be a rather bald re-statement of *sola Scriptura*.[99] Scripture is not to be interpreted "by any particular tradition... chosen to suit a preconceived theory."[100] For Barth the Scripture principle unites the particularism of Scripture and the community of God by his insistence that theology "is a function of the Church".[101] If the Word of God is the primary witness, then the community of faith is the secondary witness.[102] This witness is "not imposed in the name and authority of some general norm of truth" rather it comes "from the Word of God that founds the community of faith."[103] In order "to serve the community of today, theology itself must be rooted in the community of yesterday... Theology does not labour... as though Church history began today."[104] The Word of God and Scripture maintain a primacy over tradition.[105]

I shall propose that the priesthood of the ordained is to be understood by an *analogia fidei*. This draws upon a notion of an analogy of proportion in which "A relates to B as C to D".[106] A*nalogia fidei* proposes there is a detectable correspondence "between an act of God and an act of a human

---

[92] McCormack, 1997, 17.
[93] McCormack, 1997, 17.
[94] *CD* II.1, § 31.2.
[95] *CD* II.1, 503.
[96] *CD* II.1, 513.
[97] *CD* II.1, 545, 547.
[98] Karl Barth, 'The Task of the Ministry', *The Word of God and the Word of Man* (ET), London, Hodder and Stoughton, 1935, 240-41.
[99] See: 113, n. 36 above.
[100] Barth, 1935, 241.
[101] McCormack, 1997, 448.
[102] Karl Barth, *Evangelical Theology: An Introduction* (ET), New York, Holt Reinhart and Winston, 1963, 37
[103] Barth, 1963, 39.
[104] Barth, 1963, 42.
[105] Barth, 1963, 46.
[106] Eberhard Jüngel, *God As The Mystery Of The World* (ET), Edinburgh, T & T Clark, 1983, 270 reflecting tracking theory (see: 10 above).

subject; the act of divine Self-revelation and the human act of faith in which that revelation is acknowledged."[107] Such a correspondence I have argued exists between on the one hand God's sovereign grace revealed in Jesus Christ and humanity's grateful response. It is precisely this pattern which I argued undergirded the narrative structure of Philippians.[108]

I have already drawn attention to the failure of both Balthasar and Moltmann to maintain a consistent trinitarian form and structure in their theological enterprise.[109] Balthasar's understanding of priesthood is governed by his concept of office and the emphasis he places upon the Marian and Petrine principles, which fails to render sufficient attention to the biblical account consequently undermining the pneumatological.[110] Conversely, Moltmann's understanding of priesthood is governed by the traditional Protestant naively realistic understanding of the biblical account and so fails to capture the dialectical nuances of the parallel existence of both a priestly testimony and counter-testimony.[111] However, as I have argued, if the particularity of the Scriptural account is addressed and the dialectic of priestly testimony and counter-testimony given due weight, an altogether different picture of priesthood can begin to emerge.

As a result Christian ministry can be described using priestly language and is representative.[112] Ministry is priestly insofar as it crosses the boundaries, demonstrating the possibility that God and man can work together provided "it is God who absolutely precedes and man can only follow." There is also "the general acceptance of their co-existence and co-inherence, of their basic unity though without any confusion or mixture or transformation of the one into the other."[113] This emphasises the asymmetry of the divine-human relationship in which God precedes and humanity follows. The Chalcedonian pattern is repeated. There is a genuine intimacy in working together while the essential integrity of both the divine and the creature is maintained.[114] Representatively priesthood, echoing the Letter to the Hebrews, is called to pioneer what it means to be the people of God.[115]

---

[107] McCormack, 1997, 17.
[108] See: 79-81 above.
[109] See: 128 above.
[110] See: 117 above.
[111] See: 128 above.
[112] The weakness of *Baptism, Eucharist and Ministry* is that it argues from a general principle to the particular. (See: FOAG, *Baptism, Eucharist and Ministry* (Paper 111), Geneva, WCC, 1982, paras. 17, 18.) There is some discussion of the roles of Timothy and Titus, in relation to *episkopé* (*BEM*, para 21.) but otherwise it remains at the level of a somewhat abstracted and general discussion.
[113] *CD* IV.3i, 63.
[114] Hunsinger, 1993, 186-87.
[115] See: 158-164 above; also Heb 2.10; 12.2.

Bishops and Deacons at Philippi

Scholars have proposed a number of possible interpretations of why Paul addresses Philippians to 'all the saints in Christ Jesus who are at Philippi, including σὺν ἐπισκόποις καὶ διακόνοις'.[116] First, that ἐπισκόποις καὶ διακόνοις refers to those who have organized the gift which the Philippians have sent to Paul.[117] Secondly, those who think that Paul wrote to resolve existing conflict and division in Philippi have argued that this reference is intended to reinforce the recognized leadership of the Church.[118] Thirdly, Barth believed the 'bishops and deacons' "were predominantly administrative in character" but that this leadership "perhaps" included "public worship".[119] But at "the very least" Paul appears "to recognize and respect a group of people who in his own absence exercise a ministry of supervision and care for Christian polity at Philippi".[120]

Ἐπισκόποις καὶ διακόνοις are not to be understood as bearing the modern ecclesiolo-technical meaning.[121] When Polycarp wrote to the Philippian Church he addressed himself to the deacons and presbyters[122] but omitted any reference to an ἐπισκοπή. Furthermore the preposition σὺν can "be taken inclusively, 'to all the saints, including the overseers and deacons', not exclusively, that is, 'to all the saints together with the overseers and deacons'"[123] denying any material division between the ordained and non-ordained.

The fact that ἐπισκόποις is plural[124] suggests Paul does not have a concept of "a monepiscopate" in view here.[125] This would seem to reflect the pattern of his ministry. Schillebeeckx's analysis of ministry in the Pauline era[126] suggests that there was no formal juridical authority in the Church; but that the authority of the leader was rooted in their 'Christ

---

[116] Phil. 1.1.

[117] J. B. Lightfoot, *Saint Paul's Epistle to the Philippians* (rev Edn), London, Macmillan and Co., 1879, 82.

[118] Gordon Fee, *Paul's Letter to the Philippians*, Grand Rapids, Eerdmans, 1995, 69.

[119] Barth, 1962, 11.

[120] Markus Bockmuehl, *The Epistle to the Philippians* (4th Edn), London, A & C Black, 1997, 55.

[121] Bockmuehl, 1997, 55, for example: The Preface to the Ordinal, BCP.

[122] Usually dated about the middle of the second century. See: Chapters 6, 7 above.

[123] O'Brien, 1991, 48.

[124] Hawthorne, 1983, 8; Fee, 1995, 67.

[125] Bockmuehl, 1997, 54.

[126] Edward Schillebeeckx, *The Church with a Human Face* (ET), London, SCM, 1985, 55.

likeness.'[127] Furthermore Paul's mission "was a collective undertaking"[128] together with his 'fellow workers,'[129] who accompanied him on his journeys, but also included indigenous people involved in the founding of local churches. In the New Testament texts there is "a complex, fluid network of local and more than local structures and authorities."[130] Paul is not interested in titles or status but rather "with what they actually do to create Christian communities... their specific functions."[131]

Two further points should be borne in mind. First, the apparent use of titles in Philippians 1.1 is indicative of "the 'formalization' of the ministry"[132] which has been identified as a sociological necessity.[133] Secondly, Paul's uses cultic language to give expression to his and his colleagues' missionary activity as a grateful response to the prevenient divinely sovereign act of grace.[134]

But is the reference to ἐπισκόποις καὶ διακόνοις in Philippians simply indicative of the transition from a charismatic to institutional ministry? Its real significance is that it implies the existence of a 'representative' ministerial group within the Philippian Church. First, as a group they are numbered among 'the saints in Christ Jesus who are at Philippi'. Secondly, the ἐπισκόποις καὶ διακόνοις form a collegial group.[135] Thirdly, this is an identifiable group recognisable to the recipients of the letter.[136] They form a group who are identifiable by the practices and roles they are engaged in. While it may have been ἐπισκόποις καὶ διακόνοις who were responsible

---

[127] Schillebeeckx, 1985, 54. Schillebeeckx formulates this negatively discussing the role of teachers of the faith stating that 'others, who also gave instruction, lost authority as a result of their behaviour.' It is instructive to compare this with Phil 3.17.

[128] Schillebeeckx, 1985, 57. Also Acts 13.2, 13; 15.2; 36-40.

[129] In all his letters Paul acknowledges the work of those he calls his fellow workers (Rom. 16.3ff; 1 Cor. 1.1; 16.19f; 2 Cor. 1.1; Phil. 4.21; 1 Thess. 1.1; Philemon 23f). A T Hanson examines Paul's use of 'we' in his letters, discerning three possible interpretations: 'I' (See Rom. 1.5; 1 Thess. 2.17-3.2); 'I and my colleagues' (See 1 Cor. 4.12; 9.6; Gal. 1.8f; 1 Thess. 1.2-9; 2.1-12); or 'I and you' (1 Cor. 2.16, again this refers to having a common mind in Christ; also Rom. 8.23; 2 Cor. 5.1-10). (See: A. T. Hanson, *The Pioneer Ministry*, London, SCM, 1961, 46-56.)

[130] Schillebeeckx, 1985, 59.

[131] Schillebeeckx, 1985, 61.

[132] Schillebeeckx, 1985, 61.

[133] See for example the discussion of the work of Max Weber and Ernst Troeltsch in Andrew Walker, *Restoring the Kingdom*, London, Hodder and Stoughton, 1985, 201-15; or H. R. Neibuhr, *The Kingdom of God in America*, New York, Harper Row, 1951, *The Social Source of Denominationalism*, New York, New American Library, 1981 on the rise of sects and denominations.

[134] David J. Bosch, *Transforming Mission*, New York, Orbis, 1999, 138-139.

[135] Barth, 1962, 11; Bockmuehl, 1997, 54; Fee, 1995, 67.

[136] See: 82 above.

for organising the gift for Paul, this was not their reason for existing. However, there remains the question about the nature of such a 'representation' in relation to the Church as the priestly people of God.

Is it possible to discern a notion of representative[137] ministry in Paul? The answer it would appear is that Paul identifies the representative nature of the Christian ministry in its being 'Christ like'. So in the particular example of Timothy and Epaphroditus[138] observable first is Paul's use of priestly and sacrificial language and secondly the vocational account of the sending of Timothy and Epaphroditus. Both motifs are connected in Paul's thought by kenosis.[139] Furthermore the account alludes to the *carmen Christi* echoing the pattern of *descensus* and *ascensus*, in which Jesus is identified in relation to God through his obedient service.[140] One analogy that Paul uses elsewhere, but which may be implicit in Philippians 2.25-30, is that of an ambassador. Ambassadors speak 'on behalf of' the one who they represent.[141] Ambassadors are engaged to travel as "duly commissioned representatives."[142] Ambassadors represent the one who commissioned them and would often face hardships in their stead. Furthermore many Roman ambassadors were also "priests... of the imperial cult".[143] With this background Paul speaks of Epaphroditus' role as an envoy in priestly and representative terms.[144]

Timothy and Epaphroditus fulfil representative roles as those who are called and 'sent' by another.[145] By themselves they are not qualified of themselves to fulfil this particular commission, but are representative exemplars of the Christian calling. The model they repeat, non-identically,

---

[137] See: Chapter 1 above.

[138] Timothy and Epaphroditus are both mentioned twice in the Epistle - Timothy as a co-author of the letter (Phil. 1.1). (See: O'Brien, 1991, 44; also Fee, 1995, 61; also Barth, 1962, 9, 85.) Epaphroditus as an envoy from the Philippians to Paul. (See: O'Brien, 1991, 313.)

[139] See: 86 above.

[140] So too Timothy is presented as one 'who has slaved selflessly in the gospel (2.22; c.f 1.1, 7.)' and Epaphroditus as one who 'almost died in the *service* of Christ (2.30).' (O'Brien, 1991, 315.)

[141] Likeness is located therefore primarily, though not exclusively in the words spoken.

[142] Anthony Bash, *Ambassadors for Christ*, Tübingen, J. C. B. Mohr, 1997, 105. For bishops as 'ambassadors of Christ see: K. D. Mackenzie, 'Sidelights From Non—Episcopal Communions', K. E. Kirk (ed), *The Apostolic Ministry*, London, Hodder and Stoughton, 1946, 491.

[143] Bash, 1997, 108.

[144] Phil. 2.25, 30 (λιετουργίασ); 4.18.

[145] Phil. 2.19, 23, 25, 28. So, Timothy is sent by Paul, Epaphroditus is doubly sent by the Philippians to Paul (4.18) and by Paul to the Philippians. But of course ultimately they are called and sent by God, a calling recognised by Paul and the Church. This echoes the Trinitarian economy whereby the Father sends the Son in the power of the Spirit.

is the model of Christ. In this they enact a sacrifice of gratitude. It appears that Epaphroditus is the one who not only delivers, but also, is himself part of the Philippians' gift to Paul.[146] Likewise Paul, whose relationship with Timothy is 'intimate,' sends him to Philippi in a costly gesture.[147] This repeats a kenotic sacrificial pattern, whereby the gift is offered and received but the giver receives back more than they have given. Timothy and Epaphroditus are priestly[148] representatives within the particular economy of the interchange of gifts between Paul and the Philippians. It is not an abstract notion but occurs only in the reality of the giving and receiving of gifts. In this interchange there is an event of kenotic re-identification in which they become, by extension, part of the gift but without loss of identity.

The Eucharist and Priesthood

I have argued from the particular examples in the Letter to the Philippians that priesthood because, it is recognizable in the practices and roles, with which it is engaged, is representative. Furthermore such a representative ministry maintains the Chalcedonian pattern but in the form of non-identical repetition. It is non-identical first in that it is imitative, and therefore a copy or likeness but not the original. Secondly, it mirrors Christ likeness in that it is only in the *a priori* revelation of God's sovereign grace in Christ that priesthood has meaning. It represents the priesthood of Christ both as testimony and counter-testimony tracing, but not effecting the crossing of the boundaries of the divine/human *diastasis* in the event of the atonement.[149] In the light of this I shall explore the relationship between priestly ministry and sacrifice in relation to the eucharist which is the supreme location of the distinctive practices and roles which defines both the community of faith and therefore those who minister. Worship, and in particular the eucharist is a public event of recognisable identification which includes both the inward and the external within its performance.[150]

---

[146] O'Brien, 1991, 333.

[147] Hawthorne, 1983, 111. (See also: O'Brien, 1991, 317.)

[148] Here I am using the word 'priestly' adjectivally. I am not suggesting that either Timothy or Epaphroditus were formally ordained to the priesthood.

[149] This is contrary to the traditional Protestant account which rejects notions of the priesthood and in particular any reference to the role of the eucharistic president. See: Steve Walton, 'Sacrifice and Priesthood in Relation to the Christian Life and Church in the New Testament', Roger T. Beckwith and Martin J. Selman (ed), *Sacrifice in the Bible*, Carlisle, Paternoster, 1995, 148-152.

[150] Stephen Sykes, *The Identity of Christianity*, Philadelphia, Fortress Press, 1984, 265-269.

Kenneth Stevenson identifies three principal themes in a narrative understanding of the eucharist.[151] The narrative begins with the 'story' as the "recitation before God of his mighty acts culminating in the life and work of Christ."[152] The middle 'gift', is rather more ambiguous "in which the prayers describe and treat the bread and wine, whether by offering them or by referring to them explicitly or implicitly as gifts."[153] The narrative ends with the 'response' of the Church "by which the faithful unite themselves to the sacrifice of Christ."[154] The crucial elements are the nature of the gift, its source, to whom the gift is directed and therefore its purpose and finally the response that is appropriately called for, raising questions about the sacrificial nature of the eucharist.

Rowan Williams articulates three primary objections to the application of sacrificial concepts to the eucharist. The importance of the objections voiced by Williams is made clear in the first one which he says is "the classical Reformation objection" which emphasizes the sufficiency of Christ's sacrifice at Calvary. Secondly, the question "who is the agent in the eucharist"? Thirdly, if "the agency of Christ is transferred to the church... at the hands of the clergy"[155] this implies a distinctive relationship between the ordained and Christ, indicative of a hierarchical structure within the Church. All three objections lie at the heart of Protestant unease with the notion of the priesthood of the ordained in relation to the eucharist. In narrative terms, these three problems are moments of reversal, so the answers to the objections Williams identifies must provide the possibility of recognition and astonishment.[156] By maintaining a dialectic and therefore refusing to speak naively realistically of the eucharist it is possible to sustain its "superabundance of meaning."[157]

It is possible to identify five markers of practice and which help to define the priestly roles, which have already emerged, concerning the nature of priesthood, sacrifice and kenosis and which form significant aspects of the eucharist within Stevenson's narrative structure.[158] First, in the eucharist there is an interchange of gifts. Secondly, the eucharist is testimony to the

---

[151] Kenneth Stevenson, *Eucharist and Offering*, New York, Pueblo Publishing Co, 1986, 4-6.
[152] Stevenson, 1986, 4.
[153] Stevenson, 1986, 5.
[154] Stevenson, 1986, 6.
[155] Rowan Williams, *Eucharistic Sacrifice – The Roots of a Metaphor*, Bramcote, Grove Books (Liturgical Studies No. 31), 1982, 3-4.
[156] Aristotle, *Poetics*, 6.
[157] David Ford, *Self and Salvation*, Cambridge, CUP, 1999, 145.
[158] The five aspects that I list all actually fall within the middle and end parts of the narrative. I am assuming that the 'recitation before God of his mighty acts culminating in the life and work of Christ' is relatively straightforward. The five aspects suggested all relate in some way to the understanding of 'gift'.

Divine *pro nobis* and hence a priestly event. Thirdly, the eucharist as a sacrificial counter-testimony enacts an event of kenotic re-identification through the self-oblation of the participants. Fourthly, the eucharist is a bloodless counter-testimony. Finally, the eucharist celebrates the sovereign and therefore superabundant generosity of God's grace.

First, for the discussion of gift and offering in the eucharist the parameters must be determined by the need to maintain the divine sovereignty and the precedence of grace within the reciprocity of sacrifice.[159] The act of giving is an act of generosity. However, eucharistic language is inherently imperative[160] apparently undermining any notion of gift. Echoing the imagery of Philippians 2, David Ford argues that obedience is the outward sign of an inner gratitude and is itself the gift.[161] Paul enjoins the Philippians to be Christ like. But the distinction between Christ and those who are 'in Christ' remains.[162] Signs are indicative "of what they are not: they are transformations of the world by re-ordering it, not destroying it, so that the tension of otherness remains".[163] The "object is relocated... [but] it is still itself in its new context".[164] The interchange is maintained and the offering made, but it is neither expiatory nor propitiatory. The gift is offered and sacrificed. It does not disappear but is returned transformed[165] and increased by the action.[166]

---

[159] See: 169 above. Dom Gregory Dix proposed (*The Shape of The Liturgy*, 1945) that the eucharist has a fourfold shape: taking and blessing, and breaking and sharing. Dix argues that the offertory was 'a physical necessity' (Gregory Dix, *The Shape of the Liturgy*, London, A & C Black, 1978, 110). Dix understood the eucharist as 'a true offering by the church in its hierarchic completeness' (Dix, 1978, 117). Furthermore the 'offertory in the original view of the rite is therefore something much more than a ceremonial action, the placing of bread and wine upon the altar... [but] a self sacrificial act by which each Christian comes to his being as a member of Christ in the "re-calling" before God of the self-sacrificial offering of Christ' (Dix, 1978, 117f.).

[160] Ford, 1999, 145.

[161] Ford, 1999, 146. See also: Rowan Williams, *On Christian Theology*, Oxford, Blackwell, 2000, 205.

[162] See the earlier discussion of Phil 3.21 (see: 211 above).

[163] Williams, 2000, 207.

[164] Williams, 2000, 207.

[165] Graham, Ward, 'Suffering and Incarnation', Graham Ward (ed), *The Blackwell Companion to Postmodern Theology*, Oxford, Blackwell, 2002, 193-208. Graham Ward proposes that the Christian economy of sacrifice is kenotic consisting of both 'emptying and filling' (Ward, 2002, 202).

[166] The interchange of gifts at the eucharist is responsive, in the same way as Paul suggests that the reason for contributing to the collection for the Jerusalem saints is 'the real basis for such generous action – the grace of the Lord Jesus Christ, who, though he was rich became poor for their sake' (Hooker, 1971, 353; c.f. 2 Cor 8. 9).

Secondly, the eucharist is testimony to the Divine *pro nobis* and a priestly event. The asymmetrical relationship between the priestly sacrifice of Jesus Christ upon the cross and the people of God reconstituted as a 'priestly people' is key.[167] Priesthood exists neither in virtue of the faithfulness of the individual believer nor the believing community "but because of the faithfulness *usque ad mortem* of the sole authentic priest... whose priestly life and death constitute the ground of all subsequent offering."[168] Morna Hooker argues that it is interchange, which offers "the real clue to Paul's understanding of the atonement." It is as "man's *representative* rather than his substitute, that Christ suffers."[169] Christ suffers as 'truly God and truly man'; alike in humanity but different in His divinity. God and humanity encounter one another in Jesus Christ and neither is diminished nor confused in a final synthesis.

The eucharist "resonates with the most common and basic practices necessary for sustaining life."[170] In their very ordinariness it is the bread and the wine, which become integral to the story that the eucharist enacts.[171] The accounts of the Last Supper both focus upon the "blessing of the ordinary"[172] and the betrayal of Judas when the bonds of the community are tested "past breaking point."[173] But Judas does not betray but 'hands over' Jesus.[174] Paul employs the notion of handing over in relation to the divine *pro nobis*.[175] Furthermore he speaks of 'handing over' "with both Father and Son as subject".[176] Moltmann thinks this indicative of "a *homoousion*, in respect of an identity of substance" of the Father and the Son upon the cross. Within the cross as a Trinitarian event there is "not only unity of substance but also the wholly and utterly different character and

---

[167] 1 Pet. 2. 9. (See: 139-145 above.)

[168] Williams, 1982, 15. This is quite different from Balthasar's understanding in which the emphasis is upon the hierarchical and institutional authority of Church. See: Balthasar, 1991, 321.

[169] Hooker, 1971, 358 – her italics.

[170] Ford, 1999, 149.

[171] *CD* IV.2, 677. *Contra* Balthasar, Barth insists that the Church 'is one human society with others' (*CD* IV.2, 688). However, it exists in relation to 'the particular happening of Christian worship... [which] embraces and orders the whole life of the community.' It is this which is derived from its relationship to Jesus Christ as 'the One who exists in a history – His own particular history – within universal history' (*CD* IV.2, 695). Thus Barth locates the Church and its activity within the particularity of Jesus Christ.

[172] Ford, 1999, 150.

[173] Ford, 1999, 151.

[174] W. H. Vanstone, *The Stature of Waiting*, London, DLT, 1982, see especially Chapter 1, 'The Deed of Judas'. For 'handing over' and kenosis see also: 59 above (in Balthasar) and 68 above (in Moltmann).

[175] Jürgen Moltmann, *The Crucified God* (ET), London, SCM, 1974, 242.

[176] Moltmann. 1974, 243.

inequality".[177] In the eucharist the bread and wine are 'handed over' and a sign of Jesus Christ, the presence of God, is handed back. This has already been suggested by the notion of the interchange of gifts and is present in the eucharist as the enactment of the story of the divine *pro nobis* in the response of the worshipper. In this act of 'handing over' there is the most profound priestly testimony in which death is risked but life is given.

Thirdly, the eucharist is a counter-testimony embodied in the kenotic re-identification of the worshippers through their self-oblation. The eucharistic sacrifice touches upon "the mysteries of divine grace and human response".[178] Kenotic re-identification is "a self-emptying *in order* to be".[179] Confronted by the story of Christ and his gracious self-giving the response of the communicant is to offer his whole life to God.[180] Such a movement can only ever be responsive to the primacy of divine sovereignty and the consequent precedence of grace. Stevenson says that Cranmer's view of the eucharistic sacrifice, combined with the absence of any formal offertory in the communion rite, suggests that we "are *not* offering gifts, we are *not* offering Mass but we *are* offering ourselves."[181] The eucharist becomes an event of priestly counter-testimony.[182]

Moltmann locates the priestly and sacrificial counter-testimony in the importance of the resurrection for the atonement[183] wherein Christ "died 'for us', to give us, 'the dead', a share in his new life of resurrection and in his future of eternal life."[184] He recognises that resurrection is fundamentally transformative (viz. Philippians), making "us sinners" while anticipating that we are also "righteous and sons of God."[185] The resurrection provides a model of non-identical repetition in which the risen

---

[177] Moltmann, 1974, 244.

[178] Mark Santer, 'Foreword', (Stevenson, 1986, vii).

[179] John Milbank, 'Stories of Sacrifice', Modern Theology (12), 1996, 52 – his italics. (See: 167 above.)

[180] Rom. 12.1 c.f. Phil. 2.5; 3.21. If the divine priestly testimony is *pro nobis* then the countertestimony is *ad deum*. Thus Cranmer's location of the 'self-oblation' "*after* communion" is motivated by the desire to show 'the essential character of this movement of humanity to God' (Stevenson, 1986, 7).

[181] Stevenson, 1986, 173 – his italics.

[182] Kenneth Stevenson draws attention to the reference made to Mal. 1.11 in the eucharistic prayer of the *Didache* and subsequently. (Stevenson, 1986, 15.) The priestly countertestimony in the First Testament (see: 154-158 above) is continued in the Letter to the Hebrews. (See: 162-166 above.)

[183] See: 179 above.

[184] Moltmann, 1974, 186.

[185] Moltmann, 1974, 187, has in mind Philippians 2. Barth also recognises this but does not give it the same prominence. (See: Timothy Gorringe, *Karl Barth Against Hegemony*, Oxford, OUP, 1999, 231.)

Jesus Christ is encountered but not immediately recognised.[186] Integral to the eucharist is the story as the recollection of God's saving acts, culminating in the story of Jesus Christ and the institution narrative.[187] Repetition "properly so called is recollected forwards"[188] wherein "the good of the past can overflow into continuing life" becoming an event of praise.[189] Repetition within the eucharistic event enacts being 'in Christ'.[190] Put another way, the sacramental repetition "traces a transition from one sort of reality to another"[191] and is "self-identifying".[192]

Fourthly, an understanding of the eucharist as a sacrificial counter-testimony appears in the texts.[193] Stevenson draws attention to the *Strasbourg* papyrus in which the *anaphora* speaks of the offering of "this reasonable and bloodless service"[194] leading into a quotation from Malachi 1.11.[195] To the rhetorical question, "What is offered?" Stevenson proposes the answer: "The commemoration of Christ's death. What is prayed for? The presence of the Spirit on the whole eucharist" which "need alarm no Protestants."[196] This is a further example of sacrificial reciprocity in which the eucharistic sacrifice is responsive to the primacy of the atoning sacrifice made by God in Christ.[197]

Finally therefore "we are led back again to the idea of the eucharist as a celebration of God's *gratuitous* love." We "cannot effect anything new through our offering, because God acted first, according to his nature".[198] It is thus possible to speak of the eucharist as a sacrificial rite but without

---

[186] Ford, 1999, 156.
[187] *CD* IV.2, 695.
[188] Ford, 1999, 153.
[189] Ford draws attention to eucharist as meaning 'thanks' (Ford, 1999, 154).
[190] C. F. D. Moule, *The Sacrifice of Christ*, London, Hodder and Stoughton, 1956, 52.
[191] Williams, 2000, 209.
[192] Williams, 2000, 204. See also: *CD* IV.2, 708.
[193] See: 227 n. 182 above.
[194] Stevenson, 1986, 25.
[195] Stevenson, 1986, 25.
[196] Stevenson, 'Eucharistic Sacrifice – What Can We Learn From Antiquity?', Colin Buchanan (ed), *Essays on Eucharistic Sacrifice in the Early Church*, Bramcote, Grove Books (LS 40), 1984, 29.
[197] According to Balthasar 'the Eucharist... is intimately connected with the Passion *pro nobis*.' Balthasar speaks of the eucharist as echoing the self giving of the Son in response to the Father's sending. But, and herein is a distinction from that which I have been attempting to outline, rather than reading forward from the events of the cross and resurrection he speaks instead of 'thinking backward from the Eucharist – the Son's ultimate self-giving – to the covenant that makes it possible' (*TD* IV, 330).
[198] Williams, 1982, 16.

suggesting that it is in any way expiatory or propitiatory.[199] It narrates the gratitude of debt whereby all humanity is an insolvent debtor.[200]

The previous five points emerged from a series of questions[201] concerning the nature of the eucharistic gift and its source; to whom is the gift directed; what is the purpose of the gift and finally what is the appropriate response? On the basis of the foregoing I suggest that the eucharist involves the recognition of a number of different gifts. First and foremost there is the gift of God who gives himself in Jesus Christ *pro nobis*. There is a secondary twofold gift. On the one hand there is the giving of the bread and the wine which is then transformed but without loss of identity in the eucharistic action.[202] On the other hand there is the self-oblation of the worshippers who give themselves to God in order to be transformed 'in Christ'. The primary offering in the eucharist is directed from God to humanity. But in return humanity offers worship *ad Deum*. It is also an act of communal self-identification. This understanding of the eucharist reflects the Chalcedonian pattern whereby the divine and uncreated encounters the creature, such that each retains its own essential nature without confusion and the dialectic is not resolved.[203]

The Asymmetrical Representation of the Priesthood

In the previous section I drew upon Stevenson's notion of the eucharist in terms of story, gift and response. I wish now to suggest a threefold relationship between priesthood and the eucharist. First, there is the relationship between the eucharist as that which narrates the identity of the Church and the priesthood. Secondly, there is the relationship between the priesthood and the giving of order in the Church and finally the ordained priesthood as representing the response of the community to God's grace. These three factors recognise that the eucharist is the locus of the self-identifying practices and roles of the Christian community and therefore its ministry.

---

[199] FOAG, *The Nature and Purpose of the Church* (Paper 181), Geneva, WCC, 1998, 39, which interestingly avoids the language of sacrifice.

[200] Gerard Loughlin, *Telling God's Story*, Cambridge, CUP, 1999, 151.

[201] See: 224 above.

[202] According to Cranmer 'bread and wine are not so changed into the flesh and blood of Christ that they be made one nature, but they remain distinct in nature'. However, he does not deny the divine presence at the sacrament suggesting 'the sacramental bread and wine be not bare signs but so pithy and effectuous' (John Cox (ed), *The Writings and Disputations of Thomas Cranmer Archbishop and Martyr, 1556, Relative to the Sacrament of the Lord's Supper*, Cambridge, The Parker Society, 1844, 198).

[203] Miri Rubin, 'Whose Eucharist? Eucharistic Identity As Historical Subject', Modern Theology (15), 1999, 206.

Previously I suggested that 1 Pet 2.4-10[204] is inherently referential, identifying the emerging Christian tradition with Israel's covenant identity which is gratuitous and priestly.[205] The three motifs which emerged of election, priesthood and covenant, are of particular significance. The importance of covenant emerges as the key to the sense of corporate identity of the early Christian community. Such an identity answers the questions: 'Where do we come from?' and 'Where are we going?' with reference to a common tradition.[206] In the Church the eucharist, as story, gift and response identifies the community by answering these questions. This is not the only role of the eucharist but it is an important role.

Barth discusses the eucharist under 'The Order of the Community'.[207] It "is essential to the up building of the community and therefore to the *communio sanctorum* that its eventuation should not be without form, or in an indefinite or haphazard form".[208] Disorder "is wrong... as the dissolution of form... the destruction of the distinctiveness of its particular relationships and connexions."[209] Right order takes concrete form in worship, through the "distribution of various interrelated responsibilities, obligations and functions to be discharged by individual Christians within the general activity of the community", the maintaining of common cause through disciplined belonging, the right relationship between different congregations and the "regulation... of the relationships of the community to other social forms".[210] But what is the form of the *communio sanctorum*? Almost thirty years earlier Barth had outlined this in a lecture delivered to a largely Catholic audience,[211] in which he argues that while both Catholics and Protestants both speak of the Church, each understands it differently. In the first part Barth sets out the understanding of the Church common to both Roman Catholic and Reformed theologies. In the second part he seeks to demonstrate that Catholics and Protestants view the Church from within

---

[204] See: 139-145 above.

[205] Stephen Sykes locates the identity of the Christianity in its worship as potentially individually and communally transformative (Sykes, 1984, 267).

[206] Ellen Juhl Christiansen, *The Covenant in Judaism and Paul*, Leiden, E J Brill, 1995, 1.

[207] *CD* IV.2, This forms a subsection of § 67 'The Holy Spirit and Upbuilding the Christian Community'. Generally Barth speaks of the Lord's Supper rather than the eucharist, however, he does speak of the Lords Supper as 'a Eucharist, a thanksgiving... [which] characterises the whole service.' (Karl Barth, *The Knowledge Of God And The Service Of God According To The Teaching Of The Reformation* (ET), London, Hodder and Stoughton, 1949, 197.)

[208] *CD* IV.2, 676.

[209] *CD* IV.2, 677.

[210] *CD* IV.2, 678.

[211] Karl Barth, 'The Concept of the Church', originally delivered to the University Association of the Centre Party in Münster, 11th July 1927.

Priesthood and the Ordained 233

radically different frameworks and hermeneutical horizons. The lecture concludes with the proposition that the form of the Church is a question of grace and that its power "does not lie in the hand of the Church... [but that] power lies wholly in the hand of him who alone can forgive sins and impute sins."[212] The form of the Church is taken from hearing the voice of "Jesus Christ as attested in Holy Scripture."[213] In obedience to Jesus Christ the Christian community must be determined by service[214] and while this may be universal, all "Christians do not have to serve equally, i.e. in the same function."[215] Barth does not understand the 'priesthood of all believers'[216] as eradicating the distinctiveness of individuals or their calling. Concretely the form of the relationship between Jesus Christ as the "Lord and Head of the community...is His own presence and lordship in its assembling for divine service, in the occurrence of confession, baptism, the Lord's Supper and prayer."[217] Liturgy and worship are the norm by which the Church exists concretely.

For Balthasar, however, the apostolicity of the Church is mediated through the ministerial succession. The "ministerial office" is "implanted in the Church" by Christ as "a permanent organ" which guarantees its "direct dependence on Christ" wherein "the Church has authority to administer the sacraments"[218] and is therefore of its *esse*. The medieval doctrine of the ordained priesthood developed, in part, from the idea that "the priest is detached from the world, even the world of the Christian laity."[219] As a result the Council of Trent identified the ordained ministry "almost exclusively with presiding at the eucharist (the power of consecrating and performing other sacramental actions)".[220] However, it is "silent on the

---

[212] Karl Barth, 'The Concept of the Church', in *Theology and Church* (ET), London, SCM, 1962, 284.

[213] *CD* IV.2, 682. Nonetheless Barth is adamant that the Church remains essentially 'one human society with others' (*CD* IV.2, 688).

[214] *CD* IV.2, 690. In a note (694) Barth further explains that he understands service as replacing any notion of office. Barth objects to 'clericalism' because it seeks to possess ministry by establishing a distinction between 'the active and the inactive (passive) Church; against every separation into the ruling and the ruled, the teaching and the hearing' (*CD* IV.2, 694). This is quite contrary to Balthasar's emphasis upon office, and his distinction between the active, objective and masculine Petrine office and the passive, subjective and female Marian principle as modelling the two parts that are the Church.

[215] *CD* IV.2, 693.

[216] *CD* IV.2, 694.

[217] *CD* IV.2, 706.

[218] *TD* III, 430.

[219] For example clerical celibacy. See: Schillebeeckx, 1985, 196.

[220] Schillebeeckx, 1985, 198.

universal priesthood of all believers."[221] Barth's starting point is the similarity of the 'priesthood of the ordained'[222] with the 'priesthood of all believers' whereas Balthasar assumes that the priesthood of the ordained must be ontologically different.[223] Furthermore he assumes that order is not only ontological but institutional, whereas Barth locates order in relation to the faithfulness of the community to Jesus Christ.[224] One problem with Balthasar's account is that he understands the Church in terms of a divinely given institution whose holiness is objectively given through the office of the ordained, whereas Barth's emphasis upon community, and emphasising the visible nature of the Church, is less static and more vocational.[225] Barth's account is responsive to God's prior saving event whereas Balthasar's account implies that the ordained priesthood is an effective participant or necessary mediator of divine grace. It is precisely this that Protestant theology has found impossible in the account of the priesthood of the ordained.

In the first two parts of this section I suggested that ministry, according to the Letter to the Philippians, was grounded in the particular examples of the 'bishops and deacons'[226] and of Timothy and Epaphroditus.[227] Another weakness of Balthasar's idealised ecclesiology, stressing the invisible over the visible Church, is that this leads to an abstract concept of the ordained

---

[221] Schillebeeckx, 1985, 200.

[222] I realise that this puts a phraseology, which he never used in Barth's mouth.

[223] Edward Schillebeeckx suggests that by the end of the Patristic era the 'ontological status obtained through the baptism of the Spirit was in practice misunderstood, whereas the ministry was reckoned to be a status, with heavy ontological connotations.' (Schillebeeckx, 1985, 157.) He further identifies this with the development of the eucharist theology as the sacrifice 'of the mass', (Schillebeeckx, 1985, 159.) a problem which he believes Vatican II did not satisfactorily address. Schillebeeckx, unlike Balthasar, does not seek the basis of ministry in a Petrine Office identified by Apostolic Succession. Schillebeeckx is clear that the root of a genuinely representative ordained ministry is not just that it is 'mandated by the church' but is coupled with 'a Christian ethic and spirituality' and 'in the consequences of belief in the gospel and the *sequela Jesu*.' (Schillebeeckx, 1985, 206.)

[224] According to Schillebeeckx, ministry 'is connected with a special concern for the preservation of the Christian identity of the community in constantly changing circumstances.' (Schillebeeckx, 1985, 91-92) Thus 'the Pastoral Epistles above all clearly have a preference for the teaching ministry as the only means of preserving Christian identity.' (Schillebeeckx, 1985, 102.) Whereas Balthasar locates apostolicity in succession from the Petrine Office.

[225] Barth speaks of the Church as *die Gemeinischaft* (community) which is the word for a corporation who come together with a shared self-understanding and way of life. He does not speak of community as *die Gesellschaft*, which exists by voluntary association. One difference is that the former carries vocational overtones absent from the latter.

[226] Phil. 1.1 (see: 219-221 above).

[227] Phil. 2.19-30; 4.18 (see: 221-222 above).

ministry. The "ordained ministry represents the Church; not some transcendental Church... but the empirical, visible Church in which they serve."[228] It emerges from the experience of particular churches and as in the case of the Philippians is modelled by particular men.[229] Further, such a representative ministry must maintain the Chalcedonian pattern in being imitative of Christ but in the form of asymmetrical, non-identical repetition. As Rowan Williams says, if the eucharist is an event of divine sovereignty revealing the primacy of grace, then stated negatively it cannot be dependent upon any supposed power inherent to the priest. It is inappropriate therefore to suggest that "Christ's sacrifice needs 'activation' [which] suggests that Christ is not now mighty to save".[230] The priest can only faithfully retell the story of Christ's saving act. The priest may receive the gifts of the faithful and make the offering, but this is neither propitiatory nor expiatory.[231] The sacrifice is the embodiment that 'what is *styled* kenosis, is itself the height of πληρησες'[232] wherein what is offered to God is returned transformed and multiplied. The priest leads the response of all who "offer... [their] souls and bodies to be a living sacrifice."[233] The interchange of gifts at the eucharist is an event of a double representation, in which God in Christ is represented and therefore revealed to humanity and at the same time humanity is invited to step beyond its boundaries and turn to God.[234]

In summary, what has emerged is that, the representative role of the priesthood of the ordained is responsive to God's prior sovereign grace. Moltmann urges the Church to "stop being a church of ministers functioning on behalf of laymen"[235] in which the "acknowledgement of a

---

[228] A. T. Hanson, *Church, Sacraments and Ministry*, London, Mowbrays, 1975, 113.

[229] The reference to 'men' is in no way intended to be a comment upon the question of women and priesthood. It is simply made because I have focused much of the discussion upon Philippians in which the chief characters are Paul, Timothy and Epaphroditus.

[230] See: 223 above. Rowan Williams, 1982, 3.

[231] Moltmann, 1977, 257.

[232] Moule, see: 100, n. 162 above. See also: 168, n. 156 above drew attention to the accounts of the feeding of the five thousand. The fact that the accounts given of this event are in all four Gospels suggests 'that the early Church regarded the feeding(s) as being among the greatest and most luminous for faith of the mighty works of Jesus.' (C. E. B. Cranfield, *The Gospel according to St Mark*, Cambridge, CUP, 1974, 216.) Morna Hooker draws attention to the eucharistic overtones, though without suggesting that it is a eucharist. (Morna Hooker, *The Gospel According To St Mark*, London, A & C Black, 1997, 164-65; see also: Cranfield, 1974, 222-23.)

[233] *Common Worship*, post communion prayer.

[234] For references to priesthood and boundary setting and crossing see: 149, 167, 203 above.

[235] Moltmann, 1977, 242.

special [priestly] ministry obscures Christ's giving of himself 'for all'".[236] Despite his apparently negative approach to the ordained ministry he recognises that one of the roles fulfilled by worship and ritual in a community is to establish "a framework of social coherences... Through ritual a group assures itself of its own character, integrates itself and portrays itself."[237] It would seem therefore that the ordained ministry through its practices and roles is called to enact the Church as the community ordered in the light of the divine *pro nobis* and externalised in the eucharist. Barth notes a "community which does not ask concerning law and order, inevitably abandoning its life to chance and caprice and confusion, will be just as much in contradiction of the Holy Spirit of Jesus".[238] The ordained ministry is representative not 'on behalf of' but rather in that it gathers "up the roles, which belong to the whole Church."[239] It is representative, not vicariously but, summatively.

"Therefore on the grounds not only of status within the community but also of charism, one of the leaders would have been the obvious person to have presided at the eucharistic assembly."[240] The *Apostolic Traditions* states that if a "confessor has been placed in chains for the Name of the Lord, hands are not laid upon him for the office of deacon or elder."[241] Ordination becomes primarily "a call to the leadership of service"; publicly acknowledged by both the community and the ordained "in the laying on of hands"[242] and prayer; thereby establishing order. This does not grant any external power[243] to the community of faith but it is appropriate that "the

---

[236] Moltmann, 1977, 246.

[237] Moltmann, 1977, 264.

[238] Barth, *CD* IV.2, 68.

[239] A. M. Ramsey, *The Christian Priest Today*, London, SPCK, 1972, 6. See also: Tim Herbert, 'To Be or to Do?: Is That the Question?', *Anvil* (7), 1990, 225-40.

[240] Paul Bradshaw, *Liturgical Presidency in the Early Church*, Bramcote, Grove Books (LS 36), 1983. In this essay Bradshaw traces the emergence of liturgical presidency in the Church from its very beginning through the Patristic era. Like most commentators (i.e. Hanson, 1961; H. Küng, *Why Priests?* (ET), London, Collins, 1972; Hans von Campenhausen, *Ecclesiastical Authority and Spiritual Power in the Church of the First Three Centuries* (ET), Peabody (Mass), Hendrickson, 1997, Hanson, 1979; Schillebeeckx, 1985.) Bradshaw understands the emergence of the ministry of the ordained as being of the *bene esse* of the Church.

[241] Hippolytus, *Apostolic Tradition*, 9, (www.bombaxo.com/hippolytus.html, 6.12.2002). One reason might be that at ordination prayers were said for the candidates that they would receive the 'relevant endowment of the Spirit' (Colin Bulley, *The Priesthood of Some Believers*, Carlisle, Paternoster, 2000, 270). The other reason may be that the Confessor is one who is recognised as having demonstrated and represented the Christian confession of faith in the public arena.

[242] Küng, 1973, 67.

[243] Küng, 1973, 80.

president of the community [the ordained leader]"[244] should celebrate the eucharist as that which 'assures itself of its own character... and portrays itself.'[245] It is analogous with the primary model set out in Philippians[246] and incarnated in a "'counter-office' of servanthood"[247] by Paul, Timothy and Epaphroditus.

Representation and Participation

The concern of this work has been to examine the appropriateness of the application of priesthood as a designation of the ordained ministry from a Protestant perspective. A number of factors have shaped the emerging narrative beginning with the activity of God in Jesus Christ.[248] Three primary markers have been established. The first is the primacy of God's sovereignty and the prevenience of grace,[249] whereby the divine and the human are, and must, remain distinct. Secondly there is the importance of the Chalcedonian pattern wherein Jesus Christ is 'truly God and truly man' but in such a way that the two natures remain unconfused. Thirdly it has been argued that the Protestant doctrine of priesthood is a matter of identity enacted through a series of practices and roles, most obviously as the eucharistic president.

As well as these primary markers a number of secondary statements have further refined the characteristics of a possible priesthood. It has been suggested that priesthood can only be apprehended dialectically.[250] Priesthood takes its form, by analogy, as a form of participation, from the kenotic relationship of God and humanity. This is enacted on the one hand through the intra-Trinitarian, and on the other the human-divine κοινωνία, which is concerned with crossing the boundaries separating God and man. Human priesthood cannot effect either expiation or propitiation and is not mediatory.[251] However, priesthood proclaims the identity of God in relation to humanity and also humanity in relation to God. Priesthood is fundamentally concerned with sacrifice, which is responsive and therefore

---

[244] Küng, 1973, 81.
[245] See: 234 n. 237 above.
[246] Phil. 2.5-11.
[247] Bockmuehl, 1997, 55 (See: Phil. 1.1; 2.22, 30).
[248] Part I.
[249] See: 173-185 above.
[250] See: Chapter 6 above and the exploration of the priestly testimony and countertestimony in both the Old Testament and the Letter to the Hebrews.
[251] This is the inherent weakness of an Adamic Christology. (See: 92-96 above.) Likewise Balthasar's theo-dramatic Christology, his emphasis upon 'standing between' in the drama and Adamic Christology. (See: 119 above.) and his understanding of Mary and Peter as mediatory figures (see: 116, 119 above.)

secondary.[252] Finally, priesthood is ascribed more widely in the New Testament to those who minister than is assumed.[253]

Tracing the Priestly Representation

In discussing the meaning of identity and representation in Chapter 1 above I drew upon Graham Ward's analysis of the threefold understanding of representation in the thought of Karl Barth. According to Ward, Barth 'articulates representation in three distinct ways';[254] of which the third form *'repraesentieren'* "is neither direct presentation [*eintreten*], nor equivocating mediation [*darstellen*], but the tracing of a repeated promise... moving between its past announcement and its future fulfilment."[255] I believe that this facet of representation will help understand priesthood as the summative (not vicarious) engagement of the ordained priesthood with the truly divine and the truly human in the context of the Church and as a public activity.

As a priestly community the Church stands between the historic event of Jesus Christ's 'once for all saving act' and the future eschatological fulfilment of the divine-human history.[256] Barth understands both Biblical exegesis and the public event of preaching as the proclamation of the Word of God as essentially priestly tasks.[257] Proclamation participates, on the one hand, in the written text, which is fixed,[258] but which, on the other hand, can never (save at the risk of doing violence to the text) be formulated propositionally.[259] The *successio apostolorum* is maintained when the Church allows "the text to speak anew for itself without restriction" so standing under "the lordship of this free power in the Bible".[260] The promise contained in the apostolic word is its witness to the "proclamation and preaching of Jesus Christ" as 'true God and true man'. The "promise of this word is therefore in effect Immanuel! God with us!"[261] It is this which the

---

[252] Sacrifice becomes part of the countertestimony and responsive praise and gratitude to the sovereign grace of God. (See: 196-97 above.)

[253] See: 90-91, 102-103, 208-212 above. See also: R. Paul Stevens, (*The Abolition of the Laity*, Carlisle, Paternoster Press, 1999 140.)

[254] See: 9 above.

[255] Ward, 1998, 243.

[256] See: Rev. 21.22 where this is made explicit the account in of the new Jerusalem in which there is neither temple nor altar, for both are rendered redundant by the fully realised presence of God.

[257] Karl Barth, *Homiletics*, Louisville, Westminster/John Knox Press, 1991b, 46.

[258] By fixed, Barth means 'canonical'. The Biblical text belongs to the Church not simply the individual believer.

[259] *CD* I.1, 119.

[260] *CD* I.1, 120.

[261] *CD* I.1, 121.

Priesthood and the Ordained

apostles and their successors hand on. Representation is caught within this dialectic of being and not being, of containing, but in a form that is both veiled and unveiled. The analogy of kenosis offers precisely the fluidity of identity revealed by God in Jesus Christ. It is in the analogous and therefore non-identical repetition of the divine identity, revealed in Jesus Christ, that priesthood exists and is apostolic.

I propose that priesthood does not exist as office inherited through a trackable lineage from the apostles (*pace* Balthasar). Neither can priesthood effect, by its actions, sacramental or otherwise, the due reconciliation of God and man. Nor does the rejection of such concepts logically imply that priesthood is not a valid concept (*pace* Barth and Moltmann). But what is left if priesthood is to be meaningful in any sense? My view is that priesthood *represents* the possibility of *the divine-human encounter*. Priesthood speaks of the possibility of traversing the *diastasis* between God and humanity. However, the priest is not the one who bridges this *diastasis* because of any power given through ordination. Instead the key lies in the Barthian concept of the Word.

According to Barth, the Word of God addressed to humanity in human language is at once veiled and unveiled. The role of the apostles as witnesses is crucial, as those who receive the Word and who hand it on to others. However, unlike Balthasar, he does not believe that their role as witnesses to Jesus is grounded "on the basis of their appointment alone."[262] The disciples do not principally identify (recognise) who Jesus is cognitively but only in the light of the cross and resurrection, the result of which is an "open-ended act of affirmation, entailing discipleship".[263]

While Barth explores the veiled, kenotic identity of God in Jesus, as the 'Way of the Son into the Far Country'[264] the 'Homecoming of the Son of Man' is concerned with the unveiled identification of Jesus Christ which occurs only in the light of the resurrection and ascension.[265] In Barth's threefold schema it is the third part, the account of the resurrection, which

---

[262] David E. Demson, *Hans Frei and Karl Barth: different ways of reading scripture*, Grand Rapids, Eerdmans, 1997, 97. Demson proposes that (Dempson, 1997, 1-4.) Barth's reading of the gospels falls into three stages: the Galilean ministry, the second stage beginning variously with the entry into Jerusalem or at Gethsemene and the third stage tells of the forty days beginning with the resurrection and culminating in the ascension. It is in this third stage that, according to Barth, the historical man Jesus (*CD* IV.1, 448.) is manifested to the disciples in the mode of God. It is in 'this manifestation Jesus exercises this power by confirming his appointment and calling of the disciples in his commissioning of them' (Demson, 1997, 17).

[263] Oliver Davies, *A Theology of Compassion*, London, SCM, 2001, 216. It is 'the resurrection that *manifests* to the disciples the secret of Jesus ministry.' (Demson, 1997, 97 – his italics.)

[264] *CD* IV.1, § 59.1. (See: 53-55 above.)

[265] *CD* IV.2, 154.

decisively confirms the first two.[266] The disciples are "the rock on which He builds His Church" because "there is no way to Him which does not lead past them."[267] They hold the keys as witnesses to the resurrection identity of Jesus Christ.[268] They exist in the Word wherein "through their witness He speaks to His community."[269] Thus Barth outlines a progression "towards externality, secondariness" that is reminiscent of the kenotic whereby "human externality manifests the essential nature" of the Church as the visible presence of Christ in "a world in which what appears is not what is."[270]

So like the apostles, for Barth, the community as the elect is God's messenger. Accordingly "he [each elect individual] may *represent* [*repraesentieren*] and portray [*abbilden*] the glory of the grace of God."[271] To this extent he 'shares' in "the office of Jesus Christ"[272] Such participation does not replace the original but is a limited and non-identical imitative repetition or enactment.[273] But because this is a consequence of the divine grace it is to be received with praise. In this the elect person reveals that they are sent by God "to be an apostle of grace"[274] which is the basis of the ordering and vocation of the community. This calling is priestly involving "a hidden but real crossing of frontiers" which God wills.[275] However, it must not be forgotten that "everything is primarily and actually the work of Jesus Christ Himself." Therefore, the "distinction between the

---

[266] Demson, 1997, 74.

[267] *CD* IV.1, 719.

[268] According to Barth the apostolic succession cannot be the transference of the work of the Holy Spirit because 'apostolicity is His [Jesus] work and a gift' (*CD* IV.1, 717). The Holy Spirit is not 'a property' owned by some or all of the Church. The apostles are distinct from all else who follow in that they 'are his direct witnesses, they belong together with Him in a unique and special way' (*CD* IV.1, 718). Again what is evident is Barth's particularism.

[269] *CD* IV.1, 720. Consequently, it is not the Church which controls the Spirit but the Holy Spirit which controls the Church and which is at the heart of the apostolic succession.

[270] Graham Ward, 'Kenosis: Death, Discourse and Resurrection', Lucy Gardiner, B. Quash, G. Ward, *Balthasar at the End of Modernity*, Edinburgh, T & T Clark, 1999, 23. (Quoted: 98, n. 149 above.)

[271] *CD* II.2, 415 – my italics. Barth uses the word *abbilden*, to make a copy, a picture one from another, not in the sense of demonstrating (*darstellen*) but much in the same way a portrait painter proceeds making a likeness, that is recognisable but not exact, a non-identical copy.

[272] *CD* II.2, 415.

[273] *CD* II.2, 417.

[274] *CD* II.2, 415.

[275] *CD* II.2, 417.

electing God and elected man remains clear."[276] Nonetheless the priestly task is to ensure that "the truth [of God's grace] is repeated" and "a new sign is erected".[277] The elect man or woman is called to live amongst others as the one who "represents and reflects the gracious God and Jesus Christ and His people" in their concern to proclaim the 'ministry of reconciliation' (2 Cor 5.19).[278] The elect are following the example of the apostles as those who are "the essence and representation (*als Inbegriff und Repraesentation*) of discipleship."[279] Priesthood embodies,[280] by tracing or retelling, through a series of practices and roles, the promise of God's saving act. What is repeated is the proclamation, whereby the 'once for all' historical event of Jesus Christ's death and resurrection is made present now in the spoken word.

Priesthood becomes the sign, which by externalising, traces of the crossing of boundaries, is a testimony to reconciliation, and atonement having been secured 'once for all' in the event of Jesus Christ. The boundaries are crossed in the moment when Jesus Christ is made known and is recognised as 'truly God and truly man'. This is only possible in the light of the resurrection and is known only through the apostolic witness.[281] Witness is always secondary to the event and therefore repetitious. Scripture, preaching and therefore the sacramental witness to God are always secondary. They take their form from Jesus Christ "Himself God and Himself man... In Him God reveals himself to man. In Him man sees and knows God."[282] Similarly Scripture which contains the Word of God repeats the Chalcedonian pattern.[283] The image is priestly, but the focus is the 'Word' as the basis "of God's revelation, God's supernatural communication to man." It is the divine Word, embodied in Jesus Christ, which proceeds "from person to person and uniting God with man."[284] It is the Word, which is never static but always an event, which crosses the

---

[276] *CD* II.2, 415.

[277] *CD* II.2, 418.

[278] *CD* II.2, 419.

[279] *CD* II.2, 431. I am indebted to Graham Ward who kindly provided me with the German original enabling me to make this crucial point.

[280] *Inbegriff* means the 'the embodiment of' discipleship which exists only in relation to Jesus Christ, the one who is the true (prophet) priest (and king) in His appointment, calling and commission. The apostolate according to Barth is 'the active participation... in... His Messianic office'. So Barth draws particular attention to Jesus' own calling as *apostolos* (Heb. 3.1). The 'apostolate consists in sharing in Jesus own mission.' In this they replicate non-identically, but are to be identifiable as 'themselves prophets, priests and kings (1 Pet. 2.9)' (*CD* II.2, 432).

[281] *CD* III.2, 448.

[282] *CD* II.2, 94.

[283] *CD* I.2, 501.

[284] *CD* II.2, 97.

boundaries.[285]

The dialectical form of the revelation of faith emerges from "the kenosis of radical discipleship" by which Oliver Davies[286] articulates the possibility of being drawn into the divine-human conversation.[287] Faith is priestly, an act of *"dialectical responsivity"* which, on the one hand, results from knowing that "the infinite Person of Christ, is to open to ourselves to unforeseeable change and radical journeying"[288] thereby crossing the boundaries and being re-identified in resemblance to Him.[289] On the other, it results in "an equivalent dispossession within us which is expressed as compassionate movement towards others"[290] by tracking and externalising the priestly act of compassion. Compassion, like love and priesthood, provides "the analogical language for divine love and mercy."[291] In Paul's writing, σπλάγχνα (compassion) "is part of the vocabulary of the Christian church" as it can be grouped with κοινωνία[292] and is overtly Christological.[293]

The word σπλάγχνα enables Paul to bring together the Christological and the affective.[294] Consequently he speaks of his participating in Christ's love for the Philippians.[295] Secondly, in Philippians 2.1 Paul's fourfold[296] exhortation under girds the injunction to his listeners to be Christ like,[297] tracing or externalising their response to God's prior saving grace in Christ. This reveals their "participation …in the Holy Spirit".[298] If God's love is portrayed analogously by reference to the love of the parent for their child, so human affection "is refigured by divine self-giving and becomes the

---

[285] *CD* I.2, 45. (See also: Gorringe, 1999, 134.)

[286] Davies, 2001, 36.

[287] Davies, 2001, 212.

[288] Davies, 2001, 213 – his italics.

[289] In other words drawing upon a fitting theory of representations (see: 10 above).

[290] Davies, 2001, 213.

[291] Davies, 2001, 246. There is an analogical participation or likeness, which repeats but is not identical.

[292] Davies, 2001, 248.

[293] Davies, 2001, 247.

[294] 'It is right for me to feel this way about you all, because I hold you in my heart, for you are partakers (συγκοινωνύς) with me of grace, both in my imprisonment and in the defence and confirmation of the gospel. For God is my witness, how I yearn for you with all the affection (σπλάγχνοις) of Christ Jesus.' (Phil. 1.7-8.)

[295] 'It is not Paul who lives within Paul, but Jesus Christ, which is why Paul is not moved by the bowels of Paul but by the bowels of Jesus Christ.' (J. A. Bengal, quoted, O'Brien, 1991, 72.)

[296] 'So if there is any encouragement in Christ, any incentive of love, any participation (κοινωνία) in the Spirit, any affection and sympathy' (σπλάγχνα) (Phil. 2.1).

[297] Phil. 2.2.

[298] O'Brien, 1991, 176.

Priesthood and the Ordained 243

foundation of the new life that is the spirit of the church."[299] This is also the basis of priesthood as the reconfiguration and externalisation of those who are publicly representative of the community of faith as those who exist in a right relationship with God. As in his incarnation God becomes externally "compassion in the flesh" likewise the people of God, in their relationship with one another, re-enact "through participation, the original mutuality of the Father, Son, and Holy Spirit."[300] Participation results in an event of non-identical repetition wherein the divine-human dialectic is maintained. The disciple is the one whose life is *god-like* as revealed supremely in the kenosis of Jesus Christ. So too the priest externalises the priesthood of Christ, precisely in the practices and roles through which it is engaged, as a mirror image through which it becomes recognisable. The incarnation and the high-priesthood of Christ is God's direct address to humanity in 'ordinary language.'[301] What is revealed in the *carmen Christi*, is "a divine, trinitarian conversation" resulting in "a new kind of human speech: one that is filled with the presence of God" in which He is represented in human speech.[302] So too the priesthood of the ordained reveals the presence of God in such that there is fluidity or elasticity but no loss of form or identity.

Κοινωνία as Participation

In Part I the progression to externality was first noted in relation to kenosis[303] and the trinitarian nature of the event of divine self-revelation. It was suggested that identity, as recognition, requires the 'one' to participate in the form of the other.[304] In Part II I suggested that the progression to externality emerged in six distinct areas relating to priesthood, sacrifice, vocation and identity.[305] Finally in Part III externalization has been evident in exemplarism and interchange, the concept of the particular and concrete and representation. Externalization repeats the Chalcedonian pattern; it has two parts: the internal and veiled, and the external and unveiled - each of which participates in the other. The ordained priesthood announces that the

---

[299] Davies, 2001, 248.
[300] Davies, 2001, 249.
[301] Davies, 2001, 271.
[302] Davies, 2001, 271.
[303] See: 56 above discussing kenosis in the thought of Barth and again in the exegesis of Phil. 2.5-11. (See: 97 above.)
[304] See: 16 above.
[305] The six indicators of a progression towards externality are: covenant identity (see: 139-145 above); the priestly testimony (see: 148-151 above); the priestly countertestimony (see: 154-158 above); the countertestimony of sacrifice (see: 166-173 above); identity both of the knowability of God (see: 21 above) but also the identity of humanity (see: 85, 109, 136 above.); vocation as gratitude embodied (see: 158 above).

divine-human boundaries have been crossed and the right ordering of God and creation are being revealed – supremely in the eucharist and the speaking of the Word of God. But priesthood does not simply participate in the divine re-ordering but also in the fullness of humanity. The key word is κοινωνία.[306]

The Letter to the Philippians is concerned with the participative identity of Paul and the Philippians whose lives are recognizable in relation to Jesus Christ. The "*κοινων-* group is most common in Paul" who uses it to speak of "the religious fellowship (participation) of the believer in Christ and Christian blessings and for the mutual fellowship of believers".[307] Examples of all of these are found in Philippians.[308] For the second group the notion of participation is of a shared commonality, of 'Christian blessings' and the third group 'the mutual fellowships of believers' contains no difficulties. However, the emphasis upon the participation 'of the believer in Christ' concerns the divine-human encounter[309] and is altogether more problematic.[310] On the one hand, it is the possibility of divine-human participation that lies at the heart of the covenant by which boundaries are crossed, while, on the other hand there remains the need to maintain an appropriate *diastasis*.

One consequence of the *carmen Christi* is that 'therefore' the Philippians are to 'work out [their] own salvation with fear and trembling'[311] as the

---

[306] Nicholas Sagovsky, *Ecumenism, Christian Origins and the Practice of Communion*, Cambridge, CUP, 2000, 18, 194.

[307] *TDNT* (ET, Vol III), 804.

[308] Phil. 1.5; 4.14,15 participation in the mutual fellowship of believers; 1.7 participation in Christian blessings; 2.1 participation of the believer in the Holy Spirit [Christ]; 3.10 participation of the believer in Christ. (I shall develop this more particularly in the next section.) The pattern I have suggested is not the same as proposed by Kittel. So for example he suggests 1.7 falls into the first category, whereas I would argue following O'Brien, that it reads more naturally as an example of the second. (O'Brien, 1991, 69.) However, despite this Kittel's categorisation is helpful.

[309] Therefore this would include 2.1, κοινωνία πνεύματος. O'Brien raises a number of key issues, 'the meaning of πνεῦμα' (O'Brien, 1991, 172.) suggesting it refers to the Holy Spirit; 'the second more difficult question has to do with the precise meaning of κοινωνία' (O'Brien, 1991, 173).

[310] Thus commenting on 1 Cor. 1.9 Anthony Thiselton insists that *κοινωνία* be translated 'communal participation' whose primary 'object is a sharing of Christ's life by his people' and only secondarily the 'fellowship of Christians one with another.' (Anthony C. Thiselton, *The First Epistle to the Corinthians*, Carlisle, Paternoster, 2000, 104.) See also: Thiselton, 2000, 762- 763.) Thiselton suggests that 1 Corinthians 10.14-22 is fundamentally concerned with a Christocentric interpretation of the covenant. (Thiselton, 2000, 750f.) See: 139-145 above covenant identity and priesthood in 1 Peter 2.

[311] Phil. 2.12. See: O'Brien, 1991, 276.

visible sign of their obedience 'in Christ'. Individually each of the words "is well known" in the New Testament, it is this combination which is distinct.[312] As they stand they "have become a crux of Protestant dogmatics and a repeatedly quoted *dictum probans* of the Catholics".[313] Barth re-orders the clause[314] by interpreting it in the light of Paul's other references to fear and trembling.[315] He reads it as a "shortened expression for: to live as a Christian, to show and prove oneself what one is as a Christian."[316] It is a call for the externalisation of faith in order to be identifiable (recognisable) in relation to God in Christ and the world, and is priestly.[317] There will be 'fear and trembling' because "everyone who puts his future salvation into practice is placed in a position of humility." Salvation is embodied, and made visible (recognisable) in the dependency of the 'self' upon 'the other', God in Christ. Humanity is "there by remembering the grace in which he *participates in Jesus Christ*."[318]

Nicholas Sagovsky believes that κοινωνία is in part concerned with mutual interchange.[319] According to Sagovsky, during the early centuries the communication between different churches and Church leaders was not just a matter of mutual concern but "was seen as a communicating of Jesus which was possible in and by the Spirit."[320] What he fails to recognise, unlike Barth, is the significance of the form of such participatory action and as a result Sagovsky inverts the order of κοινωνία. Thus he says that the "centre of the Christian faith is that which is shared between Christians (and between Christians and God)."[321] Ultimately this reveals a tendency towards the idealistic at the expense of the particular. Rowan Williams criticises what he identifies as the traditional "incarnationalist consensus"[322] adopted by ecumenists (among others). Instead he argues that fellowship or belonging is not just human but is completely reordered in relation to the divine. As the "gospels make it harshly clear that belonging with Jesus

---

[312] O'Brien, 1991, 276.

[313] Barth, 1962, 72.

[314] **'with fear and trembling** work out your salvation!' (Barth, 1962, 71 – his emphasis.)

[315] 1 Cor. 2.3; 2 Cor 7.15; Eph 6.5.

[316] Barth, 1962, 72.

[317] John Webster refering to 1 Pet. 2.9, suggests '[h]oliness is visible as testimony' (Webster, 2003, 75).

[318] Barth, 1962, 73 – my italics.

[319] Sagovsky, 2000, 142 drawing upon an essay by Rowan Williams. ('Does it make sense to speak of pre-Nicene Orthodoxy', R. D. Williams (ed), *The Making of Orthodoxy*, Cambridge, CUP, 1989.)

[320] Sagovsky, 2000, 142.

[321] Sagovsky, 2000, 145.

[322] Rowan Williams, 'Incarnation and the Renewal of Community' in *On Christian Theology*, Oxford, Blackwell, 2000, 227.

upsets all other kinds of belonging – of family, of status, even of membership of the children of Abraham."[323] This results from the identification of Jesus

> not simply as a god but as the God of Jewish scripture in two respects: he creates a people by covenant (as in the ancient and widespread tradition of the Last Supper), and by a summons that makes something radically new.[324]

For Barth "God himself has spoken"[325] and therefore made himself known. This is the objective basis of all revelation, consummated in the incarnation of Jesus Christ, the divine Logos in whom God, who is veiled, is revealed, without compromising his absolute otherness.[326] Only then can Barth proceed to consider "the subjective possibility of revelation, that is, human receptivity for it... God's address to us, an address that is heard."[327] His concern is to explore being 'in Christ' which in "Roman Catholic theology... would undoubtedly read: 'Participation in the Holy Sacraments'"[328] for to do so would be to participate in grace. However, he cannot accept this, though he prefers it to Protestant fideism.[329] Instead he looks to Philippians 2.12 ('with fear and trembling') where he sees the basis for the subjective possibility of revelation to be found "by truly and unequivocally associating Word and sacrament"[330] which he develops further in *Church Dogmatics*.[331]

The evidence of the possibility of a participative divine-human encounter is that while God speaks through human language "the divine self-Word does not cease to be itself".[332] Sacraments are further evidence of this possibility. The initiative lies with God who has commissioned the Church to proclaim the truth about him. Obedience is the external evidence that the Word, which commissions, has been heard. Therefore the form of proclamation should meet the listening and answering in the Church as the representation of God's Word, demands in some sense a setting apart, a

---

[323] Williams, 2000, 229.
[324] Williams, 2000, 231.
[325] Barth, 1991a, 45, 134.
[326] Barth, 1991a, 134-35, also 154-55.
[327] Barth, 1991a, 168. It is important to notice at once that within his structure Barth is able to ensure both divine sovereignty and the precedence of grace.
[328] Barth, 1991a, 169.
[329] Barth, 1991a, 170-71.
[330] Barth, 1991a, 171.
[331] *CD* I.1, 51-79.
[332] *CD* I.1, 57.

special imperative calling of the man who is to function here.[333]

First, God speaks and reveals his story which is given to the Church, which in turn gives itself in its response through proclamation in Word and sacrament. Secondly, the one who is called does not cease to be, but participates with "the Word as the divine event".[334] Because it is participative the two natures are maintained[335] in the mimetic act in which the promise of God's presence,[336] made to the Church, is repeated afresh. Thirdly, this is the action of the Holy Spirit who establishes "his own work, in the preacher's mouth and the hearer's ear".[337] Finally, therefore, the sacrament is responsive to the prior Word of God.[338]

The eucharist "is not something absolute; it is always the being present of something or someone."[339] The words of institution, 'This is my body which was broken for you' must not be read separating the "identifying 'is'" and "the promise 'for you'."[340] The eucharist is a sign of God's promissory presence. The promise makes credible the presence. But nonetheless difference and distinction remains.[341] Moltmann maintains an understanding of the eucharist as an event which looks back to the particular history of Jesus Christ[342] while at the same time it announces the presence "of the crucified one in the spirit of the resurrection"[343] and anticipates "the coming kingdom in history."[344] As such it is an act of gratitude[345] and therefore responsive to the sovereignty of God made manifest in the grace of Christ.[346]

Balthasar, even though he does not speak of κοινωνία, appears to share a similar understanding to Barth and Moltmann. The "liturgy [of the eucharist] constantly connects these two words: 'we recall and offer'...

---

[333] *CD* I.1, 64.

[334] *CD* I.1, 65.

[335] Thereby repeating, albeit non-identically, the two natures of Jesus Christ.

[336] What 'such a man may claim to utter as God's Word in the exercise of proclamation, cannot be the actual Word of God as such, but only the repetition of His promise, repetition of the promise, "Lo, I am with you always" (Matt 28.20). Proclamation must mean announcement – announcement, met by the real "I am with you," as the future fulfilment.' (*CD* I.1, 64.)

[337] *CD* I.1, 66.

[338] *CD* I.1, 79.

[339] Jürgen Moltmann, *The Church in the Power of the Spirit* (ET), London, SCM, 1977, 254.

[340] Moltmann, 1977, 255.

[341] Moltmann, 1977, 255.

[342] Moltmann, 1977, 249.

[343] Moltmann, 1977, 250.

[344] Moltmann, 1977, 251.

[345] Moltmann, 1977, 257.

[346] Moltmann, 1977, 259.

showing the relationship between the present action and what took place then."³⁴⁷ So too the "fundamental presupposition is that the Person of Jesus is really present".³⁴⁸ But at this point Balthasar introduces two factors. First, that Jesus is engaged in "a perpetual, eternal self-offering to the Father on behalf of mankind."³⁴⁹ This raises questions in turn about the nature of the eucharistic sacrifice. Therefore, secondly, it cannot simply be one of 'praise and thanksgiving' for "what is ultimately offered to God is no longer earthly food but Christ's body and blood".³⁵⁰ The question becomes who offers what and to whom? As a consequence the two natures become one. According to Balthasar the bread and wine *become* rather than *signify* Christ's body and blood. He speaks of mediation, rather than participation.³⁵¹ The eucharist becomes the activity of the Church in the power of the ordained.³⁵² The priesthood of the ordained is no longer summative but vicarious, primary and not responsive.

Barth holds, in contrast to Balthasar, that the Word of God mediates between God and man through the participation of the divine Word communicated in human words. The representation of the divine is possible because the divine has participation in the created. There is no synthesis, no idealised mediator. The Chalcedonian pattern remains; the divine-human encounter is an act of κοινωνία.

Participation, Κοινωνία and the Eucharist as a Theologia Crucis

Paul also makes "significant use of κοινωνία [is] for the fellowship which arises in the Lord's Supper"³⁵³ as participation in Christ. The "nature of the Lord's Supper is... [one of] fellowship with the person of Christ, namely κοινωνία with His body and blood".³⁵⁴ As a result "those who partake of the cultic meal become companions of the god", therefore by "analogy those who partake of the Lord's Supper are Christ's companions."³⁵⁵ It is important to draw out the implications of such a statement and its

---

[347] *TD* IV, 391.

[348] *TD* IV, 391-92.

[349] *TD* IV, 392. For Protestant theology this opens the door to the undermining of the 'once for all' nature of the event of the cross.

[350] *TD* IV, 394.

[351] *TD* IV, 395. See: 92-96 above. for a full discussion of the weakness of Adamic Christology. Balthasar further undermines the divine sovereignty by intruding Mary as an idealised and semi-divine figure. (See: 113-118 above., for a fuller discussion of Balthasar's Mariology)

[352] See: 232 n. 223 above.

[353] *TDNT*. (ET, Vol. III), 805.

[354] *TDNT*. (ET, Vol. III), 805.

[355] *TDNT*. (ET, Vol. III), 805.

significance in terms of priesthood.

In 1 Corinthians "**communal participation** [κοινωνία] in the Passover **cup of blessing** of Christ's redemptive **blood**" is fundamentally covenantal.[356] God gives the cup in an act of sovereign grace, which together with bread is shared and constitutes the community's oneness. The sacrifice offered "**to God** [is] not of the Lord's Supper as such but of the *life and lifestyle* which express its Christomorphic, Christocentric orientation".[357] This is not simply a legalistic commercial exchange but an affective and covenantal event. The image is not the contract but the betrothal.[358] This is precisely the point made by Paul when writing to the Philippians[359] in which the pattern of story, gift and response is evident.

Paul also speaks of sharing in Christ's sufferings and death.[360] In Philippians 3.10 Paul inverts the order of 2.5-11, so that *ascensus* is followed by *descensus*.[361] The "genitive παθημάτων is objective, denoting that in which one participates, that is, 'share in his sufferings.'"[362] O'Brien is clear that 'sufferings' is not to be read in terms of "Christ's redemptive death".[363] 'Sufferings' refers to the birth pangs of the Messianic age which God's people must endure, 'that I may know (γνῶναι) him' following from 3.8 is indicative of "an intimate personal relationship".[364] Paul employs the unusual word συμμορφιζόμενοσ,[365] a compound of μορφή which involves participation in the οὐσία also for μορφή implies not the external accidents but the essential attributes.[366] So Paul seems to be articulating Christian identity as embodying a recognisable but non-identical or asymmetrical repetition of the example of Christ (see: Philippians 2.6-11). This includes the metaphorical death and resurrection

---

[356] 1 Cor. 10.16. (Thiselton, 2000, 759 – his emphasis.)

[357] Thiselton, 2000, 751- his emphasis.

[358] Thiselton, 2000, 759. Thiselton draws attention to the 'parallel between 1 Cor. 10.14-22 and 2 Cor. 6.14-7.1' in which the '**cup of blessing** of covenant participation also finds a parallel with "the metaphor of the betrothal contract" in 2 Cor. 11.1-2' (his emphasis).

[359] Phil. 1.21, 27; 2.1-4, 5; 3.7-8; also 2.12. For Paul's supposed use of commercial imagery (4.18), which is priestly language (see: 90 above). Furthermore this is also participative language (4.14).

[360] 'I may know (γνῶναι) him and the power of his resurrection, and may share (κοινωνίαν) his sufferings (παθημάτων), becoming like (συμμορφιζόμενος) him in his death' (Phil. 3.10).

[361] J-F. Collange (*The Epistle of Saint Paul to the Philippians* (ET), London, Epworth, 1979, 13.) suggests the inversion is for polemical purposes.

[362] O'Brien, 1991, 405.

[363] O'Brien, 1991, 405.

[364] O'Brien, 1991, 402. (See: Collange, 1979, 131; Bockmuehl, 1997, 213.)

[365] Barth, 1962, 103.

[366] Lightfoot, 1879, 130-133.

of the person. There is no confusion of form since the person does not become divine but truly human. They are seen to be Christ like in the mirror of Christ.

This is a priestly event where boundaries are crossed and right order is restored. Κοινωνία "is rooted in the order of creation" which is made explicit in the covenantal relationship "established by God, between God and the chosen people".[367] The following verse points to the future hope of a completeness of resurrection living which although it is not yet, it is nonetheless anticipated.[368] This is not just an individual but ecclesial matter of being the people of God. Paul speaks of the intimacy of the δύναμιν τῆς ἀναστάσεωσ αὐτοῦ καὶ κοινωνίαν πατημάτων. Through "identification with the death and resurrection of Christ by the power of the Holy Spirit, Christians enter into fellowship (κοινωνία) with God and with one another".[369] However, κοινωνία is only possible "by virtue of God's grace through Jesus Christ".[370] This is in turn possible only by "the power of the Holy Spirit"[371] and κοινωνία is only "partially realized"[372] in the present.

Conclusion

Balthasar's ecclesiology fails because it emphasises the Marian and Petrine principles at the expense of pneumatology.[373] In its place he emphasizes the Office of the Church and the ordained ministry as the objective representation of the continuing divine-human encounter. This has a twofold effect.

First it identifies apostolicity specifically with the ordained ministry. Apostolicity is important. The creedal confession of the Church is to believe in the 'one, holy, catholic and apostolic Church.' Balthasar appears to maintain an objective notion of apostolicity grounded in an Enlightenment understanding of history.[374] He maintains the branch theory of apostolic succession, as providing a verifiable line of episcopal succession initiated by Christ through Peter and the apostles, which is

---

[367] WCC, *The Nature and Purpose of the Church*, Faith and Order Paper 181, Geneva, 1998, 24, para. 49.

[368] Earlier (see: 86 above.) I suggested that Phil. 3 falls into a threefold dialectic in which 3.1-6 describes false (or mistaken) identity; 3.7-11 describes true identity; and 3.12-21 identity which is not yet completed.

[369] FOAG (181), 1998, 25 para 53.

[370] FOAG (181), 1998, 25 para 55.

[371] FOAG (181), 1998, 26 para 59.

[372] FOAG (181), 1998, 27 para 60.

[373] See: 116, n. 71 above.

[374] See: 230 above.

historically traceable. Furthermore this is exclusively located in the Roman Catholic Church.[375] The presence of the Holy Spirit is confirmed and undergirded by "the indefectibility of the Petrine Office".[376] The unity of the Church divinely instituted is focused in the episcopate, embodied in the Bishop of Rome and incorporating "both the communion of love and the (strongly emphasized) legal authority that upholds the purity of faith and love as it did in the times of the apostles".[377] The "Petrine Office is both central and 'eccentric'... in the centre of the Church".[378] Infallibility resides in the office, which stands in a particular relationship to the Holy Spirit and not the person.[379] Balthasar believes that "Christ having implanted in the Church a permanent organ (which through apostolic succession, must remain so) securing and guaranteeing the direct dependence on Christ. Such is the ministerial office."[380] Because the Church receives authority from Christ through the apostles she can administer the sacraments and through their successors hand it on.[381] However, as John Webster says, "[f]orms cannot guarantee authenticity".[382]

In 1 Corinthians 15.3 Paul introduces the creedal statement[383] saying 'I delivered to you... what I also received'. Marcion omits *what I also received* "to avoid any implication that Paul depends on apostolic tradition rather than direct revelation".[384] Paul does not claim mere "historical continuity and tradition entitle no one to be regarded as a specially privileged person or source of authoritative decisions".[385] The continuity that Paul speaks of would seem to be the content of the tradition and not of office. Authority is located in relation to the faithful receiving and handing on of the gospel. This theme is one that is developed by the Roman

---

[375] Hans Urs von Balthasar, *The Office of Peter and the Structure of the Church*, San Francisco, Ignatius Press, 1986, 273.
[376] Balthasar, 1986, 125.
[377] Balthasar, 1986, 164.
[378] Balthasar, 1986, 181.
[379] Balthasar, 1986, 218.
[380] *TD* III, 430.
[381] Curiously Balthasar finds support for his understanding of apostolic succession from Newman (a former Anglican) and Richard Hooker who he thinks argues that 'the bishop's spiritual authority comes to him in virtue of apostolic succession' (Balthasar, 1986, 271). However, Balthasar appears to misunderstand Hooker. (*Laws*, VII. xiii. 3.)
[382] John Webster, 'The Self-Organizing Power Of The Gospel of Christ: Episcopacy And Community Formation', John Webster, *Word and Church*, Edinburgh, T & T Clark, 2001, 208.
[383] 1 Cor. 15.3b-4.
[384] Thiselton, 2000, 1186.
[385] Hans von Campenhausen, *Ecclesiastical Authority and Spiritual Power in the Church of the First Three Centuries* (ET), Peabody Mass., Hendrickson Publishers, 1997, 37.

Catholic theologians Hans Küng and Edward Schillebeeckx.

According to Küng apostolicity resides in the whole church and not simply the office of the ordained. The Apostles are unique. What "remains is the task and a commission"[386] to hand on the message received from the apostle. The apostolicity of the Church is the "original and fundamental ... source and norm of the Church's existence in preaching, faith and action... in all times and places."[387] Apostolicity is not "something that can be simply stated and proved from history."[388] Apostolic succession

> entails a continuing living confrontation of the Church with the original, fundamental testimony of Scripture... the Bible does not remain a book... but is a living voice of witness, to be heard and believed... [it] means following the faith and confession of the apostles.[389]

Edward Schillebeeckx similarly understands apostolicity as constituted by the succession of the faith, received and faithfully handed on.[390] He notes "in the New Testament one striking fact is that ministry did not develop from and around the eucharist or the liturgy, but from the apostolic building up of the community through preaching, admonition and leadership."[391] The Greek Orthodox theologian John Zizioulas proposes a variant understanding. He says Balthasar is wrong to believe that apostolicity and truth is simply a matter "of a *historical transmission*." History is not just "a succession of events moving from past to present linearly". For Zizioulas the truth, and apostolicity, is maintained within the eucharist which is rooted in the whole community. Because the bishop presides, leading the Church in the liturgical event engaging with both the "*anamnetic* and *epicletic* character of the eucharist"[392] apostolicity "is less to do with transmission and much more to do with identity or authenticity".[393]

Secondly, because it is pneumatically deficient it distorts the trinitarian structure of Balthasar's theology. In Barth's language, all three cited above

---

[386] Hans Küng, *The Church* (ET), Tunbridge Wells, Search Press, 1986, 355.
[387] Küng, 1986, 356.
[388] Küng, 1986, 358.
[389] Küng, 1986, 357.
[390] Schillebeeckx, 1985, 115-119.
[391] Schillebeeckx, 1985, 118.
[392] John Zizioulas, *Being as Communion*, Crestwood, NY, St Vladimir's Seminary Press, 1985, 115 – his italics. Accordingly Balthasar's institutional model of the Church and the traditional notion of the Apostolic Succession exemplifies externality in which Christian identity is lodged in certain external features. Whereas as it is understood by Moltmann, Küng, Schillebeeckx and Zizioulas it exemplifies the 'inner, spiritual reality... transformed by God.' (Stephen Sykes, 1984, 231.)
[393] Webster, 2001, 208.

acknowledge apostolicity, like the Word of God, as an 'event'.[394] The "apostolocity of the Church cannot and must not be sought on historical and juridical grounds." Such a basis is ultimately independent of the Holy Spirit and instead takes its authority from an "uncritical or critical archaeological knowledge of the lists."[395]

In so doing Balthasar introduces an unhelpful hierarchical structure into the relationship between God and humanity. Balthasar is concerned to establish that the Church and the ordained ministry stand outside the secular and are not subordinated to the state,[396] but by emphasising the institutional model of the Church he seeks to control the Holy Spirit. It is the failure of the pneumatological that is the great weakness of Balthasar's ecclesiology. As a result he equates ordination to the priesthood with the reception of the *potestas* to consecrate the eucharist. Thus he understands the ordained priesthood of the Church as standing within the priestly testimony of First Testament. According to the priestly testimony both the priesthood and the monarchy in Israel are figures of power and authority. Priesthood articulates a *theologia gloriae*,[397] whereas the analogy of kenosis is one of a priestly testimony *and* countertestimony grounded in a *theologia crucis*. God's saving act in Jesus Christ redefines priesthood. Jesus Christ bears within himself both a testimony and counter-testimony to priesthood.[398] Balthasar's understanding of priesthood fails to repeat the Chalcedonian dialectic.[399] Ultimately it is unimaginative in its claims to be a naively realistic account of an objective reality.

The analogy of the priesthood of the ordained with kenosis requires that priesthood is understood within critically dialectic realism. This, together with the essential definition of priesthood through its practices and roles can, perhaps, be illustrated by reference to Canon 6 of Chacledon. The Canons covered a range of issues evident in the visible, externalised life of the Church. Canon 6 sets the pattern, which has governed ordination ever since, by insisting that there can be no such thing as absolute ordination. For an ordination to be valid the person must be ordained to a named title.[400] In so doing it analogously replicates the christological definition of the two natures by defining ordination as consisting of two equal parts. On the one hand, there is the liturgical act of ordination through prayer and the laying on of hands but, on the other hand, and equally importantly, ordination is

---

[394] *CD* IV.1, 714.
[395] *CD* IV.1, 715.
[396] Balthasar, 1986, 270.
[397] See: 150 above.
[398] See: 160-166 above.
[399] Balthasar, however, is convinced that the priesthood of the ordained is a priestly testimony. See: *TD* IV, 394; 399-400..
[400] J. Stevenson (ed), *Creeds, Councils and Controversies*, London, SPCK, 1973, 326.

embodied and externalised in the task given.[401] The two parts *together* effect ordination. If either is absent the person is not validly ordained. The asymmetry is maintained in the ontology of being the priest and the task or function to which the person is ordained. Both are essential for the distinction of the priestly character. The lay person may share the priestly task but not the liturgical ordination. There is no confusion; both lay and ordained are recognised together, but remain distinct.[402]

Paul speaks of his own ministry as a priestly counter-testimony in form of the proclamation of the gospel[403] and in so doing offers himself both to God and to the people to whom he is sent.[404] As he has responded 'in Christ' to the story so he calls upon others to join with him.[405] The counter-testimony is essentially one of self-oblation,[406] responsive to God's prior sovereign act of grace. Paul presents himself as the pioneer[407] whom others will follow. He calls on the Philippians to continue to show their identification with him in Christ by joining in this mimetic non-identical repetition.[408] Paul addresses the Philippians as those who have shared (συγκοινωνήσαντες)[409] in his troubles, and a Church which has entered into partnership (ἐκοινώνησεν)[410] with him in his task as witnessed by the interchange of gifts between them.[411]

These verses are not isolated asides but continue a theme present throughout the letter. This is both the starting point of Paul's narrative[412] and is repeated in his own story, 'For me to live is Christ, and to die is

---

[401] Schillebeeckx, London, 1985, 154.

[402] Letter XIV, Leo the Great to Anastasius, Bishop of Thessalonica, *The Nicene and Post Nicene Fathers* (Series 2), Vol XII, *Christian Classics Ethereal Library*, 2000 (CD 1003)

[403] He tells the story of Christ's saving action.

[404] Phil. 2.17; c.f. Rom. 12.1; 15.16.

[405] Phil. 3.17.

[406] Ps. 51.16, 17. (See: 175 above)

[407] 'join in imitating me' Phil. 3.17.

[408] In 3.17 Paul uses the otherwise unknown word συμμιμητησ (fellow imitator). The implication being that they are part of a tradition of non-identical repetition that extends beyond Paul and which points back to the imitation of Christ himself. It has to be recalled that this injunction falls within Paul's dialectic of identity, within the third part, in which identity is not yet but must be understood in terms of a continuing event. (See: 107 above.)

[409] Phil. 4.14.

[410] Phil. 4.15.

[411] Paul has brought them the gospel and the knowledge of God in Jesus Christ and they have given their financial support.

[412] Phil. 2.5-11. (See: 79 above.)

Priesthood and the Ordained 255

gain.'[413] The kenotic identity of Jesus Christ, 'truly God and truly man' is non-identically repeated in Paul's own account of his kenotic self-understanding. Paul combines within himself his physical and natural presence while yet participating 'in the Spirit'[414] and therefore in Christ. Thus Paul receives a new identity[415] in relation to Jesus Christ.

Barth maintains the dialectic of ministry[416] as universal but ordered. This is revealed in the divine self-revelation, which transforms humanity through the crossing of the divine-human boundaries. In crossing the divine-human boundaries neither party loses their identity but each gain from participation in the other. Priestly testimony remains, but it is to the divine sovereignty and grace. The priesthood of the ordained does not possess 'power' conferred upon it by the Church. Rather the priest represents the testimony in the imagination of the community, which lives its transformation through its essential practices and roles as those who are known and know Christ and are possessed by his righteousness.[417] It traces the divine priesthood by externalising it, being 'like', a recognisable representation, a sign pointing to the original, but not identical. Discussing preaching Barth offers a definition that could equally describe priesthood suggesting, "God is the one who makes himself heard, who speaks, and not we, who simply have the role of announcing what God wants to say."[418] Preaching is both the activity of the preacher, recognised and authorised, but it is also the activity of the Church.

---

[413] Phil 1.21. c.f. 'Even if I am to be poured out as a libation upon the sacrificial offering of your faith, I am glad and rejoice with you' (2.17); 'I count everything as loss because of the surpassing worth of knowing Christ Jesus my Lord.' (3.8; see 3.7-9.)
[414] Phil. 2.1.
[415] Phil. 1.13. Indeed famously after his conversion on the Damascus road Saul the Jewish persecutor of the Church is renamed as Paul to mark his new identity.
[416] I would add 'and priesthood' but as a Reformed theologian this word has a very limited place in his theological vocabulary.
[417] Phil. 3.8.
[418] Barth, 1991b, 46.

PART IV

Conclusion

Chapter 9

Priesthood: Tracing the Promise of God's Saving Act

In this thesis I have explored kenosis and priesthood in order to suggest that a Protestant re-evaluation of the nature of the ordained ministry is possible. However, by locating the understanding of priesthood by reference to kenosis, and in particular kenosis understood in relation to the divine identity it does have trinitarian implications. At this late stage it is I shall simply list four trinitarian implications, in terms of the divine-human encounter that are raised by my thesis. First, and fundamentally, there is the trinitarian nature of God and his relationship to creation and therefore humanity. This has particular significance for the understanding of grace. Secondly, both kenosis and priesthood ask important questions about the possibilities of interchange and mutuality and therefore the possibility of divine-human encounter. Thirdly, there is a question about the relationship between *perichoresis* and catholicity. *Perichoresis* speaks of the mutual coinherence of the three persons of the Trinity, so that none is isolated from the others. So too catholicity is concerned with the unity, the oneness of the Church. Fourthly, therefore there is the relationship between ecclesiology and the Trinity. Very briefly this will have implications for all notions of hierarchy, but also for the oneness of the Church. "If the triune God is *unam multiplex in se ipso* (John Scotus Erigena), if unity and multiplicity are equiprimal in him, then God is the ground of both unity and multiplicity."[1] Furthermore some Protestant theology has suggested that the basis for ecclesiology is located in a covenant with God rather than the Trinity and the divine *missio*.

However there are, I suggest, four further trinitarian implications of my thesis in terms of the human-divine engagement. First, the failure of the nineteenth century accounts of both kenosis and priesthood is at least in part a consequence of their narrowly christological basis and their failure to recognize the importance of the Trinity. Secondly, that vocation is above all an event of trinitarian *missio*.[2] To speak of vocation as a divine calling is

---

[1] Miroslav Volf, *The Church as the Image of the Trinity*, Grand Rapids, Eerdmans,1998, 193.
[2] Balthasar hints at this when he suggests that human being while being endowed with 'infinite freedom' is only her or himself when they accept their role as 'God's partner'. (*TD* II. 335.) Kenotically understood vocation becomes an event of self-giving, self-

implicit of a notion of the Trinity as the key to any divine-human participation. Consequently if "Christian initiation is a trinitarian event, then the church must speak of the Trinity as its determining reality."[3] Thirdly, it is the Trinity, which as the basis of the divine self-revelation and therefore its knowability, within which priesthood exists through leading worship as the appropriate human response. Finally therefore, as I suggested at the very start of my thesis the fundamental concern of theology is the question of salvation. Kenosis and priesthood are both rightly concerned with salvation asking: "how [does] the vision of the triune God's coming into the world of sin ought to inform the way in which we live in a world suffused with deception, injustice and violence."[4]

Furthermore, my thesis as well as raising a number of trinitarian implications also has christological implications. This is evident, following Barth, in the emphasis I have placed upon the Chalcedonian pattern in which Christ is both 'truly God and truly man.' Most notably there is the pattern of the divine-human participation without confusion. Secondly, this has implications for the understanding of the *communicatio idiomatum*. Thirdly, the trinitarian emphasis questions the "tradition of causal effect in the history of the Church between the events of the life of Jesus"[5] and the nature of the ordained ministry. Finally, this has implications for the christological and the *imago dei*.

Acknowledging these trinitarian and christological implications I shall conclude this narrative by imaginatively[6] attempting to draw together a series of a strands, which have emerged from my thesis in order to trace a picture of priesthood.

Identity and Recognition

Kenosis, as it is traditionally espoused, misunderstands the identity of Jesus Christ and therefore the nature of the divine-human relationship. It was important to establish an understanding of kenosis as an intra-trinitarian event by which God in his sovereignty reveals himself as an event of grace. In the light of which in the first part of the narrative, the study of kenosis

---

emptying in which there exists 'a community constituted by differences which desire' each other so that *missio* exists within the 'amatory desire' of the *processio*. (Graham Ward, 'Kenosis and naming: beyond analogy and towards allegoria amoris', Paul Heelas and David Martin, *Religion, Modernity and Postmodernity*, Oxford, Blackwells, 1998, 242.)

[3] Volf, 1998, 195.

[4] Volf, 1998, 6.

[5] Robin Greenwood, *Transforming Priesthood*, London, SPCK, 1994, 87.

[6] Robert P. Scharlemann, *The Reason of Following*, Chicago, The University of Chicago Press, 1991, 92.

provided the fundamental analogy for priesthood. This brought to the fore the importance of identity as recognition, which requires that an identity can be maintained across both time and location. Kenosis is the revelation of God in Jesus Christ and a 'progression towards externality' in which God, who is other and otherwise unknowable, is revealed and therefore becomes knowable. The progression "towards human externality"[7] is evident in the language of the *carmen Christi*. This raises the key notions of 'form' and 'likeness' in relation to an understanding of identity which is fluid but unconfused and so recognisable.

The 'progression towards externality' is sacramental,[8] in which the truth of the form is made visible and is portrayed as 'being like' the other but not identical to it. Priesthood, I have argued, traces the divine-human encounter. It announces that Jesus Christ has effected atonement in his death and resurrection and the divine-human boundaries have been crossed. This is the narrative embodied and so made visible by priesthood. Priesthood is an attribute of Jesus Christ that is non-identically repeated by man (Philippians 2.5); it is only ever represented or signified but never truly present.[9]

Importantly, kenosis is a public event, which proclaims God's presence in and to his creation. The *carmen Christi* is an account of the vocation of Jesus Christ, the second person of the Trinity, who is both 'truly God and truly man.' It serves to establish by making him recognizable, his true character. Ordination is a similarly public event and an act of externalization.[10] The language of priesthood signifies the ministry of the

---

[7] Graham Ward, 'Kenosis: Death, Discourse and Resurrection' in Lucy Gardiner, B. Quash, G. Ward, *Balthasar at the End of Modernity*, Edinburgh, T & T Clark, 1999, 23. See: 98, n. 149 above.

[8] A sacrament is 'an outward and visible sign of an inward and spiritual grace.' (The Catechism, *The Book of Common Prayer*) I have not included any analysis of sacramental theology in my thesis. This is deliberate. First most Protestant theology speaks of there being just two sacraments, baptism and the eucharist. Secondly, therefore, to introduce a notion of sacramentality into the discussion of priesthood can cloud the issue. Pannenberg discussing the sacraments (baptism and the Lord's Supper) speaks of them as participatory, 'fellowship [κοινωνία?] of individuals with Jesus Christ' They are 'significatory acts, "signs of the nearness of God"' and representative of 'the future consummation of the church's fellowship' (*Syst* III, 238). Augustine partly discusses the notion of sign and signification in his discussion of sacrifice. Accordingly the 'visible sacrifice is the sacrament, the sacred sign, of the invisible sacrifice.' According to Augustine sacrificial countertestimony becomes the testimony. The outward sacrificial act is effective insofar as it enacts the inner truth. (*City of God*, X.5) In other words, sacraments externalise by unveiling the presence of the divine.

[9] See: 218-19., 221-22., 230 above.

[10] Edward Schillebeeckx, *The Church with a Human Face* (ET), London, SCM, 1985, 154-156.

ordained and is appropriate, just as it is for the people of God's covenant, bringing together vocation and sacrifice. Vocation, understood within the framework of narrative identity, is to know where one stands, within the stories in which one finds oneself a participant. It therefore takes its shape from the divine-human drama.[11] For both Barth and Balthasar these are public experiences that take place in and through the Church. It is therefore appropriate that eucharistic presidency is associated with the role of the ordained.[12] The ordained are those who are identified and recognized by the Church as being called by God. Their standing within the apostolic tradition is not guaranteed by the objectivity of the office, but is evident in their faithful witness to Jesus Christ through the proclamation of the gospel as received and handed from the apostles, in other words in their essential practices and roles. Human 'externality manifests the essential nature of the Church as the visible presence of Christ.'[13]

Priesthood is an important concept and analogous of Christ's saving act bridging the divine-human *diastasis*. Its dismissal by Protestant theology because of its cultic overtones or for reasons of complexity[14] is both unconvincing and impoverishes the tradition. Indeed tradition is itself significant as being part of a dialectic of the inward and the external, by which the recognizable outward and visible character traits embody the inward and otherwise invisible beliefs of the community.[15] Indeed, as I have just outlined priesthood, it is a missionary concept called to proclaim the divine *missio* and to call forth a human response. Its importance lies in its witness to the fluidity of identity and the needful crossing of the divine-human boundaries, which are at the heart of salvation and represented by priesthood. If God is not an empty abstraction it is imperative that there is the possibility of divine-human participation. However, such participation cannot result in the eradication of the divine-human *diastasis* through the dissolution of the necessary dialectic, which governs the divine-human relationship. This would be contrary to the fundamental Chalcedonian pattern and would result in the loss of both the divine and human identities. Priesthood, understood as counter-testimony, witnesses to the divine

---

[11] Balthasar understands vocation in terms of role and personhood within the Theodrama in terms of mission (see: 115-6 above.) or as Barth suggests in the encounter between God and humanity. (See: 134 above.)

[12] This is not dependent upon any *potestas* given through ordination nor upon the nature of the office as inherited from the apostles.

[13] Graham Ward, quoted, see: 236 above.

[14] See: 177 above.

[15] Stephen Sykes, *The Identity of Christianity*, Philadelphia, Fortress Press, 1984, 232. According to Sykes whereas the Roman Catholic emphasis upon tradition betokens externality, Protestantism through its emphasis upon the Word and 'doctrinal orthodoxy' (Sykes, 1984, 233.) is essentially inwardly focused.

testimony of the priesthood of Christ. The priesthood of the ordained is mimetic of the priesthood of Christ, in so far as it is repetitious, but non-identically so, repeating[16] but not the same as the priesthood of Christ.[17] Because it is mimetic it copies the prior priesthood of Jesus Christ, which is indicative of the sovereignty of God and his prevenient grace. The priesthood of the ordained is part of an unresolved dialectic, in which it exists metaphorically, by saying 'more than what is actual' by encompassing the familiar and the strange.[18] It proclaims that which it is not, but yet by which it is recognizable. The priesthood of the ordained is a testimony to the priestly testimony of Christ and a counter-testimony because of what it is not.[19]

Kenosis articulates the veiling and unveiling of the divine in Jesus Christ. By analogy priesthood does not effect the crossing of the divine-human boundaries but represents by analogy the veiling and unveiling of the presence of the divine through the crossing of the boundaries in Jesus Christ.

Character and Diversity

The middle part of the narrative[20] focused upon the methodological, primarily by reference to the Chalcedonian pattern of the two natures and the consequent dialectic. This was then examined in Part III of this thesis. In Chapter 7 I suggested that the failure of both Protestant and Catholic theologians to agree a common understanding of priesthood was an inevitable result of attempting to understand priesthood propositionally. What has emerged is that priesthood exists in two primary dialectics, which are the Chalcedonian pattern and the priestly testimonies and counter-testimonies evident in the Bible. These are underlined by a series of lesser dialectics. First there is the ontological and functional.[21] Secondly there is the dialectic of identity 'in Christ' as non-identical 'Christ likeness'. Thirdly there is grace which is a divinely sovereign event and to which gratitude is the appropriate human response. Finally there is the tension between order and charismatic freedom.

---

[16] A copy is always a likeness, similar but not the same as the original it seeks to repeat.

[17] See: 222-23 above.

[18] See: 199-200 above, drawing upon the work of Eberhard Jüngel, 'Metaphorical Truth', *Theological Essays* I (ET), Edinburgh, T & T Clark, 1989, 17, 57, 68.

[19] A Biblical example of one who is but yet is not might be John the Baptist (Jn 1.19-34).

[20] Part II.

[21] Ordination is effected by a combination of prayer and the laying on of hands and being licensed to serve a title.

The failure of the traditional Protestant account of priesthood is in part hermeneutical. In the First Testament account there is clear evidence of the parallel existence of both a priestly testimony and counter-testimony. Furthermore this pattern is maintained in the person and work of Jesus in the Second Testament. In the First, priesthood is both a testimony to the presence of God and the right ordering of God's covenant people[22] and also a counter-testimony, calling for the self-oblation and kenotic re-identification of the worshipper as a member of God's covenant people.[23] Jesus' priesthood according to the Second Testament is both real and effective. It is not simply a metaphor exploring the meaning of Christ's atoning and expiatory death upon the cross.[24] And at the same time Jesus is a priestly counter-testimony enacted in his life of perfect obedience to his heavenly Father.[25]

Ordination requires that there is both prayer and the laying on of hands and also title and license. Therefore I drew attention[26] to the definition of valid ordination according to Canon 6 of the Council of Chalcedon, which repeats non-identically the Christological pattern of the definition, in condemning absolute consecration as invalid. Ordination "is an appointment or 'incorporation' as minister to a community".[27] It combines both the ontological liturgical event with the function of license and task. It is incarnational insofar as it externalizes and embodies the internal truth. Therefore Canon 13 of the Chalcedonian Canons forbids "Foreign clerics and those who are unknown",[28] in other words those clergy who are not recognizable by or identified with the community from performing divine service.

To speak of identity 'in Christ' is essentially dialectical. This emerged in the study of Philippians and Paul's call to be Christ like.[29] It is representative association with Christ that constitutes selfhood.[30] In Balthasar's language, personhood is constituted in the engagement with the divine mission in Christ.[31] But to be 'in Christ' is not the same as being identical with Christ. So the priesthood of the ordained is meaningful only in the experience of the priesthood of Christ; nonetheless it can only ever be 'like' but never the 'same as'.

---

[22] See: 148-151 above.
[23] See: 151-54 above.
[24] See: 160 above.
[25] Phil. 2.5-11.
[26] See: 251-52 above.
[27] Schillebeeckx, 1985, 154.
[28] J. Stevenson (ed), *Creeds Councils and Controversies*, London, SPCK, 1973, 328.
[29] Phil. 2.5: also 1.27; 2.1-2; 3.9-10, 17, 21.
[30] David Ford quoted: 84 n. 55 above.
[31] See: 109-110 above.

Grace is a divinely sovereign event, to which praise is the human response.[32] Both grace and praise or gratitude are closely interwoven. Grace is divine, primary and sovereign. Praise is always responsive, secondary and is never sovereign or initiatory. Priesthood articulates gratitude and is the subjective response to the objective divine sovereignty of grace.

Finally there is the tension between order on the one hand and charismatic freedom on the other. This is evident in the tension between Balthasar's emphasis upon office[33] and Moltmann's pneumatic model.[34]

A further important element in the narrative is characterisation. Priesthood can refer both to 'the priesthood of all believers' and the 'ordained' as well as Christ. First, its characterisation must encompass all within the family likeness.[35] So the mimetic economy of 1 Peter 2 identifies a family likeness in the Church as God's covenant and priestly people, defined in relation to Jesus Christ.[36] Secondly, the application of priestly language to the Christian ministers and ministry in the Second Testament is more extensive than is usually allowed. It is Barth's emphasis upon the particularism of biblical texts which draws attention to how Paul uses the language of priesthood, both of his own ministry and that of his fellow workers.[37] This suggests some notion of a likeness between the Christian ministry and the priestly testimony and counter-testimony of the First Testament.

Protestants have repeatedly stumbled over the question of sacrifice as a fundamental aspect of the characterisation of priesthood.[38] Traditionally the weakness of most theologies of priesthood has been the need to establish meaningful and effective sacrifice, which has tended to result in doctrines of an expiatory or propitiatory priesthood. Such theories have failed to maintain the precedence of divine sovereignty and grace. What I have sought to establish is a concept of non-pernicious sacrifice as 'giving grateful thanks' in response to God's prevenient grace.[39] Sacrifice becomes a counter-testimony[40] and an act of identification in the recognition of the

---

[32] See: 132 above.

[33] See: 113-14 above.

[34] See: 122, 124 above.

[35] See: 207 above.

[36] See: 139-145 above.

[37] For example of Paul's own ministry (see: 85 above) and Epaphroditus (Phil 2.25, 30: See: 86 above).

[38] See: 166, n. 145 above.

[39] See: 166-67 above.

[40] See: 227 above. The handing over of the bread and the wine, but also the self at the eucharist is supremely a moment of enrichment. In the earlier discussion of handing over in the work of Balthasar and Vanstone, where handing over is indicative of being placed in good hands, obedience to vocation speaks of Christ's atoning work. (See: 59 n 69 above.) Similarly Moltmann emphasises the Trinitarian structure of the handing over

self's dependence upon the generosity of the other. It is the external sign of boundaries that have been transcended and of right order revealed.[41] One such example explored was the generosity of the Philippian Church in their sacrificial support of Paul.[42]

Thirdly the characterisation of priesthood is non-identical in its repetition as it traces the priesthood of Christ. It is asymmetrically non-identical because it can only respond to the precedence of sovereignty and grace as a divine initiative.[43] This repeats the Chalcedonian pattern, in which God and man co-exist asymmetrically.[44] If Christ's atoning role presents God *pro nobis*, priesthood is a statement of humanity *ad deum*.[45] So Paul deliberately reverses the order of the words associated with representation[46] in Philippians 2.5-11 when applying them to the Philippians,[47] suggesting their identity reflects asymmetrically the form of Christ.[48] The call to the *imitatio Christi* is not a call to be the 'same as' but to be 'like' or recognizable in the image of Christ who is known in the man Jesus. In speaking of exemplarism there is no intention to suggest that the act of imitation is ever salvific.[49] The enactment of the interchange of gifts is the recognition of salvation, received and participated in, through the responsive re-ordering of lives. Jesus Christ is the pioneer of redeemed humanity.[50] Humanity is called to follow. So Paul's ministry, sometimes described using priestly language, is also pioneering. He too offers himself as a public model of Christian living. In this Paul simply replicates the original, inviting others to join him in becoming God's covenant partners.[51] But a copy is never the same as the original and therefore always non-

---

of Jesus in his atoning death. (See: 68 above.) In this moment of kenotic re-identification the person receives a new name in relation to Christ. It therefore repeats, but non-identically the climax of the *carmen Christi* when after the 'descent from a logic of identity into a world of shifting appearances... there is a return to the logic of identity' (Ward, Gardiner *et al*, 1999, 23: quoted: 98. n149 above.) which culminates in the moment of renaming. So too 'the kenosis of radical discipleship' is ultimately one in which the person is renamed 'in Christ.' Handing oneself over is not an event of self-negation but the recovery of the self in obedience to the divine Word.

[41] See: 171 above.
[42] See: 89 above.
[43] See: 168 above.
[44] See: 204 above.
[45] See: 174 above.
[46] Ward, 1999, 23. (See: 95 n. 149 above.)
[47] Phil. 3.21.
[48] A mirror image is asymmetrically repetitious. An obvious if childish example would be mirror writing, which is only readable when reflected in a mirror.
[49] See: 214 above.
[50] Heb. 2.10; 12.2. (See: 159 above.)
[51] Phil. 2.17; 3.2-11; 3.17. They are to be 'like' Paul in being 'Christlike'.

identical, and because it is a reflection it is asymmetrical. Thus the dialectic of the Chalcedonian pattern is maintained. There is participation between the divine and human but both retain their essential character identities, without confusion, each recognizable and nameable to the other though not to the same degree.

The Eucharist, Sacrifice and Externalisation

In the final part the key lies in the Eucharist as story, gift and response.[52] This narrative attempt to trace priesthood could itself be understood as an exercise in story,[53] gift[54] and response.[55] In this final section I shall now attempt to trace a fourfold priestly response externalised in a series of practices and roles, and supremely the eucharist.

First, the response is liturgical.[56] The eucharist is an event of mutual interchange raising two issues concerning the nature of representation and participation. The eucharist enacts an account of Christian identity as being named in relation to Christ.[57] The story is an event of the Word, retelling God's saving acts. The gift is first and foremost the gift of God who in Christ gives himself *pro nobis*. Only secondly is there the gift of the bread and the wine, which though re-identified by the story do not cease to exist.[58] This externalizes the asymmetrical nature of the divine-human relationship through the eucharist. On the one hand, the 'once for all' nature of the event of Christ's atoning death and resurrection is proclaimed as a priestly event, in which boundaries are crossed and right order between God and creation enunciated. On the other, the priest leads the Church in its kenotic re-identification of responsive self-oblation.

Secondly, the response of the priesthood of the ordained is the ordering of the Church. Ordination combines the ontological events of prayer and the laying on of hands, and the functional giving of the ministerial task through appointment to a title. The one who is ordained is acknowledged to be

---

[52] See: 224 above.

[53] Kenosis is the fundamental metanarrative which tells the story of God in Jesus Christ as a priestly event *pro nobis*.

[54] The Chalcedonian pattern and the ensuing dialectic are the gift which enable *koinonia* or participation such that neither God nor humanity are dissolved into another but each retains their own integrity in relation to the other.

[55] Therefore praise and gratitude become the human response to the prior event of God's grace.

[56] 'What is the chief end of man? To glorify God and enjoy Him for ever.' (*The Shorter Westminster Catechism*)

[57] *Syst.* III, 307-08.

[58] The bread and wine remain but they signify the presence of Christ but without the essential human-divine *diastasis* being eradicated. The divine-human dialectic is thereby maintained.

publicly representative of the Church. They are therefore the appropriate one to preside at the eucharist.[59] They externalize and represent the body of the ordained by their participation in the priesthood of both Jesus Christ but also of the Church in its self-identifying roles and practices. This is not a vicarious representation, but a summative one. The priest manifests[60] both the testimony and counter-testimony by which God's saving grace is made visible. Indeed salvation is itself a statement of the right ordering of God and creation. Disorder "is wrong, not merely as participation in chaos, but as the dissolution of form".[61] The Church as the 'body of Christ' is the visible externalized form[62] of the promised presence of the divine, in which the Word is spoken and heard.

Thirdly, priesthood is the response to atonement wherein life is re-ordered. The priesthood of the ordained does not effect atonement, which is an event of sovereign divine grace. Atonement gains its significance from the resurrection, not simply as an historic event but is eschatological being concerned with vindication and renewal.[63] The resurrection is the key to the revealed identity of Jesus Christ. But at the resurrection it is Jesus who finds the disciples, not vice versa,[64] in a sovereign act of self-revelation to which they can only respond.[65] If vocation is a call to 'the kenosis of radical discipleship,' priesthood is the externalization of kenosis not as a pernicious sacrifice but as resurrection πληρόω. It announces that the divine-human *diastasis* has been overcome, 'God and man at table are sat down';[66] both retain their identity but yet each can participate in the other. It does not dissolve the *diastasis* but it demonstrates the Chalcedonian pattern whereby it is possible for the truly divine and the truly human to encounter one another, without confusion.

Finally, therefore, the response of the ordained priesthood is to fulfil the vocation to be a pioneer ministry, by embodying the Christian identity. The priest is identified as being 'Christ like.' Stanley Hauerwas suggests that Protestants, in demoting the "sacerdotal functions of the ministry" have emphasized the expectation that clergy will "conform to an

---

[59] Jürgen Moltmann, *The Church in the Power of the Spirit* (ET), London, SCM, 1977, 260.
[60] To manifest is necessarily part of a 'progression towards externalisation.'
[61] *CD* IV.2, 677.
[62] *CD* IV.2, 719.
[63] See: 202-203 above.
[64] *CD* IV.2, 144.
[65] *CD* IV.2, 144. In Moltmann's words, the 'resurrection expresses the significance of the cross.' (Jürgen Moltmann, *The Crucified God* (ET), London, SCM, 1974, 182.)
[66] 'God and man at table are sat down', (67 SLW), *Combined Sounds of Living Waters and Fresh Sounds*, London, Hodder and Stoughton, 1980.

uncompromising moral ideal."[67] But priesthood is not to be equated with the self-justifying moral life. Priesthood must offer a counter-testimony to a *theologia gloriae* by announcing that humanity is simply human and God is God. The encounter between the human and the divine is possible only in the sacrifice of a *theologia crucis* where all boundaries are crossed and new lives not only announced, but enacted in the essential practices and roles that identify those whose lives have been transformed. At the beginning[68] of my thesis, drawing upon Eberhard Jüngel's study of justification, I argued that the fundamental concern of theology is the question of salvation. Jüngel contends that justification concerns both the "identity of God and of the creatures of God."[69] Towards the end of his essay Jüngel suggests that the consequence of justification for the vital practices and roles[70] is the recognition that believers, though never sure of themselves are "sure of God and his grace".[71] Quoting Luther, he states that believers do "not become righteous by doing righteous deeds but, having been made righteous, we do righteous deeds."[72] Priesthood understood within this framework bears witness to the re-establishment of right order, which it traces by non-identically repeating the example of Christ. As such it offers a trace of the presence of God and charts a pilgrimage in which it calls others to participate in a journey of discipleship. Priesthood unveils and externalizes a way of life.

---

[67] Stanley Hauerwas, 'Clerical Character', *Christian Existence Today*, Grand Rapids, Brazos Press, 2001, 133.
[68] See: 29 above.
[69] John Webster in the 'Introduction', Eberhard Jüngel, *Justification* (ET), Edinburgh, T & T Clark, 2001, viii.
[70] Hart, 2000, 194 (quoted: 228 above).
[71] Jüngel, 2001, 246.
[72] Jüngel, 2001, 247.

Bibliography

Achtemeier, Paul J., *1 Peter*, Minneapolis, Augsburg Fortress, 1996
Alexander, Loveday, 'Helenistic Letter Forms and the Structure of Philippians', *JSNT* (37), 1989, 87-101
Altizer, Thomas J. J., *The Gospel of Christian Atheism*, London, Collins, 1967
Altizer, Thomas J. J. and Hamilton, William, *Radical Theology and the Death of God*, London, Pelican, 1968
Anderson, A. A., *Psalms* (Vol. 1), London, Marshall Morgan and Scott, 1977a - *Psalms* (Vol. 2), London, Marshall Morgan and Scott, 1977b
Anglican-Lutheran Dialogue, The Report of the European Commission, London, SPCK, 1983
The Report of the Anglican-Reformed International Commission, *God's Reign & Our Unity*, London, SPCK, 1984
Aquinas, St Thomas, *Summa Theologiciae*, (Vol. 3), *Knowing and Naming God*, (ET), London, Eyre & Spottiswode, 1963
ARCIC, *The Final Report*, London, CTS/SPCK, 1981
Aristotle, *Poetics* (ET), London, Penguin, 1996
Augustine, *City of God*, London, Penguin, 1972
- *The Trinity*, (ET), NY, New City Press, 1991
- *The Confessions of St Augustine* (ET), London, Hodder and Stoughton, 1997
Auerbach, Erich, *Mimesis: The Representation of Reality in Western Literature*, Princeton, Princeton University Press, 1974
Badcock, Gary, *The Way of Life*, Grand Rapids, Eerdmans, 1998
Balthasar, Hans Urs von, *A Theology of History* (ET), London, Sheed and Ward, 1963
- *A Theological Anthropology* (ET), New York, Sheed and Ward, 1967
- *The Theology of Karl Barth* (ET), New York, Holt, Rinehart and Winston, 1971
- *The Christian State of Life* (ET), San Francisco, Ignatius Press, 1983
- *The Glory of the Lord*, Studies in Theological Style: Clerical Styles (ET, Vol. II), Edinburgh, T & T Clark, 1984
- *The Office of Peter and the Structure of the Church* (ET), San Francisco, Ignatius Press, 1986
- *Theo-Drama, Prologomena* (ET Vol. I), San Francisco, Ignatius Press, 1988
- *Theo-Drama, Dramatis Personae: Man in God,* (ET Vol. II), San Francisco, Ignatius Press, 1990a
- *Mysterium Paschale* (ET), Edinburgh, T & T Clark, 1990b
- *The Glory of the Lord* (Vol. VI), *Theology of the Old Covenant* (ET), Edinburgh, T & T Clark, 1991a
- *Explorations in Theology II*, (ET) San Francisco, Ignatius Press, 1991b
- *Theo-Drama, Dramatis Personae: Persons in Christ* (ET Vol. III), San Francisco, Ignatius Press, 1992
- *Theo-Drama, The Action* (ET Vol. IV), San Francisco, Ignatius Press, 1994

- *Theo-Drama, The Last Act* (ET Vol. V), San Francisco, Ignatius Press, 1998
Barker, Margaret, *The Gate of Heaven*, London, SPCK, 1991
- *On Heaven as It Is in Heaven*, Edinburgh, T & T Clark, 1995
Barnett, James M., *The Diaconate*, New York, Seabury Press, 1981
Barnett, Paul, *The Second Epistle To The Philippians*, Grand Rapids, Eerdmans, 1997
Barrett, C. K., *The First Epistle to the Corinthians*, London, A & C Black, 1971
- *The Second Epistle to the Corinthians*, London, A & C Black, 1973
Barth, Karl, *The Word of God and the Word of Man* (ET), London, Hodder and Stoughton, 1935
- *The Epistle to the Romans* (6th Edn, ET), London, OUP, 1957
- *Church Dogmatics* (ET, Vol. I.1) Edinburgh, T & T Clark, 1963
- *Church Dogmatics* (ET, Vol. I.2) Edinburgh, T & T Clark, 1963
- *Church Dogmatics* (ET, Vol. II.1) Edinburgh, T & T Clark, 1964
- *Church Dogmatics* (ET, Vol. II.2) Edinburgh, T & T Clark, 1957
- *Church Dogmatics* (ET, Vol. III.1) Edinburgh, T & T Clark, 1958
- *Church Dogmatics* (ET, Vol. III.2) Edinburgh, T & T Clark, 1960
- *Church Dogmatics* (ET, Vol. III.3) Edinburgh, T & T Clark, 1961
- *Church Dogmatics* (ET, Vol. IV.1) Edinburgh, T & T Clark, 1956
- *Church Dogmatics* (ET, Vol. IV.2) Edinburgh, T & T Clark, 1958
- *Church Dogmatics* (ET, Vol. IV.3i) Edinburgh, T & T Clark, 1961
- *Church Dogmatics* (ET, Vol. IV.3ii) Edinburgh, T & T Clark, 1962
- *Church Dogmatics* (ET, Vol. IV.4) Edinburgh, T & T Clark, 1969
- *The Faith of the Church* (ET), London, Fontana, 1960
- *The Epistle to the Philippians* (ET), London, SCM, 1962
- *Theology and the Church* (ET), London, SCM, 1962
- *Evangelical Theology* (ET), New York, Holt Rinehart and Winston, 1963
- *The Christian Life* (ET), Edinburgh, T & T Clark, 1981
- *The Humanity of God* (ET), Atlanta, John Knox Press, 1982
- *The Göttingen Dogmatics* (Vol. 1; ET), Grand Rapids, Eerdmans, 1991a
- *Homiletics* (ET), Louisville, Westminster/John Knox Press, 1991b
- *Protestant Theology in the Nineteenth Century* (ET), London, SCM, 2001
Bartholomew, Craig, Geene, Colin, Möller, Karl (eds), *Renewing Biblical Interpretation*, Carlisle, Paternoster, 2001
- *After Pentecost Language and Biblical Interpretation*, Carlisle, Paternoster, 2001
Barton. Stephen C., 'New Testament Interpretation as Performance', *SJT*, 52 (1999), 179-208
Barton, John, (ed), *The Cambridge Companion to Biblical Interpretation*, Cambridge, CUP, 1998
Bash, Anthony, *Ambassadors for Christ*, Tubingen, J C B Mohr, 1997
Bauckham, Richard J., *Moltmann: Messianic Theology in the Making*, Basingstoke, Marshall Morgan and Scott, 1987
- *The Theology of Jürgen Moltmann*, Edinburgh, T & T Clark, 1995
- *God Crucified, Monotheism and Christology in the New Testament*, Carlisle, Paternoster, 1998

- 'The Worship of Jesus in Philippians 2.9-11', Ralph P. Martin, Brian J. Dodd (ed), *Where Christology Began*, Louisville, Westminster John Knox Press, 1998
Baxter, Christina, 'The Christian Ministry, J B Lightfoot', *Anvil* (7), 1990, 247-251
Beare, F. W., *A Commentary on the Epistle to the Philippians*, London, A & C Black, 1959
Beckwith, Roger T. and Selman, Martin J. (ed), *Sacrifice in the Bible*, Carlisle, Paternoster, 1995
Berkhof, Louis, *Systematic Theology*, Edinburgh, Banner of Truth, 1984,
Berkouwer, G. C., *The Triumph of Grace In The Theology of Karl Barth* (ET), London, Paternoster, 1956
Best, Ernest, *1 Peter*, London, Oliphants, 1977
Bettenson, Henry (ed), *Documents of the Christian Church* (2nd Edn), Oxford, OUP, 1975
Blenkinsopp, Joseph, *Sage, Priest, Prophet*, Louisville, Westminster John Knox Press, 1995
Bloomquist, L. Gregory, *The Function of Suffering in Philippians*, Sheffield, JSNTS, Sheffield Academic Press, 1993
Bockmuehl, Marcus, 'A Commentator's Approach to the 'Effective History' of Philippians', JSNT (60), 1995, 57-88
- *The Epistle to the Philippians* (4th Edn), London, A & C Black, 1997
Bonhoeffer, Dietrich, *The Cost of Discipleship* (ET), London, SCM, 1976
- *Letters and Papers From Prison* (ET), London, SCM, 1979
- *Ethics* (ET), London, SCM, 1985
- *The Way to Freedom* (ET), London, Fontana, 1972
The Book of Common Prayer
Booth, Gordon, 'The Fruits of Sacrifice: Sigmund Freud and William Robertson Smith', *The Expository Times* (113), 2002, 258-264
Bosch, David J., *Transforming Mission*, New York, Orbis Books, 1991
Bradley, Ian, *The Power of Sacrifice*, London, DLT, 1995
Bradshaw, Paul, *Liturgical Presidency in the Early Church*, Bramcote, Grove Books, 1983
Bradshaw, Timothy, *The Olive Branch*, Carlisle, Paternoster, 1992
Briggs, Richard S., 'Getting Involved: Speech Acts and Biblical Interpretation' *Anvil* (20), 2003, 25-34
Bromiley, Geoffrey W., *Introduction to the Theology of Karl Barth*, Edinburgh, T & T Clark, 1979
Brown, David, *The Divine Trinity*, London, Duckworth, 1985
- *Tradition and Imagination*, Oxford, OUP, 1999
Bruce, F. F., *The Epistle to the Hebrews*, Eerdmans, Grand Rapids, 1979
Brueggeman, Walter, *Texts under Negotiation, The Bible and Postmodern Imagination*, Minneapolis, Fortress Press, 1993
- *Theology of the Old Testament*, Minneapolis, Fortress Press, 'Covenanting as Human Vocation', Interpretation (33), 1979, 115-129
Buchanan, Colin (ed), *Essays on Eucharistic Sacrifice in the Early Church*,

Bramcote, Grove Books, 1984
Bulley, Colin, *The Priesthood of Some Believers*, Carlisle, Paternoster, 2000
Burridge, Richard A., *What are the Gospels?* Cambridge, CUP, 1995
Butin, Phil, 'Two Early Reformed Catechisms, The Threefold Office, And The Shape Of Karl Barth's Christology', SJT (44), 1991, 195-214
Butler, Judith, *Subjects of Desire* (Paperback Edn), New York, Columbia University Press, 1999
Butterfield, Herbert, *Christianity And History*, London, G Bell and Sons Ltd., 1949
Butterworth, G. W., *Origen on First Principles*, London, SPCK, 1936
Calvin, J., *Institutes of Christian Religion*, (John T McNeill (ed)), The Library of Christian Classics, Philadelphia, The Westminster Press, 1960
- *The Epistles of Paul the Apostle to the Galatians, Ephesians, Philippians and Colossians*, (tr. T H L Parker), Carlisle, Paternoster, 1996
von Campenhausen, Hans, *Ecclesiastical Authority and Spiritual Power in the Church of the First Three Centuries* (ET), Peabody (Mass), Hendrickson, 1997
le Carré, John, *Tinker, Tailor, Soldier, Spy*, London, Hodder and Stoughton, 1974
Carroll, Lewis, *Alice in Wonderland*, and *Alice through the Looking Glass*, London, Collins, 1954
Charry, Ellen T., *By the Renewing of Your Minds*, Oxford, OUP, 1997
Chia, Roland, 'Theological Aesthetics Or Aesthetic Theology?' *SJT*, 49, 1996, 75-95
Chilton, Bruce, *The Temple of Jesus*, Pennsylvania, The Pennsylvania State University Press, 1992
Christiansen, Ellen Juhl, *The Covenant in Judaism and Paul*, Leiden, E J Brill, 1995
Clark, Mary T. (ed), *An Aquinas Reader*, London, Hodder and Stoughton, 1972
Augustine, London, Geoffrey Chapman, 1996
Clutterbuck, Richard, 'Jürgen Moltmann As A Doctrinal Theologian: The Nature Of Doctrine And The Possibilities For Its Development', *SJT* (48), 1995, 489-505
Coakley, Sarah, 'Creaturehood before God', *Theology*, (XCIII), 1990, 343-354
- 'Kenosis and Subversion' in D. Hampson (ed), *Swallowing a Fishbone?* London, SPCK, 1996, 82-111
Cocksworth, Christopher and Brown, Rosalind, *Being A Priest Today*, Norwich, Canterbury Press, 2002
Collange, Jean-François, *The Epistle Of Saint Paul To The Philippians* (ET), London, Epworth, 1979
Congar, Yves, *Lay People in the Church*, Geoffrey Chapman, London, 1965
Countryman, L. William, *The Language of Ordination*, Philadelphia, Trinity Press International, 1992
Cranfield, C. E. B., *The Gospel according to St Mark*, Cambridge, CUP, 1974
Cranmer, Thomas, (John Cox (ed), *The Writings and Disputations of Thomas Cranmer Archbishop and Martyr, 1556, Relative to the Sacrament of the*

Lord's Supper, Cambridge, The Parker Society, 1844,
Cross, Brenda, 'The Christology of Bishop Frank Weston', Theology (LXXIV), 387-391
Crouzel Henri, *Origen* (ET), Edinburgh, T & T Clark, 1989
Cuming, Geoffrey, *Hippolytus: A Text for Students*, Bramcote, Grove Books, 1979
- *Essays on Hippolytus*, Bramcote, Grove Books, 1978
- *A History of Anglican Liturgy* (2nd Edn), London, Macmillan, 1982
Cunliffe-Jones, Hubert with Drewery, Benjamin, *A History of Christian Doctrine*, Edinburgh, T & T Clark, 1980
Cupitt, Don, 'Religion without superstition', *The Listener*, 13.9.84
Daly, Mary, *The Church and the Second Sex*, London, Geoffrey Chapman, 1968
Davids, Peter H., *The First Epistle of Peter*, Grand Rapids, Eerdmans, 1990
Davidson, Robert, *The Vitality of Worship*, Grand Rapids, Eerdmans, 1998
Davies, Oliver, 'Von Balthasar and the Problem of Being', *New Blackfriars*, Vol. 79 (923), 1997, 11-17
- *A Theology of Compassion*, London, SCM, 2001
Dawes, D. G., 'A Fresh Look at the Kenotic Christologies', *SJT*, (XV), 1962, 337-349
Deddo, Garry, 'The Grammar of Barth's Theology of Personal Relations', *SJT* (47), 1994, 183-222
Demson, David E., *Hans Frei and Karl Barth, Different Ways of Reading Scripture*, Grand Rapids, Eerdmans, 1997
Dix, Dom Gregory, *The Shape Of The Liturgy*, London, A & C Black, 1978
Drewery, Bemjamin, *Origen and the Doctrine of Grace*, London, Epworth, 1960
Dulles, Avery, *Models of the Church*, Gill and Macmillan, Dublin, 1976
- *Models of Revelation*, Gill and Macmillan, Dublin, 1983
Dunn, James D. G., *Unity and Diversity in the New Testament*, London, SCM, 1977
- *Romans 1-8*, Dallas, Word Books, 1988a
- *Romans 9-16*, Dallas, Word Books, 1988b
- *Christology in the Making* (2nd Ed), SCM, London, 1989
- *The Theology of Paul the Apostle*, Edinburgh, T & T Clark, 1998
- 'What Makes a Good Exposition', *The Expository Times*, (114), 2003, 147-157
Dunnill, John, *Covenant and sacrifice in the Letter to the Hebrews*, Cambridge, CUP, 1992
Eco, Umberto, *Kant and the Platypus* (ET), London, Vintage, 2000
Eichrodt, Walther, *The Theology of the Old Testament* (Vol. 1, ET), London, SCM, 1961
Elliott, J. H., *The Elect and the Holy: An Exegetical Examination of 1 Peter 2.4-10 and the Phrase Basíleion ieráteuma*, Novum Testamentum Supplement, Leiden, Brill, 1966
Eucharistic Presidency (GS 1248), London, Church House Publishing, 1997

Evans, Richard J., *In Defense Of History*, London, Granta Books, 2000
Faith and Order Paper (111), *Baptism, Eucharist and Ministry*, Geneva, WCC, 1982
Faith and Order Paper (153), *Confessing One Faith*, Geneva, WCC, 1999
- (?) (181), *The Nature and Purpose of the Church*, Geneva, WCC, 1998
Farrer, Austin, *Interpretation and Belief*, London, SPCK, 1976
Farrow, Douglas B., 'In the End Is The Beginning: A Review Of Jürgen Moltmann's Systematic Contributions', *Modern Theology* (14), 1998, 425-447
Fee, G. D., *Paul's Letter to the Philippians*, Grand Rapids, Eerdmans, 1995
Fiddes, Paul S., *Participating in God*, London, Dartman, Longman and Todd, 2000
Fish, Stanley, *Is There A Text In This Class?* Cambridge (Mass), Harvard University Press, 1980
Flannery, Austin, OP (ed.), *The Basic Sixteen Documents Vatican Council II: Constitutions Decrees Declarations* (Revised Translation), Dublin, Dominican Publications, 1996, 27.
Ford, David, 'Barth's interpretation of the Bible', S. W. Sykes, *Karl Barth, Studies in his Theological Method*, Oxford, Clarendon Press, 1979, 55-87
- 'What Happens At The Eucharist?' *SJT* (48), 1995, 359-381
- *Self and Salvation*, Cambridge, CUP, 1999
Forrester, Duncan, *Truthful Action, Explorations in Practical Theology*, Edinburgh, T & T Clark, 2000
Forsyth, P. T., *The Person and Place of Jesus Christ*, London, Independent Press, 1946
Fowler, James, *Becoming Adult, Becoming Christian*, San Francisco, Jossey-Bass, 2000
Franklin, R. William (ed), *Anglican Orders*, London, Mowbray, 1996
Frei, Hans, *The Identity of Jesus Christ*, Philadelphia, Fortress Press, 1975
Gardner, Lucy, Moss, David, Quash, Ben, Ward, Graham, *Balthasar at the End of Modernity*, Edinburgh, T & T Clark, 1999
Geertz, Clifford, *The Interpretation of Cultures*, New York, Basic Books Inc., 1973
Goergen, Donald J., Garrido, Ann, (ed), *The Theology Of Priesthood*, The Liturgical Press, Collegeville (Minnesota), 2000
Goldingay, John, *Models for Scripture*, Paternoster, Carlisle, 1994
- *Models for the Interpretation of Scripture*, Paternoster, Carlisle, 1995
Gorringe, Timothy, *God's Just Vengeance*, Cambridge, CUP, 1996
- *Karl Barth, Against Hegemony*, Oxford, OUP, 1999
Gore, C., *Dissertations on Subjects Connected with the Incarnation*, London, John Murray, 1895
- *The Church and the Ministry* (4th Edn), Longmans, Green and Co, London, 1900
Graham, Elaine L., 'Gender, Personhood and Theology' *SJT* (48), 1995, 341-358
Green, Garrett, *Theology, Hermeneutics, and Imagination*, Cambridge, CUP,

2000
Greene, Colin J. D., '"In the Arms of the Angels": Biblical Interpretation, Christology and the Philosophy of History', Craig Bartholomew, Colin Greene, Karl Möller (ed), *Renewing Biblical Interpretation*, Carlisle, Paternoster, 2000, 202
Greenwood, Robin, *Transforming Priesthood*, London, SPCK, 1994
Grey-Wilson, Christopher, *The Illustrated Flora of Britain and Northern Europe*, London, Hodder and Stoughton, 1989
Grillmeier, A., *Christ in Christian Tradition* (2nd Edn Rev, Vol. 1, ET), Oxford, Mowbrays, 1975
Guiver, George, (ed), *Priests in a People's Church*, SPCK, London, 2001
Gunton, Colin E., *The Actuality of Atonement*, Edinburgh, T & T Clark, 1988
- *The Cambridge Companion to Christian Doctrine*, Cambridge, CUP, 1997
- *Act and Being*, London, SCM, 2002
Gunton, Colin E., and Hardy, Daniel W., (ed), *On Being The Church*, Edinburgh, T & T Clark, 1989
Hanson, Anthony T., *The Pioneer Ministry*, London, SCM, 1961
- *Church, Sacraments and Ministry*, London, Mowbrays, 1975
Hanson, R. P. C., *Christian Priesthood Examined*, Guildford, Lutterworth, 1979
Harris, Harriet, 'Should We Say That Personhood Is Relational?' *SJT* (51), 1998, 214-234
Hart, Trevor, *Regarding Karl Barth*, Carlisle, Paternoster, 1999
- *The Dictionary of Historical Theology*, Carlisle, Paternoster, 2000
Harvey, A. E., *Priest or President?* London, SPCK, 1975
Hatch, Edwin, *The Organization of the Early Christian Churches* (2nd Edn Rev.), London, Rivingtons, 1882
Hauerwas, Stanley and Jones, L. Gregory (eds), *Why Narrative? Readings in Narrative Theology*, Grand Rapids, Eerdmans, 1989
- 'What Could It Mean For The Church To Be Christ's Body?' *SJT*, 48, 1995, 1-21
- *Christian Existence Today*, Grand Rapids, Brazo Press, 2001
- *With the Grain of the Universe*, London, SCM, 2002
Hawthorne, Gerald F., *Philippians*, Waco (Texas), Word Books, 1983
Hegel, G. W. F., *The Phenomenology of Mind* (ET 2nd Edn), London, Allen and Unwin, 1971
- *The Christian Religion, Lectures on the Philosophy of Religion Part III* (ET), Missoula (Montana), Scholars Press, 1979
Hennessey, Roger, 'Priests as Objects and Subjects: Keeping the Balance', *Theology* (CVI), 2003, 168-177.
Herbert, Tim, 'To Be or To Do: Is That the Question', *Anvil* (7), 1990, 225-40
Herrick, Vanessa and Mann, Ivan, *Jesus Wept*, London, DLT, 1998
Higton, Mike, 'Frei's Christology and Linbeck's Cultural-Linguistic Theory' *SJT* (50), 1997, 83-95
Holmstrand, Jonas, *Markers and Meaning in Paul* (ET), Stockholm, Almqvist & Wiksell International, 1997

Hooker, Morna, 'Interchange in Christ', *JTS* (22), 1971, 349-61
- *The Gospel According to St Mark*, London, A & C Black, 1997
Hooker, Richard, *Laws of Ecclesiastical Polity*, Oxford, OUP, 1890
Hoover, Roy W., 'The Harpagmos Enigma: A Philosophical Solution,' *HTR* (64), 1971, 95-119
Hort, F. J. A., *The First Epistle of St Peter I.1-II.7*, London, Macmillan and Co, 1898
Horton, John and Mendus, Susan, (ed), *After MacIntyre*, Oxford, Polity Press, 1996
Horwood, William, *The Willows in Winter*, London, HarperCollins, 1995
Houlden, J. L., *Paul's Letters from Prison*, London, SCM, 1977
Hurdado, Larry, *At the Origins of Christian Worship*, Grand Rapids, Eerdmans, 2000
Hunter, J. F. M., *Wittgenstein on Words as Instruments*, Edinburgh, Edinburgh University Press, 1990
Hurst, L. D., 'Re-Enter the Pre-Existent Christ in Philippians 2.5-11', *NTS* (32), 1986, 449-454
Hyman, Gavin, *The Predicament of Postmodern Theology*, Louisville, Westminster John Knox Press, 2001
Jinkins, Michael, '*De*-scribing The Church: Ecclesiology In Semiotic Dialogue', *SJT* (51), 1998, 188-213
Jüngel, Eberhard, *The Doctrine of the Trinity, God's Being is Becoming* (ET), Edinburgh, Scottish Academic Press, 1976
- *God as the Mystery of the World* (ET), Grand Rapids, Eerdmans, 1983
- *Karl Barth, a Theological Legacy* (ET), Philadelphia, Westminster Press, 1986
- *Theological Essays I* (ET,), Edinburgh, T & T Clark, 1989
- *Justification* (ET,), Edinburgh, T & T Clark, 2001
Kelly, J. N. D., *Early Christian Doctrines* (5th Rev. Edn), London, A & C Black, 1977
Kelsey, David H., *The Uses of Scripture in Recent Theology*, London, SCM, 1975
Kerr, Fergus, *Theology after Wittgenstein* (2nd Edn), London, SPCK, 1997
Kittel, G. and Friedrich, G. (eds), *Theological Dictionary of the New Testament* (ET), Grand Rapids, Eerdmans, 1968
Kirk, K. E., (ed), *The Apostolic Ministry*, London, Hodder and Stoughton, 1946
Küng, Hans, *The Church* (ET), Tunbridge Wells, Search Press, 1968
- *Why Priests?* (ET), London, Fontana, 1972
- *The Incarnation of God* (ET), Edinburgh, T & T Clark, 1987
- *A Theology of the New Testament*, Guildford, Lutterworth Press, 1975
Lane, William L., *Hebrews 1-8*, Waco, Word Books, 1991a
- *Hebrews 9-13*, Waco, Word Books, 1991b
Lang, U. M., 'Anhypostatos-Enhypostatos: Church Fathers, Protestant Orthodoxy And Karl Barth', *JTS* (49), 1998, 630-657
Leadbetter, Shannon, 'Vocation and our Understanding of God', *Modern Believing* (42), 2001, 39-49

Leahy, Brendan, *The Marian Profile, In the Ecclesiology of Hans Urs von Balthasar*, London, New City, 2000

Lewis, Alan E. 'Kenosis and Kerygma: The Realism and the Risk of Preaching', Trevor Hart and Daniel Thimell (ed), *Christ in our Place*, Exeter, Paternoster, 1989

Lewis, C. S., *An Experiment in Criticism*, Cambridge, CUP, 1961

Lightfoot, J. B., *St Paul's Epistle to the Philippians* (New Edn), London, Macmillan, 1879

Lincoln, Andrew T. and Wedderburn, A. J. M., *The Theology of the Later Pauline Letters*, Cambridge, CUP, 1996

Lincoln, Andrew T., *Ephesians*, Dallas, Word Books, 1990

Lindars, Barnabas, *The Theology of the Letter To The Hebrews*, Cambridge, CUP, 1991

Lindbeck, George, *The Nature of Doctrine*, Philadelphia, Westminster Press, 1984

Loades, Ann, *Searching for Lost Coins*, London, SPCK, 1978

- 'The Virgin Mary and the Feminist Quest', Janet Martin Soskice (ed), *After Eve*, London, Marshall Pickering, 1990

Loofs, Friedrich, 'Kenosis', in J Hastings (ed), *Encyclopaedia of Religion and Ethics*, (Vol. VII), T & T Clark, Edinburgh, 1914, 680-7

Lohse, Bernhard, *Martin Luther's Theology* (ET), Edinburgh, T & T Clark, 1999

Longenecker, Bruce W. (ed), *Narrative Dynamics in Paul*, Louisville, Westminster John Knox Press, 2002

Loughlin, Gerard, *Telling God's Story*, Cambridge, CUP, 1999

- 'Christianity At The End Of The Story or The Return Of The Master-Narrative', *Modern Theology* (8), 1992, 365-384

de Lubac, Henri, *Catholicism* (ET), London, Burn & Oates, 1962

Luther, M., *A Commentary on St Paul's Epistle to the Galatians*, (Middleton Edition, 1575), London, James Clarke & Co Ltd, 1953

- *Luther's Works* (Vol. 28, American Edn), Saint Louis, Concordia Publishing House, 1973

- *Luther's Works* (Vol. 36, American Edn), Philadelphia, Muhlenberg Press, 1959

- *Luther's Works* (Vol. 39, American Edn), Philadelphia, Fortress Press, 1970

- *Luther's Works* (Vol. 40, American Edn), Philadelphia, Muhlenberg Press, 1958

- *Luther's Works* (Vol. 44, American Edn), Philadelphia, Fortress Press, 1966

- *Luther: Early Theological Works* (ET, The Library of Christian Classics), London, SCM, 1962

Lyons, J. A., *The Cosmic Christ in Origen and Teilhard de Chardin*, Oxford, OUP, 1982

McCant, Jerry W., *2 Corinthians*, Sheffield, Sheffield Academic Press, 1999

McClendon, James Jr. with Kallenberg, Brad J., 'Ludwig Wittgenstein: A Christian In Philosophy', *SJT* (51), 1998, 131-161

McCormack, Bruce L., Article Review: Graham Ward's *Barth, Derrida And*

The Language of Theology', *JTS* (49), 1996
- *Karl Barth's Critically Realistic Dialectic*, Oxford, OUP, 1997
MacDonald, Dennis R., (ed), *Mimesis and Intertextuality in Antiquity and Christianity*, Harrisburg PA, Trinity Press International, 2001
MacDonald, Neil B., *Karl Barth and the Strange New World within the Bible*, Carlisle, Paternoster, 2000
McGrath, Alister E., *Reformation Thought* (2nd Edn), Oxford, Blackwell, 1993a
- *Reformation Thought* (2nd Edn), Oxford, Blackwell, 1993b
- *The Christian Theology Reader*, Oxford, Blackwells, 1995
McGregor, Bede and Norris, Thomas, *The Beauty of Christ*, Edinburgh, T & T Clark, 1994
McGinn, Marie, *Wittgenstein and the Philosophical Investigations*, London, Routledge, 1997
Mackintosh, H. R., *The Person of Jesus Christ*, Edinburgh, T & T Clark, 1912
MacIntyre, Alasdair, *After Virtue* (2nd Ed), London, Duckworth, 1999
Macquarrie, John, 'Kenoticism Reconsidered', *Theology* (LXXVII), 1974, 115-124
- *Principles of Christian Theology*, London, SCM, 1977
- *Jesus Christ in Modern Thought*, London, SCM, 1997
Martin, Ralph P., *A Hymn of Christ*, Downers Grove, Illinois, IVP, 1997
- *Philippians*, London, Marshall Morgan and Scott, 1985
Martin, Ralph P., Dodd, Brian J., (ed), *Where Christology Began*, Louisville (Kentucky), Westminster John Knox Press, 1998
Mayes, A. D. H., *Deuteronomy*, Marshall Morgan and Scott, London, 1979
Michaels, J. Ramsey, *1 Peter*, Waco, World Books, 1988
Middleton, J. Richard, and Walsh, Brian J., *Truth is stranger than it used to be*, London, SPCK, 1995
Milbank, John, 'Stories of Sacrifice', *Modern Theology* (12), 1996, 27-56
- *The Word Made Strange*, Oxford, Blackwell, 1997
Miller, Rabbi Jeffrey, 'All the Jeffrey Millers', *The Expository Times* (110), 1999, 179-181
Moberly, R. C., *Ministerial Priesthood*, London, Macmillan, 1897
Moltmann, Jürgen, *Theology of Hope* (ET), London, SCM, 1967
- *The Crucified God* (ET), London, SCM, 1974
- *Man* (ET), London, SPCK, 1974
- *The Church in the Power of the Spirit* (ET), London, SCM, 1977
- *The Open Church* (ET), London, SCM, 1978
- *The Future of Creation* (ET), London, SCM, 1979
- *The Trinity and the Kingdom of God* (ET), London, SCM, 1981
- *The Power of the Powerless* (ET), London, SCM, 1983
- *The Way of Jesus Christ* (ET), London, SCM, 1990
Moore, Andrew, 'Who are the Liberals now? History, Science, and Christology in N. T. Wright and Alister McGrath', *Anvil* (20), 2003, 9-24
- *Realism and Christian Faith*, Cambridge, CUP, 2003
Moses, John, *The Sacrifice of God*, Norwich, Canterbury Press, 1992
Moss, David and Gardner, Lucy, 'Difference – The Immaculate Concept? The

Laws Of Sexual Difference In The Theology Of Hans Urs Von Balthasar', *Modern Theology* (14), 1998, 377-401

Moule, C. F. D., *The Sacrifice of Christ*, London, Hodder and Stoughton, 1956
- 'Further Reflexions on Philippians 2:5-11, Gasque, W. W., and Martin, R. P., (eds) *Apostolic History and the Gospels*, Grand Rapids, Eerdmans, 1970
- *The Origin of Christology*, Cambridge, CUP, 1979
- *The Birth of the New Testament* (3rd Ed), London, A & C Black, 1981

Murphy, Francesca, '"Whence Comes This Love As Strong As Death?": The Presence of Franz Rozenweig's "Philosophy As Narrative" in Hans Urs Von Balthasar's Theo-Drama', *The Journal of Literature and Theology* (7), 1993, 227-247
- *Christ The Form Of Beauty*, Edinburgh, T & T Clark, 1995
- 'Inclusion and Exclusion in the Ethos of Von Balthasar's Theo-Drama', in *New Blackfriars*, (79), 1997, 56-64

Neibuhr, H. R., *The Kingdom of God in America*, New York, Harper Row, 1951,
- *The Social Source of Denominationalism*, New York, New American Library, 1981

Nelson, Richard D., *Raising Up a Faithful Priest*, Louisville, Westminster/John Knox Press, 1993

Newbigin, Lesslie, 'Lay Presidency at the Eucharist', *Theology* (XCIX), 1996, 366-370

Newman, John Henry, *A Grammar of Assent* (New Edn), London, Longmans, Green, and Co., 1891

Nichols, Aiden, *Holy Order*, Dublin, Veritas Publications, 1990,
- *The Word Has Been Abroad, A Guide Through Balthasar's Aesthetics*, Edinburgh, T & T Clark, 1998
- *No Bloodless Myth, A Guide Through Balthasar's Dramatics*, Edinburgh, T & T Clark, 2000

O'Brien, Peter T., *The Epistle to the Philippians*, Grand Rapids, Eerdmans, 1991

O'Donnell, John J., 'The Doctrine of the Trinity in Recent German Theology', *The Heythrop Journal* (23), 1982, 153-167

Packer, J. I., *Knowing God*, London, Hodder and Stoughton, 1975
- *Celebrating the Saving Work of God*, Carlisle, Paternoster, 1998

Pannenberg, Wolfhart, *Jesus - God and Man* (ET), SCM, 1968
- *Systematic Theology* (Vol. 1, ET), Edinburgh, T & T Clark 1991
- *Systematic Theology* (Vol. 2, ET), Edinburgh, T & T Clark, 1994
- *Systematic Theology* (Vol. 3, ET), Edinburgh, T & T Clark, 1998

Paton, Margaret, 'Representation in Eucharistic Theology', *Theology* (XCVII), 1994, 2-8

Percy, Martyn, *Power and the Church*, London, Cassell, 1998

Pelikan, Jaroslav, *The Emergence of the Catholic Tradition (100-600)*, The University of Chicago Press, London, 1971
- *The Reformation of Church and Dogma (1300-1700)*, The University of Chicago Press, London, 1985

- *Christian Doctrine and Modern Culture (since 1700)*, Chicago, Chicago University Press, 1989
Pickstock, Catherine, 'Necrophilia: The Middle Of Modernity A Study Of Death, Signs, And The Eucharist', *Modern Theology* (12), 1996, 405-433
Polkinghorne, John (ed.), *The Work of Love*, London, SPCK, 2001
Porter, Roy, *Enlightenment*, London, Penguin, 2000
Power, Kim, *Veiled Desire*, London, DLT, 1995
Pulkingham, Betty and Harper, Jeanne (ed), *Combined Sounds of Living Waters and Fresh Sounds*, London, Hodder and Stoughton, 1980
Quash, J. B., 'Between The Brutally Given, And The Brutally, Banally Free': Von Balthasar Theology Of Drama In Dialogue With Hegel', *Modern Theology* (13), 1997, 293-318
- 'Von Balthasar and the Dialogue with Karl Barth', *New Blackfriars*, (79), 1997, 45-55
von Rad, Gerhard, *Genesis* (ET), London, SCM, 1972
Ramsey, A. M., *The Gospel And The Catholic Church*, London, Longmans, Green and Co., 1936
- *The Christian Priest Today*, London, SPCK, 1972
Rausch, Thomas P., *Priesthood Today: An Appraisal*, New York, The Paulist Press, 1992
Ricoeur, Paul, *Oneself as Another* (ET), Chicago, Chicago University Press, 1994
- *Hermeneutics and The Human Sciences* (ET), Cambridge, CUP, 1989
Roberts, A. and Donaldson, J., *The Ante-Nicene Fathers* Vol. II, 'Clement of Alexandria', Edinburgh, T & T Clark, 1993
- *The Ante-Nicene Fathers* (Vol. III), 'Tertullian', Edinburgh, T & T Clark, 1993
Robinson, J. A. T., *The Human Face of God*, London, SCM, 1994
Rooke, Deborah W., *Zadok's Heirs: The Role and Development of the High Priesthood in Ancient Israel*, Oxford, OUP, 2000
Ross, D., *Aristotle* (5th Edn), London, Methuen, 1971
Rubin, Miri, 'Whose Eucharist? Eucharistic Identity As Historical Subject', *Modern Theology* (15), 1999, 197-207
Rupp, E. G. and Drewery, Benjamin, (ed), *Martin Luther*, Edward Arnold, London, 1971
Sanday, W., (ed), *Priesthood and Sacrifice*, London, Longmans, Green and Co, 1900
Sanders, E. P., *Paul and Palestinian Judaism*, London, SCM, 1981
- *Jesus and Judaism*, London, SCM, 1985
Saye, Scott C., 'The Wild And Crooked Tree: Barth, Fish, And Interpretitive Communities', Modern Theology (12), 1996, 435-458
Schaff, P. and Wace, Henry (ed), *The Nicene and Post Nicene Fathers of the Christian Church* (Second series Vol. V), 'Gregory of Nyssa', Edinburgh, T & T Clark, 1994
Scharlemann, Robert P., *The Reason of Following*, Chicago, Chicago University Press, 1991

Schillebeeckx, Edward, *Christ* (ET), SCM, London, 1980
- *The Church with a Human Face* (ET), London, SCM, 1985
Schola, Angelo, *Hans Urs Von Balthasar* (ET), Edinburgh, T & T Clark, 1995
Scruton, Roger, *Modern Philosophy*, London, Pimlico, 1994
Selden, Raman, Widdowson, Peter, Brooker, Peter, *A Reader's Guide to Contemporary Literary Theory* (4th Edn), London, Prentice Hall, 1997
Selwyn, E. G., *The First Epistle of St Peter*, London, Macmillan & Co Ltd, 1946
Slee, Nicola, 'Parables and Women's Experience', *Modern Churchman* (26), 1984, 20-31
Sluga, Hans, Stern, David, (eds), *The Cambridge Companion to Wittgenstein*, Cambridge, CUP, 1999
Soskice, Janet Martin, *Metaphor and Religious Language*, Oxford, OUP, 1987
Stackhouse, John G. Jr., (ed), *Evangelical Futures*, Liecester, Apollos, 2000
Steenburg, D., 'The Worship of Adam and Christ as the Image of God', *JSNT* (39), 1990, 95-109
Stevenson, Kenneth, *Eucharist and Offering*, New York, Pueblo Publishing Company, 1986
Stevenson, J., (ed), *A New Eusebius*, London, SPCK, 1974
- *Creeds, Councils and Controversies*, London, SPCK, 1973
Stroup, George W., *The Promise of Narrative Theology*, London, SCM, 1984
Swete, H. B., (ed), *The Early History of the Church and the Ministry*, London, Macmillan and Co, 1921
Sykes, Stephen W., *The Integrity of Anglicanism*, London, Mowbrays, 1978
- *The Identity of Christianity*, Philadelphia, Fortress Press, 1984
- *Karl Barth: Centenary Essays*, Cambridge, CUP, 1989
- *Sacrifice and Redemption*, Cambridge, CUP, 1991
Sykes, Stephen W., (ed), *Karl Barth, Studies in his Theological Method*, Oxford, Clarendon Press, 1979
Sykes, Stephen W. and Booty, John, (ed), *The Study of Anglicanism*, London/Minneapolis, SPCK/Fortress, 1993
Taylor, Charles, *Sources of the Self, The Making of Modern Identity*, Cambridge, CUP, 2000
Thiselton, Anthony C., *New Horizons in Hermeneutics*, London, HarperCollins, 1992,
- 'Speech-Act Theory And The Claim That God Speaks: Nicholas Woltersdorff's *Divine Discourse*', *SJT*, 50, 1997, 97-110
- 'Biblical studies and theoretical hermeneutics', in Barton, John (ed), *The Cambridge Companion to Biblical Interpretation*, Cambridge, CUP, 1998
- 'Communicative Action and Promise in Interdisciplinary, Biblical, and Theological Hermeneutics', Lundin, Roger, Walhout, Clarence, Thiselton, Anthony C., *The Promise of Hermeneutics*, Grand Rapids, Eerdmans, 1999
- '"Behind" and "In Front Of" the Text', Craig Batholomew, Colin Greene, Karl Möller (ed), *After Pentecost Language and Biblical Interpretation*, Carlisle, Paternoster Press, 2001
Thompson, William M., 'Women And "Conformity To Christ's Image": The

Challenge Of Avoiding Docetism And Affirming Inclusivism', *SJT* (48), 1995, 23-35

Thurian, Max, *Priesthood and Ministry* (ET), Oxford, Mowbray, 1983

Tillard, Jean M. R., *What Priesthood has the Ministry?* Bramcote, Grove Books, 1977

Torrance, James B., 'The Place of Jesus Christ in Worship' in Ray S. Anderson (ed) *Theological Foundations for Ministry*, Edinburgh, T & T Clark, 1979

Torrance, Thomas F., *The Ground and Grammar of Theology*, Belfast, Christian Journals Limited, 1980

- *Royal Priesthood* (2nd Edn), Edinburgh, T & T Clark, 1993

Vanhoozer, Kevin J., *Biblical Narrative in the Philosophy of Paul Ricoeur*, Cambridge, CUP, 1990

- 'Does Trinity Belong in a Theology of Religions? On Angling in the Rubicon and the "Identity" of God', Vanhoozer, K J, (ed), *The Trinity in a Pluralistic Age*, Grand Rapids, Eerdmans, 1997

- *Is there a meaning in this text?* Leicester, Apollos, 1998

Vanstone, W. H., *Love's Endeavour, Love's Expense*, London, DLT, 1977

- *The Stature of Waiting*, London, DLT, 1982

Volf, Miroslav, *After Our Likeness*, Grand Rapids, Eerdmans, 1998

Walhout, Clarence, 'Narrative Hermeneutics', Lundin, Roger, Walhout, Clarence, Thiselton, Anthony, *The Promise of Hermeneutics*, Carlisle, Paternoster, 1999

Walker, Andrew, *Restoring the Kingdom*, London, Hodder and Stoughton, 1985,

Wannamaker, C. A., 'Philippians 2.6-11: Son of God or Adamic Christology', *NTS* (33), 1987, 179-193

Ward, Graham 'Mimesis: The Measure of Mark's Christology', *The Journal of Literature and Theology* (8), 1994, 1-29

- *Barth, Derrida and the Language of Theology*, Cambridge, CUP, 1998

- 'Kenosis and Naming: beyond analogy and towards *allegoria amoris*', Heelas, Paul and Martin, David, (ed), *Religion, Modernity and Postmodernity*, Oxford, Blackwells, 1998

- 'Kenosis: Death, Discourse and Resurrection', Gardiner, Lucy, Moss, David, Quash, Ben, Ward, Graham, *Balthasar at the End of Modernity*, Edinburgh, T & T Clark, 1999

- 'Bodies: The displaced body of Christ', John Milbank, Catherine Pickstock and Graham Ward, (ed), *Radical Orthodoxy*, London, Routledge, 1999

'Suffering and Incarnation', Graham Ward (ed) *True Religion*, Oxford, Blackwell, 2002

Warfield, B. B., *The Inspiration and Authority of the Bible*, The Presbyterian and Reformed Publishing Company, Philadelphia, 1948

Webster, John, *The Theology of Eberhard Jüngel*, Cambridge, CUP, 1986

- 'Ministry and Priesthood', Sykes, S W and Booty, John, (ed), *The Study of Anglicanism*, London, SPCK, 1988

- 'Hermeneutics in Modern Theology: Some Doctrinal Reflections', *SJT* (51), 1998, 307-341

- *Word And Church*, Edinburgh, T & T Clark, 2001
- *Holiness*, London, SCM, 2003
Webster, John, (ed), *The Cambridge Companion to Karl Barth*, Cambridge, CUP, 2000
Weinandy, Thomas G., *Does God Suffer?* Edinburgh, T & T Clark, 2000
Welch, Claude, (ed), *God and Incarnation in Mid-Nineteenth Century German Theology*, New York, OUP, 1965
West, Angela, *Deadly Innocence*, London, Cassell, 1995
Westcott, B. F., *The Epistle to the Hebrews*, London, Macmillan and Co., 1889
The Westminster Confession of Faith, together with The Larger Catechism and The Shorter Catechism, with Scripture Proofs (3rd Edn), The Committee for Christian Education and Publications, The Presbyterian Church of America Bookstore, Atlanta, 1990
Wiles, Maurice, *The Christian Fathers*, London, SCM, 1977
Williams, Rowan, *The Wound of Knowledge*, London, DLT, 1979
- *Eucharistic Sacrifice – The Roots of a Metaphor*, Bramcote, Grove Books, 1982
- *Arius*, London, DLT, 1987
- *On Christian Theology*, Oxford, Blackwell, 2000
Williamson, H. G. M., *1 and 2 Chronicles*, London, Marshall, Morgan and Scott, 1982
Wingren, Gustav, *Luther on Vocation* (ET), Philadelphia, Muhlenberg Press, 1957
Wittgenstein, Ludwig, *Tractatus Logico-Philosophicus* (ET, C K Ogden, 1922), London, Routledge & Kegan Paul Ltd, 1988
- *Philosophical Investigations* (ET, G E M Anscombe), Oxford, Blackwell, 2000
Wolterstorff, Nicholas, 'The Promise of Speech-act Theory for Biblical Interpretation', Craig Batholomew, Colin Greene, Karl Möller (ed), *After Pentecost Language and Biblical Interpretation*, Carlisle, Paternoster Press, 2001
Worthen, Jeremy, 'Theology and the History of the Metanarrative: Clarifying the Postmodern Question', Modern Believing (42), 2001, 15-23
Wright, N. T., *The Climax of the Covenant*, Edinburgh, T & T Clark, 1991
- *The New Testament and the People of God*, London, SPCK, 1993
- *Jesus and the Victory of God*, London, SPCK, 1996
- *The Resurrection of the Son of God*, London, SPCK, 2003
Young, Frances, *Sacrifice and the Death of Christ*, London, SPCK, 1975
Zizioulas, John, *Being as Communion*, Crestwood, NY, St Vladimir's Seminary Press, 1993

Internet Sources

www.creeds.net/reformed/helvetic.htm (4.2.02)
www.bombaxo.com/hippolytus.html (6.12.2002)

CD ROM

Christian Classics Ethereal Library, 2000 (CD 1003)

Index

Aaron 162
Aaronic priesthood 163
Abelard, Peter 215n. 65
Allen, R. E. 35
Altizer, Thomas J. J. 7, 28–9, 30, 31
ambassadors 224
analogia fidei 219–21
analogy 202–3, 208–19
Anglican orders, validity 194
Anglican-Methodist Re-Union Scheme (1968) 2n. 6
annunciation, Balthasar on 114
Anselm, St, Balthasar's criticisms of views on the atonement 178n. 241
anthropology 185–6
   Balthasar's and Moltmann's views 125–6, 128–9
   Balthasar's kenotic theology 108, 110–11, 116, 118–20
   Barth's views 129–31, 135–6, 182
   Bonhoeffer's views 123n. 125
   Moltmann's views 64, 120–9
anthropomorphism, Jüngel on 153n. 44
anti-realism 7–8
   on language and external and objective truths 4
Apostolic Succession 196, 196nn. 41 and 42, 250–3
   Barth's views 238–40, 240n. 268, 241n. 280
   Moltmann's views 127
apostolicity 234n. 224
Aquinas, Thomas, St 56, 57n. 60, 109–10
Aristotle
   on characterization 48, 52, 95
   on narrative in tragedy 78
   on representation 96
   use of metaphor 202
Arius and Arianism 17, 22, 95
   Christology 23, 32, 32n. 70, 34–6, 39, 41
   Luther's rejection 43
ἁρπαγμός 96, 98
atonement 168, 228
   and priesthood 171–2, 268
   Augustine of Hippo 39
   Balthasar's views 178–9, 180, 181
   Barth's views 52–3, 173–7, 180, 181–5
   Day of Atonement 160–1, 162, 165n. 137
   Evangelical Alliance Statement of Faith on substitutionary atonement 177n. 236
   Luther's views 42
   Moberly's views 196
   Moltmann's views 179–81
   resurrection's importance 229–30
   substitutionary atonement 176–7
   see also Jesus Christ, priesthood
Augustine of Hippo, St 4, 76n. 1
   anti-Pelagianism 115
   on analogy 208
   on sacrifice and sacraments 261n. 8
   on the Trinity and Christology 39–40
aversion 171n. 188

Balthasar, Hans Urs von 17, 88n. 84, 210, 228nn. 168 and 171
   Christology 237n. 251
   ecclesiology 133, 134, 138, 198–9, 250–1, 252n. 392, 253
   and anthropology 186
   and priesthood 205, 234–5
   emphasis upon office in the Church 233n. 214
   kenotic theology 47, 55–63, 66–7, 71–2, 107–8
   and vocation 108–20
   compared to Moltmann's 120–1, 125–8

Mariology 248n. 351
on Apostolic Succession 196n. 42, 239
on apostolicity 234n. 224
on authorial intent 109
on blood's significance for sacrifice 172
on covenantal sacrifice 170
on handing over 265n. 40
on Jesus' apostleship 163
on priesthood 129, 221, 265
on priestly testimony in the First Testament 152n. 34
on the atonement 178–9, 180, 181
on the eucharist 230n. 197, 247–8
on vocation 213, 214, 259n. 2, 262n. 11
theo-drama 55–6, 62, 108–20
utilizes narrative 79
views on sexuality compared with those of Barth 130n. 192
Baptism, Eucharist and Ministry 221n. 112
Barmen Declaration, The 133n. 214
Barnett, Paul 213n. 46
Barrett, C. K. 213
Barth, Karl 17, 229n. 185
  Adamic Christology 93
  and the imagination 199
  anthropology 145, 182, 186
  doctrine of the Trinity 69
  ecclesiology 121n. 113, 134, 135, 186, 228n. 171, 234n. 225
  historical criticism 48
  kenotic theology 47, 48–55, 62, 63, 71, 72, 107, 108
  on biblical interpretation 48–50
  on Christian living, in Philippians 85
  on human knowledge 12–13
  on Jesus Christ's priesthood 174n. 206
  on κοινωνία 248
  on ministry 255
  on narrative in the divine-human encounter 56
  on narrative emplotment 49, 51–2
  on ordained priesthood 236
  on preaching 10, 255
  on priesthood of Israel 141
  on representation 9–10
  on representation through the priesthood 238–43
  on revelation 246
  on sacrifice 168–9
  on scripture principle 220
  on sin 131, 134n. 223
  on the *analogia fidei* 219–20
  on the atonement 173–7, 180, 181–5
  on the eucharist in relation to priesthood 232–4
  on the Word of God 158
  on vocation 129–38, 214, 262n. 11
  theological methodology 8–9
  theology of the cross 64, 65–6
  use of narrative 78n. 13, 79
  views of language about God 209–10
Bauckham, Richard 93–5, 99–100
Beare, F. W. 86
Berkhof, Louis 161
Bernard, E. R. 192nn. 2 and 3
Bible
  foundationalist understandings of 6
  interpretation, Barth's views 48–50
  priesthood in 147, 211, 264, 265
  see also First Testament
Biedermann, A. E. 27
bishops
  ἐπίσκοπος 81–2
  ἐπισκόποις καὶ διακόνοις (Philippians 1.1) 222–4
  Philippian church 222–5
  supremacy 193
Blenkinsopp, Joseph 154
blood, significance in relation both to covenant and sacrifice 172
Bockmuehl, Marcus 87
Bonhoeffer, Dietrich 68
  experience of God in Jesus Christ 31
  on call and calling 123n. 125
  on suffering as making the Christian 122
  rejection of atheism 30
  religionless Christianity 28–9, 29n.

Index

46
Bradshaw, Paul 236n. 240
British kenoticists 22, 24–5
Bruce, F. F. 97, 158n. 81, 166
Brueggemann, Walter 156n. 64, 159n. 84
  and countertestimony 148n. 2
  on Eichrodt and covenant 151n. 29
  on Israel as Yahweh's partner 155–6
  on priesthood and the cult in Israel 151
  on the reading of Scripture 113n. 33
Bulley, Colin 5, 6
Butin, Phil 174n. 210
Butterfield, Herbert 13n. 94, 16n. 113

call and calling 123n. 125, 128
  see also election
Calvin, John 174
Campbell, John Mcleod, *The Nature of Atonement* 196n. 38
Cappadocian Fathers, on the Trinity 38
carmen Christi 261
  in Philippians 203
  see also Christology
Catholicism, understanding of ministerial priesthood 1–2
catholicity, and *perichoresis* 259
Chalcedon, Council of, on ordination 175n. 216, 253–4, 264
Chalcedonian Definition 21, 41, 47
  Barth's use 50, 52
  metanarrative 78n. 13
character 15n. 106
characterization 48, 52, 95
charismatic freedom, in priesthood 265
chiasmic structure, in Hebrews 161n. 102
Christian identity, in worship 232
Christian living
  as sacrifice 158
  identification with Jesus Christ, in Philippians 84–6
Christian response to God 107
Christiansen, Ellen Juhl 139n. 277, 142n. 297, 143n. 300

Christology
  Adamic Christology 92–6, 237n. 251
  and kenoticism 22–5
  and pneumatology 176
  and the Trinity 31–41, 42–5
  as the dominant theme of ecclesiology, Moltmann's views 121–4
  Barth's views 129–30, 136–7
  in Philippians 2.6–11 96–101
  see also carmen Christi; Jesus Christ
Church
  and covenant 155n. 58
  as the body of Christ 268
  as priestly community 238
  priesthood 147
  Roman Catholic and Reformed understandings of 232–3
  witness to God 220
  see also ecclesiology
circumcision 80
clean/unclean 149
Coakley, Sarah, on Balthasar's Mariology 116–17
communicatio idiomata 23, 44, 45, 260
communication 204
communio sanctorum 232
compassion (σπλάγχνα) 242–3
confessors 236n. 241
countertestimony 148n. 2
  and testimony 155n. 58
covenant
  and Christian identity 232
  and priesthood 151–8
  Barth's views 108, 129
  blood's significance for 172
  in 1 Peter 2.4–10 139, 142–5
  in Hebrews 160, 164
  in Leviticus 171n. 186
covenant identity 170, 243n. 305
covenant people, identity ἐν Χριστῷ Ἰησοῦ, in Philippians 87
Cranmer, Thomas 164n. 127
  on God's presence in the eucharist 231n. 202

on office 114n. 44
on orders of ministry 192n. 4
on the eucharist 229, 229n. 180
ordinals 194n. 27
creation
order of 150
Wellhausen's views 148n. 3
critical realism 83n. 51
on kenosis and priesthood 9
cross 228
Luther's views 42–5
Moltmann's views 63–8, 70, 71, 124
cult, in Israel 151
cultic sacrifice, in Philippians 86
Cupitt, Don 7

Daly, Mary 115
darstellen 10, 11
Davidic dynasty 157
Davids, Peter H. 141n. 288, 145n. 318
Davies, Oliver 107, 242
Davison, Dr 192nn. 2 and 3
Day of Atonement, in Hebrews 160–1, 162, 165n. 137
deacons, Philippian church 222–5
Death of God
and kenosis 22, 27–31
Radical Theology and Death of God (Altizer and Hamilton) 7
Death of God theologians 17
Demson, David E. 239nn. 262 and 263
διακόνοις 81–2
diastasis 8n. 52, 75
Didache 229n. 182
Didymus 37n. 105
disciples 243
discipleship
and God's identity 107–8
Bonhoeffer on 123n. 125
disobedience 155
disorder 268
divine-human encounter
and kenosis 2–3, 6, 72, 73, 75
and ordained priesthood 2–3, 244–8, 259
and priesthood 68, 210, 239

Balthasar's views 56–7
dialectical nature 47
in Jesus Christ 50–5, 56, 175–6
see also God
Dix, Gregory, Dom 227n. 159
Docetic Gnosticism 27
docetism 26
doctrine 7, 8, 27, 73
Lindbeck's views 177n. 236
dogs 86–7
Dorner, Isaak 23–4
Dostoevsky, Fyodor 67
δοῦλοι 81
drama, *see* theo-drama
Dulles, Avery 134n. 227
Dunn, James D. G.
on Adamic Christology, in Philippians 92
on ἐν Χριστῷ and ἐν κυρίῳ 81n. 31
on Jesus as Lord 80
on Paul's apostleship 80n. 30
on Paul's use of priestly language 2–3
on service as priesthood 103
on σῶμα, in Philippians 89
Dunnill, John 166–7, 171, 172

ecclesiology 185–6
and the Trinity 259
Balthasar's kenotic theology 108, 109, 113, 114–15, 116, 117–20
Barth's views 133–4, 228n. 171, 234n. 225
in Philippians 222–5
Moltmann's views 121–4, 127–8
see also Church
Eco, Umberto 111n. 28
Eichrodt, Walther 151
eintreten 9, 10
ἐκένωσεν 96, 98, 99
elasticity 16
election
Barth's views 108, 129
in 1 Peter 2.4–10 139–41
see also calling
elementary propositions 3–4
emplotment 79

ἐν Χριστῷ in Philippians 81, 87–8
εν κυρίῳ, in Philippians 81, 89
Epaphroditus, in Philippians 224–5, 224n. 140
epistles, narrative in 77–8
Erigena, John Scotus 259
ἐταπείνωσεν 96, 98, 99
eucharist 247–8
   and ordained priesthood 231–7, 267–8
   and the atonement, Balthasar's views 178–9
   gift and offering in 226, 227
   in 1 Corinthians 249
   Moltmann's views 126
   presidency 262
   representative nature of the priesthood 219, 225–31
Euodia 89
Evangelical Alliance Statement of Faith, on substitutionary atonement 177n. 236
Evans, Richard 13n. 91
exemplarism 64, 215–19
expiation 171n. 188
externalization 243–4

Fairburn, A. M. 192nn. 2, 3 and 195
faith
   and revelation 107
   in Hebrews 159
   priestly nature 242
false consciousness 26
feeding of five thousand 168n. 156, 235n. 232
fellowship (κοινόν), in Philippians 102
Feuerbach, L. A. 11n. 77, 26, 49n. 10
fiction, and history 198
1 Peter 17
   Barth's anthropology 145
   Barth's kenotic theology 108
   Christian identity 232
   election, priesthood and covenant in 139–45
   on the Church and covenant 155n. 58
   priesthood in 147, 212n. 36, 265

First Testament
   Paul's use of 78
   priesthood in 148–58, 164–5
   see also Bible
fitting theories 10–11, 165
Ford, David 83n. 45, 84, 227
forma Dei 184n. 289
Formula of Concord 23
Forsyth, P. T. 11–12, 24, 25, 26, 192nn. 2 and 3
foundationalism 6
foundationlist objectivism 200n. 73
Franklin, R. William 194
Freud, Sigmund 26, 49n. 10

Gadamer, Hans-Georg 100–1
Gardiner, Lucy 112n. 32
Geertz, Clifford 12n. 86
generosity, in Philippians 91
Gess, Wolfgang Friedrich 27–8
gnosis 87
God
   absence 155–6
   Barth's understanding of 8
   character 48
   Christian response to 107
   constancy and omnipotence of 220
   death of, *see* death of God
   doctrine of 40
   encounter with humanity in Jesus Christ 228
   form of (μορφῆ Θεου) 97
   identity
      and Christology 92–6
      and human identity 103–4
      Moltmann's views 120
   kenosis 14, 107–8, 123–4
   knowability 75, 175n. 211, 184n. 296
   love
      given in the eucharist 230
      see also eucharist
   nature of 7
   power 210
   presence in Israel 152–3
   relationship to Jesus in Philippians 75
   relationship with humanity 131–3,

135–7, 237–8
revelation 56, 110n. 17, 203–4
seen as metaphor 4
sovereignty 47
suffering 67, 68–9
Word of, *see* Word of God
see also divine-human encounter;
  Holy Spirit; pneumatology; Trinity
Gore, Charles 192n. 4, 192nn. 2 and 3
kenotic understanding of priesthood
  11–12
kenoticism 24–5, 24n. 20, 26
on ordained ministry 193–4, 193n.
  17, 196n. 42, 197n. 49
on priesthood 5–6
Gorringe, Timothy 177n. 235,' 196n.
  38
grace 265
gratitude/praise 132–3, 136, 137, 174,
  265
Green, Garrett 26, 49, 198, 200n. 73
Gregory of Nyssa 38
Grenz, Stanley 198n. 57
Grillmeier, A. 33–4, 37n. 105

Hamilton, William 7
handing over 59–60, 265–6n. 40
παραδίδωμι 69
hands, imposition of 193
Hanson, A. T. 223n. 129
Hart, Trevor 205–6
Hatch, Edwin 5n. 32, 193, 195
Hauerwas, Stanley 268
Headlam, A. C. 192nn. 2 and 3
Hebrews (epistle)
  and the atonement 183
  priesthood in 158–66, 201
  sacrifice in 166n. 146, 169–70
Hegel, G. W. F. 24, 29, 30, 108
Herod the Great 153n. 49
Herrmann, Wilhelm 9
Hilary of Poitiers 36–8
Hippolytus, *Apostolic Tradition*, on
  ordination 236
history
  and fiction 198
  theology 53, 112n. 29
Holy Saturday, *descensus* motif 62

Holy Spirit 240nn. 268 and 269
  Barth's ecclesiology 134, 137
  processio 38
  role in vocation 126–7
  see also God; pneumatology;
    Trinity
holy/profanity 149–50
homousios 37
Hooker, Morna
  on exemplarism in Paul 216–17
  on Paul's understanding of
    atonement 228
  on the feeding of the five thousand
    235n. 232
Hooker, Richard 195
  on apostolic succession 251n. 381
  on ordained ministry 204n. 116
  views of priesthood 208, 209
Hort, F. J. A. 140n. 280, 141n. 289,
  142n. 293
Hosea, on priesthood 154n. 56
humanity, distinction from God, in
  relation to priesthood 237–8
Hunsinger, George 130n. 192
Hyman, Gavin 169n. 169

idealism, speculative idealism 64
identity 14–16, 185, 186, 243n. 305
  and memory 126
  Balthasar's views 58, 111
  collective identity 139n. 277
  covenant identity 170
  God's identity and human identity
    103–4
  Hilary of Poitiers's understanding of
    37
  in Philippians 75–6, 80–1, 81–2,
    101–2, 103–4
  as participation in the other 90–2
  Christian living 84–6
  Paul's identity 82–4
  true and false identity 86–90
  link between kenosis and priesthood
    73
  true identity 143n. 300
Ignatius of Antioch 127n. 164
imagination
  and reality 26

Barth's views 12–13, 49
priesthood as an act of 197–206
'in Christ' 15n. 110, 216
Incarnation 11, 203
　and the Trinity 36–8
　Balthasar's views 58–9
　in Philippians 2.6–11 98
　kenotic accounts of 11
　Milbank on 168n. 158
　see also Jesus Christ
interpretation, linguistic interpretation 210
Israel 80
　Barth's views of 133n. 223
　identity 139n. 277, 151
　priesthood 141

Jeremiah
　establishment of a new covenant 164
　on the cult 155n. 58
Jesuology 64
Jesus Christ 9
　and ministerial priesthood 3
　and the church 228n. 171
　and the eucharist 248
　as divine-human encounter 50–5, 56
　betrayal 228
　Christ as title 174
　Christian living as identification with, in Philippians 84–6
　death of 59–61, 66, 67
　identification of 246
　identification with, in Philippians 87–9, 91
　identity in 264
　imitation of 217–19
　in Philippians 75–6, 80, 83–4
　kenotic consciousness 28
　nature 21, 22–3, 25, 26, 47, 260
　　and atonement 196
　　and priesthood 237
　Paul's identification with, in Philippians 83–4
　person of 41
　priesthood 147, 168–70, 174–6, 186–7, 191, 264
　　and human priesthood 261, 262–3, 266–7, 268–9
　　and ordained priesthood 206, 207–8, 218, 225, 240–1, 243
　　compared with human priesthood 167
　　in Hebrews 158–66, 201
　　Luther's views 45
　　see also atonement
　priestly sacrifice 228
　relationship with God, in Philippians 82
　resurrection 59–61
　role in theo-drama 110, 115, 116n. 64, 118, 119
　salvific action 9n. 60
　self-representation of God's revelation 56–7
　sufferings and death, sharing in 249–50
　vocation 109–11, 214–15
　see also Christology; Incarnation
Jewish worldview 144
John, St
　Christology 33
　on the Word becoming flesh 60
Judaizers 80, 87
Judas, betrayal of Jesus 228
Jüngel, Eberhard
　on anthropomorphism 153n. 44
　on justification 269
　on Mariology 116n. 67
　on metaphors and textual truth 201, 202
　on priesthood 203
　on the Death of God 29
　on truth in texts 197n. 45
justification 69, 269
Justin Martyr 193

kenosis 72–3, 207, 267n. 53
　and God's identity 14
　and priesthood 2–3, 11–12, 16–18, 45–6, 185, 205–6, 239, 253, 260–3
　and the divine-human encounter 75
　and the Incarnation 11
　as the Death of God 27–31
　Balthasar's theology 47, 55–62, 63, 66, 67, 71, 72

Barth's theology 47, 48–55, 62, 63, 71, 72, 137, 168
   critical realism on 9
   emergence of 21–7
   English kenoticists 17
   in Philippians 75–6, 85–6, 89, 98, 102, 103–4, 107
   Moltmann's theology 47, 62–73, 120–9
   representation 6, 8
Kerr, Fergus 12–13
Kierkegaard, Søren 48
Kirk, K. E. 196nn. 40 and 42
Kittel, G. 99, 244n. 308
knowledge, Barth's understanding of human knowledge 12–13
κοινωνία, as participation 82n. 41, 102, 243–8, 248, 250
κοινωνίαν 87
krypsis 37, 42
Küng, Hans 252, 253n. 392

Lane, William L. 157
Lang, Cosmo Gordon 192nn. 2 and 3, 195n. 37
language games 4, 208–9
law, Wellhausen's views 148n. 4
λειτουργία 86, 211
Leo XIII, Pope, *Apostolicae curae*, on Anglican orders 194, 194n. 27, 196n. 42
Leviticus, covenant in 171n. 186
Lightfoot, J. B. 89, 92
   on Philippians 2.6–11 97
   on φωστῆρεσ 85n. 63
   rejection of ministerial priesthood 200–1, 203, 204
   'The Christian Ministry' 192, 193–4, 195
Lima Statement, on priesthood 5n. 32
Lindars, Barnabas 159–60, 161, 166n. 146
Lindbeck, George 8, 177n. 236
liturgical presidency 236n. 240
living stones 143nn. 299 and 300, 144n. 317
Logos Christology 32
Lord's Supper *see* eucharist

Loughlin, Gerard 13, 198
love 75n. 1, 101
Lubac, Henri de 117n. 75
Luther, Martin
   Balthasar's criticisms of views on the atonement 178
   Christology and the Trinity 42–5
   Jesus Christ's natures 23
   on God's being 123
   on God's handing over 59n. 69
   on history 112n. 32
   on Jesus' apostleship 163
   on justification 69, 269
   on priesthood 149n. 6
   on vocation 123n. 125
   theology of the cross 17, 22, 47, 64, 66–7

Maccabee, Jonathan 150n. 21
Maccabee, Simon 150n. 21
McCormack, Bruce L. 8–9, 210
MacIntyre, Alasdair 77
Malachi, on priesthood 154
Marcion 152
Martin, Ralph P. 97, 99
Marx, Karl 11n. 78, 26, 49n. 10
Mary (Jesus' mother), vocation 109, 112, 113–18, 119–20
meaning 209
Melchizedek 156–7, 163
metaphors, in religious truth 201–2
Michaels, J. Ramsey 141n. 292, 142n. 297
Middleton, J. Richard 13n. 95
Milbank, John 167–9, 170
mimetic theory 96
ministerial priesthood *see* ordained priesthood; priesthood
missio 39, 163
   and *processio* 109–10
mission 118, 122
Moberly, R. C. 5n. 32, 192nn. 2 and 3, 194–6, 197, 204
modalism 54
Möller, Karl 12n. 86
Moltmann, Jürgen 17, 253n. 392
   anthropology 186
   ecclesiology 138, 186

kenotic theology 47, 62–73, 107, 108, 120–9
  on baptism 125
  on 'death in God' 30
  on handing over 265n. 40
  on identity of Father and Son on the cross 228
  on priesthood 221, 235–6, 265
  on the atonement 179–81
  on the eucharist 247
  on the resurrection 229, 268n. 65
  on vocation 123n. 125, 214
  priestly countertestimony 199
  rejection of ordained priesthood 201
  utilizes narrative 79
monarchy, and priesthood, in Israel 150
Monophysitism 40, 44, 57–8
μορφή 96, 97, 98–9
Moses 162
Moss, David 112n. 32
Moule, C. F. D. 98–9, 100
Moule, H. C. G. 192n. 2

naïve realism 6, 200n. 73
narrative 2, 3, 13, 77–9
  and identity 15–16
  and the eucharist 226
  biblical narrative 210
  mimetic narratives 101
narrative emplotment, Barth's views 49, 51–2
Nelson, Richard. D. 149–50
Nestorianism 40, 44, 57–8
Nestorius 37n. 105
Newman, J. H. 251n. 381
Nicea, Council of 68
Nichols, Aidan 61, 114n. 51, 119
Nietzsche, F. W. 26, 30, 49n. 10

O'Brien, Peter T. 85, 244nn. 308 and 309, 249
office, Balthasar on 113–15, 117
officium 127n. 166
Old Testament *see* First Testament
ὁμοίωμα 97
ὀνόματι 96
ὄνομα 96

ordained priesthood 1–3, 191, 204–5, 237–8, 262, 267–8
  and Jesus Christ's priesthood 218
  and kenosis 253
  and the divine-human encounter 244–8
  and the eucharist 219, 225–31, 231–7
  and the Trinity 259–60
  Balthasar's views 119–20
  boundary markers 47
  in Philippians 101–3
  Oxford Conference (December 1899) 191–2, 195–7, 198, 205
  Protestant views of 207–8
  representative nature 219–25, 238–43
order, in priesthood 265
ordination 253–4, 261, 263n. 21, 264, 267–8
  Chalcedonian Canons on 175n. 216
  Hippolytus, *Apostolic Tradition* 236
Origen 32–4, 38, 54
ὀσμὴν εὐωδίας 91
Oxford Conference (December 1899), on ordained priesthood 191–2, 195–7, 198, 205

Packer, James I. 178n. 236
Pannenberg, Wolfhart
  on God's deity 67
  on Jesus Christ's priesthood 177n. 232
  on patristic theology 36
  on sacraments 261n. 8
  on the Trinity 54
παραδίδωμι 102n. 177
participation 16, 185
  κοινωνία 243–8, 250
participatory mediation 176n. 220
passion narrative, Balthasar's views 56
πάθημα 102
patricompassion 65
Paul, St
  apostleship 80–1
  as a prototype of vocation, in Philippians 116

exemplarism 215–19
identification with fellow workers 223n. 129
identification with Jesus Christ, in Philippians 75, 76, 83–4
identification with the Philippians 82–3
ministry 254–5, 266
on atonement 228
on God's handing over 59n. 69
priestly and sacrificial language 211–15
use of priestly language 2–3
see also Philippians (epistle)
Pelagianism 27
perichoresis, and catholicity 259
permanence 15n. 106
personality 25–6
personhood 118, 264
Peter, St, vocation 109, 112, 113–15, 116, 117–18, 119–20
Philippians (epistle) 76–81
Adamic Christology 92, 92–6
atonement in 180
Carmen Christi in 203
Christology 33, 96–101
divine-human encounter in 244–5
ecclesiology 222–5
identity in 14, 81–2
kenosis 17, 75–6, 107
ministry 254–5
narrative structure 79–80
Paul offers himself as a prototype of vocation 116
priesthood in 75–6, 101–3, 107, 213, 214
theo-drama, Balthasar's views 62
vocation in 136
Philippians (people)
Paul's identification with 82–3
relation to Jesus 75, 76
Philo of Alexandria 35
φαίνασθε 85n. 63
physis, and *prosopon* 37n. 105
πλήρωμα 82–3, 91
Plotinus 35
plots, narrative 78
pneumatology
and Christology 176
Balthasar's views 116–17
Moltmann's views 121–2
see also Holy Spirit
political theology 121n. 109
Polycarp of Smyrna 222
Porphyry 35
power, re-imagining of 63, 72
praise/gratitude 132–3, 136, 137, 174, 265
preaching, Barth's views 10, 255
presbyters 208
priesthood 21–2, 75, 186–7, 191
and Adamic Christology 93
and analogy 208–19
and atonement 171–2, 268
and Christian living, in Philippians 85
and covenant 151–8
and eucharist 267–8
and kenosis 11–12, 16–18, 45–6, 185, 205–6, 239, 260–3
and sacrifice 145–6, 173
as act of imagination 197–206
countertestimony and testimony 243n. 305
critical realism on 9
dialectical understanding 147, 263–7
First Testament 148–58
Hooker's views 208, 209
Hosea's views 154n. 56
human priesthood compared with that of Jesus 167
humanity's distinction from God 237–8
identity 14, 16
in 1 Peter 2.4–10 139, 141–2, 143–4
in Hebrews 158–66
in Philippians 75–6, 79, 91, 103, 107
in relation to the divine-human encounter 68
in relation to the Trinity 50
Luther's views 123n. 125
Malachi's views 154
Moltmann's views 122–7, 128–9
recognition of the distinctive natures

Index

of God and humanity 65
representation 4–8
see also Jesus Christ, priesthood;
ordained priesthood
'priesthood of all believers', Barth's
views 233–4
processio, and *missio* 109–10
proclamation 247, 247n. 336
Barth's views 10, 238
prodigal son, parable, Barth's
interpretation 51–2
profanity/holy 149–50
prophets
on cult and priesthood 154
role 152, 152n. 41
prosopon, and *physis* 37n. 105
Protestant foundationalism,
understanding of reality 198–200
Protestantism
on ordained priesthood 1–2, 207–8
on priesthood 75, 237, 264
Psalm 110 on Melchizedek and the
priesthood 157
Psalm 118 143
Puller, Father 192nn. 2 and 3

Quash, Ben 115nn. 54 and 57
Qumran Community 141n. 292

Radical Theology and Death of God
(Altizer and Hamilton) 7
Rahner, Karl 66
Rashdall, Hastings 215n. 65
realism
Evans on 13n. 91
and representation 3–4
reality
and imagination 26, 200
Protestant foundationalism's
understanding of 198–200
recognition 15
reconciliation, doctrine of 174n. 211
Reformers, on the reading of Scripture
113
religion 11nn. 77 and 78
and salvation 7
religionless Christianity 28–9, 29n. 46
repetition, in the eucharist 230

representation 96, 185
and identity 101, 104
and realism 3–4
Barth's understanding 9–10
Barth's views of priesthood 238–43
fitting and tracking theories, in
Philippians 2.6–11 98
repraesentieren 10, 11
resurrection 268
and apostolic witness to Jesus Christ
239n. 263, 240
and atonement 179–81, 229–30
in Philippians 2.6–11 98
revelation
and faith 107
Barth's views 199, 246
Ricoeur, Paul 13, 15, 16, 26, 78
right living, in Philippians 91–2
roles, in theo-drama 118
Rooke, Deborah 149
Ryle, Gilbert 12n. 86
Ryle, J. C. 192nn. 2 and 3

sacraments 10, 261n. 8
sacrifice 186, 227n. 165, 238n. 252
and priesthood 141–2, 145–6, 147,
173, 195, 196–7, 265–6
and the eucharist 226
Christian living as 158
counter-testimony and testimony
166–73, 243n. 305
First Testament understanding 211
language
in Hebrews 164–5
in Philippians 91
Paul's understanding of 213
reciprocity, in the eucharist 230
Sagovsky, Nicholas 245
Salmond, Dr 192nn. 2 and, 3
salvation 260
and religion 7
as an act of sovereign grace 47
in Philippians 84
Moltmann's views 71
Sanday, William 191–2
σχήματι 96, 97
Schillebeeckx, Edward 222–3, 234nn.
223 and 234, 252, 253n. 392

Schleiermacher, Friedrich Daniel Ernst 24
Scola, Angelo 110n. 17
Scott Holland, Canon 192nn. 2 and 3
scripture 241
  Balthasar's reading of 112–13
scripture principle, Barth's views 220
Sea of Faith, The (TV series) 7
Second Testament *see* Bible
Second Vatican Council, on the ordained ministry 1n. 4
Selwyn, E. G. 141n. 287, 143n. 301
Servant of the Lord 95, 100
sexuality, Barth's and Balthasar's views 130n. 192
Shema 94n. 125
signs 227
sin, Barth's views 131, 134n. 223
σῶμα 89
Son of God *see* Jesus Christ
soteriology, and vocation 111
soul, pre-existence 32
σπλάγχνα (compassion) 242–3
Stevenson, Kenneth 226, 229, 230
stories 77
Strasbourg papyrus 230
Strauss, D. F. *Life of Jesus Critically Examined* 24n. 19
stumbling 143
subordinationism 33, 54
successio apostolorum see Apostolic Succession
suffering 68, 84
Summerfield, Donna 11
συμμιμητή (fellow imitator) 254n. 408
συμμορφιζόμενο 249
suspicion, hermeneutics of 49
Swete, H. B. 196nn. 40 and 42
Sykes, Stephen 86n. 70, 155n. 58, 197n. 49, 232n. 205, 262n. 15
Syntyche 89

Taylor, Charles 15n. 110
Temple, Wright's views 153
Ten Propositions, the (1982) 2n. 6
testimony, and countertestimony 155n. 58
texts 77
theo-drama, Balthasar's use of 55–6, 62, 108–20
Theodoret 37n. 105
theologia crucis see cross, theology
theologia gloriae, Moltmann's views 124
theology 185, 220
thick descriptions 12, 203–4
Thielicke, Helmut 179
thin descriptions 12
Thiselton, Anthony C. 77, 78, 244n. 310
Thomas, Arnold 192nn. 2 and 3
Thomasius, Gottfried 17, 22–3, 24, 42, 45
Thompson, William 215n. 62
Timothy, in Philippians 224–5, 224n. 140
Tinker Tailor Soldier Spy (John Le Carré) 78n. 17
tracking theories 10–11, 83n. 51, 165
Tradition 113n. 35, 262
tragedy 78
Trent, Council of
  on Scripture and Tradition 113n. 35
  on the ordained ministry 233–4
Trinity
  and Christology 31–41, 42–5
  and kenoticism 70, 71, 72
  and ordained priesthood 259–60
  and priesthood 50
  Balthasar's views 178
  Cappadocian Fathers on 38
  doctrine of 69
  Hegel's understanding 29–30
  Jesus' death and resurrection 61, 66, 67
  metanarrative 78n. 13
  openness of 122, 122n. 117
  Pannenberg's views 54
  revelation 57–8
  see also God; Holy Spirit
Troeltsch, Ernst 117n. 117
truth 8, 201–3
Turner, C. H. 5n. 32
two natures doctrine 37, 70

unclean/clean 149

Vanhoozer, Kevin 203–4
Vanstone, W. H. 59n. 69, 265n. 40
vertreten 11
vocation 27, 186, 213–15, 216, 243n.
  305, 259–60, 262, 268
  and God's identity 107–8
  Augustine of Hippo on 39
  Balthasar's kenotic theology 108,
    108–20, 119–20
  Barth's views 129–38, 135–8
  Bonhoeffer's views 123n. 125
  in Philippians 86
  Moltmann's views 120–9, 123n.
    125, 126, 128
  priestly nature 102
Walsh, Brian J. 13n. 95
Ward, Graham 9–10, 61, 97, 100n.
  161, 227n. 165, 238
Webster, John 117n. 74, 196n. 41,
  251
Wellhausen, Julius 148–9, 167n. 154

Westcott, B. F. 164
Weston, Frank 24–5, 26
Williams, Rowan 32n. 70, 35–6, 226,
  235, 245–6
Wilson, Archdeacon 192nn. 2 and 3
witness 241
Wittgenstein, Ludwig 3–4, 208–9
women, ordination, and
  understandings of priesthood 5n.
  32
Word of God 3
  as revelation 220
  Barth's views 130, 135, 158, 239,
    241–2
  in Philippians 79–80
worldviews 13n. 95, 77
worship 225
  Christian identity in 232
Wright, N. T. 77–8, 80, 93, 144, 153

Zizioulas, John 252, 253n. 392
Zwingli, Ulrich 23

Paternoster Biblical Monographs

(All titles uniform with this volume)
Dates in bold are of projected publication

Joseph Abraham
Eve: Accused or Acquitted?
A Reconsideration of Feminist Readings of the Creation Narrative Texts in Genesis 1–3
Two contrary views dominate contemporary feminist biblical scholarship. One finds in the Bible an unequivocal equality between the sexes from the very creation of humanity, whilst the other sees the biblical text as irredeemably patriarchal and androcentric. Dr Abraham enters into dialogue with both camps as well as introducing his own method of approach. An invaluable tool for any one who is interested in this contemporary debate.
2002 / 0-85364-971-5 / xxiv + 272pp

Octavian D. Baban
Mimesis and Luke's on the Road Encounters in Luke-Acts
Luke's Theology of the Way and its Literary Representation
The book argues on theological and literary (mimetic) grounds that Luke's on-the-road encounters, especially those belonging to the post-Easter period, are part of his complex theology of the Way. Jesus' teaching and that of the apostles is presented by Luke as a challenging answer to the Hellenistic reader's thirst for adventure, good literature, and existential paradigms.
2005 */ 1-84227-253-5 / approx. 374pp*

Paul Barker
The Triumph of Grace in Deuteronomy
This book is a textual and theological analysis of the interaction between the sin and faithlessness of Israel and the grace of Yahweh in response, looking especially at Deuteronomy chapters 1–3, 8–10 and 29–30. The author argues that the grace of Yahweh is determinative for the ongoing relationship between Yahweh and Israel and that Deuteronomy anticipates and fully expects Israel to be faithless.
2004 / 1-84227-226-8 / xxii + 270pp

Jonathan F. Bayes
The Weakness of the Law
God's Law and the Christian in New Testament Perspective
A study of the four New Testament books which refer to the law as weak (Acts, Romans, Galatians, Hebrews) leads to a defence of the third use in the Reformed debate about the law in the life of the believer.
2000 / 0-85364-957-X / xii + 244pp

Mark Bonnington
The Antioch Episode of Galatians 2:11-14 in Historical and Cultural Context

The Galatians 2 'incident' in Antioch over table-fellowship suggests significant disagreement between the leading apostles. This book analyses the background to the disagreement by locating the incident within the dynamics of social interaction between Jews and Gentiles. It proposes a new way of understanding the relationship between the individuals and issues involved.

2005 / 1-84227-050-8 / approx. 350pp

David Bostock
A Portrayal of Trust
The Theme of Faith in the Hezekiah Narratives

This study provides detailed and sensitive readings of the Hezekiah narratives (2 Kings 18–20 and Isaiah 36–39) from a theological perspective. It concentrates on the theme of faith, using narrative criticism as its methodology. Attention is paid especially to setting, plot, point of view and characterization within the narratives. A largely positive portrayal of Hezekiah emerges that underlines the importance and relevance of scripture.

2005 / 1-84227-314-0 / approx. 300pp

Mark Bredin
Jesus, Revolutionary of Peace
A Non-violent Christology in the Book of Revelation

This book aims to demonstrate that the figure of Jesus in the Book of Revelation can best be understood as an active non-violent revolutionary.

2003 / 1-84227-153-9 / xviii + 262pp

Robinson Butarbutar
Paul and Conflict Resolution
An Exegetical Study of Paul's Apostolic Paradigm in 1 Corinthians 9

The author sees the apostolic paradigm in 1 Corinthians 9 as part of Paul's unified arguments in 1 Corinthians 8–10 in which he seeks to mediate in the dispute over the issue of food offered to idols. The book also sees its relevance for dispute-resolution today, taking the conflict within the author's church as an example.

2006 / 1-84227-315-9 / approx. 280pp

Daniel J-S Chae
Paul as Apostle to the Gentiles
His Apostolic Self-awareness and its Influence on the Soteriological Argument in Romans

Opposing 'the post-Holocaust interpretation of Romans', Daniel Chae competently demonstrates that Paul argues for the equality of Jew and Gentile in Romans. Chae's fresh exegetical interpretation is academically outstanding and spiritually encouraging.

1997 / 0-85364-829-8 / xiv + 378pp

Luke L. Cheung
The Genre, Composition and Hermeneutics of the Epistle of James

The present work examines the employment of the wisdom genre with a certain compositional structure and the interpretation of the law through the Jesus tradition of the double love command by the author of the Epistle of James to serve his purpose in promoting perfection and warning against doubleness among the eschatologically renewed people of God in the Diaspora.

2003 / 1-84227-062-1 / xvi + 372pp

Youngmo Cho
Spirit and Kingdom in the Writings of Luke and Paul

The relationship between Spirit and Kingdom is a relatively unexplored area in Lukan and Pauline studies. This book offers a fresh perspective of two biblical writers on the subject. It explores the difference between Luke's and Paul's understanding of the Spirit by examining the specific question of the relationship of the concept of the Spirit to the concept of the Kingdom of God in each writer.

2005 / 1-84227-316-7 / approx. 270pp

Andrew C. Clark
Parallel Lives
The Relation of Paul to the Apostles in the Lucan Perspective

This study of the Peter-Paul parallels in Acts argues that their purpose was to emphasize the themes of continuity in salvation history and the unity of the Jewish and Gentile missions. New light is shed on Luke's literary techniques, partly through a comparison with Plutarch.

2001 / 1-84227-035-4 / xviii + 386pp

Andrew D. Clarke
Secular and Christian Leadership in Corinth
A Socio-Historical and Exegetical Study of 1 Corinthians 1–6

This volume is an investigation into the leadership structures and dynamics of first-century Roman Corinth. These are compared with the practice of leadership in the Corinthian Christian community which are reflected in 1 Corinthians 1–6, and contrasted with Paul's own principles of Christian leadership.

2005 / 1-84227-229-2 / 200pp

Stephen Finamore
God, Order and Chaos
René Girard and the Apocalypse

Readers are often disturbed by the images of destruction in the book of Revelation and unsure why they are unleashed after the exaltation of Jesus. This book examines past approaches to these texts and uses René Girard's theories to revive some old ideas and propose some new ones.

2005 / 1-84227-197-0 / approx. 344pp

David G. Firth
Surrendering Retribution in the Psalms
Responses to Violence in the Individual Complaints

In *Surrendering Retribution in the Psalms*, David Firth examines the ways in which the book of Psalms inculcates a model response to violence through the repetition of standard patterns of prayer. Rather than seeking justification for retributive violence, Psalms encourages not only a surrender of the right of retribution to Yahweh, but also sets limits on the retribution that can be sought in imprecations. Arising initially from the author's experience in South Africa, the possibilities of this model to a particular context of violence is then briefly explored.

2005 / 1-84227-337-X / xviii + 154pp

Scott J. Hafemann
Suffering and Ministry in the Spirit
Paul's Defence of His Ministry in II Corinthians 2:14–3:3

Shedding new light on the way Paul defended his apostleship, the author offers a careful, detailed study of 2 Corinthians 2:14–3:3 linked with other key passages throughout 1 and 2 Corinthians. Demonstrating the unity and coherence of Paul's argument in this passage, the author shows that Paul's suffering served as the vehicle for revealing God's power and glory through the Spirit.

2000 / 0-85364-967-7 / xiv + 262pp

Scott J. Hafemann
Paul, Moses and the History of Israel
The Letter/Spirit Contrast and the Argument from Scripture in 2 Corinthians 3
An exegetical study of the call of Moses, the second giving of the Law (Exodus 32–34), the new covenant, and the prophetic understanding of the history of Israel in 2 Corinthians 3. Hafemann's work demonstrates Paul's contextual use of the Old Testament and the essential unity between the Law and the Gospel within the context of the distinctive ministries of Moses and Paul.
2005 / 1-84227-317-5 / xii + 498pp

Douglas S. McComiskey
Lukan Theology in the Light of the Gospel's Literary Structure
Luke's Gospel was purposefully written with theology embedded in its patterned literary structure. A critical analysis of this cyclical structure provides new windows into Luke's interpretation of the individual pericopes comprising the Gospel and illuminates several of his theological interests.
2004 / 1-84227-148-2 / xviii + 388pp

Stephen Motyer
Your Father the Devil?
A New Approach to John and 'The Jews'
Who are 'the Jews' in John's Gospel? Defending John against the charge of antisemitism, Motyer argues that, far from demonising the Jews, the Gospel seeks to present Jesus as 'Good News for Jews' in a late first century setting.
1997 / 0-85364-832-8 / xiv + 260pp

Esther Ng
Reconstructing Christian Origins?
The Feminist Theology of Elizabeth Schüssler Fiorenza: An Evaluation
In a detailed evaluation, the author challenges Elizabeth Schüssler Fiorenza's reconstruction of early Christian origins and her underlying presuppositions. The author also presents her own views on women's roles both then and now.
2002 / 1-84227-055-9 / xxiv + 468pp

Robin Parry
Old Testament Story and Christian Ethics
The Rape of Dinah as a Case Study

What is the role of story in ethics and, more particularly, what is the role of Old Testament story in Christian ethics? This book, drawing on the work of contemporary philosophers, argues that narrative is crucial in the ethical shaping of people and, drawing on the work of contemporary Old Testament scholars, that story plays a key role in Old Testament ethics. Parry then argues that when situated in canonical context Old Testament stories can be reappropriated by Christian readers in their own ethical formation. The shocking story of the rape of Dinah and the massacre of the Shechemites provides a fascinating case study for exploring the parameters within which Christian ethical appropriations of Old Testament stories can live.

2004 / 1-84227-210-1 / xx + 350pp

Ian Paul
Power to See the World Anew
The Value of Paul Ricoeur's Hermeneutic of Metaphor in Interpreting the Symbolism of Revelation 12 and 13

This book is a study of the hermeneutics of metaphor of Paul Ricoeur, one of the most important writers on hermeneutics and metaphor of the last century. It sets out the key points of his theory, important criticisms of his work, and how his approach, modified in the light of these criticisms, offers a methodological framework for reading apocalyptic texts.

2006 / 1-84227-056-7 / approx. 350pp

Robert L. Plummer
Paul's Understanding of the Church's Mission
Did the Apostle Paul Expect the Early Christian Communities to Evangelize?

This book engages in a careful study of Paul's letters to determine if the apostle expected the communities to which he wrote to engage in missionary activity. It helpfully summarizes the discussion on this debated issue, judiciously handling contested texts, and provides a way forward in addressing this critical question. While admitting that Paul rarely explicitly commands the communities he founded to evangelize, Plummer amasses significant incidental data to provide a convincing case that Paul did indeed expect his churches to engage in mission activity. Throughout the study, Plummer progressively builds a theological basis for the church's mission that is both distinctively Pauline and compelling.

2006 / 1-84227-333-7 / approx. 324pp

David Powys
'Hell': A Hard Look at a Hard Question
The Fate of the Unrighteous in New Testament Thought
This comprehensive treatment seeks to unlock the original meaning of terms and phrases long thought to support the traditional doctrine of hell. It concludes that there is an alternative—one which is more biblical, and which can positively revive the rationale for Christian mission.
1997 / 0-85364-831-X / xxii + 478pp

Sorin Sabou
Between Horror and Hope
Paul's Metaphorical Language of Death in Romans 6.1-11
This book argues that Paul's metaphorical language of death in Romans 6.1-11 conveys two aspects: horror and hope. The 'horror' aspect is conveyed by the 'crucifixion' language, and the 'hope' aspect by 'burial' language. The life of the Christian believer is understood, as relationship with sin is concerned ('death to sin'), between these two realities: horror and hope.
2005 / 1-84227-322-1 / approx. 224pp

Rosalind Selby
The Comical Doctrine
The Epistemology of New Testament Hermeneutics
This book argues that the gospel breaks through postmodernity's critique of truth and the referential possibilities of textuality with its gift of grace. With a rigorous, philosophical challenge to modernist and postmodernist assumptions, Selby offers an alternative epistemology to all who would still read with faith *and* with academic credibility.
2005 / 1-84227-212-8 / approx. 350pp

Kiwoong Son
Zion Symbolism in Hebrews
Hebrews 12.18-24 as a Hermeneutical Key to the Epistle
This book challenges the general tendency of understanding the Epistle to the Hebrews against a Hellenistic background and suggests that the Epistle should be understood in the light of the Jewish apocalyptic tradition. The author especially argues for the importance of the theological symbolism of Sinai and Zion (Heb. 12:18-24) as it provides the Epistle's theological background as well as the rhetorical basis of the superiority motif of Jesus throughout the Epistle.
2005 / 1-84227-368-X / approx. 280pp

Kevin Walton
Thou Traveller Unknown
The Presence and Absence of God in the Jacob Narrative
The author offers a fresh reading of the story of Jacob in the book of Genesis through the paradox of divine presence and absence. The work also seeks to make a contribution to Pentateuchal studies by bringing together a close reading of the final text with historical critical insights, doing justice to the text's historical depth, final form and canonical status.
2003 / 1-84227-059-1 / xvi + 238pp

George M. Wieland
The Significance of Salvation
A Study of Salvation Language in the Pastoral Epistles
The language and ideas of salvation pervade the three Pastoral Epistles. This study offers a close examination of their soteriological statements. In all three letters the idea of salvation is found to play a vital paraenetic role, but each also exhibits distinctive soteriological emphases. The results challenge common assumptions about the Pastoral Epistles as a corpus.
2005 / 1-84227-257-8 / approx. 324pp

Alistair Wilson
When Will These Things Happen?
A Study of Jesus as Judge in Matthew 21–25
This study seeks to allow Matthew's carefully constructed presentation of Jesus to be given full weight in the modern evaluation of Jesus' eschatology. Careful analysis of the text of Matthew 21–25 reveals Jesus to be standing firmly in the Jewish prophetic and wisdom traditions as he proclaims and enacts imminent judgement on the Jewish authorities then boldly claims the central role in the final and universal judgement.
2004 / 1-84227-146-6 / xxii + 272pp

Lindsay Wilson
Joseph Wise and Otherwise
The Intersection of Covenant and Wisdom in Genesis 37–50
This book offers a careful literary reading of Genesis 37–50 that argues that the Joseph story contains both strong covenant themes and many wisdom-like elements. The connections between the two helps to explore how covenant and wisdom might intersect in an integrated biblical theology.
2004 / 1-84227-140-7 / xvi + 340pp

Stephen I. Wright
The Voice of Jesus
Studies in the Interpretation of Six Gospel Parables
This literary study considers how the 'voice' of Jesus has been heard in different periods of parable interpretation, and how the categories of figure and trope may help us towards a sensitive reading of the parables today.
2000 / 0-85364-975-8 / xiv + 280pp

Paternoster:
thinking faith

Paternoster
9 Holdom Avenue,
Bletchley,
Milton Keynes MK1 1QR,
United Kingdom
Web: www.authenticmedia.co.uk/paternoster

July 2005

Paternoster Theological Monographs
(All titles uniform with this volume)
Dates in bold are of projected publication

Emil Bartos
Deification in Eastern Orthodox Theology
An Evaluation and Critique of the Theology of Dumitru Staniloae

Bartos studies a fundamental yet neglected aspect of Orthodox theology: deification. By examining the doctrines of anthropology, christology, soteriology and ecclesiology as they relate to deification, he provides an important contribution to contemporary dialogue between Eastern and Western theologians.

1999 / 0-85364-956-1 / xii + 370pp

Graham Buxton
The Trinity, Creation and Pastoral Ministry
Imaging the Perichoretic God

In this book the author proposes a three-way conversation between theology, science and pastoral ministry. His approach draws on a Trinitarian understanding of God as a relational being of love, whose life 'spills over' into all created reality, human and non-human. By locating human meaning and purpose within God's 'creation-community' this book offers the possibility of a transforming engagement between those in pastoral ministry and the scientific community.

2005 / 1-84227-369-8 / approx. 380 pp

Iain D. Campbell
Fixing the Indemnity
The Life and Work of George Adam Smith

When Old Testament scholar George Adam Smith (1856–1942) delivered the Lyman Beecher lectures at Yale University in 1899, he confidently declared that 'modern criticism has won its war against traditional theories. It only remains to fix the amount of the indemnity.' In this biography, Iain D. Campbell assesses Smith's critical approach to the Old Testament and evaluates its consequences, showing that Smith's life and work still raises questions about the relationship between biblical scholarship and evangelical faith.

2004 / 1-84227-228-4 / xx + 256pp

July 2005

Tim Chester
Mission and the Coming of God
Eschatology, the Trinity and Mission in the Theology of Jürgen Moltmann
This book explores the theology and missiology of the influential contemporary theologian, Jürgen Moltmann. It highlights the important contribution Moltmann has made while offering a critique of his thought from an evangelical perspective. In so doing, it touches on pertinent issues for evangelical missiology. The conclusion takes Calvin as a starting point, proposing 'an eschatology of the cross' which offers a critique of the over-realised eschatologies in liberation theology and certain forms of evangelicalism.
2006 / 1-84227-320-5 / approx. 224pp

Sylvia Wilkey Collinson
Making Disciples
The Significance of Jesus' Educational Strategy for Today's Church
This study examines the biblical practice of discipling, formulates a definition, and makes comparisons with modern models of education. A recommendation is made for greater attention to its practice today.
2004 / 1-84227-116-4 / xiv + 278pp

Darrell Cosden
A Theology of Work
Work and the New Creation
Through dialogue with Moltmann, Pope John Paul II and others, this book develops a genitive 'theology of work', presenting a theological definition of work and a model for a theological ethics of work that shows work's nature, value and meaning now and eschatologically. Work is shown to be a transformative activity consisting of three dynamically inter-related dimensions: the instrumental, relational and ontological.
2005 / 1-84227-332-9 / xvi + 208pp

Stephen M. Dunning
The Crisis and the Quest
A Kierkegaardian Reading of Charles Williams
Employing Kierkegaardian categories and analysis, this study investigates both the central crisis in Charles Williams's authorship between hermetism and Christianity (Kierkegaard's Religions A and B), and the quest to resolve this crisis, a quest that ultimately presses the bounds of orthodoxy.
2000 / 0-85364-985-5 / xxiv + 254pp

Keith Ferdinando
The Triumph of Christ in African Perspective
A Study of Demonology and Redemption in the African Context
The book explores the implications of the gospel for traditional African fears of occult aggression. It analyses such traditional approaches to suffering and biblical responses to fears of demonic evil, concluding with an evaluation of African beliefs from the perspective of the gospel.
1999 / 0-85364-830-1 / xviii + 450pp

Andrew Goddard
Living the Word, Resisting the World
The Life and Thought of Jacques Ellul
This work offers a definitive study of both the life and thought of the French Reformed thinker Jacques Ellul (1912-1994). It will prove an indispensable resource for those interested in this influential theologian and sociologist and for Christian ethics and political thought generally.
2002 / 1-84227-053-2 / xxiv + 378pp

David Hilborn
The Words of our Lips
Language-Use in Free Church Worship
Studies of liturgical language have tended to focus on the written canons of Roman Catholic and Anglican communities. By contrast, David Hilborn analyses the more extemporary approach of English Nonconformity. Drawing on recent developments in linguistic pragmatics, he explores similarities and differences between 'fixed' and 'free' worship, and argues for the interdependence of each.
2006 / 0-85364-977-4 / approx. 350pp

Roger Hitching
The Church and Deaf People
A Study of Identity, Communication and Relationships with Special Reference to the Ecclesiology of Jürgen Moltmann
In *The Church and Deaf People* Roger Hitching sensitively examines the history and present experience of deaf people and finds similarities between aspects of sign language and Moltmann's theological method that 'open up' new ways of understanding theological concepts.
2003 / 1-84227-222-5 / xxii + 236pp

John G. Kelly
One God, One People
The Differentiated Unity of the People of God in the Theology of Jürgen Moltmann
The author expounds and critiques Moltmann's doctrine of God and highlights the systematic connections between it and Moltmann's influential discussion of Israel. He then proposes a fresh approach to Jewish–Christian relations building on Moltmann's work using insights from Habermas and Rawls.
2005 / 0-85346-969-3 / approx. 350pp

Mark F.W. Lovatt
Confronting the Will-to-Power
A Reconsideration of the Theology of Reinhold Niebuhr
Confronting the Will-to-Power is an analysis of the theology of Reinhold Niebuhr, arguing that his work is an attempt to identify, and provide a practical theological answer to, the existence and nature of human evil.
2001 / 1-84227-054-0 / xviii + 216pp

Neil B. MacDonald
Karl Barth and the Strange New World within the Bible
Barth, Wittgenstein, and the Metadilemmas of the Enlightenment
Barth's discovery of the strange new world within the Bible is examined in the context of Kant, Hume, Overbeck, and, most importantly, Wittgenstein. MacDonald covers some fundamental issues in theology today: epistemology, the final form of the text and biblical truth-claims.
2000 / 0-85364-970-7 / xxvi + 374pp

Keith A. Mascord
Alvin Plantinga and Christian Apologetics
This book draws together the contributions of the philosopher Alvin Plantinga to the major contemporary challenges to Christian belief, highlighting in particular his ground-breaking work in epistemology and the problem of evil. Plantinga's theory that both theistic and Christian belief is warrantedly basic is explored and critiqued, and an assessment offered as to the significance of his work for apologetic theory and practice.
2005 / 1-84227-256-X / approx. 304pp

Gillian McCulloch
The Deconstruction of Dualism in Theology
With Reference to Ecofeminist Theology and New Age Spirituality

This book challenges eco-theological anti-dualism in Christian theology, arguing that dualism has a twofold function in Christian religious discourse. Firstly, it enables us to express the discontinuities and divisions that are part of the process of reality. Secondly, dualistic language allows us to express the mysteries of divine transcendence/immanence and the survival of the soul without collapsing into monism and materialism, both of which are problematic for Christian epistemology.

2002 / 1-84227-044-3 / xii + 282pp

Leslie McCurdy
Attributes and Atonement
The Holy Love of God in the Theology of P.T. Forsyth

Attributes and Atonement is an intriguing full-length study of P.T. Forsyth's doctrine of the cross as it relates particularly to God's holy love. It includes an unparalleled bibliography of both primary and secondary material relating to Forsyth.

1999 / 0-85364-833-6 / xiv + 328pp

Nozomu Miyahira
Towards a Theology of the Concord of God
A Japanese Perspective on the Trinity

This book introduces a new Japanese theology and a unique Trinitarian formula based on the Japanese intellectual climate: three betweennesses and one concord. It also presents a new interpretation of the Trinity, a co-subordinationism, which is in line with orthodox Trinitarianism; each single person of the Trinity is eternally and equally subordinate (or serviceable) to the other persons, so that they retain the mutual dynamic equality.

2000 / 0-85364-863-8 / xiv + 256pp

Eddy José Muskus
The Origins and Early Development of Liberation Theology in Latin America
With Particular Reference to Gustavo Gutiérrez

This work challenges the fundamental premise of Liberation Theology, 'opting for the poor', and its claim that Christ is found in them. It also argues that Liberation Theology emerged as a direct result of the failure of the Roman Catholic Church in Latin America.

2002 / 0-85364-974-X / xiv + 296pp

Jim Purves
The Triune God and the Charismatic Movement
A Critical Appraisal from a Scottish Perspective
All emotion and no theology? Or a fundamental challenge to reappraise and realign our trinitarian theology in the light of Christian experience? This study of charismatic renewal as it found expression within Scotland at the end of the twentieth century evaluates the use of Patristic, Reformed and contemporary models of the Trinity in explaining the workings of the Holy Spirit.
2004 / 1-84227-321-3 / xxiv + 246pp

Anna Robbins
Methods in the Madness
Diversity in Twentieth-Century Christian Social Ethics
The author compares the ethical methods of Walter Rauschenbusch, Reinhold Niebuhr and others. She argues that unless Christians are clear about the ways that theology and philosophy are expressed practically they may lose the ability to discuss social ethics across contexts, let alone reach effective agreements.
2004 / 1-84227-211-X / xx + 294pp

Ed Rybarczyk
Beyond Salvation
Eastern Orthodoxy and Classical Pentecostalism on Becoming Like Christ
At first glance eastern Orthodoxy and classical Pentecostalism seem quite distinct. This ground-breaking study shows they share much in common, especially as it concerns the experiential elements of following Christ. Both traditions assert that authentic Christianity transcends the wooden categories of modernism.
2004 / 1-84227-144-X / xii + 356pp

Signe Sandsmark
Is World View Neutral Education Possible and Desirable?
A Christian Response to Liberal Arguments
(Published jointly with The Stapleford Centre)
This book discusses reasons for belief in world view neutrality, and argues that 'neutral' education will have a hidden, but strong world view influence. It discusses the place for Christian education in the common school.
2000 / 0-85364-973-1 / xiv + 182pp

Hazel Sherman
Reading Zechariah
The Allegorical Tradition of Biblical Interpretation through the Commentary of Didymus the Blind and Theodore of Mopsuestia
A close reading of the commentary on Zechariah by Didymus the Blind alongside that of Theodore of Mopsuestia suggests that popular categorising of Antiochene and Alexandrian biblical exegesis as 'historical' or 'allegorical' is inadequate and misleading.
2005 / 1-84227-213-6 / approx. 280pp

Andrew Sloane
On Being a Christian in the Academy
Nicholas Wolterstorff and the Practice of Christian Scholarship
An exposition and critical appraisal of Nicholas Wolterstorff's epistemology in the light of the philosophy of science, and an application of his thought to the practice of Christian scholarship.
2003 / 1-84227-058-3 / xvi + 274pp

Damon W.K. So
Jesus' Revelation of His Father
A Narrative-Conceptual Study of the Trinity with Special Reference to Karl Barth
This book explores the trinitarian dynamics in the context of Jesus' revelation of his Father in his earthly ministry with references to key passages in Matthew's Gospel. It develops from the exegeses of these passages a non-linear concept of revelation which links Jesus' communion with his Father to his revelatory words and actions through a nuanced understanding of the Holy Spirit, with references to K. Barth, G.W.H. Lampe, J.D.G. Dunn and E. Irving.
2005 / 1-84227-323-X / approx. 380pp

Daniel Strange
The Possibility of Salvation Among the Unevangelised
An Analysis of Inclusivism in Recent Evangelical Theology
For evangelical theologians the 'fate of the unevangelised' impinges upon fundamental tenets of evangelical identity. The position known as 'inclusivism', defined by the belief that the unevangelised can be ontologically saved by Christ whilst being epistemologically unaware of him, has been defended most vigorously by the Canadian evangelical Clark H. Pinnock. Through a detailed analysis and critique of Pinnock's work, this book examines a cluster of issues surrounding the unevangelised and its implications for christology, soteriology and the doctrine of revelation.
2002 / 1-84227-047-8 / xviii + 362pp

Scott Swain
God According to the Gospel
Biblical Narrative and the Identity of God in the Theology of Robert W. Jenson
Robert W. Jenson is one of the leading voices in contemporary Trinitarian theology. His boldest contribution in this area concerns his use of biblical narrative both to ground and explicate the Christian doctrine of God. *God According to the Gospel* critically examines Jenson's proposal and suggests an alternative way of reading the biblical portrayal of the triune God.
2006 / 1-84227-258-6 / approx. 180pp

Justyn Terry
The Justifying Judgement of God
A Reassessment of the Place of Judgement in the Saving Work of Christ
The argument of this book is that judgement, understood as the whole process of bringing justice, is the primary metaphor of atonement, with others, such as victory, redemption and sacrifice, subordinate to it. Judgement also provides the proper context for understanding penal substitution and the call to repentance, baptism, eucharist and holiness.
2005 / 1-84227-370-1 / approx. 274 pp

Graham Tomlin
The Power of the Cross
Theology and the Death of Christ in Paul, Luther and Pascal
This book explores the theology of the cross in St Paul, Luther and Pascal. It offers new perspectives on the theology of each, and some implications for the nature of power, apologetics, theology and church life in a postmodern context.
1999 / 0-85364-984-7 / xiv + 344pp

Adonis Vidu
Postliberal Theological Method
A Critical Study
The postliberal theology of Hans Frei, George Lindbeck, Ronald Thiemann, John Milbank and others is one of the more influential contemporary options. This book focuses on several aspects pertaining to its theological method, specifically its understanding of background, hermeneutics, epistemic justification, ontology, the nature of doctrine and, finally, Christological method.
2005 / 1-84227-395-7 / approx. 324pp

Graham J. Watts
Revelation and the Spirit
A Comparative Study of the Relationship between the Doctrine of Revelation and Pneumatology in the Theology of Eberhard Jüngel and of Wolfhart Pannenberg

The relationship between revelation and pneumatology is relatively unexplored. This approach offers a fresh angle on two important twentieth century theologians and raises pneumatological questions which are theologically crucial and relevant to mission in a postmodern culture.

2005 / 1-84227-104-0 / xxii + 232pp

Nigel G. Wright
Disavowing Constantine
Mission, Church and the Social Order in the Theologies of John Howard Yoder and Jürgen Moltmann

This book is a timely restatement of a radical theology of church and state in the Anabaptist and Baptist tradition. Dr Wright constructs his argument in dialogue and debate with Yoder and Moltmann, major contributors to a free church perspective.

2000 / 0-85364-978-2 / xvi + 252pp

Paternoster:
thinking faith

Paternoster
9 Holdom Avenue,
Bletchley,
Milton Keynes MK1 1QR,
United Kingdom
Web: www.authenticmedia.co.uk/paternoster

July 2005